The Information Broker's Handbook

Sue Rugge
Alfred Glossbrenner

Foreword by Reva Basch
Past President
Association of Independent
Information Professionals

Windcrest®/McGraw-Hill

FIRST EDITION
THIRD PRINTING

Library of Congress Cataloging-in-Publication Data

Rugge, Sue.
    The information broker's handbook / by Sue Rugge and Alfred
Glossbrenner.
      p. cm.
    Includes index.
    ISBN 0-8306-3798-2 (h)   ISBN 0-8306-3797-4 (p)
    1. Information services industry—Management.   2. Information
services.   3. Information scientists.   I. Glossbrenner, Alfred.
II. Title.
HD9999.I492R84   1992
025.5′2′068—dc20   91-44822
                                 CIP

Acquisitions Editor: Brad Schepp
Book Editor: David M. McCandless
Director of Production: Katherine G. Brown
Book Design: Jaclyn J. Boone
Paperbound Cover: Sandra Blair Design and
   Brent Blair Photography, Harrisburg, Pa.

Contents

8 The telephone: Your most powerful tool   95

Part III *Electronic options and alternatives*

9 Welcome to the electronic universe!   113

Part IV   *The business side of information brokering*

Foreword

THE FIRST WORDS I EVER HEARD FROM SUE RUGGE'S OFFICE WERE "YOU'RE TALKING to a desperate woman! When can you start?"

Actually, the words were those of Sue's Director of Research, Barbara Newlin Bernstein. I'd just moved back to California after a stint as an engineering company librarian in Reading, Pennsylvania, and I was looking for work. I'd heard of Sue Rugge and her pioneering efforts in what was then called the fee-based information business. So when I came across the ad for a research associate at her firm, Information on Demand, I leaped for the phone.

IOD, in turn, leaped for me. They were short two researchers, it turned out, and had more work than they could handle. What I'd assumed would be a one-hour job interview turned out to be the first day of almost six years with Information on Demand. No resume or references changed hands that day; Sue and Barbara had a warm body and a passable intellect in their grasp, and they weren't about to let go. I was given a desk, a telephone, and a few simple guidelines. Seven hours later, I could tell you anything you wanted to know about water-pumping windmills.

Those words of Barbara's proved to be prophetic. The demand for information, and for knowledgeable people to retrieve, manage, and massage it, has continued to accelerate. Hundreds of new entrepreneurs have entered the business since 1981, the year I was semi-kidnapped into it. Some of their ventures have succeeded, but the majority, I suspect, have failed.

Why? One major reason is a lack of solid, straight-from-the-shoulder information about the information industry in general and the information brokering profession in particular.

That's why a book like this is so refreshing and so essential. Sue Rugge has no illusions about the independent research business. She has no vested interest other than helping to maintain the profession's high standards and making the world aware of all that it has to offer.

Sue's concern for the profession led to her early involvement in the Association of Independent Information Professionals (AIIP), an organization she headed as President in 1988-1989. Her pragmatic view of the industry has been invaluable to me, to other AIIP officers, to hundreds of seasoned information brokers, and to thousands who aspire to enter the profession.

When people ask me for advice on becoming an information broker, I recommend Sue's seminars, telling them that the registration fee is a small price to pay for a reality check—for insurance against making a career move that might *not* be in their best interest.

Sue knows what kind of training, experience, and personality traits make a good information broker. As an industry pioneer, she is passionate about getting good people more involved. She is equally passionate about dissuading those who see the opportunity to make a quick buck, or for whom the fit just doesn't seem right.

Sue Rugge knows, in short, what *you* need to know. And she and Alfred Glossbrenner have captured in this book as much of that expertise as it is possible to transfer from human brain cells to the printed page.

Alfred has been writing books about computers and computer communications since 1981. We met through Sue, several years ago, when we all "performed" at the same small information-oriented conference. We hit it off instantly, and I know that much of the chemistry among the three of us lay in Alfred's ability to become totally engrossed in the concerns and interests of the people he is conversing with. He asks intelligent questions, absorbs what you know about the subject, draws you out, and internalizes the knowledge that you have to offer. The result is a detailed conceptual map of a subject, presented with crystalline clarity in easy, conversational tones.

Information brokering has come a long way since the early days at IOD. As in the past, most successful practitioners today have a library background, but that's changing. We're seeing more people with years of experience in a particular industry, or with a background in marketing or business management, who are willing to *learn* to do research, or to partner with someone who knows how. This increasing diversity of experience and perspective is a good thing; we can all learn from each other.

From what I've seen, there's plenty of business out there. The information profession can *always* use good people. If you are good, and if you work hard, you have an excellent chance of carving out a tidy market niche for yourself, especially if you have expertise in a hot industry or technology, or access to unique resources.

One thing that has characterized this profession from its inception is a spirit of cooperation, rather than competition, among its members. This has its roots, I think, in the library world, where the thrill of the hunt, and of *finding* what you're looking for, is something to be shared with your colleagues. If this excitement—this love of research for its own sake—resonates with you, you're already ahead of the game. Now it's time for you to listen to Sue and Alfred.

Reva Basch, Past President 1991–1992
Association of Independent Information Professionals

Introduction
TANSTAAFL

THERE'S A LOT OF MISINFORMATION AROUND ABOUT THE INFORMATION BROKERING profession. So we owe it to you to set the record straight right from the start.

You've all seen those pie-in-the-sky ads, the ones that promise to let you in on the "secrets" of how to make a good living working for yourself, in your spare time, at home. No bosses, no time cards, no worries. Nothing much to do, apparently, but trundle on down to the mailbox each day and pick up those fat checks your customers are so eager to send.

And all this from what? Stuffing envelopes? Selling magazine subscriptions over the phone? Enlisting people as soap salesmen in your "direct marketing" pyramid?

Well, maybe. It's possible that some people really have discovered a magic formula. But we've never known anyone like that. We've certainly never known any information brokers who've managed to make money so effortlessly. Our experience, in fact, tracks more with the philosophy stated by the late science fiction writer Robert A. Heinlein. Heinlein summed up his opinion in a nine-character expression: TANSTAAFL.

Translated, this means "There ain't no such thing as a free lunch!" And, of course, it's true. If it weren't, the world's taverns, pubs, and assorted watering holes—the originators of the "free lunch" concept—would soon go out of business. Somebody *always* pays. And unless you happen to own a savings and loan or other government-backed institution, that someone is almost always you.

We bring this up because for the last several years the old get-rich-quick offers of the past have been updated for the 90's. The pitch today is not so much to the desire we all have to make a ton of money, though that is still a strong undercurrent. The main focus now is on personal independence, entrepreneurship, working for yourself, making your own hours, and working from home.

Unfortunately, the profession that has long been called "information brokering" has received greater attention in these ads than ever before. After all, it offers everything a pitchman could want, starting with a very plausible story:

An information broker is someone who finds answers for money, right? And as we all know, lots of people need answers—doctors, lawyers, Fortune 500 companies, investors—you name it. Best of all, we live in the Information Age, where answers can be found virtually lying on the ground, like apples fallen from a tree. All you have to do is fire up your computer and your "telephone modem" and go get 'em. Then deliver them to the client, and collect a hefty fee.

Anyone can do it! Best of all, you can work for yourself, at home, setting your own hours.

The pitch is irresistible. And, aside from the part about the insatiable demand, the hefty fees, and the ease with which answers can be found, it's all true. Mostly. Of course, all it takes is a computer and a modem, which the pitchman may be willing to sell you for a modest fee. Plus the pitchman's "exclusive" kit and home study guide, offered for a distinctly immodest fee.

But, hey, you're worth it. Besides, this is your career we're talking about here. In a few weeks, the cost won't matter because after that, you'll be raking in the big bucks.

Best of all, the pitchman has the perfect out: "What? You say you've followed the program for six months and haven't gotten a single client? Well, you're probably not doing it right. There must be something you've missed. Maybe you should buy the Phase II kit and home study guide to *sharpen up your skills*."

You know the routine. What you probably don't know is that in this country of over 250 million people there are at most a few thousand full-time information brokers—men and women who earn enough money finding and delivering information for clients that they don't have to do anything else. There are a few hundred more who work at the profession part-time. Many of these folks hold down full-time jobs as professional librarians and corporate information center managers and do their information brokering after normal working hours.

Whether full-time or part-time, many of the people working as information brokers today have advanced degrees, often in information and library science. They are very, very good at finding answers. Yet, as noted, only a fraction of them can make a living as full-time information brokers.

That should tell you something. It should tell you that the world is not beating a path to the information broker's door. On the contrary, while most people pay lip service to the Information Age, when it comes to actually *paying* for information or the services of an information professional, most people and companies are extremely reluctant to part with their dollars.

Most simply find a way to do without. And the thing of it is, most *succeed*! Or at least they are successful enough to get by. The fact that they might have done even better and had even greater success if they had used the services of an information professional is difficult to prove.

We know it's true. We know that day in and day out, the company or concern that has the best information is going to out-perform those that are merely getting by. But often, in this era of mediocrity, getting by is more than sufficient.

Not until Company A is repeatedly beaten by Company B on bids, on contracts, and on sales will Company A begin to ask "Why?" Hopefully some bright bulb at Company A will realize that the reason the firm is getting its hind quarters kicked from here to November is that Company B has superior information. Only then will Company A eagerly seek out the services of an information broker.

In the meantime, if you want to make a living at this profession, you are going to have to spend a great deal of your time marketing your services. Or you are going to have to team up with someone who can do it for you. You do *not* have to have a computer and a modem. That kind of equipment is extremely helpful, to be sure, but it is not absolutely essential. What you really need is a telephone and the imagination and tenacity of a crack investigative reporter.

You'll also need a good head for business, and you will need patience, for what we have told you so far is the bad news. The good news is that information consciousness is growing. The Company A's of the world are beginning to ask why they are always on the losing side, and they are beginning to conclude that the answer lies in having the right information.

The opportunities are there. But you have to know how and where to look for them. You have to be willing to master a set of new skills and patiently, tirelessly build your business. But then, that's true of any business or profession.

Though our evidence is only anecdotal, it does appear that the opportunities for professional information services are growing. Once you know more about the incredible depth and diversity of information that *is* available—either through the skilled use of a computer and modem or through the imaginative use of the telephone—you will agree that the rise of the professional information consultant is inevitable.

There is definitely money to be made. And there is a growing demand for professional information services. But there's still no such thing as a free lunch.

If you want the freedom and independence that information brokering can provide, you can have it. You'll have to have a certain aptitude, and, like all self-employed people, you'll have to be willing to work like hell—in learning your trade, in marketing your services, and in delivering what you promise.

This book will show you how to accomplish all of these tasks. We'll show you what the profession of information broker is all about. We'll give you the tips and techniques you need to market your services. And we'll show you how and where to look for the answers to your clients' questions. We'll also tell you how to run an information consulting business.

The rest is up to you. If you enjoy information, but take no pleasure in the hunt—in the process of throwing your mind, imagination, and skills against a problem—then you may want to team up with someone who does. You could be the marketing arm, and your partner could be the search arm of an excellent business.

If you don't see yourself as a marketer and have no special *love* for information, then you should probably investigate other self-employment opportunities. Of course, we're biased. But then, we also know a thing or two about what it takes to be a *successful* information broker. It's not the same as selling soap, three-penny nails, or accounting services.

These are all honorable pursuits, and most of them are better paid. And in those jobs, you don't have to love the product to be a success. In contrast, if you don't "love" information and have a profound respect for its value, its power, and the thrill of finding answers, you'll never be happy as an information broker.

On the other hand, if you have a natural curiosity about things, if you are willing to work, and if you're willing to sell or team up with someone who can, then you really can become a self-employed information professional. You really can make a living at it.

This book will show you how.

How to use this book

THIS BOOK HAS BEEN DESIGNED TO GIVE YOU EVERYTHING YOU NEED TO KNOW TO become a successful information broker, regardless of your previous level of information-related experience. We are very much aware, however, that the distance separating the most experienced reader from the least experienced is likely to be very great indeed. If you are a trained librarian or information professional, or if you have a strong information background, you have one set of needs. If you have no formal training but have a strong interest in the profession, you have a different set of needs.

As we all know, no single book can be precisely tuned to every requirement every reader may have. So let us tell you what we have done, show you how the book is arranged, and offer some suggestions on how to make the most of it.

In our opinion, there is a certain quantum of knowledge anyone must have to become a successful information broker. Therefore, we begin at the beginning with a discussion of the current market for information and then offer some insights on how an intelligent, curious, *motivated* person can seize the opportunities that exist in this field. The book continues straight through this continuum of essential information, ending with a chapter on how to set up your office, followed by several information-laden appendices.

If you are new to the information field, we strongly suggest that you begin by surveying all of the chapters in this book, pausing now and again to read passages that catch your eye, and then return to the Introduction and read straight through. In general, each chapter assumes that you have read all of the chapters that precede it on the "continuum."

On the other hand, if you have had some experience in an information-related field, you may want to approach things a bit differently. You may wish to review the table of contents, select a chapter of interest, and read it in toto. You may wish to jump around. We would like to suggest, however, that you at least skim every chapter, even those that appear to cover topics long familiar to you. You never know where or when you might pick up some useful tip, technique, or tidbit.

The table of contents is largely self-explanatory, so we will not preview each chapter here. As you will notice, however, the book is divided into four main parts. Part One discusses the information business in general. It offers a no-holds-barred, straight-from-the-shoulder analysis of the market, the pluses and minuses, and your chances for success.

Part Two assumes that, despite our best attempts in the first five chapters to scare you off, that you really do have what it takes to become a successful information broker. (Or at least you think you do.) That's why Part Two focuses on the basic techniques of information gathering every information broker needs to master.

Part Three continues the tutorial by discussing the incredible array of electronic databases and online systems that are yours to mine for the raw material you need. It concludes with a chapter on CD-ROM (Compact Disk—Read Only Memory), a technology that promises to revolutionize the traditional information business.

With Part Four, we really get down to business. Here you will find the most thorough, comprehensive, and downright useful compilation of information about what it *really* takes to establish and run a successful information brokering firm available anywhere. You can be the most skilled online searcher in the world . . . you can have an armload of advanced degrees . . . but if you fail to project an image of credibility, if you neglect marketing and sales, you will *not* succeed as an independent information professional.

We are simplifying greatly here, but in a nutshell, Sue Rugge's message to all prospective information brokers is this: If you can search, join forces with someone who can sell, and if you can sell, team up with someone who can search. Either way, you will find the chapters in Part Four invaluable.

The book concludes with six appendices designed to, one way or another, provide you with the tools you need to get off to a good start. There are addresses, contacts, information sources, reference works and directories, and ''free'' business-related programs to know about.

There is also the disk that accompanies this book. As Appendix F explains, all you need do is put the disk in a drive and key in INSTALL. The installation procedure completes with a snazzy menu that offers you instant access to the information broker forms, contacts, and addresses printed in the book. But—and this is very important—the disk includes information not found in these pages, including a sample services contract, an actual information broker report, and a variety of actual cover letters sent to information broker clients. (There are also some nifty little utility programs that can make working with any IBM-compatible computer much easier.)

Our goal with the accompanying disk was to come as close as possible to providing you with a "turn-key" information broker operation. Print out the forms. Mark them up and customize them to your own needs. Then load the appropriate file on the disk into your favorite word processing program and make the modifications. What might have taken hours if you had to start from scratch can be done in minutes when you use the files on the accompanying disk as your starting point. (Replacement disks or 3.5″ media can be obtained using the order form in Appendix D.)

In conclusion, we think you will be fascinated by the dynamic profession of information brokering. It's exciting, frustrating, demanding, and immensely rewarding, all at the same time. It is definitely not for everyone. But, by the time you finish this book, you will know whether or not it is for you.

Part I
The information business

1

The market for information

CAN *YOU* MAKE A LIVING AS AN INFORMATION BROKER? THERE'S NO WAY TO TELL for sure. But one thing is certain: you'll never even get off the ground until you have an appreciation of just what it is you're dealing with. So let's talk for a moment about the commodity we're supposedly in the business of finding, packaging, selling, or otherwise "brokering." Let's talk about *information*.

In the first place, successful information brokers do not sell information. What they sell is their *expertise* in searching for information. That may seem like a subtle distinction to you right now, but it's crucial. A client who believes that what he or she is buying from you is information is likely to gauge your worth on the quantity—not the quality—of information you deliver. If you know anything about information retrieval, you know how short-sighted that is on the client's part. But if you know anything about human nature, you know that it is inevitable—if you position yourself as a seller of information.

Thus, one of the first jobs of every information broker is to educate the client about information and the "Information Age." The "Information Age" is a phrase used so frequently that it has become a cliché. In fact, it's worse than a cliché, for as tired and shopworn as even the most common cliché may be, at least everyone knows what it means.

We all know what "Closing the barn door after the horses have escaped" or "As scarce as hen's teeth" means, even though very few of us have ever owned a horse or peered into the open beak of a chicken. The Information Age is far less clear and far more nebulous. Most of the time, with Lewis Carroll's Alice, we make the words mean whatever we want them to mean at the time.

And that's the point. The Information Age may mean cable television, with

3

more channels than ever before and round the clock up-to-the-minute news, weather, sports, and financial reports. It may mean the explosion of magazines and paperback books stuffed into store shelves, supermarket racks, and even vending machines. It may also mean the increased use of electronics—computers, fax machines, cellular telephones, databases, and satellite dishes—in nearly every industry or profession.

There is simply no clear definition of what constitutes the Information Age. Yet the Information Age itself defines the seas we must all swim in as information professionals. The Information Age *is* today's reality.

Fortunately, while no one can agree on its details, nearly everyone would agree that the two most important characteristics of the Information Age are quantity and availability. It is those two features we will consider next, especially as they relate to the information profession and the market for information-related services.

Quantity: Miles and miles of pretty files

The breadth and scope of the information that exists on virtually any topic, person, or place today is simply staggering. If you are new to the information business, you probably accept that statement the way one accepts the statement that the planet Jupiter is 1300 times the size of Earth. Your intellect acknowledges its accuracy, but your gut doesn't feel its truth.

As a prospective information broker, however, it is essential to truly experience this fact, to feel it in your soul. A stroll through your local library won't do it. As impressive as they are, most public libraries hold only a tiny fraction of all that's available on any subject.

To even glimpse the kind of quantity we're talking about, you would have to spend a couple of days prowling the stacks at a major metropolitan or university library: floor after floor containing mile after mile of books, racks of microfilm, and entire rooms piled high with back issues of magazines, journals, and newsletters.

Yet this isn't even the tip of the iceberg. After all, most metropolitan and university libraries not only have a main building but many subsidiary buildings as well, each of which houses a separate collection. At one university we know of, for example, there is not only a huge main library—three floors of which are underground—but also separate buildings for materials on art and architecture, chemistry, engineering, and psychology, to say nothing of the little niche libraries tucked away in smaller buildings on campus. Each one of these buildings houses more subject-specific books and publications than you'll find in all the branches of many county library systems.

We don't want to belabor the point. But until you've felt your heart pounding and your breath grow short when confronting the vast quantities of information available—until you have been *overwhelmed*—you'll never be a full-fledged information consultant.

This is not some macho rite of passage. It is pure practicality. After all, if you were a king, who would you rather send to slay the fire-breathing dragon? An over-confident new recruit who has never actually seen the beast? Or a seasoned warrior who in the past has been toasted by its flames? Which of these individuals is likely to give you the most accurate advice on just what can be accomplished and how long it will take? More to the point, which is likely to make the more credible presentation?

Throughout this book you'll find numerous ways to expose yourself to the dragon's fire. If you follow our advice, you'll come away with a healthy respect for what you're up against. Equally important, you'll come away with confidence. Confidence in your ability to do what others cannot do. Indeed, what most people have no idea *how* to do—retrieve information. You must never forget that what you're selling as an information broker is not really the information itself. It is your skill and ability to retrieve it.

Availability: All you have to do is ask

The other major characteristic of the Information Age is the availability of information. It is important to realize that, judged by the standards of the times, a great deal of information about a great many things has *always* existed. Record-keeping has long been a human habit.

Government bureaucracy, to take but one example, did not start with the invention of the typewriter. Even today, archaeologists continue to turn up literally mounds of contracts, property transaction records, bills of sale, and other mundane "documents" dating more than a thousand years B.C.

Many of these ancient documents were punched into soft clay tablets with the wedge-shaped implement that is the hallmark of cuneiform. The tablets were then baked into stone, yielding what one must naturally refer to as the world's first "hard copy."

Or the records were scratched on sheep guts (vellum) with a stylus and ink of carbon black and olive oil. Or written with a quill pen on parchment, with a dollop of hot sealing wax embossed with the signer's personal crest to testify to authenticity. But they were "information" all the same.

Today, in keeping with the "bigger, better, faster, more complete, more complex" orientation of modern civilization, documents are more detailed, and there are many, many more of them. But today, the documents are also *available*. And that makes all the difference.

Today, you don't have to book passage across the Mediterranean to consult the scrolls tucked inside the leather cylinders of the library at Alexandria. You don't have to be a noble or a scholar to gain access to your county's file of deeds or property transactions.

Democracy, the great leveler, gives every citizen access to vast quantities of government information. Indeed, in some states, if you have a personal computer and a modem and know what numbers to dial, you may not even have to leave your home or office to obtain the local government information you want or need. A number of counties, for example, have made their databases of real estate transactions available in this way.

And this is only government information. Even more information is published by commercial sources, much of it available by personal computer, at libraries, through the inter-library loan network, and via the many other systems that have been created for the sole purpose of making information available.

The forms are changing as well. Co-author Glossbrenner, for example, uses a CD-ROM product sold by the Ziff-Davis Publishing Company to instantly access the full text of literally hundreds of computer magazines and newsletters. The product is called Computer Select, and subscriptions run about $1000 a year.

That's a stiff price, to be sure. But consider the alternative: box after box of printed magazines in the attic, all of which take up space and none of which is easily accessible due to poor or nonexistent indexes. Add to this the fact that the CD-ROM product includes publications of interest that your co-author would not normally subscribe to, and the price begins to look much more reasonable.

Ziff-Davis's Computer Select has only been available since 1988. But it is part of a trend toward making more and more information more easily available to an ever widening audience. (More on this in Chapter 14.)

What *is* information?

This, then, is the Information Age: an incredible amount of information on an infinite variety of topics readily available to virtually everyone. This is the realm in which every prospective information broker must make a living. It is a realm that needs an information broker's services because, while all of this information is indeed available, in reality, considerable skill and expertise is required to retrieve it.

There's just one thing missing from this broad definition—a more concrete idea of just what is meant by "information." The term, like the "Age," has prodigious elasticity. Which is to say, it is used to cover nearly everything.

When RNA molecules pass on a cell's genetic code, they are said to be transferring "information." Television commercials for everything from pain killers to breakfast cereal often claim they are providing "important information" about the products they were designed to sell. Not for them the crass sales pitches of the competition. They're providing you with *information*.

And presumably the half-hour "infomercials" for everything from stain removers to Chinese woks or vegetable juicers are of an even higher caliber since they are providing you with even more "information."

The list goes on and on, and of course it includes "relative value" type data. To you, a scrap of paper bearing a sequence of digits may be about as valuable as a gum wrapper. But to someone who knows that the numbers are the combination to the office safe, the password to a secure database, or a government official's private phone number, that paper could be priceless.

In some instances, even the fact that there is *no* information on a particular topic is in itself valuable information. Imagine you're an inventor who wants to patent an invention, or a marketer interested in establishing a new brand name, or a personnel officer interested in making sure that a candidate you plan to recommend for a high level position has never been indicted. (Police records are not publicly available, but newspaper accounts and court transcripts certainly are.) In all of these cases, the fact that there is no similar patent or brand name or record of a run-in with the law is in itself valuable information.

Clearly, it is impossible to come up with a universal definition of what constitutes information. But for our purposes as information brokers, we can define it quite precisely:

Information is whatever someone wants to know—and is willing to pay to find out.

Anything. Anything at *all*.

Your role as an information broker is to find whatever it is your client wants to know, using whatever *legal* means are available and working within whatever the client's budget will allow. Information brokers may offer other services as well, but fundamentally, information brokering is about finding information.

As such, you have a great deal going for you right off the bat. In the United States, an individual with the proper skills and unwavering dedication can find out nearly anything he or she wants to know. This is an awesome prospect: anything at all that you or your client wants to know can be discovered, given sufficient time and sufficient financial resources.

Of course there are limits. You can't break the law. You must respect a person's right to privacy. You must maintain the highest ethical standard at all times—even if it means turning down assignments because you know they would force you to sail close to the wind. And undoubtedly, there are some things you cannot legally discover. But before you assume that the exceptions are large and significant, consider the case of Tom Clancy, best-selling author.

The case of Red October

Consider what happened after the publication of *The Hunt for Red October*—Clancy's novel about a Soviet submarine commander who defects and takes his submarine with him. The author was summoned by the C.I.A. and asked in no uncertain terms to name his sources. Who, the Agency wanted to know, had leaked the classified information that enabled him to give his book such authoritative and accurate descriptions of secret submarine weapons systems?

Clancy replied that far from having a mole in the Pentagon, he had found all the information he needed in the public record. And not just in obscure government studies and documents. Clancy freely admitted to reading *Aviation Week and Space Technology*, for example, a widely available technical and trade journal.

Yes, he had extrapolated. Yes, he had made some educated guesses. But there's no escaping the fact that here was a former insurance executive—not even an engineer—who had come uncomfortably close to some of the Navy's most closely guarded secrets. All from paying careful attention to publicly available documents. It gave our military people pause, to say the least.

The point is simply this: In the Information Age, for all intents and purposes, the information your client wants *is* available. The money may not be there to pay the costs of obtaining all of it, but it both exists and is available.

Complete confidence

As an information professional you are not selling a bag of hot air. You are selling something very real and very valuable—your ability to find information that you have every reason to believe does indeed exist. (And if the information does not exist, you have every reason to be confident that you will discover that fact as well, which in itself is often valuable information.)

It's like being a nuclear physicist probing the innards of an atom. You may never have seen a particular particle, but through knowledge and experience you *know* it must exist, and you know that it must have certain well-defined properties. When, after a good deal of effort and the smashing of a few billion atoms, the particle one day leaves its unmistakable signature in the cloud chamber, no one is less surprised than you. You knew it was there all the time, it was simply a matter of bringing it to light.

How can you profit from your skills?

With this brief introduction to today's world of information as background, let us now look more closely at the market for information. Or more precisely, the market for information retrieval skills.

Let's think about how someone with information retrieval skills can make money from those skills. We start by asking the basic question, the question anyone in our position would ask: what is the demand for information? Who is likely to be interested in our services?

The answer is that the demand for information is limitless. There is hardly anyone who wouldn't like to know more about a topic of personal, professional, or business interest. People will be glad to accept anything you can provide.

But don't ask them to pay for it.

To give them the benefit of the doubt—never call anyone ''cheap'' if you can avoid it—most people haven't a clue about what information costs. They don't know about online database subscriptions and connect time charges or the search training you have paid for. They have no idea how to work a library or the time, effort, and sheer running around that can be involved in locating the right books and documents. They don't know about copyright clearance fees, or the unbilled time you must spend reading journals and manuals to keep current in your profession.

All they know is that you have told them there is a good chance you can find the information they want, and that you want them to pay you for this service. It is at this point that the lip service most people pay to the Information Age stops and we really get down to cases. The fact is that when the subject is dollars and cents instead of smart sounding but vague generalities like ''the information economy,'' most people find a way to do without.

In fairness, you really can't blame them. Information resource awareness is today at about the same level that environmentalism was prior to the publication of Rachel Carson's *Silent Spring*. It is all but nonexistent. Combine this lack of awareness with the nebulous nature of information, and you're looking at a very tough sales job. People who have gotten along for years quite nicely without the kind of services you can provide will be inclined to continue to do so. Particularly if they can see no tangible benefit stemming from this most intangible of products.

Follow the money, find the market

Our problem here is that we've asked the wrong question. Demand alone doesn't make a market. Money makes a market. Follow the money, and you'll find your market.

Thus the question every prospective information broker should start with is: Who is willing to pay for information and the retrieval skills I can bring to bear? You may encounter an occasional client willing to hire you to settle a bet or merely to satisfy his or her curiosity. But most people, businesses, and professionals will spend money on information only if they believe that the information will help them make *more* money.

What is the market for information? The market consists of anyone in a position to materially benefit from that information. The corollary follows naturally: The more a client can expect to make from the information you provide, the more he or she will be willing to pay you for your services.

Who wants to know?

Now we're getting somewhere. Instead of looking at who would be interested in the information you can provide, you're zeroing in on those who can make money from that information.

Consider a simplistic example. An investment banking firm involved in corporate takeovers where hundreds of millions of dollars change hands with the stroke of a pen would think nothing of paying thousands of dollars for an in-depth report on the target company. Yet you could spend the same amount of time researching the love life of Jonathan Swift for a college English professor and be lucky if his or her grant covered your expenses.

The lesson once again is this: everyone wants information, but not everyone is willing or able to pay for it. So go where the money is. Focus your efforts on those people, professions, and companies who are in a position to profit from the information you can provide.

Insurance and investment companies

We've already identified one promising category—investment banking. Unfortunately, though it's hard to believe if you lived through the 1980's, investment bankers are relatively few and far between. And the successful ones either have an in-house research staff or long-standing relationships with established information consultants or both.

So who else stands to make more money from the money they invest in you? The ideal client is someone who constantly needs information on a constantly changing list of topics. Insurance companies are a possibility—think of all the different risks they cover. But unless you live in Hartford, Connecticut, or are otherwise close to an insurance company's home office, your opportunities here may be limited. It isn't likely that your local Prudential representative will have the authority to hire someone like yourself. But then again, he or she may, so it could be worth checking.

The same goes for your local Merrill Lynch stock broker. Stock brokers and investment advisers are constantly looking at new companies, entire industries, corporate executives, S.E.C. data, and more. As you might suspect, however, most are well supplied with information. But there may be a niche they've overlooked or something you can do for them faster and better than it is currently being done. It doesn't hurt to check.

Stock brokers and insurance agents have something obvious in common: both can materially benefit from the information you can supply. In addition, both professions often deal with a wide range of ever-changing subjects. But they have something else in common as well, something that is not immediately evident. The insurance and financial industries depend for their very existence on computers and computerized information.

For the people who work in these professions, a modicum of computer literacy is virtually a condition of employment. Even in the smallest of towns. In fact, *especially* in the smallest of towns where computer communications offers the only link to the markets, the home office, and their fellow employees.

Later in this book you will find two complete chapters devoted to marketing and sales. But even at this early stage it's a good idea to begin thinking about where you will sell your services. Start following the money—literally—by focusing on companies involved in investment and finance.

Advertising, public relations, and attorneys

Of course, financial people aren't the only good prospects. Two of the professions at the top of our list, for example, are attorneys and advertising or public relations agencies.

In any given month, an attorney in general practice might need information on half a dozen corporations (balance sheet, income statement, profiles of top executives, etc.), personal biographies of assorted plaintiffs and defendants, a year's worth of magazine articles on a particular drug, industrial process, or social phenomenon, background for prior art in a patent litigation, and a list of expert witnesses on auto safety, combined with copies of every article each has ever written on the subject.

An advertising agency always needs to know what a client's competition is doing. Agencies also need background information for ad campaigns or for their own marketing purposes. The more clients the agency has, the more reports it will need. It needs marketing studies and surveys for a wide range of products and services. It needs government data and reports. It might even need to know the personal preferences and prejudices of a key executive at a company it hopes to win as an account.

The Rugge Group has always found ad agencies to be an excellent source of business. For example, a leading agency once asked for a report on the origins of wine corks. The final report included not only text but pictures of traditional cork makers hand carving their products in Portugal. The research was later used in a series of commercials promoting Gallo's line of "better" wines. The Rugge Group also developed crucial information used in campaigns for PIP printing and in the past has supplied ad agencies with everything from pictures of the sinking of the *Titanic* to an erupting volcano to an exploding atomic bomb.

Public relations firms or the PR departments of small ad agencies have a similarly varied list of needs. They need to know about local issues and angles, individuals, movers and shakers, and buttonmen. All of them desperately need reports on how their press releases or publicity campaigns are playing.

Companies in general

These are only three general possibilities. There are many other less obvious opportunities. Large companies, for example, rarely rely exclusively on their advertising agency for market research and competitor analysis. Most have departments to address these needs, and all of them are potential clients.

At small companies, the need for information retrieval services is even more acute. (Though often it is not recognized.) Most small firms cannot afford to maintain a well-equipped, fully staffed corporate library or "information center" as such facilities are often called. Yet most could benefit greatly from the services an information consultant can provide.

So much information is available that at the very least, your services could put even a small company on a nearly equal footing with a corporate giant. The fact that such services are available on a freelance, independent-contractor basis is ideally suited to a tight budget.

In short, even if you do as we suggest and rule out all those clients who are unable or unwilling to pay you what you are worth, even if you only "follow the money," the potential market for information and the services of an information consultant is huge.

The one thing the market definitely is not, however, is well-defined. Information is such a nebulous commodity, and client needs can be so incredibly varied, that nothing is cut and dried. Every time you go in to sell yourself, you are, in effect, selling a highly customized, one-of-a-kind service. You can't just open your samples case and say "I've got this, this, and this. Would you like them in blue or in green?"

Similarly, every prospective "information broker's" situation is different. If you were selling dental office supplies or auto mechanic tools, we could easily tell you how to develop a list of prime prospects, and we could offer some reasonably accurate assessments of the extent of the market.

But information and information consulting services, as we have been at pains to emphasize in this chapter, are different. It is entirely possible, for example, that there simply is no market for information consulting in your area. There are ways to extend your reach electronically, but without a solid base of local clients, you start at a tremendous disadvantage. Some brokers have been able to overcome this because their particular skills—like chemical patent researching—are in such demand. Others have brought with them a client base developed through some other endeavor.

But, in general, you should begin by trying to establish a local base. And that may not be too difficult to do. It may be that your particular area is rife with opportunities.

There is simply no way to tell until you go look for yourself. The best anyone can do is to guide you in the right general direction and hopefully keep you from making the same mistakes we have made. We will go into more detail later in this book.

One thing we can tell you for certain: It *is* possible to make a living as an information broker. There *is* a market for what we all offer, and it is growing. But it is not rocketing through the roof. This is not at all like the early days of the fast food business when anyone able to raise the capital to buy a McDonald's franchise was guaranteed to make a fortune.

Also, regardless of where you live, information brokering is hard work. To be successful, you must be of above average intelligence, you must have a healthy amount of innate curiosity, and you must have the creativity and imagination of the finest investigative journalist or consulting detective.

It's a tall order. Yet the way things are today, even these skills and abilities aren't enough to *ensure* your success. To have a chance, you must also be able to overcome the disadvantage suffered by all information consultants. This is the previously mentioned lack of information consciousness on the part of the vast majority of people.

You will find, for example, that prospective clients don't ask you for data they think is impossible to obtain. They don't understand the depth of information that is available or the sophistication of the tools an information broker uses. So they can't conceive of asking someone to do something they think is impossible.

Earlier we compared the staggering amount of information available today to a fire-breathing dragon, and we postulated two knights, one who knew about the dragon but had never confronted it and one who could personally testify to its ferocity and strength. The plain, unvarnished truth is that most of your potential clients don't even know there *is* a dragon, let alone appreciate the skills required to bring it to heel. To say nothing of understanding the costs involved.

This means that you are going to have to spend the first precious minutes of a 25-minute sales call educating your potential client. You'll have to spend even more time sensing what it is he or she is trying to accomplish. Then you'll have to draw on your knowledge and skill to propose on the spot an information "product" customized to answer those needs. And, oh, yes, you'll also have to figure out what to charge for delivering this product and when it will be ready.

Clearly, it takes a special kind of person to be a successful information broker. No one has yet come up with a slogan to match "The few. The proud. The Marines." But if our profession had a slogan, it would be along those lines.

(Though somehow "The few. The proud. The Informed." doesn't quite do it.) If you've got what it takes, there's a job for you as an information professional. You won't get rich, but you'll never be bored. And, as we'll see in the next chapter, the avenues open to you are as limitless as the Information Age itself.

2

What *is* an
information broker?

IN THIS CHAPTER WE'LL INTRODUCE YOU TO THE WIDE WORLD OF PRACTICING
information brokers. You'll get a glimpse of the kinds of projects successful practitioners take on and the challenges they accept. You will be amazed at the depth
and variety of the information specialist's world. But search as you may, you
won't find any activity that can legitimately be called "brokering."

Defining the terms

This leads to an important point that must be addressed before we go any further.
The term "information broker" is one of the great misnomers of the age. This is
particularly ironic since, if any profession prides itself on accuracy, it is ours.

The general press and even some professional journals can use the term all
they want. That won't change the fact that the men and women commonly
referred to as "information brokers" don't broker anything. A broker, after all
(according to *Webster's Ninth Collegiate Dictionary*), is someone who "acts as an
intermediary," who serves as "an agent who arranges marriages," or "negotiates
contracts of purchase and sale (as of real estate, commodities, or securities)."

It is certainly true that today's information brokers act as intermediaries
between information resources and the people who need the information. But as
it is used today, the term really applies to someone who is actively sought out by
both buyers and sellers and who profits by taking a commission on the sales he or
she arranges.

By this definition, an information broker has far more in common with an attorney or a doctor than with brokers who deal in securities, real estate, or pork bellies. As you will see, the people whose hard work and success have defined the profession are consultants, or specialists, or professional searchers. They don't sell information, and they don't take a commission for arranging such a "sale." Like doctors, lawyers, and certified public accountants, they charge a fee for professional services. They are not "brokers" of anything.

Co-author Sue Rugge used to describe Information On Demand, the firm she founded, as "a fee-based information gathering company." Others have suggested the term "information intermediary." Helen Burwell, publisher of the only directory of information specialists, began by referring to the profession as "fee-based information services." (The word "fee" was included in both cases to emphasize the distinction between the services provided by free public libraries and money-making information firms.)

One could debate the proper terminology for hours. But in the end, you would inevitably conclude that the activities and job descriptions of information brokers are so varied that no single term will ever be totally accurate. Yet the public—and your potential clients—demand a quick handle. And "information broker" is fast becoming the recognized tag. Even the latest edition of Ms. Burwell's famous directory is called *The Burwell Directory of Information Brokers*.

Parenthetically, it is worth noting that the term "fee-based" service is being used extensively in Europe, and increasingly in the United States, to distinguish corporate, public, and academic information services from the independent, entrepreneurial professionals we normally think of as information brokers.

The terminology, in short, is a mess. In general, the momentum behind "information broker" appears to be too strong for it to be derailed in favor of a more accurate term. That's the term the public is coming to associate with the kind of activities discussed in this book, so that's the term we will use, either as "information broker" or "IB."

Incidentally, since we can now talk one-on-one, from here on we'll refer to ourselves as Sue and Alfred instead of co-author Rugge and co-author Glossbrenner. No point in standing on formality.

Job description

Now let's look at the job of the information broker. Let's look at the kinds of things you'll be doing to earn your bread once you enter the profession.

If this were an ordinary book about an ordinary profession—like being a lawyer, accountant, or salesperson—we could click off in short order the duties, tasks, responsibilities, rate of pay, types of assignments, and skills that would be required. Presenting you with an accurate and fairly complete job description would be no problem.

Alfred has done this many times in the past with pieces like "How to Get a Job in Construction," "Reserving Your Seat in the Travel Industry," and the unforgettable "Food Service and You," all written for a career encyclopedia published by the Baker & Taylor Companies in the 1970's. If nothing else, being able to tick off a definitive description of the job of information broker would appeal to Alfred's sense of organization.

But Alfred and everyone else who likes things tied up in neat little packages is forever doomed to be disappointed when describing the job of information broker. Because frankly, there *is* no job description. You've heard about those positions in corporate America where you're told "Joan/John, you can make this job anything you want"? Well, being an information broker is exactly like that and then some.

The reason for this isn't hard to find. As we said in Chapter 1, information itself is nebulous, and the needs of clients for information services are incredibly varied. Under the circumstances, it would be impossible for the information broker's job not to be equally nebulous and varied. Consequently, no two information brokers' jobs are exactly alike.

Two pillars of the profession: Retrieval and organization

Fortunately, while specific projects and assignments vary widely, it *is* possible to classify virtually all information broker activities under one of two major headings. These are information retrieval and information organization.

Information retrieval and a database thumbnail

By information retrieval we mean any activity involved in finding out what the client wants to know. Many times, the activity involved will be searching an online electronic database.

At this point we should take time out for just a moment in deference to those of you who have only the vaguest notion of what an online database is and how to access it. You'll find lots of hands-on details later in the book, but since we are going to be referring to online databases quite frequently, a quick thumbnail sketch is crucial to those who have never used one.

Vast stores of information exist today in electronic form, either because they were keyed in at a computer when they were created or because someone has paid to have them keyed in or electronically scanned after publication. A number of companies have collected information of this sort and put it into their mainframe computers. These computers are connected to special phone networks that make it possible for you to dial into them with your own personal computer.

To do so, you will need communications software and a modem, a black box that connects your computer to the phone lines. You will also need an account number and password to get into the system you want to call. The systems have names like DIALOG, The Knowledge Index, Mead Data Central (LEXIS/NEXIS), Maxwell Online (BRS and ORBIT), NewsNet, Vu/Text, DataTimes, and Dow Jones News/Retrieval. All of them charge you for the time you spend online and most charge for the information you retrieve as well.

The two final points you need to know for now are first that the online industry as a whole consists of some 4000 databases available through some 500 online systems. The industry covers *everything*. Patents and trademarks; information from Dun & Bradstreet, Standard and Poor's, and Moody's; all the leading newswires; almost every magazine, journal, newspaper or newsletter (available either as a citation or as the full text of the publication); chemical formulas; engineering specifications; doctoral dissertations; the entire Library of Congress; and on, and on, and on.

Second, in most cases, these online systems are not designed for use by the general public. Even those that claim to be "user friendly" aren't. Tapping an online database requires practice, skill, and often, special training, which most database vendors will be only too happy to provide—for a fee. (To be fair, some online systems like D&B, Predicasts, and Information Access Corporation do offer free classes and seminars.)

Returning to retrieval

To the information broker, an online database often offers the fastest, cheapest, and sometimes, only way to fulfill a client's request. But though online database searching gets most of the press coverage, it is only part of the job. After all, huge amounts of information still are not recorded or indexed in databases. Indeed, at any given moment, the most current information doesn't exist in print—it exists inside the brains of experts in the field. Interviewing these experts and other authorities on the phone also constitutes information retrieval. So, too, are market research assignments in which both multiple online searches and multiple interviews may be conducted.

There is also "document delivery," the most basic form of information retrieval. Information brokers are frequently asked to supply either photocopies or originals of magazine and newspaper articles, government reports, oversight agency filings, and just about any other piece of printed matter you can think of. In fact, there is an entire industry of document delivery brokers who can get you a copy of any article you see referenced in an online search. (More on this in Chapter 15.)

Sometimes "retrieval" requests are anything but conventional. FIND/SVP, one of the largest information gathering firms in the world, reports that clients have asked them to locate and deliver everything from theater tickets to the front end of a 1977 Toyota.

Finders Keepers, Inc.

Even stranger requests have been made of Jim Tice, founder of a firm called Finders Keepers, Inc. Tice began in the advertising business in the 1970s, where he earned a reputation for being able to find anything needed for any production, particularly unusual objects used as backdrops or accessories in TV commercials.

He went into business for himself and now gets some 4000 queries a year for everything from 300,000 ladybugs for a landscaping project to the cigarette lighter used by Humphrey Bogart in *The Maltese Falcon* to a Howdy Doody rocking chair of the sort popular between 1949 and 1955.

Tice and Finders Keepers have even tracked down an impossible-to-find perfume for singer Dolly Parton. "She had gotten the perfume 17 years ago, and all she had was an empty bottle," Tice says. The bottle had no name and there was no perfume left inside.

"We found out the company had gone out of business, but we found the maker and had a couple of ounces recreated for Ms. Parton," Tice says. Mr. Tice demurs when asked how much the assignment cost. But he notes that a major part of his operation is the Freelance Finders Network. Members pay about $20 a year to receive tips on search techniques and lists of searches under way. The finders fee is split with the freelancer who locates the object or person or supplies information leading to the correct location.

While Finders Keepers is not the "traditional" type of information brokerage, it does illustrate an important truth: Everybody must find his or her own niche in the marketplace.

Mr. Tice has found, and made the most of, a very interesting one.

Hospital floor plans to a Bahrainian palace

Sue and IOD also got their share of unusual requests. For example, there was once a client who wanted the floor plans to a particular Czechoslovakian hospital. This was during the Cold War, so information flow in and out of Eastern Europe was not exactly free. Surprisingly, Sue found the plans in a back issue of *Architectural Digest*.

In retrospect, it wasn't that difficult an assignment, but the client was sufficiently amazed. One of the rewards of this business is that you become a miracle worker on a regular basis.

Along a similar theme, a firm in Houston was once hired by the sheik of Bahrain (one of the Arab emirates) to build a new palace. The stipulation was—and here is the kicker—that the palace had to be in the Bahrainian architectural style.

The Texas firm could have handled everything from Georgian to Bauhaus, but it had no idea what constituted Bahrainian. Sue was undaunted, however. The information had to be heavily illustrated, for obvious reasons, and there is at present no way to satisfy such a request online. Online citations specify whether or not the source article contains illustrations, but one cannot usually obtain those illustrations electronically. So Sue and her assistants concentrated on books. Books of history and architecture. Her firm's proximity to the libraries of the Berkeley campus—especially the School of Environmental Design—was thus a major advantage.

Other retrieval services are more ordinary. If you have private investigators among your clients, for example, you may find yourself searching Consumer Product Safety Commission records, newspapers, and trade literature for background information related to product liability and malpractice suits. Or you may be asked to find expert witnesses or determine what opposing experts have written and where they have testified.

At IOD Sue used to get requests for product samples. The idea was that Company A would not want Company B to know that it was interested in samples of Company B's products and thus would use an information broker as an intermediary. One time, for instance, a load of carpet arrived at IOD's door, ordered by the firm for a client. Sue ran out to the truck and told the driver not to unload but to ship it to the client's address.

At the Rugge Group, Sue has also been asked to determine the worldwide manufacturing capacity for a particular chemical needed for certain drugs. This involved many, many hours of phone interviews and fax exchanges with chemical company personnel located all over the world, and long distance charges in the thousands of dollars.

Competitive intelligence, either company-specific or industry-based, is also frequently requested. Among the actual projects the large information firm Find/SVP has completed, for example, are finding the answers to questions like: What ad campaigns has McCall's Magazine run for itself in the past few years? Is anyone actively promoting the sale of milk in glass bottles? What are the leading men's fashion magazines in Japan, and can you get us sample copies? What major articles have been written in the business press on fast-food chicken restaurants in the past five years?

Market research by phone

The Rugge Group does a lot of competitive intelligence, even for large companies that have their own in-house research departments. Of course these companies hire us for our outstanding work. That goes without saying! But there's also the very real need for confidentiality. If you work for a company, you may be able to call out without revealing the name of your firm. But when someone calls you back, they will usually get the switchboard, and all will be revealed.

Typically, clients will want to know what their competition is doing, what the rest of the industry sees for the future. And they can get that sort of information more easily through an intermediary than if they were to assign an assistant VP, because that person would have to identify his or her affiliation.

In addition, as an information broker, you're independent and objective. Clients tell us that they've done research internally on a topic, and have come to The Rugge Group to confirm or disprove the results they found. Their people may have had even a subliminal vested interest that would inadvertently cant things a certain way.

Requests for copies of a competing firm's Securities and Exchange Commission (S.E.C.) filings are common. As are requests for brief biographies of the company's leading executives. Companies also like to know things on an ongoing basis, so you may get requests like ''Tell me whenever Company B files for a patent,'' or ''Give me a copy of every article mentioning the firm whenever it appears.''

SDI services

Requests like these have led some information brokers to offer what in the library profession is known as an "SDI service." This stands for "selective dissemination of information." That's a librarian's term that simply means "current awareness." As you will see, it is possible to tell an online database to conduct a search for the information you specify each time new information is added to the database.

This makes it relatively easy to offer a current awareness service to your clients. And it is a good idea to try to do so. You probably won't make a great deal of money at it, but a monthly or weekly report from your firm helps keep the client aware of *you* as well.

Information organization

The heart and soul of the information broker's job is information retrieval. But many individuals also offer information organization services as well. These include assembling and preparing bibliographies, cataloguing book and materials collections, book indexing, library management, and consulting on library or information center design and management.

You may well wonder what doing something like cataloguing all the books in a company's library has to do with, say, preparing an in-depth competitive analysis for the same company. Where's the common thread? Are all information brokers supposed to have library management skills?

The answer once again lies in the elasticity of the information broker job description. The people who offer information organization services do so because they have had training or experience in these areas. Most hold advanced degrees in library science and thus operate as "freelance librarians" as well as search and retrieval specialists. The common thread is library science, a discipline that embraces both information organization and retrieval. Quite naturally, its masters tend to be skilled in both areas.

Go with what you know

The point every reader should take away from this, however, is not that all successful information brokers must hold a Master of Library Science (MLS) degree. (Neither Sue nor Alfred hold advanced degrees.) This idea couldn't be further from the truth. The key point is that successful information brokers draw upon the training and experience they already have, whatever that may be.

For example, if you've spent the last ten years of your life as a stock broker, you can't tell us that you don't know much more than most people do about how to read a balance sheet or how to interpret financial data. You don't have to have a clue about how to prepare a bibliography or organize a library collection. Simply go with what you know.

If two years from now you've built a business offering investment research to people who prefer to deal with discount brokerage firms (which provide no research at all), your type of service could easily become "one of the things information brokers do"—simply because you're an information broker and you're doing them.

But we're not playing fair. A stock broker is too easy an example. Let's assume instead that you've spent the last decade as a dispatcher for a trucking company, a purchasing agent for a manufacturing firm, or a lab technician for a pharmaceutical company. Whatever it is, it's a business you know inside and out. You know how it works, you know the major problems, you know lots of people—and you know what information needs are not being met.

It is simply impossible to believe that once you have a better understanding of information, how to retrieve it, and how to package and present it that there isn't some service you could provide that the industry you know so well would pay you to offer.

This is a broad statement, to be sure. There are undoubtedly some exceptions. But knowing what we know about information and about the sorry state of information-related services in all American industries, it's a statement we make with confidence. No matter what you do for a living right now, somewhere there's an information niche in that field that is not being filled.

We would never claim that filling it will be easy, though you may be surprised at how readily your proposals will be accepted. We certainly wouldn't claim that you can make a living at it. But we *know* the niches exist. As a prospective information broker, your first job should be to find them. That will give you a base from which you can branch out to encompass industries and areas with which you may not be so familiar.

The most crucial component

We've given you just a small sampling of the kinds of things practicing information brokers do. It simply is not possible to be any more precise. Information brokers do all *kinds* of things.

You know the expression about charging "whatever the traffic will bear?" Well, when you're an information broker, you may find yourself offering "whatever the client may want." (And charging whatever the traffic will bear as well!) You may not be able to provide the service by doing the work yourself. But if you're any good at your profession, you will be able to find someone else who can. You will review the results to make sure they are up to your quality standards, add a mark-up, and present the product to the client.

In the "old days"

It takes some time to learn the mechanics of information retrieval. And you will never stop learning about all that is available. It is true that the more imagination and creativity you can bring to the job, the better off you will be. But the fundamentals of information retrieval can be learned by any intelligent, motivated person.

The real trick—whether you're an information broker, freelance writer, consultant, or some other self-employed professional—is to find out what the client really wants, what he or she is trying to accomplish. That can be the greatest information retrieval trick of all, since clients don't always know themselves what they really want or need. This is where the sheep part company from the goats, for it is the single most important skill you must develop.

There was a time, for example, when it was possible to walk into a client's office and thump a two-inch-thick computer printout of a database search on his or her desk, and say, "Here it is. All the information you asked for." From about 1971 to about 1976 or so, you could be a miracle worker by handing somebody a printout created from an online database search.

Nobody knew that this kind of thing was possible. Where did all this come from? How did it get into your computer? They were amazed. Sue used to respond by explaining that the printed information was just half a loaf and then take the opportunity to explain the other services her firm could provide—like following up leads brought to light by the initial search, conducting phone interviews, obtaining actual copies of the documents referred to in the printout, and so on.

No solutions. No answers

Today, the results of an online database search are more like a third of a loaf. Today, people need—indeed, demand—more than just raw information.

This brings up an important point. As information brokers, we shouldn't consider ourselves capable of providing solutions. Let the people who call themselves "consultants" or subject "experts" do that.

What we *can* provide, and what sets a really good information broker apart from the rest, are resources. We can provide the client with the kinds of information he or she needs—the statistics or lists or reports that make it possible for individuals to solve their problems.

That is probably as close as it is possible to come to defining the essence of information brokering. The mechanics of actually getting the information are, in the end, just mechanics. Performing an online search requires a good deal of knowledge and skill, for example. But any intelligent person can learn how to do it. An information broker needs something more.

What does the client *really* want?

We can illustrate the point with a basic example. The process begins with the initial meeting and continues throughout the project, but it is perhaps most evident in what professional librarians and information brokers alike call the "reference interview." The *reference interview* is the conversation you have with the client to determine the goal the client is trying to achieve and the particular kind of information most likely to help him or her achieve it. Not surprisingly, it is of major importance since your ability to ask the right questions is crucial to delivering what the client needs.

Now, it is not at all uncommon for a client to say something like "I want everything there is on solar energy." As an information broker, however, you're familiar with the information dragon. You might not know anything about solar energy yourself, but you know enough about information to be aware that literally tons of material exist on the subject. Clearly that's not what the client really wants. It is thus your job to help the client more clearly express his or her goals. So instead of saying, "Yup, everything there is on solar energy. Got it. Anything else?", you might respond with "What are you trying to find out? What goals are you trying to achieve?"

To which the client may very well respond "Just give me everything on solar energy." As we said in the previous chapter, most people have no idea that the information dragon even exists, let alone how to tame it. So you have to be patient. You have to avoid making them feel foolish. After all, information isn't *their* profession.

Somewhere buried within their request is the goal they're trying to achieve. It is your job to find it. So thinking quickly, you gently suggest that there is a great deal, a *very* great deal of information on solar energy. Perhaps the client could help you out by narrowing things down a bit.

In general, you'll find that new clients either don't really have a clear idea themselves what they're after, or they don't think you can find what they want. So they make their requests as broad as possible. Through no fault of their own, their awareness of the breadth and scope of the information available on any topic and their familiarity with what can be accomplished by a skilled information broker is virtually nil.

Fortunately this is gradually changing. There is indeed a growing body of well-informed clients who recognize the need for a professional but who are also savvy enough to know what they need and what it should cost. In general, such people make very good clients since you don't have to spend your time explaining things to them. They also tend to appreciate your skills since they know what it takes to do a good job.

Narrowing it down

What they don't know is that you want them to make their request as narrow as possible because that makes things infinitely easier. Among other things, narrowing things down is the whole point of using a computer. If you use the computer and get 500 citations, there's no benefit—you can whip up 500 citations in a library. But if the request is narrow enough, you can come up with perhaps *five* citations that are absolutely on target.

The biggest asset an information broker offers a client is being able to pinpoint what he or she really needs to know. Or more accurately, working with the individual, asking the right questions, and offering seasoned guidance to help him or her clearly define the information needed.

It is impossible to emphasize this point too strongly. If you think about it for just a moment, you'll see why. Anyone can meet with a client and blindly accept the request to provide everything there is on solar energy. And many people are familiar with the mechanics of information retrieval, particularly on such a broad topic as solar energy.

What sets the information broker apart is the ability to help a client more clearly define the goal. Without this crucial ingredient, the client will be literally inundated with information—98 percent of which is guaranteed to be useless. In fact, it's worse than useless—it is time-consuming to review, and it is expensive to provide.

As an information broker, you can save the client all that time and all that needless expense by helping the individual clarify what he or she really wants to know. After all, it takes no skill to attack a problem with an axe or a meat cleaver. Some people who call themselves information brokers actually operate that way. The true professional, on the other hand, always uses a scalpel.

The solar energy request is a perfect example. It is drawn from an actual project Sue completed for a corporate executive. As it turned out, what the person really wanted was not everything there is on solar energy. He merely wanted to build a greenhouse in his backyard to raise tomatoes. But he simply didn't think it was possible to get information specific to that problem. Then again, he had never heard of the information dragon.

Sell, sell, sell

As you can see, an information broker is and does many things. But there's one thing that all successful information brokers do and do well. Every one of them knows how to sell.

It doesn't matter how good a searcher you are, how good a librarian, or how much you read or know. If you can't *sell*, you will never make a living as an information broker.

If you can't sell yourself, if you can't be credible to your prospective clients, they're not going to hire you. That's often true in other professions, but it is doubly true here. You must never forget that, to most of your clients, information is a stepchild to their own professions. It's not recognized as a legitimate profession on its own by most other professionals—chemists, biologists, management consultants, and especially engineers.

All those people think that because it's *their* subject, they're better able to gather the information they need than you are. If you're not an engineer or a chemist, how can you possibly know anything about "my" field?

It is a reaction you encounter in any freelance profession. After writing everything from a home economics textbook to sales brochures and speeches for Merrill Lynch, Alfred wrote two best-selling books on baseball with Charley Lau—even though he had no knowledge of the game. Then he wrote a book about computer communications. Then one on all available kinds of software. Recently Osborne/McGraw-Hill published his guide to hard disk drives, and Random House published his guide to Microsoft's DOS 5.

Eventually—after you've actually done it a few times and have samples to show—the questions and doubts cease. Sue has had the same experience. If someone doubts that The Rugge Group can handle a job, they have only to look at Sue's track record.

Now this is not to say that you should expect to be equally skilled in all topics. There are some subjects—like chemical structure searching, patents, and biotechnology—that are best left to those information professionals with training in those areas. It is important to know your limits.

At the same time, if you know the information field and are skilled at using retrieval techniques and tools, you can obtain excellent results in many different subject areas. Naturally, that doesn't stop some people from being skeptical. Part of it no doubt has to do with the client defending his or her territory. Part of it is ego. It is painful, particularly for those who have spent their lives in the soft embrace of academically oriented professions, to accept the fact that an outsider—with no scholarly dissertations, no conference papers, no sabbaticals in Europe—could possibly find what they're looking for.

"But you don't know anything about the field," they say. If you try to tell them, "But I'm an information professional," they're likely to respond, "What's that? You mean you're a librarian?"

Nix on "librarian"

A word to the wise. You want the word "librarian" to stay as far away from this profession as possible—even if you happen to be one. It's nothing personal—some of our best friends and clients are librarians, and most successful information brokers are or once were card-carrying librarians. It is strictly a matter of image.

The public image of a librarian is of someone who has all these sources at his or her disposal, and all of them are mysterious. This is overlaid with the impression that somehow librarians see themselves as priests and priestesses whose responsibility it is to guard "their" information from the grubby hands of the general public.

This couldn't be further from the truth, of course. Though there are inevitably one or two bad apples, as a group, you will never find a more selfless, giving, and generous collection of people than the country's librarians. Far from jealously guarding "their" information, those that we know are positively bursting to share the sheer joy of knowledge, particularly with young minds.

Yet the image of "Marion, Madame Librarian" presented by the 1962 movie *The Music Man* is still very much with us: a repressed female, hair in a bun, glasses, the severest of makeup—and very strict about "her" books. To say nothing of people speaking above a whisper in "her" library. It is hard to say whether the movie took its cue from the public or whether public sentiment was formed by the movie. But the fact is that this general image persists, and as an information broker you would do well to steer as clear of it and the word "librarian" as possible.

You might also want to steer clear of certain professions. You want advertising agencies, public relations firms, management consultants, and attorneys. Those are the kinds of people who are continually bombarded with new subjects, new companies, new products, new types of cases. They are the people who have to become instant experts overnight. So not only do they need your services, they understand completely that you don't have to have a degree in a subject to be able to find information about it.

Avoid academics and engineers

The professions to avoid are academics and engineers. Among Sue's best clients is a firm of engineering consultants who specialize in supplying needed expertise to patent attorneys. But these enlightened folks are the exception that proves the rule. In general, it has been our experience that engineers can be among the worst clients to work for. An engineer has his or her own colleague network. They'll go down the hall. If Joe or Jane doesn't know, it probably doesn't need to be known or isn't worth finding out.

Engineers like to think that they are on the leading edge. If it has already been published in a journal, it's not worth getting because everybody already knows about it.

Chemists, in contrast, tend to be much better clients. A chemist goes to college and learns how to use *Chemical Abstracts*. We've never met an engineer who's even heard of *Engineering Index*. Yet EI started in 1898, the same time that Chem Abs started. (The online version of EI is called "Compendex.")

Whether you're selling to chemists, attorneys, ad agencies, or even engineers, the key component is confidence. You simply must be credible. You have got to know the information field.

You have got to believe in your own abilities.

To use a quick example, imagine that you're a contractor called in to bid on a particular home repair job. No two jobs are ever identical, but if you are good at your profession, you can look at the job and make a credible presentation. You may not know exactly how you will handle this specific job, but based on past experience, you know you can do it. Or you know that you can't.

Either way, your competence and the confidence it generates comes through. The homeowner knows even less about what might be involved than you do. But he or she can tell in an instant whether you know what you're talking about. This is not something you can fake.

To look at things the other way, you may be a crackerjack online searcher and you may have all the confidence in the world in your ability to find anything anyone asks you to find. But if you don't get out there and sell your services, clients are not going to beat a path to your door.

Search and sell—you have to be able and enthusiastically willing to do both if you want to be a success as an information broker. Either that, or you've got to find a partner who is good at whichever activity you are not good at. Any number of successful information firms have been founded by an ace searcher and an ace salesperson, the talents of one complementing those of the other.

A day in the life

At this point you should have at least a general idea of what an information broker is and does. You've been introduced to the two basic pillars of the field (retrieval and organization), and you've seen how varied the activities within each can be. You've been told to go with what you know in focusing your initial efforts. And you know that the most important talent an information broker can have is the ability to help the client determine what he or she really wants or needs to know. We've also told you how important it is never to cease in selling your services.

We'll close with what might be called "a day in the life of an information broker." Our goal here is to give you some idea of what your workdays may be like once you enter the profession. Obviously, this is only an approximation, and it compresses into a single day activities and tasks that may actually be done over several days. But it's the flavor we're after. As you read this day-in-the-life, ask yourself if you can see yourself doing these kinds of things on a regular basis.

Morning

Get up, get coffee, scan the papers. You'll want a local paper, of course. But you should also consider subscribing to a major metropolitan daily (*New York Times*, *San Francisco Chronicle*, *Cleveland Plain Dealer*, etc.) and, if you can afford it, the *Wall Street Journal*. As an information broker, you're an information omnivore—you can never tell when something you come across in the papers will have a bearing on a current or future project.

Go to the office and boot up your computer. Sign on to CompuServe, MCI Mail, GEnie, and whatever other electronic mail services you use. Pick up and print out your mail. Answer the "hot" letters and queries immediately. Save the others for later.

Check your daily appointment book. Is anybody coming? Is there anybody you are scheduled to go see? Are there any other "to-do's" for the day?

Return to the marketing study you were writing up for Client A. Answer the phone and field inquiries. It breaks your train of thought, but any call could be a client with an assignment.

Print out the report and type up the necessary Federal Express airbill. But don't call FedEx yet. The day is still young. Between now and the 6:00 P.M. cutoff, you may have other packages to send. (Your FedEx cutoff will vary with your location.)

Take a call from a current client. He wants to know about the progress of a corporate profile you are working on. Reassure the client. After you hang up, make a note to try to get the profile done tonight.

Take another call. It's someone who has read your article in the *XYZ Magazine*. Would it be possible for you to find everything that has been published in the last five years on a certain industrial process? Explain your terms. The prospective client promises to FedEx you a check for half the fee immediately—or she decides to think about it.

Afternoon

Time for lunch. You eat at your desk, reading *Business Week*, *Time*, or *Newsweek*, or some other magazine. After lunch, and more phone calls, you spend an hour working on the speech you will be giving next week at the local Rotary Club. It's a speech on information brokers, of course, and it is designed to both inform and, subtly, sell your services.

Tired of writing for the time being, you decide to take a break and catch up on your reading. You read two articles in *Online* magazine, scan DIALOG's *Chronolog*, and update your Bluesheets collection (explained in Part Three of this book).

At about 2:00 P.M., you start your daily round of business development phone calls. Your goal is to make appointments to get in to see people at local ad agencies, law offices, and corporations. By 3:00 you've got one luke-warm prospect who thinks he might be able to see you next month some time. You make a note to call him back to firm up a date next week.

It's 3:30 now and you're just about to pop out to pick up some office supplies when one of your very best clients calls.

"I need all you can find on artificial sweeteners, and I need it now." You calm the client down and help her more clearly define her goals. Then you agree to take a swing at it and call her back.

Forty-five minutes later, you have searched nine databases and have a pretty impressive wad of information on disk. You call the client and offer to fax it to her. She says, no, "Can you send it to me via MCI Mail?" No problem. You sign on to that system and upload the entire, unedited text file to her address. Then you make a hard copy printout and put it into a FedEx envelope. You will bill her later, once you have checked to make sure she is satisfied.

Evening

The evening rush hour has begun. No point in going out for office supplies now. You've still got a proposal to write for a prospective client. But you decide that you've worked enough for the time being, and besides, you'll be working tonight. So you spend an hour puttering around the house or working in the garage, if you have a home office. Getting dinner started also offers a nice change of pace.

Or you make a few phone calls. Or maybe you simply take the time to think about how you will approach the next project on your list. Who will you call? What databases will you search? Do you have any contacts who could help you on this one? You make notes to yourself, of course. When you're juggling five or six projects at a time, it's the only way to remember where you were on each.

It's a quarter to six in the evening, and it is also the end of the month. Bill-paying time. Time to do the books. And next week your quarterly tax payment is due. You spend the hour with the books and the checkbook. While you're at it, you make a note to send second notices to several clients who are more than 30 days past due.

At 7:00 you break for dinner. But you are back at your machine by 9:00. You've got three online searches to do, and some online systems cut their rates dramatically after 6:00 P.M. Some databases never go down in price, but it only makes good sense to do whatever searching you can at the low, evening rate.

By midnight, you're exhausted. You think you've got all you need for two projects and have started the third. But your eyes are beginning to blur and you're no longer as sharp as you were when you started. You sign off and decide to postpone cleaning up and printing out the information you have captured until tomorrow.

Before going to sleep you either watch that television show you taped earlier in the evening or you read a novel or non-fiction book that has nothing to do with computers or the information industry. You have found that if you don't do this, if you simply climb into bed, your mind keeps replaying the last search and helpfully suggesting additional avenues of inquiry.

At the end of the day

Though hypothetical, this is very much what you can expect your days to be like as an information broker. You do spend a good portion of your day actually practicing your profession. But there are also speeches to give, articles to write, and sales calls to make. There are the mind-numbing but necessary details of paying the bills, balancing the books, and keeping the office well-supplied. There are phone calls to take—both desired and unwanted—letters to write, rush jobs to complete, and publications to read.

But there is also the freedom to come and go as you please. To make your own hours. To run an errand in the middle of the afternoon—provided a client doesn't call with an immediate need—without asking anyone's permission. To work as long and as hard as you like, or to not work at all—provided you get the check to the mortgage company on time.

No job is perfect. But some are more perfect than others. Given the fact that we must all work for a living, we must all do *something*, you could do far worse than to become an information broker. Provided that you love information.

In the next chapter we will elaborate on this theme. We will look with a cold, rational eye at the pros and cons of the information business.

3

Pros and cons of the information business

IN THIS CHAPTER IT IS OUR GOAL TO SCARE THE DAYLIGHTS OUT OF YOU. WE'RE going to tell you everything that's wrong with the information industry as a whole and the profession of information broker in particular. There is no need to exaggerate or in any way stretch the truth, even if we were inclined to do so. The reality alone says it all. We need only present the facts.

If, after absorbing those facts, you *still* want to become an information broker, you will find that the profession has its rewards. We'll tell you about them as well. But you should be aware that there's a fundamental imbalance between the cons and the pros. Knowing what we know, our advice is this: If there's anything else you can do for a living that meets your own personal goals, by all means do it. You will never be able to make a rational, cost-justified case for choosing this profession. The choice has to come from the heart.

We will begin by considering the information industry as a whole. Then we'll narrow the focus to a more personal level and look at the process of starting up the business, the daily work, the financial potential, and competition. We will close with some thoughts on the challenges anyone seeking to set up a small business or become self-employed faces. In each case, we will present the negative aspects and then the positive aspects, if any, as we see them.

You're free to agree or disagree as you choose. We simply want to make you aware of the pitfalls as well as the joys of the profession. If you get into it and later decide that "this information broker stuff is not for me," you'll have only yourself to blame. No one can say you weren't warned.

Problems in the online information industry

The online industry has been good to us. We know and count as our friends lots of the people involved. They are good, bright, hard working men and women wrestling with what amounts to nothing less than a force of nature. In addition, due to the relatively small numbers of online customers, these folks generally don't have large budgets to work with. But they do the best with what they have.

At the same time, however, as your guides into this realm, we have a responsibility to tell you the unvarnished truth. The truth is that if you approach online information and the companies that provide it as if this were a mature industry, you are likely to become disappointed, frustrated, and confused. If you approach it as a good consumer, your feelings may border on outrage, for the online information industry has a lot of weaknesses. Though, as one commentator we know has pointed out, the weakness never extends to prices. In good times or bad, it seems, the urge is ever upward when it comes to prices.

In short, the online information industry has more than its share of really good people. But, as Alfred says, it's still a wild and woolly place, particularly for new users. Our goal in the criticisms levelled throughout this chapter is to alert you to this fact. Keep your eyes open, and, until you feel you know what you're doing, keep your wallet close to your chest.

A product without value

We've said this so often that you're undoubtedly tired of hearing it by now, but information and the industry that has grown up to collect, catalogue, disseminate, and profit from it is the very paradigm of the word *nebulous*. None of us even knows what information actually is, let alone how to price the services required to retrieve it.

For one person, the journal articles you provide on some new anti-pollution process are definitely "information." But for another person, the *number* of articles that have been written on this process is the crucial point. To such a person, the actual content of the articles themselves may be totally irrelevant. As we mentioned in Chapter 1, often the simple fact that there *is* no information available on a particular topic can be valuable information in and of itself.

Information, in other words, has no clearly defined value. As such, the information industry has no clearly defined image in the minds of the people you plan to sell your services to. Many of them will know very little (if anything) about personal computers. And, while awareness is increasing, they will probably know even less about modems and online electronic databases. Worse still, those who do have some knowledge will assume that all an information broker has to do is type a few keywords into a database and—presto—the desired information appears on the screen.

"Com'on, how much time can that take? If I wasn't so busy, I'd do it myself and save your fee." Every information broker encounters clients like this. While the temptation is to plead your case and attempt some instant education, if you don't absolutely need the job, the best response is "Mr. Client, meet The Dragon. And good luck to you."

No one, in short, knows what you really do because they don't understand how it's done. People who willingly acknowledge the special talents and training of a doctor, lawyer, or tax accountant will thus not accord you the same respect. At least not until you knock their stockings off with a killer report or online search. That means that you start at a serious disadvantage with nearly every prospective client. You really do have to prove yourself every day.

On the plus side, once you have successfully handled an assignment or two, a satisfied client will become your biggest supporter. Often you will develop a personal relationship that probably has more in common with the doctor-patient relationship than with any standard business association. You'll become their personal miracle worker. They don't have to know what you do. All they know is you find them the information they need.

The problem of duplicate data

Like any other industry, the information industry has its own internal technical problems. At best, these problems make your tasks more difficult. At worst, they can raise serious questions about liability.

Let's take a real-life example. ABC News White House reporter Brit Hume writes a computer column for the *Washington Post*. Larry Shannon and Peter Lewis each write computer columns for the *New York Times*. All three columns are excellent sources, and, as it happens, each can be found online. Let's assume that the *Washington Post* and *New York Times* are each available as a separate database. (That is indeed the case, though the *Post* is included in many multi-publication databases as well.)

So far, so good. You sign on to the appropriate systems and search the appropriate databases. Perhaps you are interested in reviews of some new computer program or hardware component. You obtain the information you want—copies of each columnist's review of the product. Then you decide to broaden your search to include additional publications. You try a database that covers perhaps 50 or more newspapers, but not the *Post* or the *Times*. You get lots of hits (i.e., matches in the database for your search terms), and you begin displaying the relevant articles.

But wait a minute. You've seen the information in many of these articles before. It turns out that the columns done by Hume, Shannon, and Lewis are *syndicated*. Like press releases, their columns get picked up and printed by many newspapers, often under completely different headlines. So there you are— you've just paid perhaps $3 apiece for eleven articles, five of which are exact duplicates of what you already have from your first search.

Sue has one searcher friend who poo-poos this problem, citing DIALOG's relatively new (1991) "duplicate detection" feature as the solution. But then, she's a long-time DIALOG employee and clearly doesn't get out much when it comes to other online systems. Most professional searchers like the idea of duplicate detection, but many will tell you that it doesn't always work.

What few people inside the industry will tell you is that there is a *lot* of duplication of data in online databases. And DIALOG or no, it is not always easy to detect. As we will see in Part Three of this book, the databases themselves don't make it easy for you to discover exactly which publications or sources they cover. There are at least two dozen databases, for example, that cover *Business Week*. But each database starts its coverage with a different year. Some offer the full text of every issue they cover. Some are limited to abstracts. And some mix the two. Naturally, all of them have attached a different set of keywords to the same articles. And oh, by the way, the prices you'll pay to search these databases differ by several orders of magnitude.

Byzantine pricing schemes

Speaking of prices, we can think of no industry with a more Byzantine pricing structure than the online information industry. It may be that some defense contractors come close. But for sheer complexity, the online industry takes the prize. We'll go into much more detail in Part Three of this book. For now, take it on faith that most of the time there is absolutely no way to compare prices across different online systems. Each has its own way of deciding how much you owe them.

When an online system is the exclusive distributor of a given database, you have no choice. But a growing number of databases are available on several systems. So as a smart businessperson, you've frequently got to try to figure out who is giving you the best deal. This is much more complicated than it sounds, since, among other things, some systems charge you on the basis of each article or citation you retrieve, while others charge you by the number of characters they transmit to your screen, and still others charge only on the basis of connect time.

In mature consumer products industries, one can assume that misleading pricing or other tricks are intentional. Do you really think, for example, that a company packing 13 ounces of gourmet coffee beans into the same size bag that for decades has always held a full pound of coffee is accidental? Of course not.

Things are different in the online industry. The industry sells a "product" whose value and price are extremely difficult to define. And in the past, the people charged with the responsibility for doing just that have not come from a marketing background. Add to this the relative immaturity of the industry and the fact that everyone wants to try doing things his or her own way, and the result is the incredibly complex pricing structure that exists today.

The inevitable result of this unintended confusion is that many people end up paying much more than they need to pay for the very same data. If you were a large company with lots of fat in the budget, a dollar here and a dollar there might not matter. As it is, even if you can pass 100 percent of the costs along, the shrewdness with which you use online resources can make or break you as an independent information broker.

Inaccurate data

You can avoid the pitfalls of pricing and duplicate data through trial and error and by learning as much as you can about the nuts and bolts of the online information industry. But how can you cope with inaccurate data?

Inaccurate. Incorrect. And just plain wrong! This is the industry's real Achilles heel. Most of us used to think that if something was in print it had to be true. We transferred this faith to television news programs, and then to online databases.

You need only to spend a week as an information broker to see what a fool's paradise you used to live in.

Again, we can offer a quick real-life example. In the course of writing *How to Look It Up Online*, Alfred searched the Library of Congress database for his last name. The search turned up a previously unknown publication written by a great-grandfather. (The sly old fox!) But it also turned up a book published in 1889 called *The Life of Bishop Glossbrenner*. The kicker was that the record was tagged with the named person identified as "Grossbrenner, Jacob John."

Somewhere along the line, someone made a typing mistake. But that doesn't change the fact that if you had told the database to focus on the named person field and searched on "Glossbrenner," you would *not* have found this record.

It's a small typo, of course. Merely a single letter. And the fact that Alfred located the record is proof that there are ways around errors of this sort. But the mere existence of such mistakes gives one pause. Suppose that instead of a single letter being typed incorrectly, the error occurred in a field containing numerical data. Suppose that as a result, the XYZ Company shows up with earnings either far greater or far less than it actually produced.

As an information intermediary, there is virtually no way you could detect the error. Yet it would be included in the printout or report and given to your client. If the client did not detect the error, he or she could easily make a major decision on the basis of faulty information.

Mistakes of this sort turn up *all the time*. If you're already a DIALOG user, you have only to EXPAND a few search terms to see clear evidence of what we mean. The EXPAND command on DIALOG displays a list of keywords showing you those above and below your target word in alphabetical order. For each keyword there is a number indicating how many times it occurs in the database. It is very common to find, say, 3000 occurrences of "automobile" and one or two occurrences of "automobiel."

Again, this is a problem for at least two reasons. First, if you are searching on "automobile" you may not find the records in which that word is misspelled. And second, if mistakes can be made in text—where they can be easily detected—they can also be made in numerical data where detection is next to impossible.

Of course, the same kinds of problems occur all the time in print publications. Or, indeed, in any publication produced by human beings. No one talks about it. No one runs ads saying "Our database has fewer errors in it than the competition." But the problem clearly exists. And as a practicing information professional, you must confront it every day.

Every database is different

In this catalogue of ills, we will pass over the often poor documentation and inadequate instructions provided by online information systems. It took DIALOG and Mead Data Central ten years to produce what is now generally considered to be good documentation. But they are but two of over 500 online systems, and one cannot help wondering why it took these two industry leaders so long to produce good manuals.

We will pass over that other little problem—the joke about how frequently a given database is updated. It's all done with the best intentions, undoubtedly. The database producer tells an online system like DIALOG that the product will be updated on a certain schedule. The online system relays that schedule to customers in printed materials.

Sometimes the advertised update schedule is not always met. This is usually the problem of the database producer. Sometimes a vendor will get a bad tape and have to ask for a new copy. But usually vendors are told by the producers that ''the update tape is in the mail.''

As a customer, you have the right to expect accurate information regarding updates. But vendors tend to feel that it is also your responsibility to notice when you are not getting hits on current topics or proper names you know should be in a database that has been updated on schedule. Call the vendor to find out what is happening.

With DIALOG, you can always tell when the last update was added to a file by reading the banner that appears each time you enter a database. If you see that a given database is several months behind its published update schedule, call DIALOG customer service and find out why before you continue your search.

We will leave aside the fact that the identical database is often implemented in different ways on different online systems. That means that not all of your knowledge about a given database is necessarily directly transferable.

But we cannot pass over the fact that every online system is different. That in itself is not bad. But the fact remains that, more than a decade after the start of the online industry, there is no common command language. The commands you learn for retrieving information on DIALOG, for example, do you no good at all on NEXIS, Vu/Text, or BRS.

The concepts of searching are the same throughout the industry. But the means and commands for employing these concepts differ widely. In essence, you will have to learn an entirely different ''language'' for every online system you wish to search. Then, of course, each online system and each database has its own little quirks. There are things you can do on DIALOG that are not possible on BRS, and vice versa.

And those are just two of the leading online systems. As a practicing information broker, you'll have to completely master four or five systems—or hire someone with these skills—just to stay in the game. CompuServe, GEnie, and other consumer-oriented systems don't count. From an information perspective, they aren't even on the chart. Though thanks to an aggressive campaign by Information Access Company and a few other database producers, CompuServe is offering more and more industrial strength information.

It is very true that online searching is only part of the information broker's job. But it can be a significant part. Even if you specialize in telephone interviews, online databases offer a wealth of names, contacts, and other starting points. We thus thought it best to clue you in right from the start.

It is far better for you to learn these things now than it is to learn them later, after you have a lot of time and money in the profession. And it is this matter that we will examine next.

Start-up costs

Every new business involves start-up costs. Compared to other professions, information brokers get off rather lightly. Dentists have to buy everything from an X-ray machine to the paper bibs they snap around your neck. Attorneys have expensive law libraries to acquire. A prospective franchisee has to not only buy equipment and supplies, but also pay a hefty franchise fee. And so on.

As an information broker, you must basically buy the things needed to equip an office: a personal computer and printer (preferably a laser printer), possibly a typewriter for labels and envelopes, a two-line phone system (at least), a fax machine and/or a fax board and scanner for your computer, stationery, a photocopier, business cards, paper clips, and all the other paraphernalia of setting up an office. You will also need a 2400 bit per second (bps) or, if you can afford it, a 9600 bps unit. And you will need software.

None of these items is unique. As you will see later in this book, there are ways to save big bucks on nearly every one of them. The start-up expenses unique to information brokers are things like subscriptions to professional journals such as *Information Today Online*, *Database*, and *Database Searcher*. In some cases, that can cost you $100 or more a year each. Please see Appendix A for details on crucial publications.

There are also subscriptions to online systems to consider. Access to DIALOG is cheap at $35 a year. But a NewsNet subscription is $15 a month, simply for access. And, unless you are a member of the Association of Independent Information Professionals (AIIP) and can take advantage of one of its special deals, you'll pay a great deal for access to NEXIS or DataTimes. Again, these fees are merely for the privilege of having an account number and password. All online and information retrieval charges are extra.

Note: The AIIP is constantly expanding the number of special deals for members. It is possible that as you read this, DIALOG, NewsNet, and other fees will be waived for AIIP members. Please see Appendix C for more information on this essential organization.

Another expense not to be overlooked is the cost of training in using various databases and online systems. In general, you should probably budget close to $1000 a year or more for training fees, travel, and living expenses associated with enrolling in various programs offered by databases and database vendors (online systems). You may be able to skip a year now and then, but these systems are constantly changing, so you will have to keep current.

You may spend several thousand dollars more attending trade shows and seminars. It can be vital to maintain a presence in the field, and of course, you never know when a speech you have given will lead to an assignment. Sue and Alfred both have given speeches, appeared on discussion panels, and written articles either for free or for nothing more than a token payment.

In any case, these thousands of dollars are simply the out-of-pocket expense. As a self-employed professional, you'll spend even more in "soft dollars." Writing an article or preparing a speech can take several days, for example. If you hope to make, say, $50,000 a year, with two weeks of vacation, you have to earn $200 a day working five days a week. A day here and a day there spent writing an article or preparing a speech adds up.

And we haven't even mentioned the time you will have to spend reading the professional journals and update sheets that will land on your doorstep like new-fallen snow. If you were a doctor or a lawyer, you'd have to do the same thing. But it still amounts to time spent, and when you are self-employed, time is money.

The daily grind

It is perhaps unfair of us to refer to the day-to-day work of an information professional as "the daily grind." But after all, there's a reason why they call it "work." If you are a certain type of person, there is no experience that compares to nailing down an elusive piece of information. Sex may come close, but it's only a momentary high. If you are a skilled information professional, the high can last for days.

Take all the mystery movies you've ever seen, add in the non-fiction shows about dedicated scientists making important discoveries, and the designers and inventors solving "insoluble" problems, and you'll have some inkling of what it can be like to be an information broker.

You may look and dress like everyone else at the supermarket. But as you load up your cart with the bacon and beans, the paper towels and toilet paper, you know that you're different. Through your knowledge of the information industry, your skill at manipulating its resources, and your creative imagination in deciding where to search, you have solved the mystery. You have found the patent, or located the crucial article, or otherwise performed feats mere mortals can't even dream of.

Reverie and delight

And tomorrow you're going to do it again. Another day, another miracle. And, by the way, "That will be $28.97, please." As the checker who has spent the last three minutes dragging your groceries over the laser-powered Universal Product Code reader interrupts your thoughts.

Would that it could all be reverie and delight. Would that every day could be spent confronting and besting the information dragon. Unfortunately, no self-employed information broker has this luxury. Exhilaration is definitely a part of the job. But so too is paying the bills. Literally. Hauling out the checkbook, deciding whom you can pay this month and which creditors you can let slide.

There is also the essential, never-ending work of selling. We provided a brief glimpse of a "day in the life" of an information broker in Chapter 2. The portrait was essentially accurate, but designed as it was to illustrate all the various activities of being an information broker, it did not sufficiently emphasize the sales component.

It is possible, but very unlikely, that you will reach a position where you do not have to concern yourself with the sources of the next month's billing. After several years in practice, you may be able to establish a large enough client base to have your "nut" (your fundamental expenses) covered each month.

But don't count on it.

Your best client, an executive at the ABC Company, may get promoted to a distant city. (Though you shouldn't let that fact stop you from trying to maintain the relationship.) People retire all the time. People come and go. It's in the nature of things. And every time you lose a client, you face the task of starting all over again. As we have tried to emphasize repeatedly, the client-information broker relationship is a personal relationship. If Jane Smith gets promoted out, you may have to start all over again with her replacement, John Jones.

So you have got to *sell*. Always. Every day. That means "cold calls" (by telephone or personal appearances when you have not been invited). It means organizing direct mail campaigns to likely prospects—and following up with phone calls. It means soliciting speech and article assignments, preparing and issuing press releases, and making unpaid guest appearances before local community groups. Most important, it means constantly thinking about ways to (inexpensively) promote your name and the services you offer, whether it be to local or worldwide clients.

Unpleasant, stupid people

Dealing with clients is also a part of the daily grind. You may of necessity have to work at times for unpleasant people. You may have to present your skills to someone who, at best, is uninformed and, at worst, is plain stupid. You will have to smile a lot, even (especially) when you don't mean it.

You will also have to deal with smart clients who think they know how to conduct an online search. Never has a little knowledge been a more aggravating thing. They'll tell you which databases to use, ask whether you have a copy of some database thesaurus and if not, would you like to borrow theirs, and generally make a nuisance of themselves.

Smile politely. Tell them how impressed you are with their knowledge of the online world. Allow as how they have some interesting ideas and suggestions. Then go out and do precisely what you want. Under no circumstances, in our opinion, should you ever let a client sit at your shoulder when you are conducting an online search.

Follow their suggestions if you feel you have to keep them happy. But charge them for it. If you have not followed their suggestions and they ask you about it later, smile pleasantly and explain that you were searching database XYZ anyway and happened to find what they needed. Say you felt certain that under the circumstances the client would not want to incur the additional fees of searching database ABC when you already had what he or she wanted. Or words to that effect.

Compliment them on their knowledge. Talk shop with them if that's what they want to do. Don't ever let them feel ignorant or inadequate. But don't let them control your approach to a problem either. In other words, be a good politician, but stick to your principles.

Financial potential

You would think that in the Information Age, someone who was a master of retrieving information would be able to write his or her own ticket. It may eventually come to that. Knowing what we do about information and its role in the modern economy, it is entirely plausible that—someday—a company's information broker will be accorded the same respect, deference, and salary given to other leading executives considered essential to the firm. But the time is not yet.

At the very least you would think that plain common sense would cause companies to accord an information broker the same respect given to its tax accountant. That simply is not the case, thanks in large measure to the nebulousness of the information field. Everyone knows what a sharp tax accountant can do. But an information broker? You're basically a librarian, right?

It is our opinion that this situation *must* change. The potential and the value of information and the people with the unique skills needed to retrieve it are simply too great to ignore. We aren't betting the farm on seeing it change in our lifetimes, however.

As a prospective information broker, this means that you can forget about fat, easily obtained paychecks. If nothing else, your cost of making a single sale—which includes all the dead ends and false leads you had to pursue to find the one ready client—is too high. You can make a living at this profession, but you're not going to make a fortune and you will never make a killing.

That's why we have said repeatedly that you simply have to love the work. It is why we say that if you can possibly do anything else, do it. You can make $50,000 a year within two or three years—*if* you can sell and if you can produce a top-notch product.

But if making $50,000 a year is your goal, you will have an easier time selling residential real estate. At a seven percent commission, you would only have to sell three or four homes at today's prices to earn that much money each year.

And at least as a real estate agent, you won't be on the hook for hundreds of dollars in online database expenses. No matter how careful you are in negotiating advance payments, there is always the possibility that a client will not pay you for your services and expenses.

When that happens, it is one thing to write off the time you have spent and other "soft dollar" expenses. But if the project has caused you to generate $250 in DIALOG expenses, you'll have to pay that bill. If you don't, you may never be allowed on the system again, and that can be the kiss of death to an information broker. In other words, an information broker, unlike, say, a real estate salesperson, incurs certain hard financial risks. And often for a lot less financial reward.

Competition

If you were thinking of investing a million dollars in a McDonald's franchise, you would certainly be interested in whether Burger King, Wendy's, or some other competing franchise had plans to open up down the street. The competition isn't nearly as intense in the information field, but that doesn't mean it does not exist. Nor does it mean that it is somehow ''bad.'' In fact, for the foreseeable future, the more truly good information brokers there are, the better for all of us.

That may sound surprising, but it's true. As information brokers, our major competition is not other information brokers. Indeed, you should think of other information brokers as your network of resources, not as your competition.

Our major competition is plain ignorance—client ignorance of what can be accomplished. As we have said before, your clients will not ask you to do what *they* think is impossible. But most clients have no idea of what is truly possible in the information field today. We—all of us—have got to educate them. Only then will they appreciate what an information broker can do. Only then will they unhesitatingly pick up the phone and say ''I've got a problem I think you can help me with . . .''

We will say it again: Other brokers are *not* your competition. If they were, do you think we would be writing this book? Do you think Sue Rugge would be criss-crossing the country conducting The Information Broker's Seminar? In your dreams. We'd keep the good stuff to ourselves. And so would you, if you were in our position.

Anyone who is responsibly marketing information brokering services benefits every information broker. No one—no one individual, no one company—is in a position to provide everything any given client needs to know. That's why *subcontracting* is vital to any broker's ability to satisfy his or her clients' needs. But to be able to successfully subcontract work, you've got to have good people in the field. Lots of them. With lots of individual specialities.

It is no small accomplishment to get that telephone on your desk to ring. It only happens through marketing. And if you have marketed yourself and your services thoroughly, and the phone rings, you deserve the client. If the client needs something that you personally cannot provide, don't refer him to a colleague. Subcontract the job to that colleague and keep the client for yourself.

This way everyone benefits. The colleague gets business that would not have occurred were it not for you. You are compensated for the time, expertise, and expense required for the marketing effort. And the client gets the best possible service.

Sue's rule of thumb is that even if you don't do the actual searching yourself, if you add something to the equation, you're entitled to the client. After all, there is no way of knowing what the individual will need the next time he or she calls.

The bottom line is that, for very tough, practical reasons, the more skilled, responsible, information brokers there are, the better for everyone—for you, for them, and for your clients.

What about libraries?

At this point we need to say a word or two about libraries and librarians. So let's lay it on the table: Are librarians competition for information brokers? The answer is a resounding "yes and no."

There has long been some bad blood between professional librarians and professional information brokers. In general, librarians do not look kindly upon information brokers who take advantage of their "free" services and their expertise to produce a report that they then deliver to a client for a fee.

There are arguments on both sides of the issue, but there is little point in rehearsing them here. In our opinion, and in the opinion of most responsible information brokers, a library's resources should be used without using the librarian's time.

It is *our* job to ferret out the needed facts. That's what we are being paid to do. It is not fair—and it may not be ethical—to ask the librarian to do it for us. The pioneers in the information brokering field have had to work very hard to establish a positive relationship with their colleagues on the other side of the reference desk. As a new information broker, it is your responsibility not to abuse or destroy this trust.

On the other hand, while most people do not know it, many libraries have long offered research services, either for free or for a charge equivalent to database expenses. And as budgets tighten, all libraries are looking for sources of additional funds. Accordingly, some libraries have begun to charge more for research services than simple pass-through database expenses.

This could be considered a change for the better from an information broker's standpoint. For, if the library is making a profit on a search, it is difficult to see how anyone can complain if you employ these services in your own work. By entering the profit-making arena, the library and the librarians become, in effect, subcontractors.

So, in a way, libraries could be considered competitors. But the stark advantage you'll have over any library is marketing. No research librarian with a steady paycheck, benefits, and all the rest will ever have the motivation of an information broker who must make a sale to make the rent each month.

In fact, as indicated above, you can turn the entire situation to your advantage. If your library offers fee-based, profit-making research services, you may find that it is to your advantage to use them as subcontractors. (Though few public librarians have the subject expertise needed to do the type of work required of most information brokers.) That would give you more time to sell and to provide the things that librarians cannot offer. Local reference and research librarians also often make excellent freelance searchers should you ever need extra help on a particular job.

Online systems and amateurs

A more serious form of competition comes from the databases and online services themselves. Whether for reasons of profit or otherwise, many online services actively promote the idea of "end user searching." This simply means that the person who needs the information—the "client" in our case—does the actual searching.

Remember that these services make their money on connect time. And who do they want to be connected to their computers? Bumbling amateurs who don't know what they're doing, of course!

As time goes on, you will also face competition from people who have no business being in the information industry at all, people who have bought into the idea that all you need is a computer and a modem to make money. Folks, this is a profession! This is a specialty. It is not something that you turn on in the morning and crank out.

The problem is that the marketplace at this point doesn't know the difference between someone who has just gotten his account on CompuServe and someone who has been wending his way through DIALOG or NEXIS for years. Amateurs and quick-buck artists won't ruin the profession, but you can count on the fact that they will appear and possibly damage your business.

They will bill themselves as information brokers, just like you. And they will promise clients things they cannot possibly deliver. When they fail to deliver, or when they provide shoddy service, the entire profession will suffer. All of which makes your job as a legitimate information broker more difficult. Someone who has been badly burned by the last supposed professional is not going to greet you with open arms. You can yell "Wait a minute! I'm different!" all you want.

Standard self-employment concerns

Since this is not a book about how to become self-employed, we will touch only lightly on the standard concerns any self-employed person must face. Our point is that these concerns are there, and they have nothing to do with how you actually earn your daily bread.

Taxes are certainly a problem. In its wisdom the federal government has chosen to tax self-employed people rather severely for being self-employed. The tax we have in mind is even called the "Self-Employment Tax," though it goes for Social Security. The "net, net" is that if you are self-employed, you will pay more in Social Security tax than your friends who work for regular companies.

On the positive side, self-employed individuals have access to more legitimate deductions—starting with all that office equipment you had to buy. But the tax code is so complex that even if you have always filed the short form before, once you become self-employed, you will almost certainly have to hire a tax specialist to see to it that you are receiving every legitimate deduction.

You may also need the services of an attorney. An attorney can help you draft standard letters of agreement and contracts for your services. He or she can also advise you on issues of liability. And between the two of them, your accountant and attorney can help you structure your business in the way best suited to your own situation.

As a businessperson, you will also have to balance the books. This doesn't have to be a major undertaking, but you will definitely have to account for income and expenses. Of course, you will have to pay business-related bills in addition to the domestic ones you already pay. Even assuming that money is not a problem, one should not underestimate the time this requires each month. (Fortunately there are programs like *Managing Your Money* and *Quicken* that can largely automate this procedure.)

As "the boss," you will of course be involved in all equipment purchases. But you will also be responsible for equipment maintenance and office supplies. And, most important of all, you will have to handle dunning notices and "reminders" for clients who have not paid their bills on time.

As a small business person, you might as well face it—you are often the last to get paid. Your claim may be just as legitimate as that of a Fortune 500 company. In fact, you may actually have a prior claim. But your creditors know that you have little recourse. If they don't pay the big company on time, that company might cause trouble. But what are you, Joe/Jane Information Broker, going to do? Sue them? Right. Your attorney's retainer fee will probably be several times the amount in question. So politely, but persistently, dunning slow-paying clients is an unavoidable part of the job.

Not dissuaded, huh?

It is our fondest hope that this chapter will bring you up short. If it has caused you to seriously re-examine whether you really want to be an information broker, then it has done its job. Again, we must emphasize that we have told you nothing but the truth. We have not exaggerated, and we have not left anything out.

If you still want to become an information broker, then more power to you. It is an enormously rewarding profession for those who are suited to it. But it is definitely not the easy path to El Dorado. If there were any money in the information profession—any *real* money—the databases and online services wouldn't be in the state they are in, the profession wouldn't be so small, and you wouldn't need a book like this. Instead, "information broker" would be a widely understood title and accepted job description, and there would be courses in all the colleges and high schools designed to train students in this skill.

As it is, we're a small band of "happy warriors" dedicated to taking on The Dragon and, against all odds, making a living at this profession. If you're still with us, turn to the next chapter, where we will help you determine whether you've got what it takes to be happy as an information broker.

4

The crucial question
Is it for you?

WITH ANY LUCK, THAT LAST CHAPTER WILL HAVE SCARED OFF ALL THE ASPIRING quick-buck artists. As you are sure to have discovered by now, there are some people with a sixth sense for "the next new thing," particularly if it is something that promises to pay a lot of money for a relatively small amount of work.

For a while it was home-based water purification systems. The "900" and "976" phone services are still big. And "network marketing" (the 1990's name for modified and therefore completely legal pyramid-style schemes) is an up-and-comer. Recently, we've seen it used to sell everything from residential homes to discount long distance phone service.

Business opportunities of this sort have a number of things in common. They all tell a plausible story. They are all "new." Most emphasize their use of computers and technology to add to the intrigue and believability. Most also share the common pitch: "Look, people *want* and *need* this product or service. And with the technology we put at your disposal, it's easy to deliver. So there is no way you won't make a killing."

We'll leave it to you to deduce who really makes the killing and who is the kill-ee in such setups. But you can see how, on the surface at least, "information brokering" would appear to be ideally suited to snaring a quick buck or two. With any luck, by showing you the truth of the profession, we have convinced you that this simply isn't so.

To be sure, we have a vested interest in seeing that the profession isn't flooded with amateurs or those who think information brokering is the perfect home-based business.

But it's not what you might think. It isn't a question of there not being enough work to go around. There is plenty of work, but you've got to sell each client one at a time. Each information broker is thus a missionary.

For nine out of ten clients, you *are* the profession of information broker. You are their only exposure to the information industry. If you are not competent, if you promise things you cannot deliver, if, in short, you don't know what you're doing, you can do enormous damage to this budding profession.

Though it is not likely that information brokers will ever be licensed, at least not any time soon, work has already begun on establishing and codifying professional ethics. That, in fact, was one of the main initial goals of the Association for Independent Information Professionals (AIIP), a group started in 1987.

The Carnegie syndrome

The AIIP is essential because existing information industry organizations don't always address the needs of information brokers. In fact, over the years, some people at the Special Libraries Association (SLA) and the American Library Association (ALA) have in the past spent a tremendous amount of time and energy trying to negate the whole concept.

In the beginning, in 1972, there was an editorial by John Berry in *Library Journal* about how Sue Rugge was going to be the downfall of the public library system. Needless to say, it came as a great surprise to Sue that she had amassed that much power.

The concept of information gathering, which is usually associated with a librarian, suffers from what we call the "Carnegie syndrome." It is the idea that somehow all information should be free.

As you may remember, Andrew Carnegie, after he created U.S. Steel, wanted to give something back to society in the early years of this century. He did a great deal of good, but he is most remembered for donating libraries. He would build and stock the facilities, on condition that local authorities provided the site and maintenance.

Over the years this established a tradition that libraries existed to dispense information for free to everyone who wanted it. This is very much a part of the librarian ethic, and it has led to tremendous debates within the profession: Should online searching be offered as part of this charter? Should it be offered for free? Should librarians offer it at all if they have to charge for it?

In our opinion, many librarians are so caught up in this issue of whether to charge for their services or not that they are missing a lucrative opportunity. And that is the possibility of supplementing their already tight budgets by offering the business community a higher level of service for which companies would be willing to pay a higher level of fees. The profits generated from such an approach would enable a library to offer more free services to the general public as a whole.

Please don't misunderstand. These are dedicated, often selfless, people. They will bend over backwards to satisfy a patron's request, no matter how seemingly insignificant the issue or how difficult the research task. But while many have excellent reference interview skills, many more have difficulty helping the patron define the problem. For that, you usually need an independent information broker.

You're going to think we're out to get librarians. We aren't. But it is impossible to deny that a lot of librarians went into their profession because of its job security. There was no risk-taking, at least until everyone began to hear the whisper of the budgetary axe. It's intellectually stimulating, but if they can't find the answer, there's no financial risk for them. It is not as though they have to perform successfully each day to be assured of being able to pay the rent.

But, boy, if you're an information broker, *everything* is on the line, both personally and financially. If you're promising things you can't deliver, you're probably not going to get paid. An information broker revels in "living dangerously," as Walter Kauffman, Alfred's philosophy professor, used to say. It takes a special personality, and it is that topic we'd like to consider next.

Five crucial elements

If you've read the first three chapters, you should have at least a sense of what the information industry is all about. You know there is definitely a market for the services information brokers can provide, and you have some idea of what the job itself is like. The next logical question is "Is this profession for me? What do you have to bring to the profession to have a chance of succeeding?"

The answer can be concentrated into five elements: brains, personality, education, background and training, and skills—and in that order. Thus of the five, brains and personality are by far the most important, so we'll look at them first.

Intelligence

There are simply no two ways about it. If you're going to be a successful information broker, you've got to be smart. In virtually every other profession, there are niches for average people. Not here. There are lawyers, accountants, college professors, and even medical doctors who spend their days doing the same routine chores over and over again. They are undoubtedly of above-average intelligence—most of us would be appalled at how truly average "average intelligence" really is— but they are not above-average people. There are no such niches for information brokers.

Now, by "smart," we don't mean that you had to get straight A's in school. We mean you've got to be clever and creative. There are no instruction manuals to show you how to solve specific problems in this field. If you're familiar with the resources available, however, you can usually figure out how to manipulate them to get the job done.

You've also got to be a quick study, able to assimilate and make sense of large numbers of facts in very little time, and you've got to have an excellent memory. You never know when something you saw last week or last year will be of value in doing the current assignment.

It is also essential to be adaptable, since one day you may be dealing with nuclear power, and the next with the manufacture of low-salt peanut butter. In fact, handling only one topic each day is a luxury, and it will probably be unprofitable. Most of the time you will have to deal with them all at once. Every time the phone rings, you will probably have to shift gears as you interact with different clients or interview sources for different projects.

Personality

Your personality is equally important. When Sue was looking for employees for IOD, she always found it very hard to find people with the right combination of personality and innate ability. Like many computer programmers, people who are good at information often aren't good at relating to other people. But what's needed in the information broker is someone who is not only great with information but also great with clients.

An information broker may find information for a living, but what he or she really does—the unique service we all offer—is to serve as an interface between a client's needs and the big wide world of information. That is the essence of the profession. You must be able to make clients feel comfortable talking to you. You have to be able to draw them out and help them express what it is they are trying to accomplish.

Alfred has always said that the trick in being a freelance writer is not delivering what the client wants—it's finding out what the person wants or needs in the first place. The plain truth is that whether it is freelance writing or information, most clients have only the vaguest notion of what they really want. It is your job to help them clarify their needs by raising possibilities, suggesting alternatives, and listening very carefully to what they are saying.

You've also got to inspire confidence. You have to convince your clients, by what you say and the way you handle the situation, that you know what you are doing and that you really are going to be able to help them. Otherwise they will never invest their money in what, despite your best efforts at education, will always remain an incomprehensible never-never land.

Not everyone can do this. If client contact is not your strong point, you are certainly not barred from the profession. But you will need to team up with someone who *can* handle the client end of things. And that person will have to have far more than just a "sales personality."

Information brokers also need perseverance and adaptability. If you're blocked in one line of inquiry, you can't simply throw up your hands and quit. You should have the kind of personality that automatically begins looking for a way around the obstacle. And since you're going to be spending a good deal of time looking for things, it will be extremely helpful if you are the kind of person who enjoys the hunt.

It goes without saying that curiosity is an essential characteristic. Successful information brokers are what Sue likes to call "eclectic generalists." They are interested in *everything*. Not because they think the information they acquire by reading a wide variety of books, magazines, and newspapers (and from watching television) will necessarily be useful in some future assignment, but simply because they find it fascinating.

Finally, successful information brokers have a lot of pride. Pride in their abilities, and pride in what they produce. Sometimes that means spending far more time on a project than you should because you can't bear to put your name on something that doesn't measure up to your standards. It also means that everything coming out of your office, from business correspondence to final reports to the voice that answers the phone, should connote professionalism.

There *are* standards, ladies and gentlemen. And nothing that has happened in the past 30 years can change that. Women no longer wear white gloves to go downtown—indeed "downtown" has moved out to the mall. Men no longer have to wear ties at all public occasions. But a business letter with even a single misspelled word is and always will be unprofessional. After all, how much faith would you as a client put in the accuracy of a report by an information broker who can't even manage to produce an accurate cover letter?

Education

The third crucial quality is education, and here you are in for a surprise. Many of your competitors in the information field will hold advanced degrees, principally in library science. And many of them are not shy about waving their degrees about. Thankfully, with the possible exception of college library schools, the pernicious practice of addressing everyone who has a Ph.D. as "Doctor" has not taken root in this field. Yet.

Probably it never will, for this is the business world. Some business people are impressed by degrees. But in general, business people don't share the need for the constant reassurance and ego stroking many college professors require. The head of a giant corporation doesn't insist that people call him or her Chairman Smith. It is much more likely to be "Bill" or "Betty." In the business world, you are known by your deeds, not by your doctorates.

This is certainly true in the world of the information broker. You don't need a degree—of any sort. What you need is the knowledge and some of the skills that are supposed to come with the degree but often don't. A prospective client is going to be much more interested in what you have done—the other projects you have completed, other clients served, etc.—than in your formal education.

If you've got a degree or special training you can boast about, by all means make the most of it. But put it in at the end of your capabilities brochure in a mini-resume section. The bulk of your brochure should highlight your accomplishments as an information broker and the benefits you can offer your clients. Otherwise don't give this issue a second thought.

If you are at all doubtful on this point, consider the fact that one of today's leading information brokers, someone who built the second largest information retrieval firm in the country—and then sold it for a comfortable profit—does not have a college degree. Her name is Sue Rugge.

Background and training

When someone calls The Rugge Group and says "I'm just retiring after 30 years in engineering, and now I want to be an information broker," Sue always tells them:

"Capitalize on that background. You have colleagues, and those are the people who should be the beginning of your client base." It's good advice, since whatever background or training you bring to the profession offers the ideal starting point.

We cannot emphasize this point strongly enough: There isn't a profession, a craft, or a trade in existence that does not have unmet information needs. The needs may not be obvious, and certainly some businesses have more of them than others. But no matter what you're doing for a living right now, look around! Somewhere there's a need for better information retrieval, packaging, or presentation.

Most of the time you don't have to be all that clever to find it. All you need is a good, solid knowledge of your business and the ability to look at it with new eyes. Once you flip that little switch in your head that illuminates the possibility of providing information services, you will be amazed at what you see.

No one is suggesting that you can count on making a living serving the information needs of your current profession. But it is definitely a start. Many an information broker has begun with a previous employer as a first client. And as your experience grows, so too will the breadth of your subject areas and assignments.

In short, just about any background and training is grist for the mill. If you've got the brains and the personality to be an information broker, your previous work history and background can only be an asset. At worst, it will be a neutral factor. It will never be a liability.

Skills

Finally, we come to the skills component. The most important single skill you can bring to your new profession is—touch typing. Most people are under the misimpression that to be able to talk to a computer you need to be fluent in BASIC, C, Pascal, COBOL, or some other computer language. That's wrong, unless you plan to be a professional programmer. The language of computing is plain old typing.

And you don't have to be able to type 58 error-free words per minute, either. The skill level to strive for is *comfort*. You want to be able to type well enough that you can think a word and have it instantly appear on the screen, without laboring over the process of getting it there.

This is important for business correspondence and reports. But it is essential to the cost-effective use of online systems. It is true that when you are conducting an online search, most of your typing is done in very short bursts. But if you have to hunt-and-peck every word, even entering a short string of characters can be a laborious process.

The extra online time you'll spend hunting and pecking is important, of course. But the real killer is the distraction. Online searches have a rhythm and flow. You enter something. The computer responds. You quickly absorb that and enter something else. And so on. You're thinking all the time. In this situation, the last thing you want to worry about is where to find the letter *S* on the keyboard.

So learn to type. Then learn to search. Good searchers are born, not made. But you'll never know whether you were born with "the right stuff" until you try your hand at it. You have to have self-confidence, and you have to have the ability to "think on your seat" when you are online. You have to be able to instantly adapt to what you find, and change your search strategy accordingly. Of course you hear the meter running as you search, but you don't let it rattle you.

Where does this kind of confidence come from? It's probably innate. Some years ago IOD had a wonderful researcher named David who was on the staff for years. He tried online searching a couple of times. We sent him to all the seminars, and he read all the manuals. After three months he said, "You know, I really don't like this. I'd rather not do this any more."

Despite David's manifest skills in other areas, he was really a lousy online searcher. And he knew it. If you like online searching, you tend to be good at it. If it scares you, if computers in general scare you, then you probably should think twice about trying to become an online searcher.

This is not to say that you can't become an information broker. As we have said repeatedly, online searching is only one part of the job, a part that you can hire out if you do not have an aptitude for it. There are many times when expert phone interviewers are essential to the success of the project. But one simply cannot escape the fact that computers in general, and online searching in particular, are essential tools of the information trade. A carpenter who can only use a hammer but has never mastered the circular saw will never be a full-fledged member of the carpenters' trade.

So, in general, learn to type. Learn to use a computer. And learn to search, both online and using conventional, library-oriented resources. And don't forget to learn to use the telephone. This is possibly an information broker's most valuable and most frequently used tool, yet few people know how to use it properly to project the friendly, interested, persona most likely to elicit information from the person on the other end of the line.

Conclusion

It is our job here to help you decide whether you have the talents, the personality, and the desire to become an information broker. We can give you our best advice. You can, and should, read what others have to say. But the best any book or any other person can do is to help focus your attention on several key aspects. Ultimately, only you can decide whether this is likely to be an agreeable way to make a living.

If, on the basis of what you've read so far, you have decided that this is probably not the right profession for you, we are very happy indeed. We've just saved you a great deal of time, effort, expense, and disappointment.

On the other hand, if some of the aspects of this crazy profession intrigue you, if you think it's something you might enjoy, there's only one way to know for sure, and that is to actually try your hand at it. That's what we'll show you how to do when we discuss "How to Get Started" in the next chapter.

5

How to get started

AS WE SAID IN CHAPTER 4, IF YOU'VE GOT THE BRAINS AND THE PERSONALITY, you can have the job. In this chapter we're going to offer some suggestions on how to get started and how to break into this business. We will look at four major steps along the way: finding your market niche, surveying the resources, self-tests and practice, and getting your first job.

Finding your market niche

The biggest mistake most new information brokers make is assuming that their business is information-driven. They assume that the first thing they must do is learn how to retrieve information and that the second step is to go out and try to sell their information retrieval skills. In reality, things are exactly the reverse.

As an information broker, you have to be *market-driven*, not information-driven. The most important thing you can do—before you develop or further polish your information retrieval and search skills—is to find your niche in the market. There are at least two reasons why this is so.

First, as your common sense will tell you, it is pointless to manufacture a product before you know what the market for that product might be. It is much better to try to find out what the market wants and design your product to satisfy those needs. If you are an information broker, your "product" is actually the service of locating information.

Second, so much information and so many resources are available that some kind of focus is necessary. No one can be an expert in every information resource.

Nor should you try to be. But how do you decide where to direct your energies? The answer is to let the market be your guide.

Capitalize on your background. Approach people you can communicate with. Probe for their information needs. (Even though they may not realize that they even have information needs.) What subjects are your potential clients interested in? What would they pay you money to find? It is crucial to ask those kinds of questions first—to find your market niche—before you begin to seriously focus on specific resources, search and retrieval techniques, and the services you wish to offer.

Unfortunately, unless you are a professional librarian or have some sort of information resource background (journalism, market research, private investigations, paralegal services, etc.), this sets up something of a "Catch-22" situation. You can't get a sense of the market if you don't have at least some idea of the information resources that are available, but we've just told you that you shouldn't focus on resources until you get a sense of the market and where you might fit.

Your authors are in a similar situation. On the one hand, we know how important it is for you to keep marketing and the goal of discovering your market niche uppermost in your mind. But we also know that many readers have only a glancing acquaintance with the kinds of information resources that are available. And you can't appreciate the marketing side of things without at least some familiarity with the resource side.

There is no neat solution to this problem. However, we do have a suggestion. If you are already an information professional, jump ahead to Part Four, "The Business Side of Information Brokering." Read Chapters 15 through 18. Then return here and continue with the book.

If you are new to the information field, finish this chapter. Then jump ahead and skim Chapters 15 through 18. Don't worry if they contain terms you don't yet understand. Return to Chapter 6, the chapter following this one, and read straight through. The *next* time you read Chapters 15 through 18, you'll have an even better appreciation for the importance of marketing and the need to find your niche and shape your services to meet its needs.

Specialization of labor

You may or may not want to follow these suggestions. But regardless of your approach, regardless of your current situation, it is vital to bear one other point in mind as you read this and the following chapters. It is a concept that will help you put everything into a personal perspective:

Figure out what you do best and then hire the rest.

It is simply not realistic, and it is extremely inefficient, to expect yourself to do *everything* required of a successful information brokerage. You will be tremendously handicapped if you try to be the researcher, marketer, and bill collector—let alone the word processor and receptionist—all by yourself. Make no mistake about it: The first year you are in business, you should expect to spend at least 70 percent of your time marketing. If you're not good at sales, find someone who is and team up with them.

One way or another, someone has got to be spending the vast majority of his or her time out there beating the bushes and scaring up business. Establishing a client base is paramount to the success of your business. If you don't do this, you will fail. It is simply impossible to over-emphasize that fact. Therefore, to be quite blunt, you've got no business spending your time doing the kinds of things—typing, filing, accounting, etc.—that you can hire temporary or part-time help to do.

Yes. We know. That means spending money. It means that even if you're a crackerjack typist, you should resist the temptation to do all the typing that needs to be done. Hire someone else to do it, and spend your time selling or dreaming up new ways to market your services. It's true that you may save a little money by trying to do everything yourself. But that's penny-wise and pound-foolish. It's like winning a battle but losing the war.

The concept of figuring out what you do best and then hiring the rest also applies if your talents lie not in marketing but in information retrieval. Though you are not likely to be able to hire an information services marketer through a temporary agency, you may very well be able to team up with a colleague or friend whose talents lie in that area. You could pay the person a commission on each assignment brought in. Or you could simply agree to divide the profits.

To summarize then, it is crucial to keep two points in mind. Never forget that your first job as an aspiring information broker is to find your niche in the market. And second, always remember that it is not efficient to try to do everything yourself. Realistically, you may be forced to be a jack of all trades when you are just starting out. But from Day 1 onward your goal should be to free up as much of your time as possible for those things you're really good at by hiring, delegating, or otherwise off-loading everything else.

Preliminaries

In the 1973 musical "Seesaw," there's a boffo production number in which Tommy Tune dances up a storm while the entire company sings "It's Not Where You Start (It's Where You Finish)."

The same sentiments apply to the profession of information broker. You really *can* start from anywhere, with little more than a smile and a shine in your eyes when you think of successfully locating some obscure piece of information.

Where you start does make a difference, however, in how hard you will have to work and in how much you will have to learn to achieve professional competence. If you have not darkened the door of a library since fourth grade, you've got some big-time catching up to do.

More than likely, if you're reading this book, you are already working at some kind of a job that has an information component. You may no longer remember how to use a library's card catalogues, many of which have been replaced by computer terminals and online catalogues in recent years. But you are thoroughly familiar with how to look up prices, specifications, rules and regulations, and other job-related pieces of information.

When the boss says, "Find out how much the DEF Company has bought from us in the last five years and how much they owe us," you're involved in information retrieval. If the boss adds, "And by the way, give me a line graph plotting their purchases by week," you're involved in information packaging and presentation. You may thus already be working as an information broker. But you're working for someone else, not for yourself.

When we say "preliminaries," we mean in part "getting the lay of the land." You are going to have to familiarize yourself with the information resources (libraries, online systems, unique sources, etc.) at your disposal. They are your tools, and you can accomplish nothing without them. Later, you will want to try to get a handle on the likely demand for your services. But focus on the tools first.

Three quick steps
Subscribe to KI

Here are three things you should do right away. First, send for the DIALOG/ Knowledge Index information kit. DIALOG is a Knight-Ridder company, and it is one of the largest online information systems in the world. At this writing, it has close to 400 different databases for you to search.

The Knowledge Index (KI) is DIALOG's low-cost, after hours service. KI contains only a fraction of the databases available on the big system, and you must search it after 6:00 P.M., your local time. But the same databases that during the day cost $125 or more per hour on DIALOG cost only $24 an hour when searched on KI.

If you're going to learn online searching, KI is the place to start. However, it is important to emphasize that you will not be able to use KI to satisfy your clients' needs. It is expressly against DIALOG's policy for this system to be used for any commercial purpose. In addition, the search protocol is somewhat different than the "real" DIALOG system.

Nonetheless, KI offers a wonderful introduction to the world of online databases and electronic information retrieval. And at $24 an hour, you can't get into too much trouble. The first time Alfred tapped into DIALOG in 1982, he quickly blew $100 and had nothing to show for it. Fortunately, at the time, DIALOG gave all new subscribers a $100 credit to get started. But Alfred didn't know that until later. It could just as easily have been real money.

DIALOG still gives new subscribers a credit of $50 to $100 good against database charges. You have 30 days from the time of your first sign-on to take advantage of this credit. DIALOG Customer Service is usually available round-the-clock Monday through Saturday. However we have known them to close at midnight Pacific Time, depending on personnel availability.

To request your free information kit, call (800) 334-2564. If you are calling from Canada, call collect at (415) 858-0321. About a week later, your information kit will arrive and you'll be on your way into the world of industrial-strength information resources. (Please see Part Three of this book for much more information on DIALOG, KI, and many other systems.)

Look at your own area

If you are a librarian, you are already well acquainted with information resources in general, and you probably have intimate knowledge of the resources available in one or more specialty areas. If you are not an information professional, the next thing you should do is make a concerted effort to get a handle on the information resources available in your own line of work or industry. If your firm has a company library, pay it an extended visit and tell the librarian exactly the kind of overview you want to have.

If there is no company library or information center, round up all the different trade journals you can find. Every industry has trade journals and specialty magazines or newspapers. Go over them thoroughly, both to widen your vision of the field and all its various aspects and to see if there are ads or articles dealing with other industry-related information sources.

You might even consider doing a little practice phone work. For example, if some company is advertising a software package or some other custom product for your industry, you might call them up and explain that you are interested in the field, could they help you learn more? Are there any books they would suggest that you read? And, golly, how did they get to learn so much about the industry to be able to write a program or create a special product for it?

They will want to send you information on their product, of course. Accept the offer gratefully and have the stuff sent to your home.

This kind of exercise has many points to recommend it. First and foremost, it gives you a chance to practice your information retrieval skills and telephone personality risk-free and cost-free. No one is paying you any money for this, so the worst that can happen is the place you call will be unable to help you. You will certainly be well-motivated since you are looking for information for yourself.

In addition, this is exactly the type of query you can expect to be asked to pursue as an information professional. And in all likelihood you would do so by asking people questions on the phone. So have at it! Plan to call several firms. Take notes, and be sure to send those people who have been helpful a short thank-you note. Who knows, you just might get lucky. One or more of these firms might eventually become your clients.

Support your local library

The third step is to pay several extended visits to your local library. Now, we know that libraries vary considerably in the extent of their facilities, so pick one that is generally considered "good" in your area, even if you have to drive a few miles to get there. The main branches of county libraries and libraries at community colleges tend to offer more than most local branches.

If you can possibly manage it, try to avoid going on a weekend or during the after-school, before-dinner period. This way there will be fewer adults and children around and the librarians can more easily answer your questions. You might even consider phoning the reference librarian first. Explain that you want to really get to know the available reference sources and ask when is the best time to come.

However—and this is extremely important—it is against the unwritten rules of the profession for an information broker to use or otherwise rely on library staff. Many public librarians resent information brokers, particularly those who don't even know how to use a library, making demands on their time.

As an information broker, you're a professional being paid to do a job. It is unfair and even unethical for you to ask a librarian to do it for you. That doesn't mean you can't ask questions or develop a cordial relationship. It doesn't mean you can't talk to a librarian, one information professional to another. But it most emphatically means that you are not to ask the individual to do your work for you.

The pioneers of the information brokering profession have worked very hard to develop a positive relationship with their colleagues on the other side of the reference desk, most of whom are over-worked and terribly underpaid. As a new information broker, it is your responsibility to honor that trust. If you don't, be aware that the information community is not all that large. People talk, and sooner or later word will get out about just what kind of information "broker" you are.

The reference section

When you get to the library, head straight for the reference section. This is the part of the library containing the big, expensive directories, books, statistical compilations, etc., that do not circulate. Choose a corner of the room or section as your starting point and plan to work your way around until you reach the end.

Your objective is to become aware of every book in the reference section. Some you will want to pass over. Others you will thumb lightly. Still others will beckon you to plunge in. We suggest you do exactly what you feel like doing. Let your curiosity be your guide. But make every effort to cover everything, even if it takes you several visits.

By all means, take a note or two if something strikes your fancy. But there is absolutely no need to make a list of the books that are available. They're all in the card catalogue, which in most libraries these days is online and electronic. So it's usually easy to make a printout when you need one. As you will see in the next chapter, there are even reference books about reference books. So there is no need to re-invent the wheel by taking copious notes.

When you've introduced yourself to all the books, ask the librarian about non-book materials like collections of maps, photos, or prints. Make a point of learning how to use the microfilm reader and the microfiche as well, if the library uses fiche.

Then zero in on the *Reader's Guide to Periodical Literature*. This is the most basic index to periodical literature, and frankly, if you've never learned how to use it, you're in for a very long learning curve on your way to becoming an information broker. It is fundamental. It is the reference work you go to when you are looking for relatively current information published in magazines. "RG" and its companions are available electronically on Wilsonline, but before you even think about that approach, learn to use the paper-based version.

Finally, return to the bookshelf and locate the multi-volume *Encyclopedia of Associations*. This could be the most crucial reference work of all since it is your key to expert information on all kinds of industries and professions. Look up the associations that are relevant to the industry or field you are currently working in and photocopy the information.

Every association worthy of the name has free pamphlets and publications to distribute. Indeed, spreading the good word about their industries or professions is one of their main reasons for existing. Most have an executive director or some-one with a similar title, and that is the person you should plan to call. Your goal is the same as that of Step 2—to learn as much as you can about the information sources that focus on what you already do for a living.

A word of warning is in order at this point. We are sending you into the lion's den here. If you don't know "information," and even if you do, it is very easy to be overwhelmed by the reference material available in even a modest library. So take your time. Plan on making several visits.

And remember—as an information broker you do not have to *know* the infor-mation, you only have to know where and how to find it. As a practicing profes-sional, you will frequently have assignments that introduce you to reference books that you will never use again. So rather than attempting to grasp all the details and specifics, try to feel the power.

Let yourself get caught up in the sweep and sheer breadth and depth of refer-ence information available in the library. Introduce yourself to The Dragon. You can worry about how to twist its tail later.

Self-test and practice

The preliminaries discussed above can easily take you several weeks. But at some point you will realize that you now know a great deal about the tools at your dis-posal, both the industry- or profession-specific tools and the standard library ref-erence tools. At that point, it's time to take a few practice runs.

In *Marathon Man*, a book and movie by William Goldman, the protagonist is an intense young man who is a doctoral candidate at Columbia. He's also a long-distance runner, and while he runs he asks himself the kinds of questions he expects to be asked during his final exams.

Though we hope you're not as tightly wrapped as Dustin Hoffman, the actor who played the lead in the movie, we suggest that you do the same kind of thing. Set yourself a few information broker-style assignments and see how you do. Don't worry about preparing a report at this point. Just concentrate on develop-ing and then executing a strategy to find the answers to the questions.

Here are a dozen general questions that you can adapt to your own particular situation. Some of them assume that you are currently employed in a particular industry or profession. If that isn't the case, simply pick an industry or profession of interest.

We suggest that you pick three of these questions and make them your assignment. We don't want you to spend any money finding these answers. The whole idea is to help you get a feel for the tools you have discovered and how to use them.

1. What is the fourth largest firm in your industry, and what were its sales last year? What is the name of its CEO, and how many children does he or she have?

2. What do industry experts (not your own personal opinion) feel are the three most significant products/services in your industry that are likely to appear in the next five years? And which company is best positioned to exploit one or more of them?

3. Who is the leading manufacturer of baking soda in the United States, and what do Wall Street experts feel are its prospects for the near future? Also, what is the chemical formula for baking soda? (A cream puff question.)

4. How are manufacturers of latex paint likely to be affected by new air pollution laws and when will the effects, if any, be felt?

5. Roughly how many plants exist to manufacture compact audio disks? Are they generally running at capacity or are more plants needed to fill the demand?

6. How do Canadians feel about orange juice? Do they drink it at breakfast like Americans? Is there evidence of an unexploited market for orange juice in Canada, and if so, fresh or frozen concentrate?

7. Are T-120 VHS video tapes still the most popular format or is there a detectable trend toward longer tapes? Can you find either the dollar value or the number of units shipped or both for each VHS tape length last year?

8. What ever happened with the trade agreement between the U.S. and Canada regarding cedar roofing shingles? Briefly summarize the history of the conflict and tell us the current state of affairs.

9. What are the demographic characteristics of the people who buy cake mixes especially designed for ''baking'' in microwave ovens? Has this product category been successful?

10. How many grocery store coupons do shoppers use in a year? And how are those coupons processed?

11. How many tons of steel did the U.S. produce last year compared to the tonnage produced by Germany and Japan? Is the fact that Germany has been re-unified likely to affect steel production in the future? If so, when?

12. For many years there has been a trend toward moving out of big cities to the suburbs. Are there any indications that this trend has reversed in recent times? What kind of statistics support your findings?

Take the test

These are exactly the kinds of questions you will be asked to research as a practicing professional. We do not know the correct answers, though we are confident that you will be able to find them using a good local library. But even if we did know the answers we would not present them, because the answers aren't the point. The point here is the *process*: What reference books will you consult? Who will you call for insight and details?

If you don't take this test, if you don't pick out three questions or create three others of similar difficulty, you will only be cheating yourself. There is much to gain. And all you have to lose is a bit of time. If you try to set up a business and your clients throw similar problems your way, you will lose a great deal more if you don't know how to solve them.

Optional assignment for extra credit

If you have answered at least three of the above questions and if you find that you enjoyed the process, then you may want to consider taking DIALOG training. DIALOG offers regular seminars and hands-on training sessions in major cities throughout the year. You want the introductory session, and you should plan on spending $140 or so for your ticket. More if you have to travel and stay overnight. The information on DIALOG and KI that you send for should include the current seminar schedule. If it doesn't, call back and ask.

The introductory DIALOG training seminar offers an ideal way to get a sense of online searching. It's cheap at the price and even cheaper when you consider the consequences of taking it. If you discover that you like online searching, you will learn much that you can use at the seminar. If, at the end of the class, you find that you do not like online searching, you will have learned something of great value regarding your future plans.

Of course neither this nor any other seminar will make you a professional. Indeed, even experienced searchers continue to attend the seminar updates given by DIALOG and many leading database producers.

Getting your first job

The third and final major step is to go out and get your first job. As we have said repeatedly, there is no one "right path" to becoming an information broker. But it should be obvious that if you are not familiar with the reference sources available, if you haven't completed a few sample assignments, if, in short, you haven't a clue about the information industry and how it works, it is going to be very tough to convince someone to pay you to retrieve information.

So we are going to assume that at this point you have done the survey, taken the tests, and have reason to feel confident about your ability to satisfy a client. Of course you'll be nervous. Every assignment is a curve ball, even after years of experience in the business. But what the years of experience teach you is that the information is almost always there to be found. All you have to do is apply your brain, your imagination, and your accumulated skill and knowledge, and most problems will yield.

At this point, you may be saying, "Hey, wait a minute. I'm not nearly ready to begin thinking about my first job." That may be so. But don't let yourself off too easily. Your goal is to discover whether you should become an information broker. We've told you about the industry, the market, what an information broker does and the pros and cons of the business. We've tried to guide you to the basic research sources, though we naturally hope you will use this merely as your starting point.

The one thing you don't know right now is whether you've got the knack of selling information services. Bear in mind that no one has asked you to make any commitment at this point. You've still got your day job, and your investment in exploring the profession has been long on time and short on dollars. But before taking the plunge, you've got to know the whole story. As we have emphasized time and time again, selling is a very large part of the story. If you can't sell yourself and your service, you won't make it as an information broker.

If you are already confident of your abilities, go ahead and set up a few sales calls. Do it right—send a letter requesting an appointment and follow up with a phone call. (See Chapters 16, 17, and 18 for more specific details.) Put on your best business clothes and arrive at the prospect's office with five or ten minutes to spare. Then have at it!

Remember, at this juncture you have nothing to lose. The worst that can happen is that the prospect will cut the interview short and politely usher you out of the office. In the best case, your personal chemistry will effortlessly click with the prospect and he or she will become your first client. More than likely, the presentation will end inconclusively, with the prospect interested but not ready to commit.

That's fine too. Both of you will have learned something—the prospect will have learned about the kinds of things that are available, and you will have experienced some real-life client contact for the first time. Follow up the next week with a brief thank-you note. Then call the client back in a month to see if he or she has any additional thoughts on hiring you.

If the chemistry is bad—if the two of you simply are not simpatico—you should still send the thank-you. But you may want to focus future efforts on someone else. There are *lots* of fish in the sea, and there is little point in pursuing someone with whom you don't match, especially in the information broker field.

Pricing

What about pricing? For that we have a trick or two to recommend. First, most clients will understand and completely accept your statement that you want to consider the job back at the office and that you will phone them with a quote. After you've had more experience, you'll be able to offer a ballpark figure on the spot. But there is usually no need to do so if you are just starting out.

The key thing is to do such a good job presenting your case that the prospect says, "Well, that is very intriguing. What will it cost to get this information?" You, of course, don't have any idea what it will cost at this point. But you don't communicate that to the client. Instead, you say, ''What level of effort did you have in mind?'' The client will respond, and you will have the opportunity to get a sense of what he or she is thinking of spending.

When you have a better idea of how the client sees the project and its budget, say ''Let me develop a complete proposal and get back to you with the figures tomorrow, or later on today.'' This is a perfectly reasonable request, and under no circumstances should you let the client pressure you into committing to a specific price at this point. After all, you can do a $500 project or a $5000 project on the same topic.

When you return to your office, sit down and map out your search strategy. Where will you look? Will any expenses be involved—long distance phone charges, photocopying, whatever? How much time do you think you will have to spend getting the answers and preparing a professional looking report? When you have a ''guesstimate'' on how many hours you will spend, add a third more hours as a safety margin and multiply the total by $75.

If you come out with an odd number, round it up. Then ask yourself how that figure compares with your reading of the interview. Would the client accept a somewhat higher figure? Or is your estimate already beyond what you think the client would pay? Pricing is an art, not a science.

Subcontracting

Now for the real stroke. Call an established information broker and ask what the cost would be to complete the identical assignment. Also, ask when the work could be completed. An experienced person should be able to come up with a quote fairly quickly. The Rugge Group is a subcontractor for many an aspiring broker and, of course, it carries our highest recommendation.

Compare your quote with the professional's quote, and again view both against your impressions of how the client interview went. At the very least this gives you a frame of reference. But it also opens other possibilities. You might, for example, decide to mark up the professional's quote and convey that figure to the client. If the client accepts, you can hire the established broker to do the work and keep the markup.

Or you might decide on reflection that your own quote was too low. You might use the established broker's figure and charge even more for the job. Again, assuming that the amount is acceptable to the client.

Handling the selling yourself and subcontracting the actual work is a really good way to start. Naturally, at the same time you would decide how you yourself would approach the problem. Then learn from what the established information broker does.

That's assuming you eventually want to search for yourself. If you just want to do the selling, keep in mind that there are more people out there who are skilled searchers than there are people who can sell the results. If you like the selling aspect, just go out and sell the work, then subcontract it. There is usually room to mark up a search by at least 25 percent. Some brokers will give you a discount because you have already secured the client. So there's usually plenty of room for your markup. If you're a good salesperson, you understand what the traffic will bear; and that has a lot to do with how you quote.

There is no apprentice program in this profession, but you may be able to create one for yourself. You might, for example, establish a relationship with a practicing information broker. You could do the selling, while the information broker did all the searching. Or perhaps the person needs someone to handle some of the more basic chores, like running down documents, setting up appointments, transcribing taped phone interviews, or taking care of bread-and-butter business correspondence.

Pay close attention to how your associate operates, how problems are attacked and solved, the resources used, and how final reports are prepared. Assuming you've picked a good broker, this will give you an excellent education in how it's done.

Such an arrangement can ultimately lead to a full-fledged partnership. Or after a time you may decide you're ready to step out on your own. Or maybe both of you will end up doing the searching and taking on someone else to do the selling. The possibilities are endless.

There's a lot more to learn about the nitty-gritty details of the information trade. And we've tried to cover most of it in the chapters that follow. The point we want to leave you with here at the end of Part One is that there is no single, regulation path for getting into this business. It isn't like becoming a doctor, dentist, or lawyer.

To get started, you merely have to *start*. Whether you follow some of our suggestions or invent some approaches of your own, starting is exactly what we hope you will do once you finish this book.

Part II

Fundamental tools and techniques

6

At the library
Non-electronic
sources and resources

LIBRARIES ARE MAGNIFICENT CREATIONS. EVEN THE SMALLEST LIBRARY OUT IN the country is a testament to human civilization and the things that really matter. Unfortunately, after listening to the required lecture in high school about how to use a library, and after pulling our share of all-nighters in college, most of us never darken a library's door again. Unless it is to drop the kids off for a little free day care.

That's a shame, of course, but it's not the topic here. We're interested in what libraries and conventional print sources have to offer practicing information brokers. The answer may surprise you: Not much. What these sources offer can be vital, and they can certainly help you round out a final report, but they are probably *not* going to supply the information and answers clients will hire you to find. At IOD and The Rugge Group, Sue always found libraries to be a tertiary source at best.

There's a very good reason for this. Libraries specialize in cataloguing and making available information that has been printed, published, or recorded in some other form. But many of the answers successful information brokers are hired to find haven't been printed, published, or recorded yet. The answers usually exist inside the brains of individual people who are experts or otherwise have special knowledge about a particular field.

This is the kind of information that, in our experience, clients are most eager to have and most willing to pay for. Clients typically want to know the state of things right *now* and, if possible, the most likely state of things in the near future. Consider a hypothetical marketing problem as an example.

A hypothetical example

Assume that the results of a study conducted at a major university have just been reported in the *New England Journal of Medicine*. The study found that when consumed in the proper quantities, a particular species of seaweed absorbs twice its weight in alcohol, chemically binding it and rendering it harmless. Five minutes after eating the stuff, people who were legally intoxicated have no trace of alcohol in their blood.

The day after the article appears (or as often seems to happen, is leaked to the press), *The Wall Street Journal*, *New York Times*, Associated Press, and others run stories. CNN picks it up, and the following day, all three network evening news programs run "special segment" features on "The Instant Sobriety Pill." Just think of the implications.

Your client, for one, has thought of them. And he wants to know a number of key facts. (For the sake of simplicity, we will use the male pronoun in this example.) Facts, like all the locations where this species of seaweed grows. What is the current world supply? Can it be grown in a tank on land? Is the process for extracting the magic substance patented, and if so, by whom? Your client's goal is to get a quick handle on the feasibility of producing an actual instant sobriety pill for the consumer market. He's got to move *fast*, because you can bet his competitors are.

Our point is that while the information you must find for this client will eventually end up in a library, it isn't there right now. The newspaper stories will be there today or tomorrow, but at least three months will pass before the first magazine stories appear, since that is the minimum lead time for most publications.

The library as an example

So do you forget the library altogether? Not exactly. As Sue says, "We just don't use libraries. Online searching and phone work take care of 90 percent of our research. About the only time we go to the library is to locate and copy a document that a client has requested."

Most information brokers would say the same thing. As one of them told us, "I recommend online databases as the starting point. Libraries are good for the specialized collections they have and for inexpensive access to hard copy resources—if all you have is *time* and no money. But library research just isn't part of our normal methodology." Or of most established information brokers. It just takes too much time. It is too labor-intensive. And it usually does not yield the kind of up-to-the-second information clients demand.

However, if you are a *prospective* information broker with no formal research training, your local library offers an excellent opportunity to hone your skills. Your only cost will be the time you spend.

For example, let's suppose that you've got a client interested in the seaweed-based sobriety pill discussed a moment ago. And let us further suppose that all you have to work with is a good library and the telephone. What can you do?

Well, for one thing, you can use the library as a source for the clues and directional arrows you need to locate the people who do have the information you seek. For example, who is the world's greatest authority on seaweed? We have no idea. But we're willing to bet that you can find a book on underwater plants and that at the end of that book there will be a bibliography. The bibliography will contain books by people who are experts in their fields, and one of them may be your man or woman.

No book available? Okay, look up "seaweed" in the encyclopedia. Who wrote the encyclopedia's article on the subject? Most encyclopedias will give you both the person's name and his or her affiliation. It's also worth checking the *Readers Guide to Periodical Literature* in the library's reference section. Seaweed farming could be a big topic. You never know. Or maybe you'll find some obscure little article that just happens to mention the names of several seaweed experts.

Ultimately, you'll come up with a list of names of people to phone who are likely to know the answers. Or, if they don't know the answers themselves, they'll know someone who does. And how can you find out where these folks live so you can get their phone numbers? There are lots of ways. The easiest may be to consult one of the many *Who's Who* volumes in the reference section. The volume focusing on "American Men and Women of Science" is an obvious choice.

If that fails, go back to the *Readers Guide* and look for the target individual's name as the author of an article. The byline of the article will certainly give you the name of the company or university the person works for. If there are no articles, look for books written by the individual, first in the library's card catalogue and then in *Books In Print*. If the library doesn't have the person's book, call the publisher to get the person's name and address (or that of his or her literary agent).

Be sure to check the *Encyclopedia of Associations* for the name of a professional or industry trade association to which the individual may belong. Then call the associations and ask them to check their membership roster. And while you have them on the phone, ask if *they* can suggest an expert.

These are merely the first steps that come to mind. They are by no means the only ways to approach this part of the problem. Think of yourself as a ladle of red-hot mercury flowing downward through the internal cracks and crevices of a chunk of volcanic rock. There are many alternative paths leading to more and more paths. Some are dead ends, but some lead downward toward your goal.

There are so many possible paths that there is simply no doubt that you will get to the bottom of things one way or another. Your library probably won't contain the information itself, but if you know how to use its resources, they will reveal potential paths.

Our point is not to suggest that you plan to use the library as a primary information resource in your information brokering business. As we have said, most of the time, you can find the information you need online or obtain it via telephone interviews. But you simply cannot beat using the library as an inexpensive way to sharpen your skills.

The key thing, ultimately, is not so much the particular resources you use. It is developing a search mentality and imagination. A good information broker and searcher will figure out a way to use the tools at hand, regardless of what those tools may be. The fundamental search skills you learn in doing library research will serve you in good stead when you move on to electronic databases.

Survey your library resources

In Chapter 5, we suggested that as a preliminary step in getting a feel for this profession you make a point of familiarizing yourself with the reference section of your local library. Now we want you to go further. Look in the Yellow Pages under ''Libraries'' or some similar heading and make a point of visiting each one in your area. Don't forget to check for community colleges as well. All of them have libraries. If you live near a state capital, check for state libraries as well since they often contain information general-public libraries don't have.

If you were going to build a manufacturing plant, you would certainly do a site survey and pay attention to the resources available in your chosen area (water, power, labor, transportation, etc.). As an information professional, you can afford to do no less for your own business. What local resources do you have to work with?

When you visit each library, give it a good going over. Ask if the library has any unique collections. Is it known to be especially strong in some area?

You will find that all libraries are not alike, even those that serve similar sized communities within the same library system. Each has its own personality. Each has certain strengths. One local library Alfred knows of, for example, has a particularly extensive collection of books and music on tape. Another has a superior collection of magazines on file. Still another is particularly good at providing business information. Yet all three are part of the same Bucks County Free Library system.

Build the tools to build the tools

As stated in Chapter 5, you have to get familiar with the mechanics. You've got to learn to use the microfilm reader, and you will want to learn how to make a photocopy of a frame of microfilm. Does the coin box attached to the machine make change, or do you have to bring nickels or dimes? Can you buy a magnetic-strip copier card to eliminate the hassle of having correct change?

What do you do if you want to look at a particular issue of a magazine? What magazines does the library have on file and how far back does the collection go? Learn, too, about union lists of periodicals. A union list is generally a publication produced by the libraries in a particular area telling you which library has which magazines on hand. Also, ask if the library has a pamphlet describing its various facilities and collections (many do), and get a copy.

This process is going to take some time. Don't feel you have to rush things here. Over time, as you do more and more assignments, you will get to know the libraries in your area very well. The key thing is to develop some initial sense of what reference tools and resources are readily available to you at your ''site.''

A second important point about libraries and the information broker is knowing enough about information to be able to *find* the tools and resources you need. This is like building the tools so you can build the tools to build a car. You couldn't have industrial robots without first having lathes to turn and shape their steel. And you couldn't have steel without blast furnaces and rolling mills. And so on.

Here we can recommend a shortcut or two. We know for a fact, without ever visiting your town, that your local library contains only a fraction of the reference books and directories that are available. The Library of Congress may contain them all, but even that is not a certainty.

You probably know enough about information now to be reasonably sure that there is a reference book for nearly any topic you can name. But simply knowing that something exists isn't much help if you don't know its author and title. It is for this reason that a number of people have produced reference books about reference books.

Highly recommended reference books

There are several titles that Alfred has collected over the years and keeps near at hand. All of them are in paperback and, as you will note, some of them are quite a few years old. However, while it is true that things change very fast in the information industry, and while it may be that some specific references cited in their pages are out of date, these books offer an excellent introduction to general research concepts.

For any aspiring information broker, the first three are likely to be the most helpful. These are:

Find it Fast: How to uncover expert information on any subject by Robert Berkman [Harper Collins, 1990]. One of the few recent titles available on research sources and methods.

Finding Facts Fast by Alden Todd [Ten Speed Press, 1979]. Mr. Todd's book is also exceptional. It is more on the order of a series of profiles of information sources and pitfalls than a textbook on how to do research. But he highlights lots of fascinating ins and outs. Please keep in mind that many of the specific details of the sources cited have changed since the book's publication.

Where to Go for What by Mara Miller [Spectrum/Prentice-Hall, 1981]. Ms. Miller has taught Basic Research Skills/How to Do Research at the Womanschool in New York City. If one were going to write a book on the nitty gritty of how to do research as an information broker, *Where to Go for What* is the ideal model. Unfortunately, it's out of print, so you won't find it in bookstores. But check for it at your local library.

Though they may not be quite as useful to an information broker as the Berkman, Todd, and Miller titles, the following three books are also quite good. The first is still being published. The other two are out of print, so look for them at the library.

The New York Times Guide to Reference Materials by Mona McCormick [New American Library, 1986].

Writer's Research Handbook by Keith M. Cottam and Robert W. Pelton [Barnes & Noble/Harper & Row, 1978].

The Basic Guide to Research Sources edited by Robert O'Brien and Joanne Soderman [Mentor/New American Library, 1975].

As an unabashed information junky, Alfred freely admits that these books have been acquired over a number of years. Indeed, any time he encounters books of this sort on a paperback rack, the impulse to buy them is irresistible: no single book ever covers everything.

Other reference books

You'll find a complete list of the reference books that should be on every working information broker's shelves in Appendix A. But Sue's staff has some personal favorites without which they would not venture forth to slay the dragon:

Business Information Sources, Revised Edition [Lorna Daniells, UC Press, 1985]. A classic book for the business researcher.

Directory of Online Databases [Gale, published semi-annually]. A comprehensive source of world-wide databases which includes a good subject index and vendor contact information.

Encyclopedia of Associations [Gale, published annually]. Essential for locating contacts in even the most narrow of industries.

Gale's Directory of Publications & Broadcast Media (formerly Director of Directories). This publication offers a good jumping off point for additional resources.

How to Find Information About Private Companies, Edition IV [Washington Researchers]. Ideas and sources for tackling private company research. Washington Researchers offers a whole range of publications. Call them at (202) 333-3499 ✓ for their catalog.

Lesko's Info Power [Information USA, also available on diskette]. Invaluable for locating almost anything in our nation's capital.

The National Directory of Addresses and Telephone Numbers [Omnigraphics, Inc., published annually]. Contains over 230,000 phone and fax numbers for businesses nationwide.

NPTA, National Trade and Professional Associations of the United States [Columbia Books Inc., published annually]. A less expensive alternative to the *Encyclopedia of Associations*, though narrower in scope.

SRDS [Standard Rate and Data Service, published monthly]. Great for locating trade publications in almost any industry.

Still more reference books

Now let's have some fun. Listed next is a highly eclectic selection of various kinds of reference books. The titles here were chosen to demonstrate the breadth and depth of reference works. The descriptions given are merely our quick handles on the publications. The reference books that describe them go into much greater detail:

Gebbie House Magazine Directory   A guide to company newsletters and house organs.

O'Dwyer's Directory of Corporate Communications   Lists on-staff public relations people for U.S. corporations.

American Architects Directory   Self-explanatory.

The Directory of World Museums   Self-explanatory.

Trade Names Dictionary   Over 100,000 trade and brand names.

Foreign Trade Marketplace   Over 5000 companies, consultants, and organizations, arranged by subject and by geographic area.

Who's Who In Finance and Industry   Only one of the many special Who's Who directories.

Reference Encyclopedia of the American Indian   Information sources and biographical information.

The Political Marketplace   Suppliers, consultants, brokers—you name it— anyone having anything to do with political campaigns.

Short Story Index   Tells you where to find a given short story by a given author.

These are just a few titles. For the titles we recommend to all practicing information brokers, please see Appendix A. But as an experiment, you might check your local library for reference books about reference books just to see what we're talking about. Such books will probably be kept in the reference section and not in the stacks. If no librarian is available, check the catalogue. All reference books in the library will be listed there.

Finally, in addition to knowing what tools are available and how to find reference books that are not available locally, you need to become intimately familiar with the works you use most often. This will happen as a matter of course. After doing a few projects in package goods marketing, for example, you will discover that you are very familiar with the reference tools that focus on that area.

This is important, because your knowledge of those tools becomes a part of you. It is what eventually lets you instinctively know which source to tap. Though not exactly a reference work example, let Alfred tell you how this kind of instinct can apply in a real-life situation.

Alfred's story

Years ago, before personal computers were even invented, I got an assignment from Berlitz, the language schools company. What they wanted was a series of booklets, written in English, that they could use in their courses. They were going after the business market and felt that business people would become bored with the "Waiter, there's a fly in my soup" approach of traditional courses.

Among other things, I ended up writing four booklets for them covering everything from banking, accounting, and finance to science, engineering, and construction. The pieces in each publication covered topics like electronic funds transfer, the Data Encryption Standard (DES), how the Coke bottle was created, celebrity product endorsements, the Eurodollar market, Lloyds of London, the Tunguska blast, and Le Corbusier.

Needless to say, I got to know the *Readers Guide* very, very well. But I got to know the leading magazines even better. You see, every piece that I eventually wrote was only one of several possibilities. I would find topics that looked like the kind of thing the client wanted, locate the articles, and together we would decide on what would actually be written up. For every piece in a booklet, there were three or four suggestions that were not used.

I freely admit that before this assignment, I did not think much about magazines. I subscribed to some, of course, but that was it. After a while, however, I began to clearly see and anticipate the approach each magazine would take on a given topic.

I noticed that the articles I would get from *Reader's Digest* would be heavy on the anecdotal side and light on statistics. Those from *Scientific American* would give me far more information than I needed. *Time* and *Newsweek* were okay, but they often did not go into enough factual detail.

At the beginning of this rather lengthy project, I would look for a topic and slavishly copy down every relevant reference—article title, publication, date, and page numbers from the *Reader's Guide* and similar reference sources. But after reading countless articles from many different magazines, I found that I could tell without actually looking how a given publication would cover a particular topic.

If that was the approach I was looking for, I would make a note. Otherwise, I would pass it by. I became very, very familiar with my sources on this project. I *knew* instinctively which articles were worth trudging after—and which would prove a waste of time.

This library had open stacks, and volumes of back issues of magazines were on the shelves right next to the books. I didn't want to borrow them, so I had to cart them down several floors to the photocopy room. So I suppose that was an added incentive to learn my sources so well. I also learned to go to a particular magazine's location without looking up its call number, even though the magazines were scattered over four or five floors.

Conclusion

As Alfred would be the first to admit, intimacy of this sort is only possible if you're dealing with a limited number of sources, in his case, popular magazines. One could never become so well-versed in *all* the reference works that are available. But since you will be choosing a niche for yourself and your information brokering services, you too will develop an instinct about the best sources to tap for a given question.

To summarize then, libraries are incredible institutions worthy of your profound respect and even awe in some cases. But as a practicing information broker, it is a mistake to assume that even the greatest library holds the answers to your client's questions.

You may want to locate books, articles, maps, photos, readily available statistics, and other materials to round out your final report. But in general, you should go to the library to find out where *else* to go or whom to call. A library may be your starting point in some cases. But it is almost never your final destination.

If you have followed the advice presented in Chapter 5 about going to your best local library and thoroughly examining its reference section, then your next step is to broaden your focus to include all local libraries. Get a good, solid idea of what's available to you. Then let your assignments control how well you get to know various resources at various libraries. And remember, while we would be the last to suggest that there is only one way to be an information broker, in our experience, most brokers rely primarily on online databases and telephone interviews to complete their work. Though none would deny the value of having a good library nearby.

In the next chapter, we'll introduce you to one of the greatest "libraries" of all—the mind-boggling amount of information produced by the U.S. government. Though it will not be a primary source in most situations, it is important for every prospective information broker to have at least some idea of the breadth and depth of information published or otherwise made available by Uncle Sam each year.

7

Government information sources

PROFESSIONAL CRITICS, AND POLITICIANS WHO ARE BETWEEN JOBS, OFTEN RAIL against government waste. But none of them ever mentions the biggest wastes of all: the huge quantities of top-quality information the government produces every day that no one ever uses.

As citizens, we are paying thousands of men and women around the country to collect, analyze, and publish information on every topic imaginable (and unimaginable!). Every week a federal agency somewhere commissions a private consultant to prepare a detailed report. Every month university professors and graduate students win government grants to study some macro or micro phenomenon.

The amount of information prepared and produced each year as a result of federal government activities is simply awesome. Equally impressive is the breadth and depth of topics covered. Since government is in some way involved in virtually every aspect of our business and personal lives, there is scarcely a topic you can name that isn't covered in one way or another. There are books, booklets, maps, charts, computer programs, filmstrips, video tapes, reports, and magazines. The number of individual items is in the scores of thousands. Even the government doesn't know for sure how many items it publishes.

Small wonder that most of us have no concept of the vast amount of material that is available, let alone how to find that one crucial publication on the "Molluscan Record from a mid-Cretaceous Borehole in Weston County, Wyoming." (At least not when we need it.) Because of this, a great deal of government information is vastly underutilized—"wasted"—each year.

Government information:
An endless cornucopia

As a practicing information broker, the endless cornucopia of government information is both good and bad. On the plus side, the U.S. Government Printing Office (GPO) can be thought of as a gigantic national library, a master source for almost all federally produced information.

The information is usually quite good and quite reasonably priced. In fact, a lot of it is either free or downright cheap, because you've already paid for it with your taxes. You might pay $3 or $4, for example, for a government-published book that would sell commercially for ten times that amount, assuming such a title were even available.

And the information is generally considered to be top-quality. For credibility, it is still difficult to beat the phrase, "A study done by the U.S. (fill in the blank with the appropriate department, commission, bureau, panel, etc.) found that. . ." Since a great deal of government information focuses on topics of interest to businesspeople, your best clients, it can be especially useful to you as an information broker.

But of course there's a down side. Many government agencies have done the best that their budgets will allow in letting citizens know what they offer. But that isn't much, compared to what commercial magazine and book publishers typically do. And, of course, dealing with any branch of any government always involves bureaucratic red tape of one sort or another. Add to this the fact that bureaucrats typically lack the motivating incentives of the marketplace, and you can see why mastering the ins and outs of obtaining information from the government can be a challenge.

As we'll see later, for example, the *GPO Monthly Catalog* and the *GPO Sales Publications Reference File* are available for searching online. NTIS, the Commerce Department's National Technical Information Service, is another prime print and online source. The NTIS database corresponds to the biweekly publication *Government Reports Announcements & Index* and covers virtually all non-classified federally funded information. Thus, locating documents that pertain to your area of inquiry can be relatively easy in many cases.

Obtaining copies of them quickly, however, is another matter. The government must field so many requests that it has rather stringent rules about the ordering information you must supply (publication numbers, codes, etc.). If you make a mistake or if your request is incomplete, your order will almost certainly be returned to you unfilled.

In addition, while we have always found GPO people to be very friendly and helpful, they *are* government employees, and they tend to go home precisely on time. Under the circumstances, you may be best off hiring a firm that specializes in quickly obtaining and shipping the federal documents you want. You'll find some suggestions below.

The potato man

As a professional information broker, you will probably make greater use of government data than you do of the information available in your local library. This is because government information often fits so well into a typical information broker's report and because so much of it pertains to business, finance, international trade, production figures, and so on—the very topics many of your clients are likely to be most interested in.

However, as with libraries, there is so much readily available government information that you may be beguiled into believing that it contains the answers to all of your queries. It doesn't. Depending on your needs, it may contain proportionally more usable information than a typical library. But the *real* information sources are still people. As with library information, government publications and reports are often best used as a way of identifying and locating *human experts*.

For example, several years ago Sue and Alfred had the enjoyable experience of speaking (on different topics) at the annual meeting of the Investigator's Online Network (ION). This is a group of private investigators who are on the leading edge of investigative technology. The luncheon speaker was Matthew Lesko, whom you may have seen on television talk shows or starring in his own late-night commercials for *Lesko's Info-Power Sourcebook*.

Lesko is probably the world's expert on information available from the U.S. government. As the sales copy for his book notes, it gives you access to ten billion dollars worth of government research and analysis, more than two million free or low-cost publications on every subject imaginable, and over 700,000 government experts.

Speaking without notes and dressed in a black suit with pink tie and matching socks (!), Matthew Lesko regaled the assembly with the tale of how he came to found Washington Researchers, a firm specializing in locating government information for clients. (The company is now part of Mr. Lesko's Information USA, Inc.) The year was 1975 and Lesko's first client was someone who wanted to know about Maine potatoes.

The client represented a group of commodity investors who were concerned to know why Maine potatoes were currently selling at double their normal price. And they needed to know *yesterday*! Lesko told us with great good humor that he knew nothing about potatoes but nonetheless agreed to take the job. He agreed that if he couldn't find the desired information in one day, he would not be paid for his efforts. (This is not a policy we recommend, but as a rank beginner nearly 20 years ago, Lesko obviously had no choice.)

He phoned the Department of Agriculture and, on a flyer, asked to talk to the department's expert on potatoes. To his surprise, the request was handled routinely. Apparently there actually *was* a U.S.D.A. expert on potatoes. As Lesko told it, he went to the man's office and there found not only every reference book one could possibly imagine about potatoes, but an amiable man who had spent his entire career studying the supply and demand for the potato.

Across from the potato expert's office was another office staffed with people whose sole job it was to compile a monthly report tracking potato production and consumption in the United States. Even the number of potato chips produced each month was (and is) tallied.

Equally amazing, down the hall from the potato expert were the offices of individuals with similar expertise in beans, wheat, corn—you name it. It was an entire building of experts. As Lesko said, the only problem is that once you get one of these experts talking, you may find it difficult to end the conversation, so thrilled are they to find someone with a genuine need seeking their expertise.

Information USA, Inc.

Matthew Lesko is an absolutely delightful speaker, and if you ever get a chance to hear him, by all means go. You will also want to get a copy of his book, *Lesko's Info-Power Sourcebook*, published by Information USA, Inc. Selling for about $35 and running to more than 1000 pages, it is a key entry point to government information. Mr. Lesko also maintains a feature on CompuServe (GO IUS) that presents much of the material in his book via a series of menus. There is no extra charge for using this feature, beyond normal CompuServe connect time rates (about $12.80 an hour). Mr. Lesko can be reached at and the book can be ordered from:

> Information USA, Inc.
> P.O. Box E
> Kensington, MD 20895
> (301) 942-6303
> CompuServe ID: 76703,4201

The lesson for all of us here is threefold. First, regardless of the topic, the government almost certainly publishes some kind of information on it. Second, that information is frequently developed by experts who are full-time government employees. And third, many of these experts are not only willing to talk to you, they are positively eager to do so. Once again: The printed information you find can be useful to support expert statements or opinions or to otherwise round out a report, but its main value is in identifying the right person to call and interview.

Get to know the GPO

The federal government publishes a host of catalogues, directories, and guides to its publications. But the two you should be most aware of are the *GPO Sales Publications Reference File* and the *Monthly Catalog of United States Government Publications*, or "GPO Monthly Catalog." You will undoubtedly be able to find both at your library. But both are also available for searching online via systems like DIALOG, Knowledge Index, BRS, and even CompuServe.

As you will learn in Part Three of this book, when something is online, you can usually search it on the basis of the keywords you select. This is almost always faster than using the printed version, and it certainly saves on the eyesight, given the thin paper and fine print of most government publications. Online searching also usually lets you look for words that are not found in the print publication's index.

Now, the main difference between "PRF" (Publications Reference File) and the *Monthly Catalog* is this: The *Monthly Catalog* covers over 280,000 items published by the federal government and indexed by the Superintendent of Documents. This does not mean *all* federally published documents, for there are many that never make it to "SuDocs," as information professionals often refer to that office. PRF, on the other hand, covers just those items that can be ordered directly from the GPO. At around 21,000 items, that amounts to less than ten percent of everything found in the *Monthly Catalog*.

PRF is thus a sub-set of the *GPO Monthly Catalog*. However, here is a professional's tip: PRF and "MoCat" (the Monthly Catalog) are usually out of synch. Historically, MoCat tends to lag behind PRF in its cataloguing. Thus, while many items in PRF eventually are included in MoCat, they typically appear in PRF first. It is therefore important to search both databases, not just the *Monthly Catalog*.

Items not available directly from the GPO (and thus not listed in PRF) must be obtained from the organizations that sponsored them. Or you must locate them in a federal depository library (about which more in a moment).

The *GPO Monthly Catalog*

The *GPO Monthly Catalog* weighs in at over 400 paperback pages. It is available on a subscription basis for $199 a year, but you can get a single copy for $32. We recommend you save your money and look at the library's copy instead.

The *GPO Monthly Catalog* lists government publications catalogued each month. It includes citations to the publications of U.S. government agencies, including the Congress. It covers Senate and House hearings on bills and laws, as well as many studies sponsored by federal agencies. Maps, fact sheets, handbooks, bibliographies, conference proceedings, computer programs, microfiche, books, pamphlets, brochures, and folders. Subjects include farming and agriculture, economics, energy, public affairs, taxes, health, law, consumer issues, and the environment.

The catalogue includes items sold by the Superintendent of Documents (the GPO), items available from the issuing agencies and other bodies, items for official use, and items sent to federal depository libraries. Each issue of the catalogue contains between 1500 and 3000 items. That works out to close to 30,000 new publications a year, more than enough to keep the many GPO printing plants and thousands of printing contractors busy day in and day out.

Although a cumulative index is issued twice a year and an annual Serials Supplement is published, you'll still have lots of volumes to check to find the publication you need if you try to do so by hand. When you search online, on the other hand, you can search the contents of all monthly issues all at once. Indeed, you can search through years of monthly catalogues, though the further back you go, the less chance there is that an item will still be in print.

Note that at least two companies offer the *GPO Monthly Catalog* on CD-ROM: Online Computer Library Center, Inc. (OCLC) and SilverPlatter Information, Inc. Subscriptions are several hundred dollars a year. You may thus wish to check at your local library to see if it offers one of these CD-ROM versions.

The *GPO Publications Reference File*

As noted, "PRF" includes only those items found in the monthly catalogue that can be ordered directly from the GPO (Superintendent of Documents). There is no printed version of "PRF." Instead, the information is published on micro-fiche—which is all the more reason to search PRF in its online database form. When you key in GO GPO on CompuServe, for example, you will be taken to a menu-driven version of PRF. The Knowledge Index offers the identical database but lets you reach it via a series of menus and then search it by selecting your own keywords. PRF is also available on DIALOG.

The coverage in PRF concentrates on the legislative and executive branches and includes books, pamphlets, periodicals, maps, posters, and other documents from over 60 major federal departments and agencies and from smaller federal bureaus. Between 17,000 to 25,000 titles are in stock at any one time. Most were issued in the last five years, but forthcoming and recently out-of-print publications are included as well. The file dates back to 1971. It is updated every other week.

A free "PRF User's Manual" is available. Contact the Records Branch of the Sales Management Division of the GPO or simply call the GPO order desk number given below. Though aimed at users of the microfiche product, the booklet does a good job of explaining the file and telling you whom to contact if you need more help.

NTIS: National Technical Information Service

Experts might argue about which is the more crucial, but practically everyone agrees that the *GPO Monthly Catalog* and the National Technical Information Service (NTIS) database are the two top directories of U.S. government-produced information. NTIS is a service of the U.S. Department of Commerce, and it covers all non-classified government-sponsored research, development, and engineering reports, plus analyses prepared by federal agencies, their contractors, and their grantees.

As the DIALOG database catalogue says, "[NTIS] is the means through which unclassified, publicly available, unlimited distribution reports are made available for sale from agencies such as NASA, DOD, DOE, HUD, DOT, Department of Commerce, and some 240 other agencies. In addition, some state and local government agencies now contribute their reports to the database."

Subjects covered include: administration and management, agriculture and food, behavior and society, building, business and economics, chemistry, civil engineering, energy, health planning, library and information science, materials science, medicine and biology, military science, and transportation.

For example, a moment ago we searched NTIS on DIALOG's Knowledge Index for articles about "mosquitoes." The system reported it had 1012 entries containing the word *mosquito* or *mosquitoes*. All such entries consist of a bibliographic citation and a brief abstract of the source article or report. Here are just a few sample titles. Please take the time to read each one:

Aquatic plant management
Joint Agency Plan, Aquatic Plant Management on Guntersville Reservoir
Research Program in Tropical Infectious Diseases
Sensor-Triggered Suction Trap for Collecting Gravid Mosquitoes
Attraction of Mosquitoes to Diethyl Methylbenzamide and Ethyl Hexanediol
Duplex Cone Trap for Collection of Adult Mosquitoes
Japanese Encephalitis—A Plague of the Orient
Toxicity of methoxychlor to fish
Highly Efficient Dry Season Transmission of Malaria in Thailand
Estimation of the Number of Malaria Sporozoites Ejected by a Feeding Mosquito
Biological Control of Pests and Insects. March 1971-May 1990 (A Bibliography)
Mosquito Transmission of Hepatitis B. Review
Improved Laboratory Test Cage for Testing Repellents on Human Volunteers
Parasitic Disease in the U.S. Navy
Comparison of Artificial Membrane with Live Host Bloodfeeding

The point here, of course, is not that NTIS contains entries offering more information than you will ever care to read about mosquitoes. The point is the breadth and the depth of the coverage. And remember, these are just a few of more than 1000 references. If NTIS contains all of this on just the mosquito, think how much it must offer on, say, the space shuttle, soy beans, or nuclear fusion.

We didn't check those topics. But we did search on "computer viruses" and came up with 83 entries. Figure 7-1 contains just one of those records.

We've shown you the record in Fig. 7-1 for several reasons. First, we want to emphasize once again the breadth and depth of coverage you can expect from NTIS. Second, we wanted you to see what an NTIS record looks like. (Records from the GPO Monthly Catalog and PRF are quite similar.) And third, we wanted to get you thinking about the next step—obtaining copies of the reports and other items referred to in government databases.

Notice, for example, that the 17-page report cited in the Fig. 7-1 record is not available from NTIS but can be ordered from the ERIC Document Reproduction Service. (Consult the first block of information in Fig. 7-1.) Virtually all records in all government publication databases contain the information you will need to order the actual document, and it is this topic we will turn to next.

How to order copies of federal government publications

There are at least four ways to obtain copies of virtually any non-classified document published by the United States Government. As we've seen in Fig. 7-1, you may be able to order a document through a specifically identified agency or organization. For other documents, you may have to turn to the Government Printing

1461341 NTIS Accession Number: ED-314 069

Computer Viruses. Legal and Policy Issues Facing Colleges and
    Universities Johnson, D. R.
American Council on Education, Washington, DC.
Corp. Source Codes: 001440000
May 89   17p
Languages: English
Journal Announcement: GRAI9015
Available from ERIC Document Reproduction Service (Computer
    Microfilm International Corporation), 3900 Wheeler Ave.,
    Alexandria, VA 22304-5110.
NTIS Prices: Not available NTIS
Country of Publication: United States

Compiled by various members of the higher educational community together with risk
managers, computer center managers, and computer industry experts, this report
recommends establishing policies on an institutional level to protect colleges and
universities from computer viruses and the accompanying liability.

Various aspects of the topic are addressed, including:

(1) what a computer virus is, how it is spread, how it can be detected, the kind of
damage it can do, how viruses are created and launched, what makes colleges and
universities especially at risk, and available technical protective measures;

(2) the legal issues, including criminal statutes, tort liability (i.e., the university's liability
for student conduct and its role as employer), contractual implications, and statutory
duties related to privacy; and

(3) specific priorities and options, such as establishing policies for student and faculty
conduct, distribution of information about viruses throughout the campus, limiting access
to college computers, establishing operational safeguards, creating an emergency action
plan, and developing plans for responding to governmental inquiries. A review of
contractual rights and obligations and suggestions for dealing with specific problems are
included. (SD).

Descriptors: Administrative policy; College faculty; *Colleges; *Computer networks;
*Computer software; Contracts; Higher education; *Legal problems; Microcomputers;
Student behavior; Telecommunications; Torts
Identifiers: *Computer Crimes; *Computer Viruses; NTISHEWERI

Fig. 7-1. A record from the National Technical Information Service (NTIS) database

Office or one of its bookstores. A third option is to contact one of the many official U.S. Government Depository Libraries across the country to see if they have a
copy you can review or use. Finally, you can often order copies through another
information broker who specializes in "document delivery."

Unfortunately, there is no single best source for obtaining all government
documents. The course you follow depends ultimately on the amount of time you
have and the money in the search budget. If time is short and money, reasonably
plentiful, you will be best off turning to a document delivery service that specializes in government publications. If you have more time than you do money, you
may want to take on the job yourself. In that case, everything depends on how the

publication originated (which agency or organization created it) and who is responsible for distributing it.

As we said at the beginning of this chapter, the up side of government information is that there is so much of it that your topic of interest has almost certainly been covered, often in great detail. And the information is usually cheap, besides. The down side is that bureaucratic complexity can make it difficult to obtain what you need in a timely fashion.

It is for this reason that we suggest you strongly consider employing a document delivery service or information broker specializing in government documents first. These folks know the ins and outs of government publications the way a professional lobbyist knows the ins and outs of Capital Hill. They know who to call, where to go, and what to ask for to get a needed publication as quickly as possible.

Information broker document delivery

As you know from Chapter 2, obtaining originals or photocopies of documents and supplying them to clients is a major aspect of the information brokering business. We'll have much more to say on the topic and the "doc del" services you might consider offering in Chapter 15. Right now it is important for you to know that, just as some brokers specialize in certain topics and fields, some document delivery services are particularly adept at obtaining certain kinds of documents.

Information On Demand (IOD), the firm Sue founded and later sold to Maxwell Communications, for example, has an in-house collection containing most documents cited in the NTIS database.

The Document Center in Belmont, California specializes in supplying specifications and standards documents (military, government, industrial, and foreign). Docutronics Information Services Corporation in New York City, can provide you with copies of all reports filed by public companies with the Securities & Exchange Commission. Maryland-based InFocus Research Services specializes in hard-to-locate technical reports and U.S. government publications. And so on.

There are lots of firms specializing in obtaining government-published documents. You will find many of them in *Burwell's Directory of Information Brokers*, the guide cited in Chapter 2. But Federal Document Retrieval (FDR) is typical. This Washington, D.C.-based firm has associates in major cities across the country. One FDR brochure is headlined "Name a Document. Name a City. Name a Deadline." The subhead reads "Get any publicly available document from any place in the U.S. And get it fast."

For about $15, plus about 38 cents per page for photocopying (or the actual document cost) and applicable delivery charges, FDR provides any publication from Congress, The White House, executive departments and federal agencies, the courts ("decisions, briefs, pleadings from any court in the U.S."), the GPO, the National Technical Information Service (NTIS), the General Accounting Office, the Consumer Product Safety Commission, the National Highway Transportation Safety Administration, and more. Photocopies of out-of-print publications are available as well.

For more information and a free brochure and current price list, contact:

Federal Document Retrieval
810 First Street, NE, Ste. 600
Washington, DC 20002
✓ (202) 789-2233

Ordering from the GPO

If you'd rather not pay a broker, the easiest way to lay your hands on a government document yourself is to simply phone the GPO order desk in Laurel, Maryland. The desk is staffed Monday through Friday, 8:00 AM to 4:30 PM, Eastern time. You may use Visa or MasterCard, or you can establish a deposit account with the Superintendent of Documents. You can also order by mail using these options or a check or money order.

If you do not know a publication's stock number, you can order up to six items per phone call, including subscriptions to most government periodicals. If you do know the stock numbers, you can order up to 10 items per call. (You get the stock numbers from PRF.) You can also enter your order online when searching PRF via a system like DIALOG.

Prices are very reasonable. The cost of a single issue of the *Congressional Record* is $1 domestic, $1.25 foreign. The cost of a single issue of the *Federal Register* is $1.50 domestic, $1.88 foreign. Postage is included in all GPO price quotes.

Here's the address to contact and the number of the GPO order desk:

Superintendent of Documents
U.S. Government Printing Office
Washington, DC 20402
Order Desk: Mon—Fri, 8AM—4:30PM
(202) 783-3238

U.S. government depository libraries

The U.S. Government Depository Library program is based on three principles. First, that with certain specified exceptions, all government publications will be made available to depository libraries. Second, that such libraries will be located in each state and congressional district to make government publications widely available. And third, that these government publications will be available for the free use of the general public.

The outline of the current program was drawn up in 1857, and documents have been accumulating ever since. By law there are two libraries per congressional district and one for each senator, plus assorted state libraries, libraries of the land-grant colleges, and so on. The total is now close to 1390 in the U.S. and its protectorates.

There are two categories of depository libraries. A full-blown depository library accepts everything. A "selective depository library" is permitted to select and obtain any government publication free of charge in return for allowing the public to have free access to it. As one librarian we spoke with put it, "The materials are on deposit with us. We don't own them, the government does."

Due to the selectivity option, not every depository library has all government publications, though the larger the library, generally the larger the collection. Selective depository libraries are presented with a list of government publications and are free to choose the ones they want to have.

GPO bookstores

You should also know that the GPO operates 25 bookstores in 21 cities around the country. While the bookstores carry only a small percentage of all that is available from the government, they typically stock the titles that are most in demand. And, of course, they can accept orders for any title not actually carried in the store.

The one exception is the GPO Retail Sales Outlet in Laurel, Maryland. As a part of the office's Retail Distribution Division, it has access to all titles currently in stock. This is why, if you need something quickly, it can be best to hire a document delivery service based in the area. They can go to Laurel, Maryland, pick up the item, and Federal Express it out to you.

All GPO bookstores and the Laurel, Maryland, location accept MasterCard, Visa, or pre-paid Superintendent of Documents deposit account charges. The addresses and phone numbers of all the bookstores are listed next.

This is the complete current list of the locations and phone numbers of all GPO bookstores in the U.S. If convenient, it can be worth your while to pay one a visit. If not, you can often order GPO documents by phone. You can obtain the necessary document reference numbers by searching the GPO database online.

Atlanta
U.S. Government Printing Office Bookstore
Room 100, Federal Building
275 Peachtree Street, NE
PO Box 56445
Atlanta, GA 30343
(404) 331-6947
FAX: (404) 331-1787

Birmingham
U.S. Government Printing Office Bookstore
O'Neill Building
2021 Third Avenue, North
Birmingham, AL 35203
(205) 731-1056
FAX: (205) 731-3444

Boston
U.S. Government Printing Office Bookstore
Thomas P. O'Neill Building
Room 179
10 Causeway Street
Boston, MA 02222
(617) 720-4180
FAX: (617) 720-5753

Chicago

U.S. Government Printing Office Bookstore
Room 1365, Federal Building
219 S. Dearborn Street
Chicago, IL 60604
(312) 353-5133
FAX: (312) 353-1590

Cleveland

U.S. Government Printing Office Bookstore
Room 1653, Federal Building
1240 East 9th Street
Cleveland, OH 44199
(216) 522-4922
FAX: (216) 522-4714

Columbus

U.S. Government Printing Office Bookstore
Room 207, Federal Building
200 N. High Street
Columbus, OH 43215
(614) 469-6956
FAX: (614) 469-5374

Dallas

U.S. Government Printing Office Bookstore
Room 1C46, Federal Building
1100 Commerce Street
Dallas, TX 75242
(214) 767-0076
FAX: (214) 767-3239

Denver

U.S. Government Printing Office Bookstore
Room 117, Federal Building
1961 Stout Street
Denver, CO 80294
(303) 844-3964
FAX: (303) 844-4000

Detroit

U.S. Government Printing Office Bookstore
Suite 160, Federal Building
477 Michigan Avenue
Detroit, MI 48226
(313) 226-7816
FAX: (313) 226-4698

Houston

U.S. Government Printing Office Bookstore
Texas Crude Building, Suite 120
801 Travis Street
Houston, TX 77002
(713) 228-1187
FAX: (713) 228-1186

Jacksonville

U.S. Government Printing Office Bookstore
Room 158, Federal Building
400 W. Bay Street
Jacksonville, FL 32202
(904) 353-0569
FAX: (904) 353-1280

Kansas City

U.S. Government Printing Office Bookstore
120 Bannister Mall
5600 E. Bannister Road
Kansas City, MO 64137
(816) 765-2256
FAX: (816) 767-8233

Laurel

U.S. Government Printing Office Bookstore
Warehouse Sales Outlet
8660 Cherry Lane
Laurel, MD 20707
(301) 953-7974
(301) 792-0262
FAX: (301) 498-9107

Los Angeles

U.S. Government Printing Office Bookstore
ARCO Plaza, C Level
505 S. Flower Street
Los Angeles, CA 90071
(213) 239-9844
FAX: (213) 239-9848

Milwaukee

U.S. Government Printing Office Bookstore
Room 190, Federal Building
517 E. Wisconsin Avenue
Milwaukee, WI 53202
(414) 297-1304
FAX: (414) 297-1300

New York
U.S. Government Printing Office Bookstore
Room 110
26 Federal Plaza
New York, NY 10278
(212) 264-3825
FAX: (212) 264-9318

Philadelphia
U.S. Government Printing Office Bookstore
Robert Morris Building
100 North 17th Street
Philadelphia, PA 19103
(215) 597-0677
FAX: (215) 597-4546

Pittsburgh
U.S. Government Printing Office Bookstore
Room 118, Federal Building
1000 Liberty Avenue
Pittsburgh, PA 15222
(412) 644-2721
FAX: (412) 644-4547

Portland
U.S. Government Print Office Bookstore
1305 SW First Avenue
Portland, OR 97201-5801
(503) 221-6217
FAX: (503) 225-0563

Pueblo
U.S. Government Printing Office Bookstore
World Savings Building
720 North Main Street
Pueblo, CO 81003
(719) 544-3142
FAX: (719) 544-6719

San Francisco
U.S. Government Printing Office Bookstore
Room 1023, Federal Building
450 Golden Gate Avenue
San Francisco, CA 94102
(415) 252-5334
FAX: (415) 252-5339

Seattle
U.S. Government Printing Office Bookstore
Room 194, Federal Building
915 Second Avenue
Seattle, WA 98174
(206) 553-4271
FAX: (206) 553-6717

Washington, DC
U.S. Government Printing Office
710 North Capitol Street, NW
Washington, DC 20401
(202) 275-2091
FAX: (202) 275-9037

U.S. Government Printing Office
1510 H Street, NW
Washington, DC 20005
(202) 653-5075
FAX: (202) 376-5056

Contacting NTIS

As we have emphasized throughout this chapter, the GPO and its catalogue is one major entry point to government information. The National Technical Information Service (NTIS) is another. For more information on the information, services, and document delivery options NTIS offers, contact:

National Technical Information Service
U.S. Department of Commerce
5285 Port Royal Road
Springfield, VA 22161
(703) 487-4807

State libraries

Researching, locating, and obtaining government information is a book-length subject in and of itself. For those with computers and modems, Alfred offers more details in his book *How to Look it Up Online*. But even that book doesn't touch on the lodes of information available from local state governments.

Space does not permit a complete treatment here, either. However, you should be aware that to a greater or lesser degree, everything we have said about federal government information applies equally well to state government information. This is the place to look when you need a sharper focus than is available through the wide-angle lens of federal information. The place to start is often with your state's library. But remember: A reputable information broker uses the sources a library offers but does not make any demands on the library staff.

Here are the numbers to call to get started looking into any state-specific topic:

Alabama State Information	(205) 261-2500
Alaska State Information	(907) 465-2111
Arizona State Information	(602) 255-4900
Arkansas State Information	(501) 371-3000
California State Information	(916) 322-9900
Colorado State Information	(303) 866-5000
Connecticut State Information	(203) 240-0222
Delaware State Information	(302) 736-4000
District of Columbia Information	(202) 727-1000
Florida State Information	(904) 488-1234
Georgia State Information	(404) 656-2000
Hawaii State Information	(808) 548-6222
Idaho State Information	(208) 334-2411
Illinois State Information	(217) 782-2000
Indiana State Information	(317) 232-1000
Iowa State Information	(515) 281-5011
Kansas State Information	(913) 296-0111
Kentucky State Information	(502) 564-3130
Louisiana State Information	(504) 342-6600
Maine State Information	(207) 289-1110
Maryland State Information	(301) 974-2000
Massachusetts State Information	(617) 727-2121
Michigan State Information	(517) 373-1837
Minnesota State Information	(612) 296-6013
Mississippi State Information	(601) 359-1000
Missouri State Information	(314) 751-2000
Montana State Information	(406) 444-2511
Nebraska State Information	(402) 471-2311
Nevada State Information	(702) 885-5000
New Hampshire State Information	(603) 271-1100
New Jersey State Information	(609) 292-2121
New Mexico State Information	(505) 827-4011
New York State Information	(518) 474-2121
North Carolina State Information	(919) 733-1110
North Dakota State Information	(701) 224-2000
Ohio State Information	(614) 466-2000
Oklahoma State Information	(405) 521-1601
Oregon State Information	(503) 378-3131
Pennsylvania State Information	(717) 787-2121
Rhode Island State Information	(401) 277-2000
South Carolina State Information	(803) 734-1000
South Dakota State Information	(605) 773-3011
Tennessee State Information	(615) 741-3011

Texas State Information	(512) 463-4630
Utah State Information	(801) 533-4000
Vermont State Information	(802) 828-1110
Virginia State Information	(804) 786-0000
Washington State Information	(206) 753-5000
West Virginia State Information	(304) 348-3456
Wisconsin State Information	(608) 266-2211
Wyoming State Information	(307) 777-7011

Conclusion

Again, it is important to emphasize that what we have provided in this chapter is merely an introduction to the vast and deep world of federal and state government information. There is much more to learn, and, should your practice take you in this direction, you will learn it as the needs of your jobs dictate.

From an information broker's viewpoint, there are two key things to remember about government information. First, regardless of the topic, there is almost certainly some government information available that relates to it. It may not always offer you exactly what you need, but, by golly, it's *something*. As you are executing a search assignment, you should always keep this fact in mind.

Second, as with library-based information, most of the time you should view government information as only the starting point. Use it as a means to identify the experts and professionals with special knowledge about your target subject. Then make a point of contacting *them* for their latest thinking, analysis, statistics, and additional information leads.

It is the contact phase of the information broker's job that we will consider in the next chapter. "Working the phone" is an essential skill for all information professionals. You've found the right person to call for the information you seek. Now what? That's what we'll address in Chapter 8.

8

The telephone
Your most powerful tool

THE TELEPHONE IS TO THE INFORMATION BROKER WHAT A SCALPEL IS TO A surgeon. And you should be just as comfortable holding it, manipulating it, and using it as conveyance of your skill. But where a scalpel is an extension of a surgeon's hand, the telephone is an extension of your personality. It is you, the pleasant person on the other end of the line, to whom the expert, the recognized authority, or the Great Man or Great Woman is yielding up information, opinions, and analysis—the very gold dust that pays your bills.

How to use the phone effectively

Needless to say, mastery of this most powerful of tools is essential. After all, there are *lots* of people skilled at doing library research. Graduate students needing extra cash, freelance or moonlighting librarians, particularly bright staff assistants and interns, and corporate information center managers come to mind immediately.

Relatively speaking, however, there are not that many people who can pick up the phone, call an authority or expert, and conduct a successful interview. As we have said throughout this book, it is the kind of information developed from interviews of this sort that most clients are most willing to pay for. As an important sidenote, mastery of the telephone is equally important in selling your services and building your business, as we will see in Chapter 17—"Marketing, the Missing Ingredient."

So let's look the situation right in the eye. We can show you some techniques and give you the pointers you need to set off in the right direction. With practice, you'll develop your own style. But if you don't have an outgoing personality to begin with, if you don't plain enjoy talking to other people, you start at a serious disadvantage.

If you've never done anything like this before or if you think of yourself as shy, don't be discouraged. The worst possible thing that can happen is that the person you call will abruptly hang up on you. It is not as though he or she could reach out and grab you by the collar. The person doesn't even know what you look like. So there is no point in being embarrassed. Besides, early 19th century English novels to the contrary, no one ever *died* of embarrassment.

More than likely, protected by the anonymity of the telephone, your shyness will drop away. Your brain will take over, and you'll be so caught up in pursuing the answers you've called to find that you'll forget to be nervous. Who knows? Lurking behind that shy, retiring image you present in person could be a dynamite telephone personality. So give it a try.

A double perspective

Over the years, Sue and Alfred have both given and done countless phone interviews. We have been on either end of the conversation. We know what it's like, for example, to have the phone ring in the midst of a project and hear a voice on the other end ask for just a few moments of our time.

Though the milk of human kindness flows through our veins and though we are, of course, the most amiable, co-operative people you would ever want to meet—if someone calls and they are unprepared, unprofessional, or unpleasant, a few moments is exactly what they'll get. A very few. (Incidently, time simply doesn't permit us to offer readers advice and counsel on the phone. So we'd appreciate it if you'd resist the temptation to call. If you'd like to talk to Sue in person, plan to attend her Information Broker's Seminar when it is held in a city near you. Please see Appendix E for details.)

We also know what it's like to be the caller, to be under a rush deadline, and to be desperate for the information we think the expert can offer. We know the frustration of interviewing someone who really doesn't know what he or she is talking about, or the frustration of a key source being unreachable (on vacation, out of the office, in a meeting, take your pick).

And we know the satisfaction of reaching someone who is both very good and very knowledgeable and personally simpatico. After conversations like these, you hang up the phone saying to yourself, ''By golly, that's what life is really all about. That's what makes this business worthwhile. Everything else just pays the bills.''

As a result of this double perspective, we have some pretty definite opinions about what goes into a successful interview. Indeed, we can break it down into four major stages or steps:

1. Preparation
2. Initial contact
3. The interview
4. Assimilation of results

Step 1: Preparation

There are two reasons why we have placed such a heavy emphasis on phone work in this book. The first is to help counteract the misimpression many people have that being an ''information broker'' is simply a matter of learning to use online databases and paying an occasional visit to the local library. The second is that in our rather long experience, phone work supplies over 50 percent of the information you need to satisfy your client. The telephone thus clearly *deserves* all the emphasis we have given it.

So, while you will want and need to use information obtained from the library, from the government, or from online databases in your final report for the client, much of the work you do in these areas is really preparation for one or more telephone interviews. This preparation takes two forms. First, library and online research will reveal the names of the people you should call. Second, the information you assemble this way will give you the background you need, to know what questions to ask when you go to the phone.

Who you gonna call?

Selecting the right people to call when you're working on a project is something of an art. But it is an art no one has even come close to mastering. At times the person who seems like he would be the perfect source turns out to be a real dud and a serious waste of time, while the person you dialed as a shot in the dark turns out to be a genuine gold mine. Authoritative pronouncements from your authors on this subject are thus impossible.

What we *can* do, however, is help get you thinking in the right direction. In fact, your thinking and your mindset is the key to the whole matter. If you wouldn't dream of calling up the clerk of an important Senate committee to get information on a pending bill, if it would never occur to you to phone the president of a large corporation, then seeing the names of these sources in print will do you absolutely no good.

You have got to get rid of the notion that calling people you don't know ''simply isn't done.'' On the contrary, it's done all the time, and not just by telemarketers trying to sell you something. There are a few truths about life and about the business world that every aspiring information broker must become aware of.

First, anyone can call anyone. You may not always get to speak to the person you call, but a surprising percentage of the time, you do. Not everyone has a secretary, and not everyone who does has that person screen incoming calls. Some people like to answer their own phone. And even if you run into an initial screen, you can always ask for a call back or ask to make an appointment to call again.

Taking advantage of opportunities

Interestingly, as Sue points out, many times you may end up speaking with the people who work for the person you had hoped to reach. That can prove to be a real opportunity, since these folks don't get to tell people what they know very often and thus may be more helpful in your quest. In general, the higher you go in an organization, the more you are apt to meet with suspicion, resistance, and lack of co-operation.

As Sue says, "I always start by asking for the ultimate person. But if they are not available, I'll say to their assistant, 'Well, maybe I don't really need him or her. Perhaps you can help.' Then I explain what I need. If the assistant cannot help, at least they then have a detailed message they can relay to their boss and, hopefully, have an answer for you when you call back. It is amazing how often this works: You can accomplish your goal even if you never get to speak to the person you set out to interview."

Second, people *like* to talk about their work. And who can blame them? We all like to talk about our work. We spend at least a third of our day and more than half our lives doing it. What makes you think some august authority on a subject is any different?

Third, most people are predisposed to help other people. Who among us wouldn't want to help someone else who was in trouble? We might not do it—if there was danger, if the cost to us was too high, or if the individual didn't appear to "deserve" assistance—but the instinct is there.

So some polite, pleasant-sounding person who has obviously done his or her homework calls you up. The person has a problem. And it turns out that not only can you help at no cost to yourself, but doing so requires you to talk about your work or area of expertise. Are you really going to say, "Go away, kid, you bother me."? Of course not. You're flattered, and you want to help. If at all possible, you're going to say, "Okay, I've got a few minutes. What can I do for you?"

Use your imagination

Now that we're agreed that anyone can call anyone else, now that we've opened our minds to this possibility, who do we call?

Often the answer is obvious. If a reporter has done a story on hi-tech hog farming, that reporter is a good place to start. The sources the reporter interviewed and quoted or credited in the article are equally good. And bear in mind when doing any phone interview that people know other people and experts know other experts. If the reporter or the quoted sources cannot themselves give you the information you seek, the chances are good that they know someone who can. Always ask, "Who else do you think I should contact?"

If the article appears in a magazine devoted to a particular subject, say like *Hog Producers Daily*, consider calling the editor. You might ask if the magazine has covered the hi-tech angle in other issues. Or you might simply ask if the editor can steer you to the leading experts in hi-tech hog farming.

If the experts are professors, there's a good chance that they've written other pieces on the subject and will love to tell you all about them. Be sure to ask. More than likely they will be happy to send you copies of their works—saving you the trouble and expense of locating them on your own. Indeed, sources like these tend to send you far more than you need (or want to look at), but you accept it all graciously and gratefully.

The *Encyclopedia of Associations* is another wonderful source of people to call. And again, each person you call is a potential gateway to other people with the expertise you need. The *Encyclopedia of Associations* is available in all but the smallest of libraries, and it can be searched online, as we will see later. But it is so useful that it is the first print media tool every information broker should consider buying.

There are trade associations for every conceivable industry, profession, and sub-specialty. Virtually all of them have a magazine of some sort. And every last one of them exists primarily to dispense information about their area of focus. A given association may be so small that it will have just an executive director and no staff. Or it may be large enough to have an entire library.

Some will not give statistics to non-members. But most are very helpful. And often they provide or suggest resources that may not have occurred to you. Incidentally, if they have a ''members only'' policy, you will want to tell your client that. The client may want to call as a potential member or actually join. It's even possible that the client may already be a member and never thought of calling.

The importance of the audit trail

You always want to tell the client every person you called, their affiliation, and provide their phone number. Providing an audit trail of your sources is part of what the client is paying you for. It also protects your credibility when the information you have been asked to find turns out to be unavailable. In addition, your clients may want to follow up on their own, even six months or a year later.

Articles, editors, and associations don't make tremendous demands on your little grey cells of imagination. These are obvious sources to any information broker. Now let's carry things a little bit further.

Your subject is hi-tech hog farming. You've got an article on the subject that focuses on machines and devices to automate the feeding process. One of the sources quoted in the piece makes a passing reference to inoculating the animals against disease. But the article does not explore this avenue.

A light bulb goes off in your head. Inoculation wasn't something you had thought of in connection with hi-tech hog farming. But clearly it is an important part of the process. No source or other reference is given. So, assuming you have not yet reached the reporter or the editor, who can you call for information on this aspect of the topic?

There are many paths you could follow, of course. But for the sake of argument, let's assume that all print and online sources are closed to you for the time being. All you've got to work with is the phone.

You might start by calling a local hog farmer and asking how the problem of innoculation is handled. That could lead to the name of a drug manufacturer or a local veterinarian. Assume it's the drug company. You call there and ask to talk to their public information or public relations office. If it's a big company, you can count on getting bounced around to three or four people.

But eventually you will find someone who can give you information about the drugs the firm makes for swine and probably the names of the companies who make the equipment for administering them. The person will probably also be able to supply you with trade journal or other articles discussing the merits of the firm's products. Accept them gratefully.

You repeat the phoning process with the equipment manufacturers suggested by the drug firm. They too have articles and press releases for you, complete with black and white glossies illustrating their latest shot-giving machines.

As we said, there are many ways to attack a problem like this. But one must agree that the "phone-alone" scenario we have just presented is entirely plausible. And, as we hope we have shown, your own imagination—your own answers to the self-imposed question "Who would know?"—is the key. That and good phone work.

Getting your ducks in a row

The final stage in your preparation is deciding exactly who you want to call and what you plan to ask. We do not want to give you the impression that you can complete most projects by simply narrowing down a list of names and phone numbers, spreading them out before you, and picking up the phone. That may indeed happen. But usually you will have no idea when you make your first call how many additional people you will be speaking to before the project is finished. In fact, if you are doing your job right, there is no way you *can* know, since one source so often leads to two or three others. You may well find that you need to grow an "information tree" for each project.

In short, you'll go through the "ducks in a row" stage many times in the course of a job. At least once for each call you place.

Start by putting the person's name, address, and phone number on a separate sheet of paper. Then list the major points you want to cover in the interview on the same sheet of paper. Leave plenty of room between your questions since you will need the space to make notes on the answers. Do not use the back of the paper. It is too easy to overlook. Instead, start a second sheet if you need more room.

Good organization is crucial. And keeping each source on a separate sheet (or sheets) of paper makes it much easier to prepare your final report to the client. You will be able to tell the client who you called, their address, what you asked, how they responded, and so on, without shuffling through a pile of disorganized notes.

It is also crucial to know what you're talking about when you call a source. Obviously you won't know the answers to your own questions. But you have got to have done your homework. Nothing turns a source off quicker than someone calling and saying, "Gee, I've got to find out about hi-tech hog farming. Can you help me out?" Remember, you are asking the source to give up time and share knowledge with you free of charge. If you yourself cannot be bothered to spend enough time to learn something about the subject, you can't expect the source to look kindly on your request for a free education.

On the other hand, if you have read enough about the subject to be able to say, "I think I have the basic concepts of the new trends in hog farming down, but there are one or two points for which I need more detail," you will get a much better reception. And if the source presses you to explain your areas of confusion, you had better be prepared to do so. Fakery and bluff is as apparent in an interviewer as it is in a source.

Is tape recording legal?

There are a number of purely mechanical details to prepare as well. First, we recommend that you consider using a telephone headset. A headset leaves your hands free to type notes at your computer or to write them by hand. And they eliminate the chronic crick in the neck that many phone users suffer from. Headsets are available from catalogues and office supply stores. But you may want to check at your local AT&T phone store. We'll discuss this item in more detail later in the book when we look at how to set up an office.

Second, you may find it convenient to use a tape recorder. Forget about the suction cup induction coil units—the ones where the pickup unit suckers onto the handset. Opt instead for a direct connect pickup that joins the phone line with your tape recorder. These units are about $25 from Radio Shack. Please note, however, that in some states—like California, for example—taping a phone conversation is not legal unless both parties are aware that a recorder is being used.

There is an important caveat to enter here. If taping a conversation is legal in your state and you decide to turn on the recorder, the tapes you make of your interviews must be held in the strictest confidence. They are for your exclusive, personal use only. In our opinion, it is unethical to either provide them to the client or to even suggest this as a possibility—unless you have notified your source at the beginning of the conversation that a tape recorder is being used. The same logic applies to transcripts. To do otherwise is to violate the unspoken trust between you and your source.

The sole reason for using a tape recorder is that it frees you from worrying about whether you have accurately noted the source's answers. This lets you concentrate on the give and take of the conversation. It lets you really listen to what the person is saying and react with follow-up questions.

One should never rely on a tape recorder alone. You will find that going back and transcribing or taking notes on a taped interview takes too much time. It is much better to make notes during the conversation—typing them at your computer, if convenient—and to assume that they are your only record of the conversation. If some point gets missed or is otherwise unclear from your notes, *then* go to the recording to check what was actually said. Tape recordings are also helpful when you want to quote one or two sentences verbatim in preparing your final report.

If you are going to use a tape recorder, make sure that it is working before you place the call. Put it on RECORD. Pick up the phone and punch a number to stop the dial tone. Then say something. The needle on the recorder should react. Verify that everything is in working order by rewinding and playing the tape you have just made.

The nuisance of call waiting

If you have Call Waiting, disable it before you make your call. You don't want the disruptive Call Waiting signal to interfere with your interview. Check the front pages of your phone book under ToneBlock for instructions. In most areas of the country, dialing 1170 or *70 will disable Call Waiting for the duration of the call. It goes into effect again as soon as you hang up.

As discussed later, whether or not you are using a recorder, Call Waiting can be a real nuisance during an interview if you forget to turn it off before placing the call. For this reason, we strongly recommend getting a second, non-Call Waiting-equipped phone line as soon as possible. Use it for your interviews and let your answering machine pick up calls coming into your original line.

Finally, make sure that you have plenty of paper nearby to take notes. The same goes for your notes on the subject, or on previous phone interviews, or any other material you may need to refer to during the conversation.

Step 2: Initial contact

Now you're ready for the second phase—actually making the call. There are a number of ways this can go. In the best of all possible worlds, you would reach every person in person the first time you tried. The interview would give you everything you need. You could write up the final report for the client that afternoon, and we could all go home early.

Sometimes that does happen. But not often. Usually you'll run into a screen of the ''And what may I say this is in reference to?'' variety. We're assuming here that you have the name of a specific individual you want to call. Calling a large company or government agency without a specific name, though necessary at times, is to be avoided whenever possible.

How to make the most of a screen

When you encounter a screen, it is important to be able to phrase your goal as succinctly as possible. You do not want to have to explain every detail to a screening secretary or executive assistant. At the same time, you want to pique the interest of the source you are trying to reach.

If the screen says, ''Perhaps there's something I can help you with,'' do not disregard the offer. You may think that the screen is just doing his or her job. And you are probably right. But as we said earlier, many ''lower-level'' people are very eager to talk. Often they know a great deal about a topic, but no one ever asks them to discuss it.

It is even possible that the person serving as a screen actually wrote the article or the program or whatever that caused you to call, although his or her boss got credit for it. Everything depends on what you are after. If nothing but the insight and analysis of the particular individual you are trying to reach will do, then you will have to make every effort to speak to that person.

Tips on technique

But if all you need is more information on a particular topic, "Perhaps I can help?" can be a wonderful opportunity. You might say, "Why, yes. I'd like to know more about your firm's automated hog inoculator." Ask your questions and really listen to the answers. Don't interrupt to ask your next question until the person has run out of things to say. Sometimes silence can be a golden source since people quite naturally feel obliged to fill it. By all means let them. Don't make the person uncomfortable, but don't rush in to raise a follow-up question until the person has finished. Instead, make a note of the follow-up point and bring it up later, during the next lull in the conversation.

Use this technique regardless of who you are speaking with, screen or target source. And don't forget to be complimentary. Extoll the article they've written. If John Doe has told you that they are the real expert in the field, be sure to tell them of Mr. Doe's recommendation. If someone else said that they would be the ideal person to talk to, tell them that as well. Never forget, these people are doing you a favor. In most cases, talking to inquiring minds who want to know is not part of their job. So be as nice as you possibly can without being insincere.

Making an ally

Of course, not all screens are information goldmines. But that does not mean you should dismiss them out of hand. Often a screen can save you some time. It may be, for example, that the source you wanted to speak with no longer covers your area of interest. The screen doesn't have to tell you that when a simple "I'm sorry, Ms. Smith is not available" will do. But if you are personable and don't treat the screen as a roadblock, you may hear something like this: "Ms. Smith no longer covers that area. The person you want to speak to is Mr. Jones. Hold on a moment, I'll ring him."

At this point, you've got an ally. The screen has become your temporary advocate within the organization. The call to Mr. Jones comes with the screen's introduction and approval. Consequently, Mr. Jones is much more inclined to be helpful than if you had called him directly.

On some occasions, you may receive a counter-request to submit your questions or query in writing. In an earlier age, submitting a written request for an interview would have been everyone's first step. But not today. Today, we advise trying the phone first. If that doesn't work, you can always fall back on sending a letter. In fact, you can FAX the person a letter so it will arrive immediately.

Seizing (and keeping) the initiative

Only you can decide whether to play this game if it is imposed upon you. It all depends upon how badly you need this particular individual's input. (And bear in mind that through no fault of their own, the sources you think you want to interview may not have the information you need.) If you do decide to send or FAX a letter, be sure to include a phrase at the end of your missive noting that you will be calling back to follow up later on today or tomorrow. You may or may not wish to give the person a bit more time, but under no circumstances should you leave the next move up to the source.

The most likely outcome of your initial call is that the person you want to speak with will not be immediately available. Your response here is to ask the screen, or whomever else you are talking to, when would be a good time to call back. Again, keep the initiative firmly planted in your own hands.

If the screen demurs, ask if there is someone else you could speak to who may be able to help. If the screen suggests Ms. Jones, do whatever you can to contact her. The idea is first to see if Ms. Jones can give you the information you need, and if not, enlist her in your quest to talk to your original source. You want to get beyond the screen, in other words. It may be that Ms. Jones will be seeing your source in a meeting tomorrow. Perhaps she could mention that you are trying to get in touch?

When you call your source again, you may then be able to say that "Ms. Jones told me she would speak to Mr. Smith and tell him I would be calling." That will give even the most diligent of screens pause. The person will almost certainly have to check with Mr. Smith to notify him that you are on the line.

These are only a few possible scenarios. The key thing, as when conducting the interview itself, is to sense your opportunities and to improvise freely. What Sue says about searching online applies equally well to working the phone—you have got to think on your seat.

You will undoubtedly find that the first few calls are the most difficult. This is because at that early stage you probably will not have "referral information." You won't be able to say, "Dr. Perkins suggested I give you a call," or "I was referred to you by John Doe." Sometimes, however, you can finesse the situation by searching to see if your target source has written any articles. As you will discover in Part Three of this book, conducting such a search can be relatively easy to do using an online database. Often if you can say, "I've just read the piece Ms. Jones did in the *Journal of Enlightened Hog Farming*, and I'd like to ask her a few questions," the screen will put you right through.

Winning at "telephone tag"

Note that it is entirely possible that all of your sources will be eager to talk to you, but be unable to do so at the time you call. In such cases, ask when would be the best time for you to call them back. If at all possible, do not leave the call back up to the source. You're the one who needs the information, after all.

Call backs are an unavoidable part of phone work. The trouble is that when you are working on a project and calling several people, you can generate a long list of people who will be calling you back in no time at all. This presents a real dilemma for which there really is no ideal solution.

You can take it as given that if you have arranged for call backs, you are tied to your office for the rest of the day. The trouble arises if you have a list of ten people to call and currently have five call backs "scheduled." What will almost certainly happen is that as you are interviewing source Number 7, source Number 3 will be trying to reach you.

If you have a single phone line equipped with Call Waiting, this does not present a technical problem. But it does present an inter-personal problem since in order to deal with the second call, you must put your current source on hold. Some people will be understanding, but everyone will resent it.

The only partial solution we can suggest is adding a second phone line. You will probably want to do this if you plan to do much online searching in any case. It can be very convenient to be able to take calls while an online database is grinding away. Equip your first line with an answering machine and give its phone number as the number your "callers back" should dial. Then make all your outgoing calls on the second line.

This way, if a source calls back while you are interviewing someone else, the answering machine will pick up and the caller can leave a message. Needless to say, as soon as you are finished with your current interview, you will want to go to the machine, find out who called, and call them back immediately. You can explain that you were out of the office momentarily.

Alternatively, you might wish to follow Sue's practice of putting a very frank message on your machine. Sue's machine says, "If you've reached this machine during regular business hours—which are nine to five Pacific time—it means that we are busy on other lines. We will call you back as soon as possible."

In addition to being more businesslike than the typical "We're not here right now, but your message is very important to us. . .," this approach assures the person that his or her call will be returned quickly, often within two or three minutes. It also eliminates the need to produce some weak excuse as to why you weren't there when you do call the person back.

Step 3: The interview

Now we're ready for the main event. You've gotten through the screen, and the person on the other end of the line is indeed the source you want to interview. Like the "friendly letter" you learned how to write (or at least *should* have learned how to write) in high school, an interview has several distinct stages.

The first is the salutation. The second is the body—the real meat of the matter. And the third is the closing and gracious good-bye.

Each stage is important, but the salutation is the most important of all. "Meeting" someone on the phone is no different than meeting them in person. First impressions count. It is not impossible to counteract a bad first impression and to turn things around in the interview, but it is not the best way to proceed.

Be yourself

The best advice we can give you about making your best first impression is simple—let your own personality shine through. If you've got a lousy personality, you probably won't be aware of it, since even those few friends you have will probably be loath to tell you. So you might as well assume that you have a wonderful personality. You're a bright, imaginative person with knowledge and interesting comments to make on a whole range of subjects. You're exactly the kind of person anyone who is also bright and imaginative would like to sit down with at a cocktail bar for a stimulating chat.

And, oh, by the way, you've got this job to do researching hi-tech hog farming. You've read up on the subject, but there are still a few points for which you need more details. Could the source possibly take just a moment to help you understand thus and so?

In other words, be yourself. Let the inner "you" shine through. Make every attempt during the salutation phase to establish rapport with the source. This should not be mechanistic. If you're the type of person who's good at phone work, it will come naturally. Be cheerful and optimistic. Leave no doubt in the source's mind that you are going to be a bright spot in his or her day.

At all times, put yourself in the shoes of the person you are calling. During the first few moments of a call, your source is wondering who the hell you are, what do you want and why do you want it, and are you going to make them look stupid by asking questions they can't answer. Are you going to be like Dan Rather or a similarly obnoxious reporter, will their name be used and are they likely to get into trouble, and how much time is all this going to take from their day?

Put the source at ease

That's why you should make every effort to put your source at ease immediately. You know the person is busy. You promise not to take much of their time. But your research leads you to believe that they hold the answer to some of your unanswered questions. In other words, take the "you approach," not the "I approach." Never forget that your sources are doing you a favor. They do not *have* to talk to you.

The best way to introduce yourself is with complete honesty. Don't volunteer more information than you're asked. But don't be coy and expect your source to accept it. One technique that Sue Rugge uses is to say something like, "I'm Sue Rugge, and I'm calling from Berkeley." Often the source assumes that Sue is calling from the University of California at Berkeley. And if they don't press the issue, she doesn't explain further.

At other times, you may have to go into more detail. Often the way you introduce yourself depends on the assignment. If you're doing competitive intelligence, you will naturally be more circumspect than if you are researching some obscure subject.

You must never lie to a source. Not ever. It is not only unethical, it is also bad business, for lies will come back to haunt you. They destroy your credibility, and as an information broker, credibility is paramount.

Protecting your client's identity

But at the same time, if it is important to protect the identity of your client, you must do so. If the source presses you further, you may simply have to end the interview. Unless you have your client's permission beforehand, you can never tell anyone who you're working for.

So you're working for a client interested in buying up a large number of hog farms and melding them into a lean, mean, high-tech hog producing machine. Tens of millions of dollars are involved. You call the editor of *Hog Producers Daily* to pursue a relevant story published in that estimable journal:

Sue   "Hello, I'm Sue Rugge from Berkeley, and I'm doing a market research study on hi-tech hog farming."

Editor   "Oh, and who are you associated with, Ms. Rugge?"

Sue   "The Rugge Group. We do market research."

Editor   "I see. And are you doing this work on speculation or for a client."

Sue   "For a client."

Editor   "And might I ask just who this client is?"

Sue   "I'm afraid that's confidential. I can't reveal the client's name. But if you would be willing to speak to them directly, I will include your name in my report."

Sometimes, that stops the conversation. The source may simply refuse to be interviewed if you don't reveal the client's name. And unfortunately, there is no way to get past this fact. The source may say, "If they tell me who they are, I'll talk to them." A lot of people will say that. They don't want to talk to an intermediary. So you can simply make a note of this fact and pass it along to the client. It may very well be that the client will want to call personally.

And what do you do if this individual is the only one in the country who has the information you need? In that case, you try to keep them on the line. Explain how much you value the information they could impart. You're sorry you can't tell them the client's name, but they really are highly respected in the industry and if they could just see their way clear to help you . . .

Does "No" mean "NO!"?

Sometimes sources will try a gambit. They may say they only talk to principals, not intermediaries, just to see what *you* will say. We're not advising "Don't take 'No!' for an answer." We merely want to point out that once a source has refused you, you have very little to lose by persisting. Nicely, of course. But it doesn't hurt to keep them talking. People's opinions change from moment to moment like the colors of a 1970s era "mood ring." So even a "No!" doesn't always mean "No! No! A thousand times, No!" Sometimes it means "Let me think about it." By keeping a source talking, you allow time for that to happen.

Another thing to remember is that all the people you talk to are potential clients. A lot of times sources are very interested in what you're doing. It occurs to them that maybe you could do the same kind of thing for them, and you end up sending out your literature to those people. This is all the more reason to represent yourself as legitimately as possible.

Go with the flow

Let's assume that you've overcome any objections and that the source has said, "Okay, what is it you want to know?" You follow with the first of your prepared questions. But the source warms to the subject and continues talking, even after you have gotten the information you need.

Here you must remember the cardinal rule of conducting an interview. We've discussed it in general terms earlier, and now here it is in all its stark glory: Never cut off a source. You might have your own agenda, your own list of questions that you want to ask. But let the source go on as long as he or she wants. You have no way of knowing what pieces of information or additional lines of inquiry the source may offer this way. Many, many times in such situations a source will mention some one or some thing you haven't thought of or considered.

When that happens, you must be ready to follow up. Don't slavishly return to Question Number 2 on your list. Listen to what the source is actually saying and engage with the person as if you were holding a real conversation, not a "Barbara Walters" style interview. It is one of the sad but typical ironies of our age that Barbara Walters is considered one of the greatest interviewers. She gets the name celebrities, yes. But as any viewer can tell, she is so focused on asking her next prepared question that she never listens to what her subjects are *saying*.

An interview should be a real conversation, with each person reacting to and building upon what the other has just said. As a skilled interviewer, you will naturally want to bring the conversation back to the questions you need to have answered. But you should also go with the flow. If you're really good, your sources won't be aware that you have a list of "must answer" questions. Instead, they will feel that they've had an enjoyable conversation about their area of expertise.

The closing

Just as the friendly letter has a natural winding down and ending—the traditional technique used by Alfred's nephews is "Well, gotta go now."—so too, with interviews. When you reach the natural end of the conversation, you might consider saying, "Gee, that covers it all. Is there anything I forgot to ask?" This gives the source one last chance to interject points that may have been passed over. And it sometimes brings to light other people or lines of inquiry you should pursue. Indeed, if no additional names or contacts surface, it doesn't hurt to press the point: "And can you direct me to any other sources on this subject?"

As the interview draws to a close, put on your most gracious self. Thank the source for cooperating. Indicate that you have really enjoyed the conversation. Summarize any promises the source may have made to send you additional information. Suggest they FAX it to you or give them your Federal Express number to emphasize the immediacy of your need. Then say "good-bye."

We have said it before, but it bears repeating. As information brokers we must never forget that an interview is an imposition. Yes, the source may willingly grant it. Yes, it may be—indeed, we hope that it will be—an enjoyable experience. But it is still a favor and good manners demand that you acknowledge that fact.

Step 4: Assimilation of results

This last stage may be the most important of all. You've hung up the phone and put the recorder on rewind. Your impulse is to either get up from your chair and do something else or, in the frenzy of the hunt, pick up the phone and make another call.

Listen to Aunt Sue and Uncle Alfred: Neither impulse is good for you.

Upon finishing a phone interview, the absolute best thing you can do is to review, annotate, and expand your notes. Your source's comments will never be fresher in your mind than they are at this very moment. Make yourself take the time to review them and, if possible, write them up. The idea is to capture the relevant points of the conversation you just had as completely as possible. This is especially important if you are not legally permitted to use a tape recorder. But even if a recorder is permissible, you will find that thoughts, questions, additional avenues to pursue, and many other ideas popped into your head during the conversation but were never verbalized and thus, never recorded.

Much of the time it is very difficult to make yourself do this right away. Your body's tired. Your brain is full. You need a break. But you will thank yourself a week from now when you must return to your notes to prepare your client's report. At this very moment, you know exactly what information the source had to convey to you. A week from now, the ashes will be cold. You'll have to spend time bringing yourself back up to speed as you try to recall the conversation. It is so much easier in the long run to bite the bullet and summarize the interview now, even if your summary is nothing more than a long note to yourself about what was asked and what was said.

Finally, you may want to consider sending your source a thank-you note. Written thank-you's are so rare anymore that anything you send is bound to make a positive impression. Only two or three lines are necessary. Just a small token symbolizing your appreciation for the time the source gave you. If appropriate, on the basis of the conversation, you may want to include literature about your information/research service.

Conclusion

No surgeon reaches for the scalpel without a good deal of advance preparation. No information broker should reach for the phone without being equally well prepared. But while successful preparation is a function of the mind, a successful interview is largely a matter of personality. Your brain has to be working all the time, but it is not your brain that the human being on the other end of the line is talking to—it's you, the person.

So just be yourself. But be yourself at your best. Try not to do an interview when you're tired or feeling glum. If need be, take a moment before you call to meditate on everything that is good about your life. Push the bad thoughts away and focus on how much you enjoy the hunt and on how this source is going to supply a key piece of the puzzle.

Always assume that the source does indeed have the information you seek and that obtaining it will not be a problem. You'd be surprised how often that proves to be the case. If your preparation and preliminary research have been thorough, there is an excellent chance that you will indeed be calling the "right" person. Even if you have your doubts, conveying a feeling of optimism that the source can help often stimulates the individual to go the extra mile for you.

And as we said earlier in the chapter, don't forget to be genuinely complimentary. If the source is an authority in the field, make it clear right up front that you are aware of that fact and grateful for the opportunity to speak with him or her. If you can say that, on the basis of your research, the source is clearly the one person who can best answer your questions, by all means say it.

People will see through blatant flattery. But by the same token, if you are aware of these kinds of facts about a source, there is no reason to leave them unspoken. By acknowledging them, you are merely being complimentary. You are also demonstrating that you have done your homework and thus automatically raised your credibility in your source's eyes.

Always take great care to listen—really listen—to what the person is saying. Nuance, inflection, hesitancy, tone, nervous laughter, and all the vocal devices people use to convey non-verbal information become crucial when you're on the phone. With no body language or other non-verbal cues to support them, they are all you have to work with. It is entirely possible for someone to convey a meaning that is completely the opposite of the words he or she speaks, merely by the way the words are spoken.

Above all, have fun with it. Normally we hate it when people say that about a task or a job. But in our experience, phone work really is fun. On many levels. It's an intellectual challenge; it's a test of your inter-personal skills; and it is always rewarding to encounter another human being.

In the next chapter, we will look at phone work of an entirely different sort. We'll introduce you to the many marvelous things you can do with a computer, a modem, and a telephone as we introduce you to the Electronic Universe of databases and online communications.

Part III

Electronic options
and alternatives

9

Welcome to the electronic universe!

IN THIS CHAPTER WE'LL INTRODUCE YOU TO THE ELECTRONIC UNIVERSE OF personal computer communications. You will see that this vast realm divides naturally into four parts: information, communication, services, and Special Interest Groups (SIGs).

We'll help you get acquainted with each of these areas and what they can do for you as an information broker. We think you'll enjoy the tour.

Don't worry about the technology just yet. In the next chapter we'll show you exactly what you need and what to do to go online. And in the chapters after that we'll go into much more detail about how to use the power that exists at your fingertips. Here we'd like you to concentrate on getting the lay of the land. We want you to start developing a feeling for the kinds of things that are available and how this universe is structured.

Why the electronic universe is essential

Sue Rugge founded her first professional research business in 1971, and for the first year or so the business was literally based in a shoebox. Not until 1974 did she buy a terminal to begin accessing the six databases the newly formed DIALOG system began offering in 1972. As you'll learn in the next chapter, a terminal is not a personal computer. The first personal computer didn't appear until 1976.

Alfred began writing professionally in 1973, using the same Royal Ultronic that had seen him through college. Some years later he bought a Smith-Corona, the one with the cartridge ribbons that load from the side and pop in and out.

Alfred wrote five books on that machine and in 1980 wanted nothing more in the world than a correcting IBM Selectric.

Things have changed considerably since then. It is hard to believe, but for a number of years, there was a good deal of doubt about whether one needed a personal computer at all. It was a nice option, apparently, but no one really understood what it could do or what it could mean. In some circles, much more effort was spent debating whether a dot matrix printer produced output of acceptable quality for business correspondence than on how a PC could boost productivity.

Alfred vividly remembers his first encounter with a dedicated word processor, a personal computer that is optimized for text production. Though a business associate swore by it, Alfred thought it was a toy. A correcting IBM Selectric, now there was a machine to conjure with.

It took an hour of "playing" at the word processor's keyboard one afternoon. After that, Alfred was hooked. Within six months, he had a CPT word processor of his own, complete with a half-screen black-on-white display and a single eight-inch disk drive. It was simply self-evident that no writer, at least no writer who makes a living at his trade, could possibly do without the power such machines made available.

The same is true in the information business. An information broker needs a personal computer for all the normal business chores—correspondence, accounting, keeping track of inventory or clients, etc. But that's not what makes it *essential*. What makes a personal computer essential these days for writers and information brokers alike is the electronic doorways it opens via the telephone.

A simple process

The basic process is easy to explain. When you hook your computer to the phone line using a device called a "modem," you can connect your machine to a distant computer. That's called "going online." Once the connection is made, each time you hit your *A* key, the code for that letter goes out over the wire, ending up inside the distant computer and being displayed on its screen. When someone sitting at that computer hits his *B* key, the process operates in the other direction, and a *B* ends up on your screen.

Now, remove that other person. In his place substitute a computer program designed to respond to the commands you send it from your keyboard. You want to know what the *Wall Street Journal* has written about the XYZ Company? The distant computer will check its files and transmit the full text of those articles to your screen, just as if they were being typed by some incredibly fast secretary.

All you have to do is tell your own computer to capture the incoming text and save it on your disk drive. You can then say good-bye to the distant computer and break the connection. Once you're offline, you can review the text you have captured with your word processing program, print it out, incorporate key paragraphs (properly credited, of course) in your report, and so on. We'll go into more detail later, but basically that's all there is to it.

The electronic universe

Obviously, the value of a service like this hinges on the remote computer and the information it has access to. If all that remote system could offer was a database of recipes or people interested in yoga, or national potato production figures, it would be of limited value.

But suppose it's a system like DIALOG, that offers over 400 separate databases including files like America: History and Life; files containing every report published by the Associated Press since 1984; the Arab Information Bank; Biography Master Index; databases of every federal or state registered trademark; a database listing every book in the Library of Congress; and a database of world patents.

All of a sudden, that system becomes very interesting indeed. For not only does it give you access to concentrations of information you aren't likely to find in any library, it also gives you the power to search through that information in the twinkling of an eye.

Imagine standing in front of your library's card catalogue—with its thousands and thousands of three by five cards neatly arranged in row upon row of little drawers. Imagine being able to stand there, snap your fingers and say, "Give me all the cards for books on home energy conservation published after 1976 but before 1983," and have them appear instantly in your hand. *That*'s the kind of power these systems place at your disposal. Indeed, that's why more and more libraries are getting rid of their card catalogues in favor of terminals that you can use in exactly this way.

Hundreds of systems, thousands of databases

Database vendors like DIALOG, however, are only part of the story. There are many, many smaller systems, some of them offering only one database, like the one operated by Bloodstock Research that gives you access to the pedigrees, breeding records, and race records of all thoroughbreds in North America since 1922. The database is called Horse, of course.

There are also consumer-oriented "online utility" systems like CompuServe, Delphi, GEnie, and Prodigy. And there are 32,000 or more free public bulletin board systems, most of which consist of a single PC sitting in someone's bedroom or basement. The online utilities and the bulletin boards do not normally offer industrial-strength information. But they can be a great place to locate people with the expertise or knowledge you need.

And we haven't even mentioned the communications-oriented systems. A system like MCI Mail, for example, lets you instantly send letters, reports, memos, and other text files to fellow subscribers. If your correspondent is not a subscriber, you can order MCI Mail to print out a copy of your document at a location near your correspondent's home or office and put it in the U.S. Mail. With MCI Mail, you can also exchange messages with any telex or TWX machine anywhere in the world, and you can transmit text files to any fax machine (a great feature if you don't happen to have a fax machine yourself). Some of these features are also available from systems like CompuServe, GEnie, or Delphi.

The features, the services, the information—the sheer power that a communications-equipped computer places at your disposal—is so vast that it constitutes nothing less than an entire universe. An "electronic universe." The phrase is as accurate now as it was when Alfred coined it in 1983, particularly since, like the physical universe of stars and planets, this one has continued to expand since then.

Guide books for the tour

There are books you can refer to for more detailed information. *The Complete Handbook of Personal Computer Communications—3rd Edition* and *How to Look It Up Online*, both by Alfred Glossbrenner, naturally carry our highest recommendation. But these aren't the only books on the subject, so check at your local library.

While you're at it, check for the *Directory of Online Databases*. Now published by Gale Research, this volume is still known by its traditional name, "The Cuadra Directory." The Cuadra Directory offers over 800 pages of database descriptions, nearly 4500 of them in all. The book's subject index will quickly identify the databases most likely to be of interest to you. Of course, you will still have to subscribe to the system offering each database (or access it via Telebase's EasyNet, discussed later). And you will have to contact the database producer for detailed documentation.

There are other database directories as well, many of them published by Gale Research. But historically the Cuadra Directory has always been the most comprehensive and current. Note that Gale also publishes a directory of databases available on CD-ROM called the *Directory of Portable Databases*.

A handle on the universe

As we suggested at the beginning of the chapter, the best way to get a handle on all of the various options at your disposal is to realize that everything in the online world falls into one of four categories:

Information
Communication
Services
Special Interest Groups (SIGs) or clubs

Of these, information and communication are the two major categories. Services and special interest groups are really just combinations of the other two, as we'll see later. For now, however, if you keep this four-part matrix in mind, you'll have a much easier time figuring out where everything fits.

Information services

The online information industry has two main types of players. There are the database producers, also called "information providers" or "IPs" (pronounced "eye-pea"). And there are the online systems or "vendors" like DIALOG, Mead Data Central (LEXIS and NEXIS), BRS, ORBIT, and the others. (BRS and ORBIT are now part of Maxwell Online, though the names and systems have remained distinct entities.)

The relationship between IP and database vendor is often very much that of wholesaler and department store. The IP supplies the database, and the vendor makes it available to the public. Often this works well for all three parties—IP, vendor, and customer. The IP is free to concentrate on database development. The vendor handles software development, updates, billing, and advertising. And the customer can take advantage of one-stop shopping, using the same set of commands to search many databases on the same system and paying one itemized monthly bill.

What's in a database?

A database can contain absolutely anything. It could consist of every article in *Time* or *Newsweek* magazine or the most important economic and demographic reports and tables from the Census Bureau or a catalogue listing and describing almost every piece of software for Macintosh computers. It could be the "Yellow Pages" or the "White Pages" of the nation's phone books, or the full text of a major reference book like *The Encyclopedia of Associations*. Basically, if there's a market for the information (and sometimes, even if there isn't), a database will be created to provide it.

It is crucial to understand the wide open nature of the field. There are no standards. Thus one company can choose to create a database that contains, say, only the cover stories published by *Time* magazine, plus "other selected articles." It may choose to begin its coverage with, say, 1962. A different company might also choose to offer *Time* magazine in its database, but include every article. Its coverage, however, might begin with 1979. Still another database could decide to include only article citations—not the full text of the articles themselves—from *Time*. All three could say in their promotional literature that they cover *Time* magazine, but as you can see, their coverage is quite different.

We confected the above example to make a point. In reality, competitive pressures virtually rule out the existence of differences in coverage as significant as those in our example. The actual differences are more subtle. But they're there, and as a professional searcher, you have to be aware of them.

What format does the information take?

Because the information in databases can vary so and be so eclectic, it is impossible to classify them by content other than to refer to their coverage: "This one covers every U.S. doctoral dissertation written since 1861, and that one covers over 300 English- and French-language Canadian periodicals."

In terms of information format, however, things are a bit more uniform. There are three major formats you can expect to encounter online: bibliographic, full text, and statistical. Not every database falls into one of these three categories—some databases offer directory listings, for example—but as a new denizen

of the electronic universe, you can't go far wrong if you keep these three categories in mind.

Most of us are familiar with statistical tables, though you may want to look at
Fig. 9-1 for a classic example of online statistics. Full text, of course, is full text—
the complete text of a magazine, newspaper, or other article. All that's missing are
any photos, graphs, or other illustrations. That can be an important omission,
since photos, graphs, and illustrations may be vital to your quest. Undoubtedly
illustrations of this sort will become available online as well one of these days.
Until this happens, however, you may find that you must still track down the
actual article.

Shown here is one of the many tables you will find in CENDATA, a database prepared by the U.S.
Census Bureau. This database is available in a command-driven format on DIALOG as File 580. An
easy-to-use menu-driven version is also available on DIALOG and on CompuServe (GO CENDATA).

Some statistical databases contain only tabular matter, in which case you must search on the basis
of the title of the table. CENDATA contains both statistics and paragraphs of text summarizing the
data. For reasons of space, we have not included the portion of the table that presented the data in
1987 dollars, and we have presented only a few paragraphs from the textual summary.

11.5.2 - November 1, 1991
TABLE 1. VALUE OF NEW CONSTRUCTION PUT IN PLACE IN THE UNITED STATES,
SEASONALLY ADJUSTED ANNUAL RATE (BILLIONS OF DOLLARS)

Type of construction	Sep(p) 1991	Aug(r) 1991	Jul(r) 1991	Jun 1991	May 1991	Sep 1990
Current dollars						
Total new construction...............	406.5	402.1	400.6	398.2	399.0	437.2
Private construction(1).....................	295.9	293.2	289.6	290.9	291.0	330.3
Residential buildings(2)................	167.7	162.9	157.8	158.3	154.6	175.4
New housing units.....................	119.0	114.6	109.7	106.7	103.2	121.6
1 unit.....................................	104.2	101.0	96.1	91.9	87.9	102.9
2 units or more.........................	14.8	13.6	13.6	14.8	15.3	18.7
Nonresidential buildings....................	90.1	91.9	93.9	94.2	99.0	117.6
Industrial.................................	20.0	20.4	20.9	20.9	20.7	22.5
Office......................................	21.3	21.6	22.2	22.6	23.2	28.6
Hotels, motels..........................	5.2	5.3	5.3	5.4	7.3	9.7
Other commercial......................	23.2	24.6	24.7	24.9	27.0	34.0
Religious..................................	3.4	3.3	3.6	3.4	3.3	4.0
Educational..............................	3.8	3.6	3.8	3.8	4.2	4.5
Hospital and institutional.............	9.0	8.7	9.0	9.1	9.2	9.9
Miscellaneous buildings...............	4.2	4.3	4.3	4.1	4.1	4.3
Telecommunications........................	(NA)	9.2	8.9	9.4	8.6	9.9
All other private.............................	3.9	3.9	3.8	3.8	3.7	3.3
Public construction..........................	110.6	108.9	111.0	107.3	108.0	106.8
Housing and redevelopment.........	3.8	3.4	3.5	3.6	3.7	3.7
Industrial.................................	4.0	1.5	1.4	2.2	1.8	2.1
Educational..............................	22.7	23.1	24.3	22.4	23.6	21.1

Fig. 9-1. CENDATA (U.S. Census) online

Hospital	2.7	2.6	2.7	2.5	2.6	2.5
Other public buildings	17.5	18.6	17.6	16.2	17.2	17.8
Highways and streets	28.2	30.0	28.7	28.8	29.2	29.8
Military facilities	2.2	1.8	1.8	1.9	1.9	2.5
Conservation and development	4.4	5.0	8.2	5.8	5.1	3.4
Sewer systems	10.8	9.8	8.9	9.9	10.1	10.2
Water supply facilities	4.6	4.9	5.1	5.2	4.8	5.3
Miscellaneous public	9.7	8.2	8.8	8.9	7.8	8.4

(NA) Not available.   (p) Preliminary.   (r) Revised.

(1) Includes the following categories of private construction not shown separately: residential improvements, railroads, electric light and power, gas, petroleum pipelines, and farm nonresidential.

(2) Includes improvements.

Textual summary:

SEPTEMBER 1991 CONSTRUCTION AT $406.5 BILLION ANNUAL RATE

New construction put in place during September 1991 was estimated at a seasonally adjusted annual rate of $406.5 billion compared to the revised August estimate of $402.1 billion, according to the U.S. Commerce Department's Bureau of the Census.

During the first 9 months of this year, $301.1 billion of new construction was put in place, 11 percent below the $337.3 billion for the same period in 1990.

(etc.)

Bibcites and abstracts

Bibliographic citations, or "bibcites," are another matter. The closest most of us have ever gotten to a bibcite is having to prepare a list of them for a high school or college term paper. (Bibcites are the items that appear in your "bibliography" when preparing such papers.) Since most electronic information exists in bibcite form, it is worth taking a moment to understand what you can expect to find online—and how to find it.

Note that most information professionals truncate the term "bibliographic citation" even further than "bibcite" and simply refer to them as "cites." We will use "bibcite" here to prevent confusion. But you will want to keep the "professional usage" in mind.

Online databases, like those you might create yourself with PFS:File, dBASE, or some other personal computer database management package, are called *files*. Each complete item in the file is called a *record*. Each piece of information in the record is called a *field*.

The easiest way to keep these terms straight is the classic example of a collection of canceled personal checks. All the checks together constitute the file. Each individual check is a record. Each piece of information on a check (the date, the payee, the numerical amount, etc.) is a field.

In Fig. 9-2, for example, all of the downloaded text constitutes a single record in the PTS PROMT (sic) database file. The fields include the article title, the name of the journal, the publication date, the publication year, and the ISSN (International Standard Serial Number) of the publication. The summary paragraph or

Here is a record from the PTS (Predicasts Terminal System) PROMT (Predicasts Overview of Markets and Technology) database file on DIALOG. The article title, the publication, the publication date, and other individual pieces of information constitute the fields. This record can be searched for and retrieved based on the contents of any of its fields, including the contents of the summary paragraphs or abstract.

Bacteriocide makers hare to face keen competition with newcomers

Japan Chemical Week January 4, 1990 p. 4
ISSN: 0047-1755

Japan: The domestic market for new-quinolone-based bacteriocides will be almost Y100 bil/yr. Four leading companies and their products are Daiichi Pharmaceutical's Tarivid with a 37% market share and sales of Y35 bil/yr; Kyorin Pharmaceutical-Torii's Baccidal with a 20% market share; Takeda's Cyproxan with a 19% market share; and Dainippon Pharmaceutical's Flumark with a 17% market share. New products entering the antibacterial market in spring-1990 include 2 based on lomefloxacin hydrochloride, Shionogi's Lomebact and Hokuriku Seiyaku's Bareon, and 2 based on tosufloxacin, Toyama Chemical's Ozex and Dainabot's Tosuxacin. Shionogi's sales target for Lomebact is Y10 bil/yr. Toyama's sales target for Ozex is Y15 bil/yr. Antibacterial products have different actions than antibiotics and a broad spectrum. They are being used more frequently against infectious diseases because bacteria do not readily develop resistance to drugs. They are frequently used in place of oral antiboiotics, which may affect the overall antibiotics market.

COMPANY:
    Daiichi Pharmaceuticals
    Kyorin Pharmaceutical
    Takeda Chemical Ind DUNS: 69-053-8228
    Dainippon Pharmaceutical

PRODUCT: Quinolone Antibiotics (2834828)
EVENT: Sales & Consumption (65); Market Information (60)
COUNTRY: Japan (9JPN)

Fig. 9-2. File, record, and field—Bibcite and Abstract

"abstract" is also considered a field, as is the collection of keywords (product, event, and country) at the end of the record.

All records in a bibliographic database contain at least two components: the bibcite and a list of keywords or *descriptors*. The bibcite includes the article title, the author's name, and all relevant facts about the source publication. Often the author information will include the person's affiliation, making it easy to reach him or her for a more in-depth interview. Ultimately, the purpose of a bibliography is to make it easy for someone to locate the books, articles, and other publications it contains or, sometimes, the author who wrote the piece.

In Fig. 9-2, the bibcite occupies the first four lines of the downloaded text. As you can see, it includes everything you need to know to quickly locate the original article in a library. But it doesn't include any real information.

Nor does it contain enough information to make it practical to search for this record. Remember, computers are nothing if not literal-minded. If a word does not exist in a record, there is no way the machine can find it, and the bibcite alone doesn't give you much to work with. For this reason, the creators of bibliographic databases almost always add a field of keywords. These words may also be called *indexing terms* or *descriptors*.

The people who add these keywords work for the database producer and are called *indexer/abstracters*. They are professionally trained to read each source article and decide which keywords best describe its contents (the issues, topics, or concepts it covers), and where it fits in the overall scheme of things. The keywords the indexer/abstracter decides on may or may not appear in the source article.

Controlled vocabularies

How does the indexer/abstracter know which words to choose? The answer is that indexing terms are almost always drawn from a pre-defined list of words called a "controlled vocabulary." The complete controlled vocabulary used to index a database is called a "thesaurus."

For example, John Wiley & Sons, the producer of the Harvard Business Review Online (HBRO) database, has established a list of 3500 "authorized index terms" that includes everything from "ordnance" to "x-ray apparatus." The words "ammunition" and "x-ray machine," in contrast, are not on the list and are thus not used as keyword descriptors. The only way to determine this fact is to look up "ammunition" in the HBRO thesaurus, where you will be told, "See ordnance." Needless to say, if you plan to do much searching of a database that uses a controlled vocabulary, it's essential to either have a copy of its thesaurus or learn how to take advantage of the online version that's sometimes incorporated in the database itself. Wiley, incidentally, sells the 400-page HBRO thesaurus for about $50. (Of course, many databases also use additional identifiers and descriptors which are not "controlled.")

Including abstracts— the other bibliographic option

A record consisting of a straight bibliographic citation and a list of key index words can be quite serviceable. Indeed when the information industry was starting and computer storage costs were high, most of the time it wasn't economical to offer anything but bibcites and keywords. Of course there were exceptions. NTIS, for one, has had searchable abstracts from the beginning.

There is also the fact that communications speeds were four to six times slower than they are now, making it impractical to transmit significant quantities of text. There were few complaints from end-users, however, since most were librarians with easy access to the source material and since online databases represented such a leap forward.

Some commercial databases, like Information Access Company's (IAC) Magazine Index, still offer nothing but bibcites and keywords. (IAC's companion product, Magazine ASAP, offers the full text of many of the articles referenced in Magazine Index.) But it is much more typical these days for the producer to include short summaries or abstracts of the source article as well. They are usually prepared by the same professionals responsible for indexing a database.

The abstract of the *Japan Chemical Week* article in Fig. 9-2 gives you a much better idea of whether it would be worthwhile to obtain a copy of the source article. Better still, a good abstract may very well contain exactly the fact, figure, or statistic you're looking for and thus eliminate the need for the source article entirely. As noted, the abstract itself is considered a field in the record, and it is almost always searchable on most vendors's systems.

How to find the information you want

As a new online searcher it is tempting to believe that because it is more "complete," a full-text database is *ipso facto* better than one offering bibcites and abstracts. But that is definitely not the case. In fact, much of the time exactly the opposite is true.

A database of abstracts is usually much easier to search, particularly if you are a new user. Unless you are looking for a very specific and unique combination of words, searching a full-text database can be treacherous. With so many words, the potential for unexpected (and thus irrelevant) combinations and occurrences of your search terms is enormous. You can easily end up retrieving and paying for articles that have nothing to do with your subject of interest.

Abstracts can also save you both time and money. For example, if you wanted information on the bacteriocide market in Japan, which would you rather read, a complete 1000-word article or a short, fact-packed abstract of the article like the one shown in Fig. 9-2? Which would you rather: pay as much as 5 dollars for the full text or about 65 cents for the bibcite and abstract?

When searching for bibcites and abstracts of interest, the fields of each record are obviously crucial. Records are what you are after when you search a database, and fields are the only way you can hit them. In fact, each time a system finds a record containing one of your keywords, it's called a "hit."

Finding information is thus a lot like the carnival game where the object is to dump the pretty girl, good-looking guy, or some other clown into the water by hitting a target with a baseball. You know someone's there. You can see him through the protective cage. But you'll never knock him into the pool unless you hit the target.

In the carnival game there is only one target. In a database record there are many. That's important because the more fields a record contains, the more precisely you can focus your search. Needless to say, the number of fields a record contains is up to the database producer and the database vendor or online system on which the database resides. In Chapter 11 we'll have much more to say about online databases and how to search them.

Communication

The second main part of the electronic universe is communication "from any machine—to any machine—any place in the world." If industries had mottos, that would be the stated goal of the various telex, fax, personal computer, and electronic mail providers and equipment makers that constitute the world's data communications industry.

Computer communications is an entire sub-universe all by itself, so we cannot cover it in depth here. As an information professional, however, it is important for you to be aware of what *can* be done if the need arises. If you happen to hook up with a particularly computer-savvy client, for example, you may want to be able to offer to deliver your search results and/or reports by electronic mail.

If you have international clients, you may want to be able to communicate via the worldwide telex system—without buying or leasing a telex machine yourself. And, of course, everyone these days knows the value of fax machines. What most people don't know, however, is how easily faxes can be sent from a personal computer. It's easy to receive faxes as well, if you have a little inexpensive equipment.

What follows, then, is a whirlwind tour of the main communications options available in the electronic universe. These include electronic mail ("e-mail"), computerized conferencing, computer-generated paper mail, file exchanges, telex/TWX connections, and facsimile messages. We'll give you names and addresses to contact when appropriate, but for a more complete treatment, see Alfred's communications handbook.

Electronic mail

All electronic mail is rooted in a single concept: the ability of computers to store messages just as they store information. It is very simple. When you want to send a letter, you go online with another computer—usually a commercial system with e-mail capabilities—and transmit the message you have prepared. The distant computer stores that message on its disks or tapes or whatever. At that point your job is over, and you can sign off.

The complementary phase occurs when the person you have sent the letter to goes online with the same host computer and, with hope in his heart, keys in a command saying in effect, "Is there any mail for me?"

The computer responds with the equivalent of a bespectacled postman leaning over an oak countertop and saying, "Why yes, Mr. Jones. I believe I did see something in your box. Would you like me to get it for you now?"

That's it. The only hardware components, other than the telephone system, are your personal computer and modem, the main computer, and your correspondent's machine. Everything in the field of electronic mail involves those three components and the options and possibilities available through each of them.

Electronic mail offers many advantages. For one thing, it gives the sender complete control over when a message is sent and the correspondent complete control over when it is received. This is something a voice telephone call cannot deliver since the recipient has to be ready to receive when the "sender" (caller) is ready to send. When you are separated by 3000 miles of real estate and three hours of time difference, as Sue and Alfred are, the "on-demand" sending and "on-demand" receiving advantages of e-mail are particularly apparent.

In addition, electronic mail is the ideal way to quickly transmit information that would be far too detailed to convey in a voice conversation. Can you imagine what it would be like to have to verbally communicate the contents of the CEN-DATA table shown in Fig. 9-1, for example? With e-mail, you simply transmit the entire file to the other person's mailbox.

Few cross-system connections

The only serious drawback to e-mail at the present time is the general lack of interconnection among e-mail systems. Some connections do exist, thanks to the X.400 standard promoted by the communications arm of the United Nations. But practically speaking, if you and a client are going to really use e-mail, you must both subscribe to the same system.

As a general rule, no client will think the worse of you if you subscribe to CompuServe and MCI Mail, since these are the most widely used systems. But if you are going to be involved in a long-term relationship with the client, you may have to subscribe to the system he or she likes to use. These can include systems like British Telecom's Dialcom, Sprintnet's Telemail, Tymnet's OnTyme, General Electric's Quick-Comm, and similar systems.

Computerized conferencing

Computerized conferencing, or "computer mediated conferencing" as it is sometimes called, is another major computer communications option. It is actually an extension of electronic mail technology. However, most conferencing enthusiasts would vigorously resist the comparison, just as they would resist the comparison with the message board "forums" of CompuServe or GEnie's "RoundTables" or the real-time "CB simulators" of those systems. They have good reason to do so. Saying that conferencing is just an electronic mail or bulletin board system is like saying that a Maserati is just an automobile. On the surface it's a true statement, but it omits the telling details.

Electronic mail, for example, is a one-to-one form of communication. Conferencing is a many-to-many medium, and special conferencing software running on the mainframe host is required to bring it off. Your messages are available for every member of a conference to read and react to. And you can react to the reactions. The conferencing software on the host provides for intricate and nearly infinite branches in the conversations and incorporates other features not available via e-mail systems or message boards. "CC" doesn't have much application for information retrieval at this time. But the various computerized conferencing systems can be good sources of experts to contact on various subjects.

PARTICIPATE (accessible via CompuServe with the command GO PARTI), The WELL, UNISON, and BIX (the *BYTE Magazine* Information Exchange) are among the leading computerized conferencing systems. For more information on PARTI and conferencing in general, contact the Electronic Networking Association, an organization that, among other things, serves as a trade association and information clearinghouse:

Electronic Networking Association
2744 Washington Street
Allentown, PA 18104-4225
(215) 821-7777

For more information on The WELL (The Whole Earth 'Lectronic Link), UNISON, and BIX, contact the following addresses:

The WELL
27 Gate Five Rd.
Sausalito, CA 94965
(415) 332-1716 (voice)

UNISON
2174 Seymour Av.
Cincinnati, OH 45237
(513) 731-2800 (voice)
(800) 334-6122 (voice)

BIX (Byte Information Exchange)
BIX/McGraw-Hill, Inc.
1 Phoenix Mill Ln.
Peterborough, NH 03458
(800) 227-2983 (voice)
(603) 924-7681 (voice)

Electronically transmitted paper mail

MCI Mail, brought to you by the phone company of the same name, is, in our opinion, the premier electronic mail system. It offers no information or databases but concentrates instead on superb person-to-person electronic communications. (At this writing, you can reach Dow Jones News/Retrieval via an MCI Mail gateway, but there is little point in doing so. You will be better off with your own DJNS subscription.) One of its most fascinating features is the option of generating paper-based mail.

The company has printing facilities at various locations around the country and around the world. If you choose the paper mail option, your text will be transmitted to the location nearest your recipient. A copy will be printed and stuffed into a distinctive MCI Mail envelope and taken to the post office to go out with the first class mail. Letters can be delivered by regular mail to any location in the world.

The cost for domestic paper mail delivery is $2 for three pages and $1 for each additional three pages. For international paper mail, the cost is $5.50 for three pages and $1 for each additional three pages. For purposes of comparison, if you were to send three pages to Europe via air mail, your cost would be $3.67.

Among other things, MCI Mail will let you put your letterhead and your signature on file with its main computer. You can then tell MCI Mail to use either or both when it is preparing a given paper mail letter. Since the company uses laser printers at all of its locations, it is easy to generate a cover letter bearing your letterhead (black ink only) and a facsimile of your signature.

If you do not use a letterhead, the system defaults to an MCI Mail letterhead informing the recipient that the letter was electronically transmitted and distrib-uted by MCI Mail. However, you can specify BLANK to cause the system to use no letterhead at all. Signatures, when specified, appear at the left margin of the letter. MCI also has an array of "holiday" letterheads. These change seasonally (Moth-er's Day, Valentine's Day, etc.), but "Happy Birthday" is always available.

If your computer does not have a "fax modem" (a modem capable of talking to remote fax machines), you can tell MCI Mail to take care of things for you. You can, for instance, send the same letter to one person's MCI Mail mailbox, another person's CompuServe mailbox (see below), and a third person's fax machine, regardless of where that third person is in the world.

In fact, as Sue reports, the MCI Mail fax option can be particularly handy, even if you have your own fax machine. If a client does not have a modem, for example, you can transmit your search results to MCI Mail and tell it to send the file to the client's fax machine. This is often much more convenient than running the same pages through your fax machine and, for technical reasons, it produces a higher quality printout on the client's machine.

More MCI mail delivery options

There are additional MCI Mail electronic delivery options as well. At this writing, you can send messages to people who subscribe to CompuServe or the French MISSIVE system. But you must know your correspondent's system address, and at this writing, the only way to obtain said address is to ask your correspondent. You can also send a message to any of the 1.8 million telex (I and II) machines in the world, about which more, later.

If you're really in a hurry, you can specify "overnight delivery," in which case the letter will be printed and delivered the next day by a courier service. Overnight courier service is available to more than 38,000 U.S. ZIP code locations and more than 100 countries abroad. The cost is $9 for the first six pages and $1 for each three-page unit after that.

You must transmit your letter or document to MCI Mail by 11:00 PM Eastern time, Monday through Friday, for guaranteed U.S. delivery by 5:00 PM the follow-ing day. (Most letters arrive before noon.) For international courier service, the posting deadline is 5:30 PM, and the cost is $12 to $30 (depending on destination) for six pages. Each additional three pages adds an extra $1 to the cost.

The prices are competitive with Federal Express, and the deadlines are more flexible. For more information, contact:

MCI Mail
Box 1001, 1900 M. St., NW
Washington, DC 20036
(800) 444-6245
(202) 833-8484, in Washington DC
Mon—Fri, 9AM to 8PM, Eastern

File exchange

It is also possible to exchange files over the phone with other computer users. Graphics or paint files (graphics files created by drawing programs like MacPaint or PC Paintbrush) are exchanged among Macintosh and IBM-compatible users all the time, for instance. Program files are exchanged as well, though only among users of compatible computers. CompuServe, GEnie, and most bulletin board systems (BBSs) actually maintain computer-specific libraries of public domain and shareware software for their users. At this writing, for example, GEnie has over 80,000 files of all kinds for users to share. CompuServe has even more.

Files can be exchanged directly, from one personal computer to another. Or they can be exchanged using the same process that is the basis of electronic mail. What distinguishes a file exchange from the kinds of communication we have discussed so far is that the files are "binary" and consist not of text but of "machine language." Spreadsheets, database data files, graphic images, and computer programs are typical examples of binary files.

Binary files cannot be displayed on the screen and thus cannot be sent like text files. In addition, it is crucial to ensure the accuracy of the transfer. If a word or two is garbled in a text transmission, the problem is easy to detect and fix. But if a binary file is similarly garbled, there is no practical way to detect or fix the damage. Most of the time, the file will be completely useless.

To solve this problem, several "error correcting protocols" have been created. Transmitting a file to a remote system is called *uploading*, while receiving a file from a system is called *downloading*, but you may hear both processes described as a "protocol file transfer." The leading protocols in the microworld have names like XMODEM, ZMODEM, Kermit, and CompuServe Quick B.

Each file transfer protocol specifies a procedure for transferring a file and for ensuring the accuracy of the transfer. For the transfer to take place, both you and the remote system must agree to use the identical protocol. The protocols available to you are a function of the communications software you use. These days, most comm programs support a wide range of protocols.

Telex and TWX

If your assignments or clients make it necessary to correspond with someone overseas, you may find that you will be asked for your telex number. Yes, it is true that telex is an outmoded form of communication, at least as far as most U.S. businesses are concerned. Indeed, as Sue freely admits, she has never once been asked to communicate with a client via telex. Alfred's experience has been different.

There is no doubt that the popularity of fax machines has caused world telex traffic to decrease. We can say this because we looked into the subject with a quick search on the NewsNet system. NewsNet specializes in offering industry and financial newsletters, and the telecommunications field is heavily covered.

Interestingly, as an article in "Computergram International" (June 21, 1991) pointed out, there's an entire world out there, and not everyone is as lucky as we are. In many countries, telex is still the *only* form of electronic international communication other than the telephone. And sometimes a country's telephone system is less than reliable.

According to Laurence Roberts, Sales Director of Comtext International, Ltd., telex sales are brisk in the Middle East and growing rapidly in Thailand, India, and Eastern Europe, due largely to the generally poor quality of the phone systems in these countries. Roberts says, "In Greece, you can't make a phone call when it rains. I don't think the people who want to build digital highways [for data networking and fax services] have travelled in these countries. I think they live in a different world."

Roberts also points out that, unlike telexes, facsimiles are still not accepted as legal documents, making telexes invaluable in shipping, financial and banking communities. "Until someone comes up with a fax that can't be easily forged," he says, "those communities will continue to need telex."

Time out for a mini-lesson

Notice how we have just used the power of online information here. A writer (Alfred) wanted to make the point that telex, while clearly outmoded, should not be completely disregarded, but he needed some facts and expert opinion to support that point. This is a perfect example of the kind of professional who needs an information broker and the kind of material information brokers may be called on to find.

If you and the writer had established a working relationship, he might phone you or send you a fax or e-mail message with his request: "John, can you find out for me whether people still use the telex system—or is fax driving it out of business?" As the information broker, you would phone the writer to discuss the assignment further. Then you would do your search, and transmit the results to the writer's fax machine or electronic mail mailbox.

The writer could make of the information what he chose, and the results might look very much like the information from "Computergram International" incorporated into the earlier text. Note that if you do not have a retainer relationship with the client, you would probably send your invoice at the same time. If your charges are reasonable, and your service, fast (most working writers are always under the pressure of deadlines), the writer is likely to call on you again and again.

Back to Telex

It may very well be that you will never have to send or receive a telex message as an information broker. But right now telex is still a major factor internationally. So if you plan to solicit international clients, it's not a bad idea to learn how to use it.

Fortunately, it's not all that difficult. If you have a personal computer and a modem, obtaining your own telex number from which you can send and receive messages is as easy as getting a subscription to MCI Mail or some other online service.

The word telex is short for "teleprinter exchange," but the machines are also called teletypewriters (TTYs) or teletypes. We'll refer to all teleprinting devices as telex machines here, with the understanding that various models differ in their capabilities.

The telex machine was developed in the 1920s and 1930s (we told you it was old) to overcome the most severe restriction imposed by the telegraph networks that existed at the time. Namely, the fact that you had to know Morse or some other code and be pretty handy with a telegraph key to send and receive messages. The telex machine was and is an electric typewriter-like device that has been plugged into the telegraph network.

Eliminating misunderstandings

Telex machines are used to send and receive messages in real time, with one person typing and the other person typing a response. But they are also used to automatically send and receive in unattended mode. Either way, like a fax, the principal advantage telex offers over a telephone conversation is that it produces a hard copy of what has been said.

It can thus eliminate misunderstandings due to a speaker's accent and it is well suited to communicating price lists, product codes, item numbers, and other information that would be tedious to provide over the phone. Besides, telex is usually much cheaper than a voice telephone connection, assuming you can even reach the person by phone.

And there are a *lot* of people available to be reached. Nearly 70 years after its invention, telex is used by some 1.8 million of your neighbors around the world. In the further reaches of civilization, it is often the only way to communicate.

TWX ("twix") machines date from the 1940's. They were created by AT&T and operate on the same principles as telex equipment. TWX is only used in North America. After extended legal action, Western Union bought the TWX network from AT&T in the 1960s. It then linked TWX with its original telex network. The company then renamed the two networks Telex I (the original) and Telex II (TWX).

Enter the personal computer

Not all that long ago, if you wanted access to the telex network, you had to buy or rent a telex machine and have a special telex line run into your office. Heavy users still do that today. But if you have an account on an online system like MCI Mail, you can send and receive telex messages just as if they were electronic letters.

You don't have to worry about the differences, but you should be aware that everything about the telex system is determined by the fact that most telex machines operate at 66-words per minute. Your messages should contain no more than 69 characters per line and no more than 100,000 characters per message. (That's the equivalent of over 50 double-spaced pages, far more than you are ever likely to need.)

You will be billed by the "telex minute." Since the machines handle 66 characters a minute, this means that you will be billed for every 66 characters you send. The charge for sending a domestic telex via MCI Mail, for example, is 75 cents per telex minute. International rates vary with the country. Sending to Abu Dhabi costs $3.65 per telex minute. Japan is $2.89. Nepal is the same price, and so is Tobago. Zimbabwe is $2.69. And so on.

How to locate Telex numbers

As you can imagine, many companies publish directories of telex numbers. The Cadillac of the field is the Jaeger-Waldmann International Directory, at $163 (including shipping) for all nine volumes. Volumes cover Countries A-F, Countries G-I, etc., plus ''Yellow Pages.'' There is also a volume organized by answerback so you can look up who a message is from. Most volumes can be purchased separately. You may be able to find a copy of the entire set in the reference section of your library. For free information on this publication, contact:

Jaeger-Waldmann
Universal Media
P.O. Box 45
Bethpage, NY 11714-0045
(516) 433-6767
TLX: 967753 INTL TLX BETH

Facsimile options

It's not impossible to do business these days without the ability to send or receive fax messages, but it is becoming increasingly difficult to do so. We would be hard-pressed to tell you which piece of equipment to buy first: a personal computer, a fax machine, or a photocopier.

It is a virtual certainty that sooner, rather than later, you are going to need to be able to send and receive facsimiles. It is quite natural to assume that this simply means buying a standard fax machine. And, indeed, for most people, this is what we would recommend.

E-mail systems and Xpedite

But you should at least be aware that there *are* other options. In the first place, if you want to send faxes, you can easily do so via MCI Mail, GEnie, CompuServe, and many other online systems. The process is identical to sending an electronic mail letter, except that instead of specifying a person's e-mail box, you specify his or her fax number.

There are two main drawbacks to this option, however. First, you can usually send only standard ASCII text files (the same sort of file you would upload to someone's e-mail address). Second, you can send, but you cannot receive faxes.

If you care to take things a step further, you might consider establishing an account on a fax specialty system like Xpedite Systems, Inc. Xpedite will accept your ASCII text files and binary graphics or paint files, convert them for fax, and send them to the fax machines you specify. It will also give you a fax address people can use to send you faxes. Incoming faxes addressed to you are converted to computer files, and you can pick them up as you would electronic mail, by calling into the Xpedite system. For more information, contact:

Xpedite Systems, Inc.
446 Highway 35
Eatontown, NJ 07724
(800) 227-9379
(201) 389-3900

PC fax boards

Still another option is to equip your PC with a fax board. The board is essentially a fax modem capable of conversing with the fax modems found at the heart of every fax machine.

When a fax machine calls Alfred's computer, for example, his fax board answers, locks on, and the transfer begins. The information is stored as a file on Alfred's hard disk, and from there it can be viewed with the fax board software or viewed and edited with a graphics/paint program and/or dumped to the computer's printer. It can also be transmitted to another fax machine (or fax board-equipped computer), or it can be uploaded to a system like CompuServe or GEnie and sent as an e-mail binary file. Fax files are really nothing more than graphics or paint files stored in a particular format, and almost every IBM-compatible or Macintosh graphics or paint program can read that format.

Most fax boards can operate "in the background." All you have to do is load the fax software and tell it that you want to use background mode. Then you can leave the program and go on with your work. Should a fax come in while you are using some other program, the board will politely put that program on hold and notify you that it is receiving. When it is finished, it will return control to whatever program you were running.

If you receive a *lot* of faxes, that could be a problem. You don't want the fax software putting you on hold while you are searching an expensive DIALOG database, for example. Only you can be the judge. But you need to be aware that faxes are not sent and received by fax machines alone.

And one of the things you should consider is computer power. With a fax board and the software that comes with it, you can arrange to have faxes sent automatically at a particular hour. You can set the system to broadcast the same fax to many people automatically. Or you can tell it to fax several files to the same number. The software will maintain a complete log file of faxes sent, received, and read. Some dedicated fax machines can do these things as well, but you will pay much more for them.

Note that there are "send-only" fax boards and boards that can both send and receive. If you are considering this option, by all means focus on a send/receive fax modem board. They don't cost that much more—about $150 for the board and software—and you will find them much more useful.

What about images and graphics?

The main drawback to the options discussed so far is this: There is no scanning capability. If all of the material you wish to fax is in the form of a plain text file that you have either created with your word processor or downloaded from some online system, this is not a problem. But if you need to fax someone a newspaper article containing a graph or pie chart, you're out of luck.

Or almost. You might consider getting a hand scanner. These devices sell for just over $200, and you can use them to scan images and text into your computer. The resulting file is a binary graphics file. The computer does not know that the image it displays on your screen contains "text." As far as the computer is concerned, the "text" consists of nothing more than paint strokes on a canvas.

The main drawback of a hand scanner is that it can only scan in a four-inch wide swath of material at a single pass. Flatbed, full-page scanners are available. But they cost about $1200, far more than one should spend just to be able to scan in faxable images.

A standard fax machine?

It is fun, and useful, to contemplate the various options technology makes available. And it may well be that in your situation one of these options will be the best solution. But most people will be served best by taking the simple route of buying a standard fax machine. Expect to pay around $500.

If you can possibly afford it, however, we strongly recommend buying a plain paper fax instead of one that uses paper on a roll. This eliminates the nuisance having to cut out and then photocopy the information you want to use. For example, often you will want to have document delivery houses and other information sources fax you material to be passed along to the client. With a plain paper fax you can simply send the person the actual pages. There is no need to cut, paste, and photocopy, and the material you send will look better.

That brings up an important point. One major drawback to a standard fax machine, compared to a fax board, is the quality of output. When you send a computer text file via a fax board, no scanning takes place and no resolution is lost. The fax that comes out of your recipient's machine will thus be much crisper than if you had sent it with a conventional fax. In addition, with a fax board (or a plain paper fax), there is no need to buy special fax paper. The fax board dumps fax files to your regular computer printer.

Some equipment sources

One fax board we know works especially well is the FAX96 from Fremont Communications Company (FRECOM). This product has received the coveted *PC Magazine Editor's Choice* award. The firm makes other boards with more capabilities, including one that contains both a fax modem and a regular modem. We suggest sticking with the garden variety plain fax board. For more information, contact:

FRECOM
46309 Warm Springs Blvd.
Fremont, CA 94539
(415) 438-5000

The hand scanner Alfred uses is the IBM-compatible Handy Scanner HS-3000 Plus from DFI (Diamond Flower Inc.). The scanner includes its own software, plus a copy of PC PaintBrush (for IBMs and compatibles). We haven't checked, but a Macintosh version is undoubtedly available as well. For more information on DFI products contact:

Diamond Flower Electric Instrument Co.
2544 Port St.
West Sacramento, CA 95691
(916) 373-1234

Services online

We're going to touch only lightly on the services aspects of the electronic universe. You need to know about them to have a well rounded picture, but more than likely, the services offered online won't have a bearing on your professional activities.

As we said at the beginning of this chapter, services and SIGs (Special Interest Groups) are really based on the larger information and communication possibilities made available online. For example, years ago when Sue was running Information On Demand (IOD), she hooked up with CompuServe and a now defunct system called The Source. People who accessed the IOD feature on these two systems were shown a file outlining what IOD could do for them as an information specialty firm. That was the information part.

If you were interested in IOD's services, you could key in a query or otherwise explain your problem or task. This would be transmitted to IOD's electronic mailbox on the system, and the next day, an IOD representative would call. That was the communications aspect.

Then, as now, most services-style features in the electronic universe are offered through general interest online utility systems like CompuServe, GEnie, Delphi, and Prodigy. Many systems, for example, give you access to Comp-U-Store, a shopping service offering discounts on over a quarter of a million brand name products. You can use the power of the remote system to search for the product or model offering exactly the features you specify. You can read a description, and if you like it and the price, you can tap a few keys and order it.

A number of systems have also created "electronic malls." These consist of a variety of "shops" sponsored by various merchants, including Waldenbooks, Long Distance Roses, Gimmee Jimmy's Cookies, Sears, and many others. All such "shops" offer only a limited selection of merchandise, but ordering any item is as easy as hitting a few keys.

It is also possible to buy and sell stocks and securities online through companies like Charles Schwab or Fidelity Investor's Express. In some cases, you can even do your banking online, either by accessing a bank through a utility service like CompuServe or by accessing a bank-sponsored service like Citibank's Direct Access system. Electronic banking has never fulfilled its initial promise, but those who use these systems can check account balances, transfer money, and pay all their bills directly from their personal computers.

At this writing, the services component of the electronic universe is thus centered around online shopping, stock trading, and to a very minor extent, online banking.

Special Interest Groups (SIGs)

The fourth and final major section of the electronic universe are the online Special Interest Groups or "SIGs." These features go by different names on different systems. On CompuServe they are officially called "forums." On GEnie they are called "RoundTables" or "RTs." But regardless of what you call them, the underlying concept is the same. Here we will call them by the generic name of SIGs.

Since a lot of information brokers are trained in traditional library science, many have little or no concept of how valuable this non-traditional source can be. Get acquainted with the SIGs on various online systems, and you just may be able to steal a march on your competitors. Or not. It all depends on the subject you have set out to investigate. But one thing's for sure: SIGs have become too important for any information broker to ignore.

Online SIGs have their roots in the computer user group movement. As personal computers were introduced and became more and more of a force, computer user groups were formed to help show members how to use them. All computer user groups are non-profit organizations staffed by volunteers. Most meet one Saturday a month at a local school, college, or other facility. Some are quite small—with perhaps only a few dozen members. Others are gigantic.

Alfred was once invited to speak at the Houston Area League of PC Users (HAL-PC; and yes, the subtle reference to the movie *2001: A Space Odyssey* is intentional). The group has over 8000 members, but Alfred was nonetheless amazed to learn that normally between 35,000 and 40,000 blank floppy disks are sold as a fund-raising activity at *each* meeting, before the formal activities begin. HAL-PC is a force to be reckoned with!

Regardless of size, however, nearly every user group has separate interest-specific committees or sub-groups. There will be a beginner's group, a group devoted to Lotus 1-2-3, a telecommunications group, and so on. These sub-groups or SIGs typically have their own meetings once a month as well. As a user group member, you can belong to as many SIGs as you want.

The online SIGs available via GEnie, CompuServe, Delphi, and other utility systems are essentially an extension of these flesh and blood groups. (Please see Fig. 9-3.) Each will have a bulletin or message board where members can raise queries and enter requests for help or information. Each also has a conferencing area where members can "chat" in real time, just as if they were on CB radio.

CompuServe offers nearly 250 "forums" or Special Interest Groups (SIGs). Shown below is the list current at this writing. The selection is so great that you will almost certainly find something of interest, so take a good look at this list.

The name of the forum is followed by the "page name" you should "Go" to in order to reach each one. To reach the Working-From-Home Forum, for example, key in GO WORK. Similar SIGs offered by GEnie and Delphi, though the list is not as extensive at this writing.

Forum	Page Name
ACIUS Forum	ACIUS
AI EXPERT Forum	AIEXPERT
ASP/Shareware Forum	ASPFORUM
Access Technology Forum	ACCTECH
Adobe Forum	ADOBE
Aldus Customer Service Forum	ALDSVC
Aldus/Silicon Beach Forum	SBSALDFORUM
Amiga Arts Forum	AMIGAARTS
Amiga Tech Forum	AMIGATECH
Amiga User's Forum	AMIGAUSER
Amiga Vendor Forum	AMIGAVENDOR
Apple II Prog. Forum	APPROG
Apple II Users Forum	APPUSER
Apple II Vendor Forum	APIIVEN
Aquaria / Fish Forum	FISHNET
Art Gallery Forum	ARTGALLERY
Ashton-Tate App. Forum	ATAPP
Ashton-Tate dBASE Forum	DBASE
Ask3Com Forum	ASKFORUM
Astronomy Forum	ASTROFORUM
Atari 8-Bit Forum	ATARI8
Atari Portfolio Forum	APORTFOLIO
Atari ST Arts Forum	ATARIARTS
Atari ST Prod. Forum	ATARIPRO
Atari Vendor Forum	ATARIVEN
Autodesk AutoCAD Forum	ACAD
Autodesk Retail Products Forum	ARETAIL
Autodesk Software Forum	ASOFT
Automobile Forum	CARS
Aviation Forum (AVSIG)	AVSIG
BASIS International Forum	BASIS
Bacchus Wine Forum	WINEFORUM
Banyan Forum	BANFORUM
Blyth Forum	BLYTH
Borland Appl. Forum	BORAPP
Borland International	BORLAND
Borland Products Forum	BORDB
Borland Prog. Forum	ABPROGA
Borland Prog. Forum	BBPROGB
Broadcast Pro Forum	BPFORUM
CADKEY Forum	CADKEY
CASE DCI Forum	CASEFORUM
CB Forum	CBFORUM
CDROM Forum	CDROM
CIM Support Forum(FREE)	CIMSUPPORT
CP/M Users Group Forum	CPMFORUM
Cancer Forum	CANCER
Canon Support Forum	CANON
Central Point Forum	CENTRAL
Client Server Computing Forum	MSNETWORKS
Coin/Stamp Collect. Forum	COLLECT
Color Computer Forum	COCO
Comics/Animation Forum	COMIC
Commodore Applications Forum	CBMAPP

Fig. 9-3. The SIGs on CompuServe

Fig. 9-3. Continued.

Commodore Arts/Games Forum	CBMART
Commodore Service Forum	CBMSERVICE
Computer Art Forum	COMART
Computer Club Forum	CLUB
Computer Consult. Forum	CONSULT
Computer Language Forum	CLMFORUM
Computer Training Forum	DPTRAIN
Computer Virus Help Forum	VIRUSFORUM
Consumer Elect. Forum	CEFORUM
Cooks Online Forum	COOKS
Crafts Forum	CRAFTS
Creative Solutions/Forth Forum	FORTH
Crosstalk Forum	XTALK
DATASTORM Forum	DATASTORM
DEC PC Forum	DECPC
DTP Vendors Forum	DTPVENDOR
Data Access Corp. Forum	DACCESS
Data Based Advisor Forum	DBADVISOR
Desktop Publishing Forum	DTPFORUM
Diabetes Forum	DIABETES
Digital Research Forum	DRFORUM
Digitalk Forum	DIGITALK
Disabilities Forum	DISABILITIES
Dr. Dobb's Forum	DDJFORUM
Education Forum	EDFORUM
Educational Res. Forum	EDRESEARCH
Engineering Automation Forum	LEAP
Epson Forum	EPSON
Financial Forums	FINFORUM
Flight Simulator Forum	FSFORUM
Florida Forum	FLORIDA
Foreign Language Forum	FLEFO
Forum Conference Schedule	OLT-120
Forum Help Area (FREE)	QAFORUM
Forums	FORUMS
Fox Software Forum	FOXFORUM
Game Forums and News	GAMECON
Game Publisher's Forum	GAMPUB
Gamers Forum	GAMERS
Genealogy Forum	ROOTS
Good Earth Forum	GOODEARTH
Graphics Corner Forum	CORNER
Graphics Forums	GRAPHICS
Graphics Support Forum	GRAPHSUPPORT
Graphics Vendor Forum	GRAPHVEN
HP Peripherials Forum	HPPER
HP Systems Forum	HPSYS
HSX Adult Forum	HSX200
HSX Open Forum	HSX100
Hamnet Forum	HAMNET
Hardware Forums	HARDWARE
Hayes Forum	HAYFORUM
Health & Fitness Forum	GOODHEALTH
IBM Applications Forum	IBMAPP
IBM Bulletin Board Forum	IBMBBS
IBM Communications Forum	IBMCOM
IBM Desktop Soft. Forum	IBMDESK
IBM European Users Forum	IBMEUROPE
IBM Hardware Forum	IBMHW
IBM New Users Forum	IBMNEW
IBM OS/2 Forum	IBMOS2
IBM Programming Forum	IBMPRO
IBM Special Needs Forum	IBMSPEC
IBM Systems/Util. Forum	IBMSYS

IBM Users Network	IBMNET
IRug Forum	REALTIME
Int'l Entrepreneurs Forum	USEN
Investors Forum	INVFORUM
Issues Forum	ISSUESFORUM
Javelin/EXPRESS Forum	IRIFORUM
Journalism Forum	JFORUM
LDC Spreadsheets Forum	LOTUSA
LDC Word Processing Forum	LOTUSWP
LDC Words & Pixels Forum	LOTUSB
LDOS/TRSDOS6 Users Forum	LDOS
LOGO Forum	LOGOFORUM
Legal Forum	LAWSIG
Literary Forum	LITFORUM
Logitech Forum	LOGITECH
MIDI Vendor Forum	MIDIVENDOR
MIDI/Music Forum	MIDIFORUM
MS Applications Forum	MSAPP
MS DOS 5.0 Forum	MSDOS
MS Operating Sys/Dev Forum	MSOPSYS
MS Windows Advanced Forum	WINADV
MS Windows SDK Forum	WINSDK
Mac A Vendor Forum	MACAVEN
Mac Applications Forum	MACAP
Mac B Vendor Forum	MACBVEN
Mac C Vendor Forum	MACCVEN
Mac CIM Support Forum (FREE)	MCIMSUP
Mac Communications Forum	MACCOMM
Mac Community/Club Forum	MACCLUB
Mac Developers Forum	MACDEV
Mac Entertainment Forum	MACFUN
Mac Hypertext Forum	MACHYPER
Mac New Users Help Forum	MACNEW
Macintosh Forums	MACINTOSH
Macintosh System 7.0 Forum	MACSEVEN
Macintosh Systems Forum	MACSYS
Medsig Forum	MEDSIG
MicroSoft BASIC Forum	MSBASIC
Microsoft Connection	MICROSOFT
Microsoft Excel Forum	MSEXCEL
Microsoft Languages Forum	MSLANG
Military Forum	MILITARY
Model Aviation Forum	MODELNET
Modem Games Forum	MODEMGAMES
Motor Sports Forum	RACING
Multi-Player Games Forum	MPGAMES
Multimedia Forum	MULTIMEDIA
Multimedia Vendor Forum	MULTIVEN
NAIC Invest. Ed. Forum	NAIC
Nantucket	NANTUCKET
Nantucket Forum	NANFORUM
Nantucket GMBH Forum	NANGMBH
NeXT Forum	NEXTFORUM
Novell Forum A	NOVA
Novell Forum B	NOVB
Novell Forum C	NOVC
Novell NetWare 2.X Forum	NETW2X
Novell NetWare 3.X Forum	NETW3X
OS9 Forum	OS9
Online Today Forum	ONLINE
Oracle Forum	ORACLE
Outdoor Forum	OUTDOORFORUM
PC Contact Forum	PCCONTACT
PC MagNet	PCMAGNET
PC Magazine(Subscribe) (FREE)	PM
PC Vendor A Forum	PCVENA

Fig. 9-3. Continued.

PC Vendor B Forum	PCVENB
PC Vendor C Forum	PCVENC
PC Vendor D Forum	PCVEND
PC Week Extra!	PCWEEK
PDP-11 Forum	PDP11
PR and Marketing Forum	PRSIG
Palmtop Forum	PALMTOP
Pets/Animal Forum	PETS
Photography Forum	PHOTOFORUM
Play-By-Mail Games Forum	PBMGAMES
Portable Prog. Forum	CODEPORT
Practical Periph. Forum	PPIFORUM
Practice Forum(FREE)	PRACTICE
Quick Picture Forum	QPICS
Religion Forum	RELIGION
Revelation Tech Forum	REVELATION
Rocknet Forum	ROCKNET
Role-Playing Games Forum	RPGAMES
SPC Forum	SPCFORUM
SYM/Norton Utility Forum	NORUTL
Safetynet Forum	SAFETYNET
Sailing Forum	SAILING
Science Fiction Forum	SCI-FI
Science/Math Ed. Forum	SCIENCE
Scuba Forum	DIVING
ShowBiz Forum	SHOWBIZ
Software Forums	SOFTWARE
Software Pub. Ass. Forum	SPAFORUM
Soviet Crisis Forum	USSRFORUM
Space/Astronomy Forum	SPACE
Spinnaker Software Forum	SPINNAKER
Sports Forum	FANS
Standard Microsystems Forum	SMC
Students' Forum	STUFO
Symantec Forum	SYMFORUM
TAPCIS Forum	TAPCIS
TBS Network Earth Forum	EARTH
Tandy Model 100 Forum	M100SIG
Tandy Professional Forum	TRS80PRO
Telecom Issues Forum	TELECOM
Texas Instruments Forum	TIFORUM
Texas Instruments News	TINEWS
The Intel Forum	INTELFORUM
Toshiba Forum	TOSHIBA
TrainNet Forum	TRAINNET
Travel Forum	TRAVSIG
UK Computing Forum	UKFORUM
UKSHARE Forum	UKSHARE
UNIX Forum	UNIXFORUM
VAX Forum	VAXFORUM
Ventura Software Forum	VENTURA
WPMA Forum	WPMA
Windows 3rd Party A Forum	WINAPA
Windows 3rd Party B Forum	WINAPB
Windows 3rd Party C Forum	WINAPC
Windows New Users Forum	WINNEW
Wolfram Research Forum	WOLFRAM
WordPerfect Supp. Group	AWPSGA
WordPerfect Supp. Group	BWPSGB
WordStar Forum	WORDSTAR
Working-From-Home Forum	WORK
Zenith Data Systems Forum	ZENITH
Zmac: MacUser/MacWeek	ZMAC

Often special guests are invited to appear in these conferences and to answer questions posed by SIG members. Among others, Steve Wozniak and John Scully have appeared as guests in Apple-related SIGs, *Entertainment Tonight's* Leonard Maltin has appeared in a SIG devoted to show business, best-selling thriller author Tom Clancy has appeared several times in a writer's SIG, and so on.

Electronic SIG libraries

SIGs also have a third section, usually called the "library." Here members can search for and download public domain and shareware programs related to the SIG's main interest area. But you can also find and download transcripts of interviews with conference guests and discussion threads on various topics. Discussion threads are usually collections of the bulletin board messages posted in response to someone's query. They can be veritable goldmines of information and expertise.

You will also find text files in SIG libraries. In the computer- or software package-specific SIGs, these text files deal with things like how to install a hard disk drive or how to do something wonderfully clever with WordPerfect, PageMaker, dBASE, Lotus, or whatever. But there are also SIGs devoted to topics like education, aviation, wine, coins and stamps, broadcasting, finance, organic gardening, law, medicine, military matters, religion, SCUBA, and many others. Their libraries often contain all kinds of topic-specific files and information, in addition to relevant software.

Note that if you are an information broker today or if you aspire to become one in the future, you cannot afford to be without a subscription to CompuServe. Brokers from all over the country meet to exchange tips in the Work-From-Home forum operated by Paul and Sarah Edwards. (Key in GO WORK once you have logged onto the CompuServe system.) This CompuServe forum is also the online home of the Association of Independent Information Professionals (AIIP). Please see Appendix C to get a better idea of the tremendous resources available to you via AIIP and this CompuServe SIG.

Conclusion

This has been but a brief overview of the electronic universe. Clearly not every aspect of it will be equally useful to every information broker. As we have said repeatedly, even the online information offerings—impressive as they are—will not be able to supply the answers to all your questions.

Regardless of whether or if you use any or all electronic universe features, it is essential that you at least have some idea of all that is available. That's what we've shown you here. In succeeding chapters, we will concentrate exclusively on the information side of things as we look at how to search an online database and how to make the most of a SIG library. But first, we've got to get you online. That's the subject we will turn to next.

10

How to go online

THIS CHAPTER WILL TELL YOU EVERYTHING YOU NEED TO KNOW TO EQUIP yourself to go online. Then it will walk you through the process step-by-step. With just a smidgen of practice, in no time at all, you'll be ready to stride into the electronic universe with confidence. Hundreds of thousands of people have done it, many, we are happy to say, with the help of Alfred's books on the subject.

However, so there won't be any misunderstanding, we should note right up front that "going online" and doing an "online search" are two very different activities. Some people may think that they mean the same thing. They don't. Going online simply means making a successful connection with a remote computer, a connection in which you type something and the distant computer responds.

Doing an online search means actually tapping into a database and looking for some of the information your client has hired you to find. Online searching is a complex, brain-intensive activity that requires an intimate familiarity with databases, online systems, and search commands. We'll give you a preview of what it's like in the next chapter. But you should know right now that years of study and experience, and a certain amount of inborn talent, are required to become a really good online searcher.

But, of course, everyone has to start somewhere, and we can say without fear of contradiction that all would-be online searchers have to start by learning how to get online in the first place. That's what we'll cover here.

What you need to go online

You don't have to be a computer expert to go online. But you do need to know a bit more about your system than how to turn it on. Either that, or you need the support of a competent computer dealer, if that phrase is not an oxymoron in your town. In truth, communications capabilities are so basic that even an incompetent dealer would have difficulty screwing it up. We are not talking about brain surgery here.

Any computer, regardless of make, model, or size can be equipped to go online. The equipment is ridiculously cheap—you can get out for slightly more than $100. You need at most five basic things: a serial port, a modem, a cable to connect the two, communications software, and a telephone line. We will start with a bit of background material and then explain each of these items in enough detail to help you see what's going on. If you need an in-depth treatment, see Glossbrenner's *Complete Handbook of Personal Computer Communications— 3rd Edition*.

Note that Sue and Alfred disagree about how much "technical" information most information brokers need. Alfred feels that it is important for every online communicator to have a genuine understanding of what's going on. Otherwise how can you hope to solve problems when they occur?

Sue feels that most information brokers would be better off spending their time drumming up business. As one of her friends says, "Who cares? The computer is a tool, like a pen. I don't want to know how they made the ink!"

Both points of view have merit. Fortunately, in a book, both can be satisfied. Thus, if you want to, feel free to skip ahead to the heading labelled "Telephone." If you are interested in more detail, some of it a bit technical, simply continue reading.

Bits, bytes, and ASCII

Computers operate with voltage pulses called *bits*, a term that is short for "binary digits." These are the famous 1's and 0's you have undoubtedly heard about. A single voltage pulse by itself doesn't amount to much. But when you put eight of them together, then you really have something. What you have, in fact, is called a *byte*. And what makes a byte useful is the large number of patterns of 1's and 0's it lets you create. In all, 256 patterns are possible, ranging from 00000000 to 11111111.

In a computer, each pattern has a different meaning. When operating in what we can call "text mode," for example, the first 128 patterns represent the letters of the alphabet. There is a separate pattern or byte for each letter in uppercase and each letter in lowercase. There is a pattern for each of the Arabic numbers from 0 through 9, and one for each major punctuation mark. About 31 patterns symbolize control functions, like "stop transmitting" or "move the cursor to the left margin," and so on.

All computers agree on what each of the first 128 patterns mean. This is what makes it possible for different kinds of machines, whether they are IBMs and

Macintoshes or mainframes, minis, and micros, to exchange information. None of this happened by accident, of course. The first 128 patterns make up what is known as the American Standard Code for Information Interchange or ASCII ("as-key") code set. The term ASCII thus means "text."

For easy reference, each pattern is referred to by its number. So each capital letter has a number—a capital *R*, for example, is an ASCII 82. Ditto for each lower-case letter—a lowercase *r* is an ASCII 114. The eight-bit patterns of 1's and 0's, you see, really *are* numbers. But they are numbers expressed in the binary or "base 2" system that is the foundation of "machine language." Human beings use the decimal or "base 10" system, and it is as decimal numbers that most people refer to each ASCII code.

If you have an IBM compatible and would like to demonstrate the ASCII code for yourself, get to the DOS command. Then hold down the Alt key and punch in 82 on your numeric keypad. When you release the Alt key, a capital *R* will appear on your screen. IBM compatible users can generate any ASCII code by holding down the Alt key and punching in the desired ASCII decimal number on the keypad.

Serial or "RS-232-C" ports and cards

Now, if you want to communicate with a remote computer, you must somehow find a way to get the patterns you are generating with your machine into the distant machine over the phone lines. That is what online communications is all about.

Your first problem is the phone line. Most wall jacks offer four wires, but only two of them are used for a telephone connection. (The other two are not used at all.) Your computer, however, uses eight-bit bytes. Inside the machine everything is connected by eight- or 16-line cables or printed circuits, and bits travel eight-abreast in "parallel" formation.

To follow the same procedure with the phone line, you would need at least eight wires going out and eight wires coming in (to carry the responses of the distant computer). Somehow you've got to convert the parallel formation of eight bits travelling together into a "serial" formation where the bits in a byte travel single-file. That is the job of the "serial card" or other circuitry lying behind your machine's serial port.

A serial port, also called an "RS-232-C" interface, is one of your computer's doors to the outside world. You will see it as a spot at the back of your machine to plug in a cable connecting the machine to some other piece of equipment.

Today, most machines of every make and model come with at least one serial port and one parallel port as standard equipment. The parallel port is typically used to connect a printer, and as its name implies, it lets the bits in a byte travel eight-abreast. Some printers, however, are designed to be plugged into a serial port, as are some mice and other peripherals.

Modem

Modems are always plugged into serial ports, for all of the reasons we've just discussed. The question now is: If the serial port takes care of rearranging the bits in a byte into a single file, why can't we just plug the phone line into the machine? Why is a modem necessary?

The simple answer is that phone lines were designed to carry sound signals generated by the microphone in the handset, not computer voltage pulses. If you want to send computer bits out over the phone, the voltage pulses must be transformed into sound. And if you want to receive computer information, the incoming sound signals must be converted back into voltage pulses.

The modem performs these transformations by "modulating" and "demodulating" the signals. The word "modem" is a combination of these two words.

Cables

The third component you will need is a cable to connect your modem to the serial port on your computer. This would hardly be worth mentioning were it not for two little twists. The first twist is plug-port compatibility. Today, two physical arrangements are widely used for serial ports—the DB-25 and the DIN plugs. Don't worry about the names. A DB-25 is a 25-pin plug or socket shaped like an elongated capital letter *D*. A DIN plug is round. ("DIN" stands for Deutsches Institute fur Normung, the German National Standards Institute.) Most modems we know of are designed to accept a DB-25 plug. And most IBM compatibles use DB-25's. Other machines accept only DIN plugs.

This means that you will either need a cable with DB-25 plugs on each end or a cable with a DB-25 on the modem end and a DIN plug on the other. This is not a problem, but it is one of those little details you should be aware of to ensure smooth sailing. When you get your modem, be sure to tell the store or mail order house what kind of computer you will be using it on.

The second twist is the existence of internal modems. Almost from the beginning of personal computing it has been possible to add a plug-in card containing a modem to your machine. If you have an internal modem, you will plug it into the phone line just as if it were an extension phone. There is no need or use for a separate data cable.

Communications software

A communications or "comm" program is needed to tie all the hardware components together and to get them functioning as they should. It is the comm program that opens the serial port and lets you talk to the modem. And it is the comm program that, on your command, records incoming information as a file on disk. Comm programs are also responsible for negotiating the connection between you and the remote system.

Communications programs are among the most widely available of all commercial and public domain or shareware programs. They all do the same basic things, and undoubtedly because of this, they tend to compete on who can offer the most exotic add-on features. Like feature-laden microwave ovens and VCR's, however, you will find that most of these extras go unused.

Telephone

Any telephone connection can be used to exchange data between two computers. It is even possible to go online with a portable or laptop computer and a car phone, though if you will be moving at the time, you will need a special cellular phone modem.

If you are just starting out, you may be tempted to get by with one phone line to handle both your voice calls and your online connections. That may indeed work for a while, but very soon you will find it convenient to have at least two lines—one for voice and one for data. The additional cost per month is not that great, and in many cases, no new wires need to be strung.

With two phone lines you will be able to take or make voice calls while you are online. This can be important if you are in the midst of a project and have left messages for several people to call you back. It means you can proceed with the next online phase of the project without tying up your incoming voice line. The same applies to fax machines and fax boards. If you have only one line, it will be completely tied up whenever you send or receive a fax.

Alfred, for example, has one "main" line equipped with Call-Waiting from the phone company, and hooked up to an answering machine. A second line is used for making modem calls and for sending and receiving fax messages from one computer. A third line is used for placing calls and going online with a second computer. The idea is to make sure that the main line is never tied up and is always answered, either by answering machine or by a human being. Sue has multiple lines as well. Although the Rugge Group has only two employees, there are five phone lines.

Multiple phone lines?

It is interesting to note that local phone companies now routinely install the number of wires required for five lines when equipping most private homes. The increasing number of fax machines, modems, and home-based businesses, to say nothing of separate lines for the children and the adults of a household, has made this policy a virtual necessity.

The bottom line is this: If you're going to be in business, you need at least two lines and probably three—one for incoming voice calls, one for outgoing modem calls, and one for fax communications. (Make sure that you leave your fax machine on and supplied with plenty of paper at all times.) If you want to keep your business and personal charges separate for tax purposes, you may even need a fourth line.

If you are just starting out in the information brokering business, you can probably get by with two lines. But you should definitely plan for and budget for more phone lines in the near future.

What kind of modem should you buy?

The most important hardware requirement is a "Hayes-compatible" modem. Hayes Microcomputer Products, Inc., was one of the first makers of so-called "smart" modems, and as a result it set the standard for computer-to-modem commands and communications. Most modems available today follow this standard, and most advertise the fact in their ads and in their literature.

Baud rates and bps

The next consideration is the matter of speed. As you may know, computer communications can take place at many different speeds, depending on the capabilities of the modems used. At this writing, there are three main speeds in the information world: 300, 1200, and 2400 bits per second (bps).

"Bits per second" and "bps?" What about "baud" and "baud rate?" The answer is that, led by *PC Magazine* and other authorities, the terminology is changing. And the reason, for once, is a move toward greater accuracy.

Traditionally data communications have been measured in units called "bauds," named after J. M. E. Baudot, inventor of the Baudot telegraph code. But technology has outstripped terminology. In reality, only "300 baud" is an accurate term. A "1200 baud" modem actually communicates at 600 baud. And things get more complex from there. Even Alfred agrees that you don't need to know the technical details.

The fact is that when there were just two widely used speeds (300 and 1200), misusing the term was understandable. But with the introduction of 2400 and 9600 units, the inaccuracy is no longer acceptable. The proper term these days is "bits per second," or "bps."

Now, for technical reasons, ten bits must be sent for each byte. (You need eight bits for a character, plus a start bit and a stop bit, for a total of ten.) So, since a byte is equivalent to a character, 300 baud is 30 characters per second (cps), 1200 is 120 cps, and 2400 is 240 cps.

These days, virtually no one uses 300 baud. Most use either 1200 or 2400 bps. So be sure to check the manual for the system you want to access and set your comm program to use the appropriate speed. As an information professional, you will be using your comm software primarily to capture incoming textual information. So be sure to check your program's manual for the command you need to open a capture buffer or otherwise write incoming information to disk as well.

Which should you get: 2400 or 9600?

When it comes to speed, we can recommend nothing less than a 2400 bps modem. (These units are available for $70 or less.) Every 2400 bps modem can also communicate at 1200 and 300 bits per second as well. So you're not locking yourself out of 1200 or 300 bps communications. The only real question is whether you should expand in the opposite direction and get a 9600 bps unit.

The answer depends on how deeply you plan to become involved in online communications. When personal computers first appeared, 300 baud was the top speed limit, though 1200 bps was waiting in the wings. A speed of 9600 bps over ordinary phone lines was simply an impossibility. Today, it is a reality, and the units that make it possible sell for as little as $500. Thanks to sophisticated error checking and techniques of "data compression," some modems rated at 9600 bps can actually put data through the line at an effective rate of 38,400 bits per second.

The catch is that today most online systems normally offer a top speed of only 2400 bps. Special arrangements may be available for large customers. But in general, even if you have a modem that can run faster than 2400 bps, it probably won't do you much good when taping leading information systems.

On the other hand, many leading bulletin board systems now offer speeds of 9600 or higher, and GEnie and CompuServe have begun to offer 9600 bps service in selected areas. (Bulletin boards are another of those wonderful resources that many traditionally trained information experts have no idea exist. You cannot afford to overlook them. And we won't, as you will see in Chapter 13.)

In our opinion, 9600 is on its way to becoming a standard feature for consumer online systems. It may take years to get here, but it is unquestionably on the way. There are as yet no indications that the leading online information systems will follow suit.

In light of this, the best general advice we can offer is to buy a Hayes-compatible 2400 bps unit. For $70 to $130, you won't be in too deep. If you find you need a faster modem sometime in the future, you can always buy a 9600 bps unit at that time, probably at an even lower price than is current today. Your 2400 bps unit can then become your backup modem.

Internal or external?

Let's assume, then, that you will buy a Hayes-compatible 2400 bps unit. The only other question is one of profile—do you want an internal or an external model? We have long favored external modems for desktop systems, and in nearly a decade of use have seen no reason to change our minds. An external modem can be used with *any* computer, but internal units or modem cards are machine-specific. If you eventually decide to change computers, this can be an important consideration.

Internal units also occupy an expansion slot, and they add heat to your system. With an external unit, you can look at front panel lights to verify that a connection has been made or to obtain other information. Internal units obviously have no front panel. Should an external unit need to go in for replacement or repairs, all you have to do is remove its connecting cable. With an internal unit, you must take your system apart to remove the modem card.

As for saving desk space, every external unit we know of will let you place a telephone on top. So, since everyone has a phone, there is no net decrease in available desk space. Obviously, an internal modem can be very convenient in a portable or a laptop, so if that is the type of computer in question, give an internal unit strong consideration.

Many companies make high-quality modems. And a modem is one thing you can safely buy through the mail. You might thus want to look at mail order ads in *Computer Resources*, *Computer Shopper*, *Computer Currents*, or in your favorite computer magazine.

Or you might want to contact the following three companies, each of which we know to offer reliable, competitively priced products:

Supra Corporation
1133 Commercial Way
Albany, OR 97321
(503) 967-9075

ZOOM Telephonics, Inc.
207 South St.
Boston, MA 02111
(617) 423-1072

U.S. Robotics
8100 North McCormick Blvd.
Skokie, IL 60076
(708) 982-5010

Micc
3255-3 Scott Blvd., Suite 102
Santa Clara, CA 95054
(408) 980-9565

Buying or obtaining communications software

Selecting a communications program today isn't nearly as tricky as it was only a few years ago. Today almost all comm programs offer the same set of basic features and differ only in the "whistles and bells" department. Though if you have purchased a 9600 or higher speed modem, you might want to make sure that the package you select supports those higher speeds.

If most of the people you'll be communicating with prefer a particular comm package, then that is a strong argument for buying that package. If you follow the computer magazines for your machine, you will certainly encounter a comprehensive round-up and review of leading comm programs in the course of a year. This kind of information is very much a standard magazine feature.

The only real decision is whether to go the commercial route (for about $125) or the shareware route (for a voluntary registration fee of $25 to $50). Again, we suggest you ask your computer-using friends what they recommend. If they are shareware users, they can legally copy the program and its documentation file and give it to you to try. If you like what you see, you are on your honor to send the program author the requested registration fee. (That's the essence of shareware.)

Shareware software is available for virtually every make and model of computer. And, although many information brokers who come from a library background aren't aware of it, shareware programs can not only be just a good as commercial products, many of them are demonstrably better. They just cost less. A *lot* less. The channels of distribution for shareware are online systems like CompuServe, GEnie, and BBSs, and local user groups. Since you won't be able to obtain a comm program from an online source until you have a comm program yourself, we suggest you look around your town for a user group.

Ask at your local computer stores for the names of groups in your area. If they can't help, contact computer teachers at local high schools and community colleges. User groups are so numerous that, once you start looking for one, it is hard to avoid finding several. If you still have no joy, consider writing to the national groups listed next. (Of course, you can always bite the bullet and buy a commercial package.)

White Knight and Red Ryder for the Macintosh

Written by Scott Watson and published by his organization, The FreeSoft Company, Red Ryder is the shareware program of choice for many in the Macintosh world. In fact, FreeSoft runs a RoundTable on GEnie to support Red Ryder and its commercial version, White Knight. Copies of Red Ryder are available from many sources, but two mail order houses we can recommend are the Public (software) Library and Educomp Computer Services. Expect to pay about $7 per disk, plus $4 per order for shipping and handling. To order or request a free catalogue, contact:

Macintosh/GEnie
The Public (software) Library
P.O. Box 35705
Houston, TX 77235-5705
(800) 242-4775

Educomp Computer Services
531 Stevens Ave.
Solana Beach, CA 92075
(619) 259-0255

Apple II Models, Apple CP/M, and compatibles

Although the public domain and shareware libraries for most computers contain dozens of communications programs, for some reason this is not the case in the Apple II world. A full-featured program called TIC ("Talk Is Cheap") used to be available as shareware. But since its author decided to go commercial, it is nearly impossible to find a public domain or shareware Apple program that will work with something other than the Hayes Micromodem (a card-mounted modem popular years ago) at a speed of 300 bits per second. One of the best of these Micromodem programs, however, is the Hayes Terminal Program disk, from the Washington Apple Pi (WAP) users group in Washington, DC. The cost is $5 for members, $8 for non-members, plus $1 for postage in both cases.

"The Pi," as it is often called, publishes a monthly magazine that normally runs about 76 desktop-published, typeset pages, and it is truly impressive. Membership is $32 for the first year and $25 a year thereafter. You will also find Pro-

DOS programs and Apple CP/M programs in the WAP library, as well as a good selection of Macintosh software. If you're interested, contact WAP at:

DISKATERIA
Washington Apple Pi, Ltd.
7910 Woodmont Ave.
Bethesda, MD 20814
(301) 654-8060

Commodore and Amiga

One of the best places to get Commodore and Amiga public domain and shareware software is the user groups associated with the Boston Computer Society (BCS). BCS is an umbrella organization of many computer and software users groups. Total BCS membership is nearly 30,000 people worldwide.

If you have a Commodore C-64 or C-128, send $4 to the Commodore group at the address below. Ask for the group's best communications disk, and make checks payable to the Boston Computer Society. Disks are normally supplied in 1541 format. If you have a 1581 drive, the cost is $5 per disk since the 3.5″ disks these drives use are more expensive.

If you have an Amiga, the procedure is pretty much the same. Send $5 to the Amiga address below with your request for the group's best communications disk. Make your check payable to the Boston Computer Society. The Amiga librarian tells us that the disk typically contains several communications programs.

Commodore User Group
c/o Boston Computer Society, Inc.
One Center Plaza
Boston, MA 02108
(617) 367-8080

Amiga User Group
c/o Boston Computer Society, Inc.
One Center Plaza
Boston, MA 02108
(617) 367-8080

ProComm for IBM-compatible users

There are many fine IBM-compatible comm programs. But in both Alfred's and Sue's opinion the shareware program ProComm from Datastorm Technologies tops them all. This package is consistently rated among the best comm programs in the IBM-compatible world, and it's available in two versions.

ProComm version 2.4.3 is shareware. It comes with a complete 97-page manual on disk for you to print out, and it offers all the capability you are likely to need. You can set the program to call your editor or word processor, for example, so you can prepare search strategies for later uploading to the host system. Better still, you can load search commands into ProComm's macro keys. That way all you need do to issue a complex command when you are online is key in Alt-1, Alt-2, or some similar easy key combination.

Perhaps the most crucial feature for anyone who does online searching is "back scrolling." You want to be able to see search results and other information that has scrolled off the screen before entering your next command.

ProComm calls this feature "redisplay," and to activate it all you have to do is enter an Alt-F6. The text that has scrolled off into space will reappear and you can use your arrow and paging keys to scroll back through it. If you like, you can tell the software to find a specific word or phrase and instantly take you to the screen containing it. You can also mark off blocks of text and write them to a file, in case you forgot to open your capture buffer.

If you prefer to use some other comm program on your IBM or compatible, just load the shareware utility FANSI-Console at boot time via your CONFIG.SYS file. Once loaded, you can use FANSI to back scroll *anything* that has appeared on the screen by simply hitting your Pause key. You can mark off sections of the screen recall buffer and write them to disk too. FANSI works so well that Alfred prefers to use it instead of the ProComm "redisplay" feature.

The requested shareware registration fee for ProComm is $50. ProComm PLUS 2.0 is the company's commercial product. It too is excellent, but you may never use many of its features. Nevertheless, at a cost of $119, it's hard to go wrong. If you'd like to try ProComm PLUS before you buy the whole package, you can get the "test drive" from the same places you get regular shareware.

ProComm is widely available from user groups and shareware disk distributors, including Glossbrenner's Choice. (Please see Appendix D for details on ProComm and FANSI-Console.)

Specialized comm programs

You should also be aware that some online systems offer communications software that has been optimized for their systems. In most cases, this special software is not required to access a given system (any comm program will do). But in some cases, the special programs can make things easier and more automatic.

In the consumer world, for example, CompuServe offers the CompuServe Information Manager (CIM). The shareware program TAPCIS is also available for those who make great use of CompuServe's forums. We'll tell you a secret: Sue almost gave up on using CompuServe until she discovered TAPCIS. Copies of the program are available on disk from Glossbrenner's Choice (Appendix D) and via the TAPCIS forum on CompuServe.

GEnie offers Aladdin to automate interactions with its RoundTables. (Available for downloading from the Aladdin RoundTable or from Glossbrenner's Choice.) Prodigy, of course, can be accessed only with special Prodigy software.

In the information world, DIALOG offers DIALOGLINK. This IBM-compatible program is particularly good at keeping track of the money you spend on the system, a great feature for any information broker. A demo copy is available from DIALOG, if you'd like to try it out. For Macintosh users, DIALOG offers Image-

Catcher, a program designed to work in conjunction with Mac telecommunications software.

Mead Data Central offers a program optimized for searching NEXIS and LEXIS. Dow Jones News/Retrieval offers combination communication and investment analysis programs. And so on.

Most of these special communications programs can be used to access other systems as well (though this is not normally their strong suit since the non-system specific features they offer tend to be rudimentary at best).

Thus, you may find that you will use different programs to search different systems. And still another program for your general communications activities.

Getting ready to go online

We urge you to read your manuals for your comm software, your modem, and the online system you plan to use. Indeed, there's really no way to escape this chore. However, we can offer a few pointed suggestions to help with the task.

First, in all likelihood, you will not have to do anything with your modem. It will probably work just fine as it comes from the factory. If you get the "OK" response whenever you key in AT before going online, then the modem is almost certainly doing everything it should. (We are assuming that you followed our advice to get a Hayes- or "AT-compatible" modem. If you did not, you will have to consult your modem manual.)

If you don't get the "OK" response, check to make sure that you used all capital letters for AT, make sure the modem is turned on, and make sure the cable connecting the modem to the computer is firmly seated. If you still don't get "OK," check your modem manual and your software manual to see if they say anything about special requirements.

Second, communications programs are capable of a variety of settings for "baud rate," "parity sense," "stop bits," and "data bits" or "word length." But only two settings are widely used, and most systems will accept either one when you call. These are "8 data bits, no parity, and one stop bit," abbreviated as 8/N/1, and "7 data bits, even parity, and one stop bit," abbreviated as 7/E/1. For technical reasons, we like to communicate at "seven, even, and one," but "eight, none, and one" will work equally well for you.

Full and half duplex

You may also encounter settings for "full" or "half" duplex. Virtually all remote systems want you to be set for full duplex. This means that you type a character, it goes down the phone lines to the target system, and the target system echoes it back to you. When your system receives the echo, it displays the character on the screen. The characters you type thus appear on the screen courtesy of the remote system.

The only remote system you are likely to access that differs from the full-duplex procedure is GEnie. GEnie operates in half duplex, meaning that if you want to see what you're typing, you will have to tell *your* computer to display it on the screen. You can do this by setting your comm program to half duplex.

Packet switching networks

Finally, you need to know about packet switching networks. These are special telephone circuits designed to carry only computer data. Packet switching networks are what make it affordable for you to call DIALOG's computers in Palo Alto, California, from your home office in Bangor, Maine. Most online systems can be reached via one or both of the leading packet switching networks, SprintNet (Telenet) or BT Tymnet. But many systems, like DIALOG, GEnie, and CompuServe, operate their own networks as well.

If you're going to call a bulletin board system, you will probably use regular phone lines and dial direct. But if you are going to call a commercial online system, you will almost certainly use a packet switcher of some sort, though most online systems have direct dial numbers as well. The key thing is to find a packet switcher access number (to connect you with a "node" on the network) that is as close to your location as possible. That way, the connection will be a local call.

Commercial online systems have a vested interest in making it as easy as possible for you to access their computers. So many supply detailed instructions on how to connect. If they don't, or if you have any questions, you can always call their customer service number and ask for help.

Putting it all together

Now let's walk through the process of going online and capturing incoming information. We can do it using the free facilities of SprintNet, the packet switching network that used to be known as Telenet. There is no need for you to have a subscription, account number, or password.

Here is the information you need about SprintNet and its phone numbers. Unless you have a 9600 bps modem, the number you will want to call will be the first one: (800) 546-1000.

SprintNet (formerly Telenet)
U.S. Sprint, Inc.
12490 Sunrise Valley Dr.
Reston, VA 22096

Free data line telephone numbers
300-2400 bps	(800) 546-1000
9600 bps (V.29)	(800) 546-2000
9600 bps (V.32)	(800) 546-2500

Voice lines for Customer Service
Customer service	(800) 336-0437
In Virginia	(703) 689-6400

Start by turning everything on, booting your system, and loading your communications software. Test your connection to the modem by keying in AT (in capital letters). The modem should respond with "OK." Then make sure you know what command to enter to tell the program to begin or stop capturing information to disk. Also check to see if there is a comm program command to tell the modem to hang up.

Next, on a separate sheet of paper write down the appropriate free SprintNet data line phone number given above. More than likely, this will be the number for 300/1200/2400 modems. Dial the access number from your keyboard by keying in ATDT followed by the number. Don't forget to key in a 1 before the area code. Your screen will look like this: ATDT 1-800-546-1000. (If you do not have TouchTone service, use the ATDP command for *pulse* dial instead.)

As soon as you hit your Enter key, you will hear the modem go off-hook and produce a dial tone. (Even internal modems have small speakers.) You will hear the numbers being transmitted. The phone will ring, and the remote system's modem will pick up the line. Some strange noises will briefly fill the air.

Connect 2400!

Once the two modems lock on, there will be silence. In most cases the modem will send a message to your screen like "CONNECT 2400" to let you know that a connection has indeed been made. Now, most online systems and bulletin boards will begin displaying some kind of text immediately. Most will prompt you to key in your account number, and then prompt you for your password.

With SprintNet, things are just a tad different. If you are signing on at 2400 bps, you will see nothing on your screen after the CONNECT 2400 message. At this point, you should hit your "at" key followed by Enter. The "at" sign looks like this @, and it can be found on the 2 key at the top of your keyboard. This lets SprintNet know that you are on at 2400 bps. If you are using a 300/1200 bps modem, simply hit your Enter key twice instead.

Please see Fig. 10-1 for an example of what you can expect to have appear on your screen at this point. You can begin saving incoming information any time you like. But please be sure to do so since that's the ultimate point of this exercise.

We will leave the joy of discovery to you and not show any more of the free SprintNet phone directory. You should know, however, that it can be very helpful to have such easy, free access to the list of SprintNet nodes. (The menu after the one shown at the end of Fig. 10-1 lets you search for node numbers by state or area code or simply call up the entire list.) It is invaluable when you are taking your portable or laptop computer on a trip and plan to be stopping in several cities.

When you are finished testing the system, tell your communications program to close its capture buffer and capture file. Then tell the program to tell the modem to hang up the phone.

Checking your results

Now for the moment of truth. Did you successfully capture incoming information to disk while you were online? To find out, get out of your comm program, load your word processor, and tell it to bring in the file your comm program used to capture text. With ProComm and other programs, you can call your editor to look at a file without actually leaving the communications software. (But unless you plan to go online again immediately, why bother?)

This is the opening series of prompts you will see after you key in @ and Enter for a 2400 bps connection or simply hit your Enter key twice for 1200 or 300 baud. The characters in italics are what you should enter in response to the SprintNet prompts.

```
TELENET
609 9C
TERMINAL = D1

YOUR AREA CODE AND LOCAL EXCHANGE (AAA,LLL) = 215,736
(Use your area code and the first three digits of your phone number here.)

@MAIL

User name? PHONES
Password? PHONES                (This ``password'' won't show as you type it.)


MONTH YEAR
Welcome to US Sprint's online directory of SprintNet local access telephone
numbers. SprintNet's Dial Access Services provide you access to the SprintNet data
network 24 hours a day for reliable data transmission across town and worldwide.
You can access the network with a local phone call from thousands of cities and
towns or by using SprintNet In-WATS service. The network is also accessible from
nearly 100 international locations. Depend on SprintNet's Dial Access Services for:

        * dial-up flexibility with access on demand
        * error protected network transmission and
        * 24-hour customer service and network management

For customer service, call toll-free 1-800/336-0437. From overseas locations with
non-WATS access, call 703/689-6400.

                    US SPRINT'S ONLINE
        LOCAL ACCESS TELEPHONE NUMBERS DIRECTORY

            1. Domestic Asynchronous Dial Service
            2. International Asynchronous Dial Service
            3. Domestic X.25 Dial Service
            4. New Access Centers and Recent Changes
            5. Product and Service Information
            6. Exit the Phones Directory

        Please enter your selection (1-6): 1
```

Fig. 10-1. Free online numbers and practice from SprintNet

As you can now see, you can edit, re-format, and print out the information you have captured just as you would with the contents of any text file, for that is exactly what this file is.

If you are not successful in looking at the file with your word processor, check to make sure that you are using the correct filename. It is entirely possible to forget the name you told your program to use, and even if you do not forget, you may have mistyped it.

If you are certain that no capture file is on the disk, load your comm program again and immediately open your capture buffer. Then key in AT several times. Your Hayes-compatible modem will obligingly supply an "OK" each time, and these will be captured. Close your capture buffer, leave your comm program, and see if the file can be looked at with your word processor. If you are successful, sign on to SprintNet again and repeat the exercise.

Two final points on the concept of capturing. First, remembering to close a capture file before leaving your comm program can be as important as remembering to open it when you think something you will want to save is about to appear. If you don't close the file and tell the comm program to stop capturing, you could lose the last few lines of text, or even the entire session, depending on how your comm program handles things.

Second, plan to capture *everything*. Open your buffer as soon as you get connected and leave it open until just after you sign off. When you are doing an online search, particularly if you are an inexperienced user, you have a great deal to think about. And the connect time meter is always ticking. The last thing you should have to worry about is deciding what you want to save to disk as it comes in on your screen.

Once you are offline, with your capture file safely stowed on disk, you can easily edit it or otherwise clean it up with your word processing software.

Conclusion

That's the basic process for going online and getting information. Clearly, there is nothing to be afraid of. It is true that there are a number of little pieces you have to bring together—access phone number, account number, password, commands for controlling the remote system, and commands for controlling your own comm program. But after you've done it a few times, it will become second nature. Besides, many comm programs offer a "script" capability that lets them automatically dial the phone and sign you on to a specific system.

When Alfred wants to sign on to CompuServe to check his mail, for example, all he does is key in CIS at the DOS prompt. This runs a batch file that loads Pro-Comm and tells it to execute the CompuServe sign-on script. Everything proceeds automatically. On instructions from ProComm, the modem dials the access number. ProComm waits for the correct prompts to appear and then issues the correct account number and password information.

The next time Alfred's input is called for is to either key in GO MAIL if Compu-Serve says there is electronic mail waiting, or OFF if there is no mail and Alfred wants to sign off the system. (Sue uses the shareware program TAPCIS, which automatically checks for and picks up her CompuServe mail.) Similarly, when accessing the Knowledge Index, Alfred merely keys in KI at the DOS prompt and doesn't have to type anything else until the Knowledge Index menu appears.

These are very simple scripts, and they are not hard to create. Our point here is that as an information broker, you should focus on how to use the online system you're calling and avoid getting caught up in the technicalities of hardware and software. In Alfred's opinion, you need enough information about how things work to be able to solve the common problems most people encounter. But what you will find in this chapter barely scratches the surface of the subject. Indeed, in this chapter, we've tried to give you exactly what you need—no more and no less—to go online.

You will want to keep these things in the back of your mind, but once you've got your sign-on scripts in place, the only thing you'll have to worry about—at least as far as your hardware and software are concerned—before going online is whether your modem is turned on. In the next chapter, we're going to show you what you can expect once you connect with an online database. We're going to introduce you to the high art of online searching.

11

Databases and
how to search them

THIS CHAPTER IS DESIGNED TO DO TWO THINGS. IT WILL GIVE YOU A SERIES OF quick snapshots of many of the leading database vendors, and it will introduce you to the art of online searching. As you would expect, there is far more to know about the systems discussed here than a mere snapshot can reveal. But the point we must emphasize in the strongest possible terms is that the discussion of online search techniques presented here is intended to serve as merely a brief *introduction* to the topic. A complete treatment is far beyond the scope of this book. Indeed, trying to learn online searching from any book or manual alone is like trying to learn open heart surgery by mail. It can't be done. Hands-on practice is essential.

Our goal here is to give you a sense of what online searching is all about. We want you to see some of the tools you'll have to work with, and we want you to try on the special mindset you must adopt when you're in search mode. If you are an experienced searcher, you know these things already. So please feel free to skim lightly over this chapter.

If you've never done an online search before, you will want to continue reading. We'll show you the doors into this part of the electronic universe and try to guide you in the right direction. But only you can turn yourself into a professional searcher.

A consummate search artist

As it happens, we have a wonderful real-life example of the level of skill you can aspire to. Several years ago Sue and Alfred spoke at a conference organized by a fellow who was very high on "online." (The adjective "online" is rapidly becoming a noun and is used by many people to refer to the entire electronic universe.) Wouldn't it be great, he thought, if a professional searcher could be available at the back of the hall? During the meetings and the speeches, the searcher could use his or her skills to locate the answers to any questions people might have. About anything.

As a promotional gesture, DIALOG was willing to provide a no-charge guest account number and password for the duration of the conference. All that was needed was someone to actually do the searching. Could Sue make any suggestions?

The conference organizer had great ideas, but he didn't really know what he was asking. It is one thing to sit down with a client, conduct a reference interview, and then return to your office where you can scream, tear your hair out, or pound your head against the desk trying to figure out where to start looking. It is quite another to sit at a PC at the back of a hotel meeting room and calmly accept any information request—*any request*—conference goers cared to throw at you.

The be-all and end-all

Alfred was in a similar situation in 1983, and the results were mixed at best. After lugging his IBM/PC and modem into New York to demonstrate "online" for the national sales staff of the firm publishing his first communications book, and after doing a dynamite demonstration of The Source and CompuServe, he had the audience in the palm of his hand.

All the sales reps were suitably amazed. They accepted without question the statement that a personal computer and a modem offer anyone the key to any kind of information he or she wants. Then a cigar-smoking sales rep from Brooklyn leaned in. "Say, can you get the race results at Hialeah on that thing?" Alfred sputtered and smiled, smiled and sputtered. He mumbled something about being pretty sure the results were available online, but not on these systems.

It was an adequate answer, and it was quite accurate. But the spell was broken. A cloud of disappointment momentarily passed across the formerly sunny faces of the attentive sales reps. They began to drift away. "This online thing is good," they seemed to say, "but not the be-all and end-all."

As it turned out, sales of that edition of the book were quite good, so some of what Alfred said must have gotten through to the reps. But it taught a very important lesson: You never know *what* someone is going to ask.

Accordingly, thoughts of someone sitting at a computer with an open line to DIALOG and accepting any and all questions are enough to send chills down your spine. Remember, DIALOG's got over 400 databases covering everything from biology to biography, from patents to philosophy, and from UPI News to USA Today. Talk about working without a net!

The very model of a modern online searcher

There are perhaps only a handful of people in the world with the knowledge and skills to take on such an assignment. And it is our great good fortune to count one of them among our very best friends. Her name is Reva Basch, and for two days she sat at her machine accepting any and all questions from conference attendees. To watch her work was like watching a harpist magically stroke DIALOG's strings to produce the most elegant melodies.

Reva, as we have told her many times, is a consummate search artist. (She's also an award-winning writer, gourmet cook, and many other things, but that's another story.) If you ask her a question, she knows immediately which three or four databases are likely to produce the best results. And not just DIALOG databases. She is equally at home using BRS, ORBIT, Dow Jones, or any of the other major systems. She knows the approach to use and the commands to enter to get the most out of these databases at the lowest possible cost.

None of this is accidental. There is no button you can push that will automatically imbue you with this kind of knowledge. You've got to be clever, and smart, and you've got to know how to imaginatively apply what you've learned. But you've got to learn it in the first place. And the only way to do that is to study and practice and study some more. Reva Basch has been searching *every day* for over 15 years, and, as she says, she continues to learn and hone her skills.

Availability of training

Professional librarians today are taught online searching in library school. However, if you are not a librarian, this fact does not put you at a major disadvantage. You may have to work a little harder to catch up with some of your information broker friends, but training is available. In fact, most industrial-strength systems offer rather extensive training programs.

For example, DIALOG's System Seminar for new users runs for an entire day and costs $140. (No previous online experience is necessary; hands-on practice and lunch are included in the fee.) Advanced DIALOG seminars focusing on single topics like patent searching, legal applications, and medical topics are also available. The ORBIT Search Service offers its Training Workshop Package for $175. BRS Information Technologies also offers basic and advanced training. And so on.

Not only that, in addition to leading database vendors, training is also available from a number of leading information providers, often free of charge. Companies like Predicasts, Dun & Bradstreet, and UMI/Data Courier, for example, hold regularly scheduled training sessions in how to search the databases they produce.

You have to have a certain amount of inborn aptitude for searching. If you don't have it, don't worry. You can always find someone to handle the online searching part of the job for you. Though, if you don't have some familiarity with what is in the databases, you won't be able to sell your firm's services effectively. In any case, you owe it to yourself to try. We'll show you how to take the first steps.

Snapshots of the leaders

The very first of these first steps is to get a handle on what it is you're dealing with. Forget about CompuServe, GEnie, Prodigy, and the other consumer-oriented services. You're out of the baby pool and into the deep end now. You've got to get to know an entirely new set of players.

Fortunately, you don't have to become intimately familiar with all 4500 databases and all 600 currently available online systems. Single-subject databases and systems, like the HORSE database we told you about in Chapter 9, are important. But most of your online searching will take place on about a dozen leading "supermarket" systems, each of which gives you access to many databases.

These systems include DIALOG, Knowledge Index, Maxwell Online (BRS and ORBIT), DataStar, NEXIS, Dow Jones News/Retrieval, Vu/Text, DataTimes, NewsNet, and possibly Wilsonline. Here are capsule summaries of these key systems. Contact each of them and request their free database catalogues and information kits. All but Dow Jones can be reached via a toll-free number.

DIALOG

Far and away the industry leader, some of DIALOG's 400 or so individual databases are DIALOG exclusives. Some can be found on other systems as well. Most offer bibliographic citations and abstracts, though many full-text databases have been added in recent years. DIALOG also carries many directory, statistical, and chemical structure databases. The trademark database offered by DIALOG even includes graphics files for various "marks." This allows you to see what various registered trademarks look like. Costs vary from $35 an hour to nearly $300 an hour, and there are additional charges tied to how much and what kind of information you opt to display.

Contact:

DIALOG Information Services, Inc.
A Knight-Ridder Company
3460 Hillview Ave.
Palo Alto, CA 94394
(415) 858-3785
(800) 334-2564

Knowledge Index

Knowledge Index (KI, pronounced "kay-eye") offers about 90 of DIALOG's databases on an after-hours basis at reduced rates. KI is available each weekday between 6:00 P.M and 5:00 A.M., your local time, and all day during the weekend. The cost is a flat $24 an hour (40 cents a minute), for everything, including telecommunications (Dialnet, BT Tymnet, and SprintNet). For more information, contact the address given above for DIALOG. Remember, though, that KI may not be used for client searching. It is a great place to practice and offers a great deal of information you will find useful in your personal life, but you are ethically bound not to use KI for information broker assignments.

BRS Search (Maxwell Online)

BRS Search is the flagship service offered by BRS Information Technologies, a division of Maxwell Online, Inc. In the broadest sense, BRS Search is very similar to DIALOG. The primary difference is that BRS offers about 100 individual databases. Its emphasis is on the biochemical and medical fields, and it offers many full-text technical journals not found elsewhere.

The main BRS system is specifically designed for information professionals. A lower-cost, after-hours system called BRS/After Dark also exists. Like KI, it has fewer databases than its parent system. Unlike KI, BRS/After Dark imposes a $12 per month minimum usage requirement.

Contact:

BRS Information Technologies
(A division of Maxwell Online, Inc.)
8000 Westpark Dr.
Suite 400
McLean, VA 22102
(703) 442-0900
(800) 289-4277

ORBIT Search Service (Maxwell Online)

Like BRS, ORBIT (at this writing) is part of Maxwell Online, Inc. ORBIT was created originally by System Development Corporation (SDC), a subsidiary of the Burroughs Corporation. Thus, you may still hear the system referred to as ''SDC.'' ORBIT is a command-driven system (no menus) offering over 70 individual databases, many of them exclusive. DIALOG, BRS, and ORBIT are the ''Big Three'' of the ''traditional'' (mainly bibliographic citations and abstracts) online information services.

Contact:

ORBIT Search Service
A division of Maxwell Online, Inc.
8000 Westpark Dr.
Suite 400
McLean, VA 22102
(703) 442-0900
(800) 456-7248

NEXIS from Mead Data Central (MDC)

Mead Data Central or ''MDC'' is a subsidiary of the Mead Corporation, the Dayton, Ohio-based paper and forest products company. It has always specialized in full-text databases offering the complete article or transcript. Its LEXIS system contains so much full-text legal information that it can virtually eliminate the need for an extensive law library. Since legal searching is a highly specialized field, we have not discussed LEXIS in this book.

The NEXIS system offers the full text of hundreds of magazines, worldwide newspapers, wire services, and industry newsletters. The only bibliographic citations and abstracts on the system are those found in The Information Bank section, a collection of databases MDC acquired from the now defunct New York

Times Information Service. The full text of the *New York Times* is available only on NEXIS.

Contact:

Mead Data Central, Inc.
P.O. Box 933
Dayton, OH 45401
(513) 865-6800
(800) 227-4908

Dow Jones News/Retrieval Service (DJN/R)

The Dow Jones News/Retrieval Service offers about 40 separate databases or services. None of them is bibliographic in the classic sense of the word. About 15 are produced in-house by Dow Jones and follow their own special formats. They include a variety of stock quotes, news, and the full text of the *Wall Street Journal*, a DJN/R exclusive.

DJN/R also offers access to the complete DataTimes database (profiled below), and it offers DowQuest, a truly unique search service based on the principles and equipment used in artificial intelligence.

Contact:

Dow Jones News/Retrieval
Dow Jones & Company, Inc.
P.O. Box 300
Princeton, NJ 08543-0300
(609) 520-4000

Vu/Text

The main focus of Vu/Text is regional newspapers. Like DIALOG, Vu/Text is a subsidiary of the Knight-Ridder Company. Indeed, although at this writing Vu/Text is still a separate system, it may one day be folded into DIALOG. Vu/Text offers the full text of well over 50 metropolitan papers (Knight-Ridder's and others), but it also offers stock quotes and a small, eclectic collection of other databases that are available on other systems.

Contact:

Vu/Text Information Services, Inc.
325 Chestnut St.
Suite 1300
Philadelphia, PA 19106
(215) 574-4400
(800) 323-2940

DataTimes

Available either by separate subscription or via Dow Jones, DataTimes gives you access to about 40 U.S.-based local newspapers and more than 40 Canadian, European, and Middle Eastern publications. Vu/Text and DataTimes compete head-to-head in offering local newspapers. Inevitably, there is a certain amount of overlap in coverage between the two.

Contact:

DataTimes
14000 Quail Springs Parkway
Suite 450
Oklahoma City, OK 73134
(405) 751-6400
(800) 642-2525

NewsNet

NewsNet offers full-text access to nearly 500 trade, industry, and investment newsletters, and over 20 separate newswires. The newsletters you'll find on NewsNet are the sorts of publications that typically charge $250 or more a year for subscriptions to their printed versions. Some 20% of NewsNet newsletters have no printed counterpart and are available only on the system. NewsNet offers many other features as well, including access to both TRW and D&B business credit reports.

Contact:

NewsNet, Inc.
945 Haverford Rd.
Bryn Mawr, PA 19010
(215) 527-8030
(800) 345-1301

Don't subscribe just yet

As noted, we strongly recommend contacting each system for its catalogue and free information. But don't subscribe just yet. The Association of Independent Information Professionals (AIIP), the professional association for information brokers, has negotiated a number of attractive special subscription arrangements with many of these systems. (Sue Rugge is a past president of AIIP.) If you're going to be an information broker, you will want to join AIIP and thus, you might as well take advantage of these deals. We'll give you more information on the AIIP in Appendix C.

Note that to qualify for these special deals and membership in the AIIP, you will have to become an independent information broker operating your own service. For obvious reasons, the various online vendors stipulate that their special AIIP offers are not valid if you work for companies, libraries, or other institutions.

Costs and account-related matters

Now let's look at the various fees you will have to pay when you set up and use an account on a database vendor's system. Unfortunately, there is no standardization. Subscription policies vary widely. In general, however, you should not be surprised to find an online system offering a subscription for a nominal amount (or even for free) and charging you for the documentation you need. The start-up fee for a DIALOG subscription, for example, is $45, but as a new user you receive $50 in free connect time. That's the good news.

The bad news is that if you want all the various manuals the company publishes, you should plan on spending an additional $100 or so. And that is just the beginning. DIALOG offers database-specific booklets as well. If you were to buy them all, you would spend much more than $100.

On the other hand, you can request a special DIALOG Starter Package that includes training and some documentation, and an additional $50 credit. There is also a $35 per year subscription fee for each password. Among other things, this fee helps cover the cost of *Chronolog*, DIALOG's monthly magazine and documentation update publication.

Policies like these are typical in the industry. If they sound confusing, good. You will be well prepared to consider the next topic—how you will be billed for using an online system.

How shall we bill you? Let us count the ways

Now, with an eye toward showing you what you're in for, let's look at how the online information industry sells its products and at what and how you will be charged. Obviously, database vendors incur certain costs. They have to pay for their computer or "host system." And there are disk farms (rooms packed with mainframe disk drives), software, maintenance, computer center and customer support personnel, plus all the traditional business expenses of rent, advertising, and taxes. They also have to pay royalties to the database producer each time you access a database, and, of course, they have to make a profit.

Given these facts, one would think that deciding how much to charge would be fairly straightforward. In reality, exactly the opposite is true. You don't have to spend much time perusing the rate cards of the various vendors to realize that the information industry has no one consistent way of pricing its products.

As an information broker, you must be very aware of costs since they can rapidly eat into your profit margin. Among the various ways online systems levy charges are these:

Connect-hour charges

Most vendors charge you for each minute you are connected to their system. You don't have to be doing anything to incur a charge. As long as the connection is open, you are at the very least using packet switcher resources and occupying a port on the host system.

The actual connect time cost varies with each database. This is due to differing royalty arrangements between the vendor and the information providers (IPs) who create the databases. A database created by the U.S. government might cost $45 an hour (including telecommunications costs), while one created by a private company might cost anywhere from $55 to nearly $300 an hour.

It is also worth noting that some vendors quote a single connect hour rate that includes everything. Others quote a basic system connect rate, a database royalty rate, and telecommunications (packet network) costs. To get the actual cost you must add all of these components together.

High-speed surcharge

In the days when there were just two speeds—300 and 1200 bits per second—it was common for a system to charge double the 300 bps rate if you connected at 1200 bps. The idea was that although you are paying double, you are obtaining your information four times as fast and will thus spend far less time connected to the system.

In more recent years, as 2400 bps has become the *de facto* standard, policies have changed. Dow Jones News/Retrieval now charges you on the basis of the number of characters they send, not on the basis of baud rate. One thousand characters (roughly one screenful) is a DJN/R "information unit."

DIALOG's 1991 price booklet says nothing about the speed of your connection. Curious, we called DIALOG Customer Service and were told that the rates quoted were the same whether you signed on at 300, 1200, 2400, or even 9600 bps (assuming you can find a packet switching node supporting that rate). We have not surveyed every system, but in general, high-speed surcharges seem to be fading from the scene in all but the consumer-oriented systems. You will be charged more for signing onto CompuServe or GEnie at 9600 bps, for example, than if you go in at 2400. As we will see in the next chapter, consumer systems can offer you a great deal of unique information not available on the traditional industrial-strength information systems.

In general, whenever there is a cost/speed differential, it makes the most sense to do your *searching* at the lowest, cheapest speed, at least when you are a new user. This way you're not paying the top rate for the time you spend thinking online. Then log off and sign back on at the higher speed and tell the system to transmit the information you've found. This assumes a speed that is quadruple but a price that is double the lower speed, as used to be the case with 300 and 1200 bps.

Prime-time premium/off-hours discount

These are two sides of the same coin. From one perspective, you pay a premium to access a vendor's system during your regular business hours; from another, you receive a discount off the "regular" rate if you wait until the midnight hour, or at least until the close of business.

The vendors that offer these discounts do so because they have excess capacity during non-business hours. One can't just shut a computer system off for the night and go home. Since the system must be up and running anyhow, it might as well be generating some revenue.

Be sure to read your contract with the vendor to make sure that you are authorized to use the system at the lower off-peak rates for business purposes. Vendor policies vary on this point, and, like everything else in the pricing equation, they tend to change fairly rapidly.

"Type" or display charge

The word *type* is a throwback to the days of printing "dumb terminals." These machines had no CRT and were basically electric typewriters hooked up to the telephone.

Though many vendors still use "type"—it is still alive and well on DIALOG, for example—the term is thankfully being replaced by the more accurate word *display*. Both terms refer to displaying information retrieved from a database on your screen. (You may also hear the terms *hit charge* or a *citation charge* used by some vendors to refer to the same thing.) Since display charges are assessed on top of connect hour charges, when they were introduced they were generally viewed as a way to raise prices without being obvious about it.

As discussed next, display charges come in several varieties and often depend upon how much of a given record you elect to view.

"Print" or offline print charge

Databases that have display charges usually give you the option of having a record or parts thereof printed offline at the vendor's computer facility instead of being displayed on your screen. The hard-copy printout is then mailed to you by the vendor.

When terminals were dumb and communications speeds were limited to 300 bits per second, offline printing was more relevant than it is today. Nonetheless, if you are not in a hurry (not likely, we know), and if you do not have a laser printer, offline prints can provide a more professional look than dot matrix output.

If you have done the search on DIALOG, you also have the option of telling the system to send the offline "prints" you have requested to your DialMail electronic mailbox. The cost is the same as a paper "print," but you will have to pay DialMail's connect time charge (20 cents per minute) to pick up your "prints." On the other hand, when you use DialMail, you will have the information within 24 hours. You won't have to wait for it to arrive by mail.

Per search charges

Mead's NEXIS is the only major database vendor to use this method. As applied by Mead, you are, in effect, charged a minimum of $6 or $7 each time you hit the Enter key to transmit a new search command. This is in addition to a basic connect rate of about $40 per hour, including telecommunications charges. You will want to review the Mead documentation and price list carefully. But in general, you can expect to pay at least $30 to $60 per search, depending on your skill and on the specific database you are searching. Mead also charges two and a half cents per line when you request certain online or offline output formats.

Pay for display

Variable display charges are almost always associated with bibliographic and directory databases, though display charges also apply to many full-text databases. A bibliographic or directory record is by its very nature divisible into discrete fields. It is thus relatively simple to impose a charge for each field a customer asks to have displayed.

It works like this. You enter a search command and the system goes away and locates the records containing your hits. Then, like a casino dealer holding his cards close to his vest, the system says in effect, "I've got all the fields for the records you asked for right here. But it's gonna cost'cha. Now, which cards would you like to see: Just the title and author? Just the title and abstract? The title, author, abstract, and indexing keywords? The full text of the article?"

Under this system, the more you ask to have displayed, the more you will pay. ORBIT, for example, offers four display options (Print Scan, Print Trial, Print Standard, and Full). DIALOG offers Formats 1 through 9 and beyond. BRS has a similar arrangement.

A DIALOG example

We can use DIALOG as our example. On this system, Format 1 displays only the accession number DIALOG assigns to each record. Format 9 usually displays the full text of the magazine article or other source material in those databases offering a full-text option. In between are options for virtually every combination of record components you can imagine.

Here are the components of the nine DIALOG display formats as implemented on ABI/INFORM, a database covering some 800 trade, business, finance, and marketing journals and magazines. Though the contents of each format are up to the database producer, the following arrangement is typical:

Format 1   DIALOG accession number
Format 2   Full record, except abstract
Format 3   Bibliographic citation
Format 4   Full record with tagged fields
Format 5   Full record
Format 6   Title
Format 7   Bibliographic citation and abstract
Format 8   Title and indexing (keywords)
Format 9   Full text (where available)

Now, here's the kicker: The actual information displayed in each format *can vary* with the database. The costs for displaying each format vary with the database as well. The database creator determines how much information is actually parcelled out in each format and how much you will pay. For example, here are the rates for displaying each format in the ABI/INFORM database. The word "types" refers to online display; "prints," to offline printouts.

Connect cost per minute: $2.20

Format	Types	Prints
1	$0.00	$0.05
2	$0.57	$0.84
3	$0.48	$0.70
4	$0.95	$1.40
5	$0.95	$1.40
6	$0.00	$0.56
7	$0.95	$1.40
8	$0.00	$0.70
9	$0.95	$1.40

Format details are provided in the documentation for each database. That's right—each of the 400 or so databases on DIALOG has its own set of instructions.

The instructions are called Bluesheets, and there is at least one Bluesheet for each database. Sometime it's two pages; sometimes it is several pages. The Bluesheet will tell you what information will be displayed for each format. The rate card will tell you what you will be charged to look at the full record. The prices for all the other formats can only be found online using the ?RATESn command, where *n* is the database number. Of course, you can also call Customer Service.

A quick-start introduction to online searching

As we have tried to emphasize, no single book can even begin to tell you every-thing you need to know about online searching. And even a book completely devoted to the subject is no substitute for actual online searching and practice.

In addition, every vendor's system is different. Every database on a vendor's system has its own little eccentricities. However, we can give you our best advice for getting started. It is a five-step process:

Step 1: Sign up for DIALOG's Knowledge Index
Call the toll-free number for DIALOG given above and ask for a Knowledge Index information kit and a customer agreement. Your one-time fee for KI will be $39.95. This gets you the KI Starter Kit, a package that includes your documenta-tion, a disk for practicing KI searches, the quarterly KI newsletter, and two free hours of search time.

This is a very good deal. Connect time is normally billed at $24 an hour, including telecommunications, and KI does not have an annual subscription fee. All charges will be billed to your chosen credit card.

Note that we are recommending KI for practice and personal use only. You are not permitted to use it to serve your information brokerage clients.

Step 2: Use KI's menu system
When your subscription is activated and you sign on, you will see a main menu offering (among other things) menu mode or command mode. Pick menu mode. Set a kitchen timer for 30 minutes and put it by your computer. Then settle back and explore. You may want to open your capture buffer to log everything to disk.

Follow this same procedure several times over the next week or so. Remem-ber, you've got two free hours to work with. The only catch is that you must use them within 30 days after signing on for the first time.

Step 3: Read the information about searching offered in this chapter
This information will give you general concepts and techniques for operating in command mode on any information system.

Step 4: Consult the Knowledge Index documentation for instructions on how to use command mode
KI puts a lot of power in your hands in command mode. You can move faster and tune your searches more precisely. Be sure to compare what the KI manual says with the general concepts below so you can make the general specific.

Step 5: Sign on to KI and opt for command mode

Give yourself an assignment. Try finding every book by your favorite author, for example. What can you discover about lead solder and domestic drinking water? What articles have been published in medical journals about some disease or condition? What substance is currently being used in place of Red Dye Number 4? And so on. The databases on KI hold the answers to all these questions—or they can tell you whom to call.

Practice what you have learned both here and from the KI manual. There is no cheaper way to learn real online information retrieval skills than with KI. In the future, you may want to try DIALOG's ONTAP databases as well. These are practice versions of many of DIALOG's most popular files. See your free DIALOG literature for more details. ONTAP databases cost $15 an hour to search, plus at least $10 per hour in telecommunications costs, for a minimum of $25 an hour.

The only drawback of ONTAP files is that they consist of a limited, non-current selection of records. If you don't find anything, it is hard to determine whether it is your fault (an inadequate search strategy) or whether the information just isn't in these severely limited databases.

A genuine value

There are a number of major advantages to following these five steps. KI may cost double the price of using CompuServe and nearly five times as much as GEnie, but by information industry standards $24 an hour for *everything* (connect time, communications charges, and display charges), is very cheap.

In addition, you get two free hours with your subscription. That's certainly enough to find out whether you absolutely cannot stand online searching or whether you take to it like a duck to water. If you find that you don't like it, the most you will be out is your $30 subscription fee. There is no yearly obligation. And you'll have access to KI from then on.

Also, Knowledge Index is a major league system. The 90 or more databases it offers contain exactly the same information available at much higher prices on the main DIALOG system. It is thus the perfect way to perfect your online information retrieval skills.

KI is not, however, the place to do the searches you will bill for. DIALOG's user agreement specifically states that KI is for *personal* searches only. If you are working for a client, you must use the main DIALOG system. We know of more than one individual whose KI and DIALOG accounts have been closed for violating this rule.

How to search a database

Now let's turn our attention to the actual search process. (Again, we can only give you a preview of what it is like.) You will find that there are two essential elements to successful online searching. The first is your mental approach to the problem at hand. The second is your familiarity with the tools available to get the job done.

The mental element is the more important of the two. Indeed it may be the most important factor of all. Certainly it's the most difficult to explain. Which is probably why most articles about online information retrieval tend to skip over it and concentrate on search commands and other clearly defined tools.

One noteworthy exception is a two-part article by Barbara Quint published in *Online* magazine [May and July, 1991; see Appendix A for details on contacting the publisher of *Online*.]. The article is called "Inside a Searcher's Mind: The Seven Stages of an Online Search," and like all of Barbara's writings and public addresses it is pungent, to the point, and packed with memorable insights.

Of course, Barbara is a personal friend. (As we have said from the beginning, this is still a very small, collegial industry.) But trust Aunt Sue and Uncle Alfred—if you ever see anything with the Barbara Quint byline, buy it, read it, and ponder it in your heart. "BQ" is truly a gem.

Here we will rush in where most others have feared to tread and attempt to offer some of our insights about online searching. We'll start with a discussion of how to develop the proper mental approach. Then we'll discuss many of the major tools and techniques you will use to start searching. We will use DIALOG's Knowledge Index as our main example. But you should know that the concepts and approaches apply to all databases, even those which, like NewsNet, NEXIS, Vu/Text, and most of Dow Jones, are not based on bibliographic citations and abstracts.

Call Customer Service

The best way to find the answers to questions about using a system is to spend some time with the database vendor's manual. Strive to get a handle on what the database contains and how it presents its information. Do your best to bring yourself up to speed. Then call Customer Service. The information industry, unlike the computer hardware and software industries, has always put a heavy emphasis on telephone support. They've got the toll-free lines, the trained staff, and the years of experience to do the job right. Top-quality customer service is part of what you're paying for when you use an online system.

Often a customer service representative will not only tell you what commands to enter, he or she will enter them at a nearby terminal to test them for you and make suggestions on how to improve on the results. You can then hang up, sign on to the system, and enter the same commands "cookbook" fashion.

But don't stop there. Learn from the experience. After you are finished, log off and *think* about how and why the search strategy worked. You can't rely on "cookbook commands" forever, after all.

IP support

The database vendor's hotline is only your first option. There is an entire second level of customer support provided by the database producers. Many IPs publish and sell their own reference manuals. The manuals and other materials explain how the database is set up, what it includes, and how to use any special codes or controlled vocabulary terms for precision searching.

Many IPs also maintain their own customer support hotlines, many of them toll-free. In fact, though it will stunt the growth of your information retrieval skills, you can often phone an IP with nothing more than a question like "How can I find information on Company X?" and receive a complete, blow-by-blow set of instructions on what commands and search terms to enter on a given system.

Mental approach: The five rules of search success

Now let's look specifically at the proper mental approach to online searching. As you will discover, it is crucial to have the right mindset when you are embarking on an online search. If you don't, you will simply burn up time and money and have nothing to show for it.

A mindset is a difficult thing to define. But we have done our best by offering what we call "The Five Rules of Search Success." And here they are:

The Five Rules of Search Success
Rule 1:   Respect your opponent
Rule 2:   Define your target
Rule 3:   Consider the source: Who would know?
Rule 4:   Don't go online unless you have to
Rule 5:   Know your databases

Rule 1:   Respect your opponent

It is vital to begin by developing a healthy respect for your opponent—the vast quantity of information that's out there. With so much information now online, it is exceptionally easy to simply dive in and drown.

Consider all the various forms the information you seek could take. If we assume, for example, that you have a client who wants to know about the market for decaffeinated tea, you could expect to find information on this topic in any or all of the following: general interest, trade, and technical newspapers and magazines; specialized newsletters; doctoral dissertations; government studies; and possibly even films, filmstrips, and video tapes. Multiply all of these by the number of countries in the world, and you can begin to appreciate the scope of what's available on this topic alone.

Rule 2: Define your target

One of the biggest mistakes new searchers make is to go online without a clearly defined idea of what they're after. If you do this, your information opponent will swallow you alive. For example, suppose your client was interested in industrial robots of the sort that weld cars together on a modern assembly line. We searched *Business Week* on the ABI/INFORM database and discovered that there were nearly 19,000 articles containing the word *industrial*, over 1200 containing the word *robot* or *robots*, and 150 containing the phrase "industrial robot(s)." That's one magazine out of the 800 that ABI/INFORM covers, and we limited things to just the last two and a half years.

Rule 3: Consider the source: Who would know?

One way to begin any search is to start with a methodical inventory of the resources at your disposal. The library card catalogue (paper or online) over here, the library's magazine and newspaper racks over there, several hundred books from A to Basque in the stacks across the room, right next to several hundred more from Cable TV to Czar.

That can be a useful approach. But it may be more productive to ask yourself, "Who would *publish* this kind of information? And how would each type of publication treat the topic?" In other words, instead of allowing your actions to be limited and channeled by what happens to be close at hand, whether it's a collection of databases or a collection of books, take control of the situation. This forces you to focus on the source material, and that has a number of benefits.

First, it emphasizes the fact that the information in an online database, whether it corresponds to a printed publication or not, has to come from somewhere. It isn't enough for an IP to say, as many do, "We've got a business database! Come search! Come search!" If information is to have any value, you've got to know where it came from. Is it from a reasonably impartial government study, a guaranteed-to-be-partial trade group, a reputable magazine, a newspaper with a particular viewpoint to sell, or what?

Focusing on source material is also one of the most important steps you can take toward ensuring successful online searches. For example, *Business Week*, *Scientific American*, *Beverage World*, and the *New York Times* could all be expected to publish information on decaffeinated tea. And you know, almost without thinking about it, that each one is going to take a different angle on the story.

Business Week could be expected to profile one or more leading firms and CEOs. *Scientific American* would report on the clinical evidence regarding the effects of regular and decaffeinated tea. Or it might go into great detail about the process of removing caffeine from tea leaves.

Beverage World, good trade magazine that it is, would zero in on market trends: who's doing what and what their plans are for the future. The *New York Times* might cover decaffeinated tea as a trend in a "Life Style" report or as a science report (if some new process were involved) or possibly as a business story (if some new company's shares were rocketing upward). But however it covered the story, the *Times* would not go into great scientific or business detail.

If you think about the kind of coverage you want, and if you think about the kinds of publications most likely to provide it, you can begin to zero in on the *databases* you should search by looking at the publications each database covers.

Rule 4: Don't go online unless you have to

Databases don't always offer the easiest solution to your information problem. It is crucial to be aware that an electronic database is only one of *many* options. It is part of a continuum of information tools that includes all of a library's standard reference, index, and directory volumes (some of which are online), encyclopedias and handbooks, the card catalogue, inter-library loan programs, and every other library resource. (Note that if you are an information broker, it isn't fair to ask public librarians to do your work for you.) This continuum also includes the telephone and the U.S. Mail.

There are lots of times when you will have to go online, of course. But when you've got a question, you might also ask yourself: "Who would know about this kind of thing?" One of your friends, contacts, or business associates? Maybe they know somebody who knows somebody you could call. No luck? Okay, let's go online. But instead of trying to find the actual information you need, consider a different approach. Instead of looking for the answers to your client's questions, use the online tools to find an expert who can tell you what you want to know.

Let the reporters do the legwork

When you're looking for an expert, you'll frequently discover that the nation's magazine and newspaper reporters have done much of the work for you. If you search for even general stories on a topic, you'll find that most will quote one or more experts and cite their credentials and affiliations. The stories will also give you important background information and alert you to issues you may not have considered. When you use a database in this way, it doesn't much matter whether the abstract or referenced article contains the exact facts and figures you're after. If it contains the name of an expert or recognized authority, you've got the entry point you need.

Sign off the system, pick up the phone, and call directory assistance to get the telephone number of the university, corporation, consulting firm, or other organization with whom the individual is associated. You may have to make several calls. The expert may or may not be able to help you. But the chances are that he or she knows someone who can, and probably has that individual's phone number in the Rolodex.

When you do make contact with the right person, you'll be able to ask questions and explore topics in a way that you will never be able to do with a computer, the inflated claims of artificial intelligence promoters notwithstanding. And, thanks to your online search, you will be able to sound more intelligent and better informed since you will have picked up the basic vocabulary, learned the issues, and discovered the current trends.

Elementary, my dear database

When searching for information it generally makes good sense to turn first to those publications and sources you know best. But no one can be familiar with every information source. The real challenge, and much of the satisfaction, comes when you apply your Holmesian powers of deductive reasoning.

For example, if you're aware that almost every industry has a trade journal of some sort, you can deduce that one exists for the industry you are interested in without ever having seen or heard of it. Similarly, you can assume that most industries have at least one trade association. Even if it is a small industry, you can assume that some investment banking concern has prepared a detailed report on it, or on one or more of its leading companies. You can also assume that it falls

under the jurisdiction of a governmental body somewhere that has probably prepared a report on it.

What are the names of the leading companies? Who are the executives of
those firms? Is it possible that one or more of them has been quoted in a national
magazine? In a local or regional newspaper? Have any of them written a book on
their experiences? You can obtain all of this information and much more from
online databases.

On becoming an information detective

Information retrieval, in short, is anything but a passive activity. It is a skill that
requires imagination, brainstorming, curiosity, and an ability to combine and
extrapolate what you know into areas you have never explored.

Consider the problem of getting financial information on privately held companies. Because they do not sell securities to the public, privately held companies
are not required by law to publicly reveal their balance sheets, income statements,
and other financial data.

At first blush, you might think, ''Well, that's that. No way to get the information.'' But one shouldn't give up so easily. Instead, ask yourself: Are there any circumstances under which a private company might voluntarily report its financials
to someone? How about when it is applying for a loan? Come to think of it, don't
most companies at one time or another have to fill out a credit report before their
suppliers will do business with them? Who would have that kind of information?

If you're a businessperson, you can probably make a pretty good guess at the
answer: Dun & Bradstreet, the country's largest credit reporting organization.
Certainly it is worth a phone call to Dun & Bradstreet (D&B) to see if the information you want is available and to find out what D&B is likely to charge you to
deliver it. Knowing what you now know about electronic information, it is also
worth checking one or more database catalogs to see if the information is online.

Either way, you would almost certainly discover a file called D&B-Dun's
Financial Records. Available on DIALOG, this file contains financial information,
sans credit and payment history, on some 700,000 firms, 98% of which are privately held. It is important for you to know, however, that while D&B information
can be helpful, it may or may not be accurate. Through no fault of Dun & Bradstreet, reports contain only the information the subject company chooses to
report. And there is usually no way to verify the accuracy of the information.

If you need credit and payment history information as well, you can get that
through the NewsNet gateways to D&B or TRW, D&B's main competitor. At this
writing, a business information report costs $45 and so does a report providing
you with payment history information. For $67.50, you can get both reports at
the same time. (D&B itself has a direct fax service called DunsExpress that charges
$60 per query.) Note that these reports apply only to companies, not to individ-
uals. And special restrictions may apply regarding what you as an information broker can do with them.

Of course things rarely work out as neatly as in this example. And no one is
suggesting that you should have been able to arrive at the same solution on your

own. The point is the *process*. The most successful searchers are those who adopt the creative, imaginative approach of an information detective.

Rule 5: Know your databases

How do you know which databases to search? How do you know which ones cover, say *Beverage World*, *Business Week*, and similar publications? It would be wonderful if there were a master database of databases that could give you an instant list of every database that covers a specific topic or every database that includes a particular publication. You could then simply search for every database that covered, say, *Time* or *Forbes*. Someday such an all-encompassing product may exist, but there is no such thing today.

Today, we have what amounts to a patchwork of database information sources. To begin with, there are the print or online versions of the leading database directories—like Gale's Computer-Readable Databases (formerly Martha Williams's Database of Databases) on DIALOG or Gale's Cuadra Directory, available online through the DataStar system—each of which offers capsule summaries of individual databases, what they cover, and the specific publications they include.

There are also the vendor catalogues with their short descriptions of the databases on their systems. There are lists of the journals covered by individual databases, available from database producers. There is the *Directory of Periodicals Online* (Vol. 1: News, Law, and Business; Vol. 2: Medicine and Science) published by Federal Document Retrieval, and Bibliodata's *Fulltext Sources Online* and Susan Bjorner's *Newspapers Online*, also from Bibliodata. And there are DIALINDEX, CROSS, and DBI, the files maintained by DIALOG, BRS, and ORBIT to help customers choose a database on those systems.

Ulrich's International Periodicals Directory, available in printed form or as a database on DIALOG or BRS, will tell you which databases index a magazine, if applicable. And DIALOG has introduced the DIALOG Journal Name Finder database (File 414) to help you find the other databases on the system that index a particular journal. The database was awarded the *Database* magazine Product of the Year Award at the ONLINE/CD-ROM '91 conference (November, 1991).

You might start by consulting one of the printed database directories. All of them are indexed by subject, but the subject headings are broad: real estate, science and technology, news, research in progress, and so on. Some of the database write-ups they contain mention the journals covered. But you can't count on it. And only a selected list is given in any case. You'll find the names of the major database directories, along with information on their availability for online searching, in Appendix B.

Ultimately, the only way to become an effective searcher is to become familiar with the databases and online systems that focus on your fields of interest. Remember, each database is a separate product, just as each computer program is a separate product. You can't expect to bring yourself up to speed on all of them overnight. As with computer software, you will probably begin by using two or three databases fairly frequently and thus get to know them well. Gradually you'll branch out, and as your familiarity grows you'll add more databases to your repertoire.

Tools and techniques

Once you've got the right mindset, the next area of concern is the collection of tools and techniques databases offer to execute your search strategy. Here is where the pedal really meets your mettle as an online searcher, for there are so many tricks, twists, and turns to online systems and the search commands they offer that you could spend a lifetime studying them.

That certainly is not our purpose here. In this book we merely want to introduce you to the process of online searching so you can get some sense of what it is like. We have made no attempt at being comprehensive and we have not included all of the various refinements a professional searcher would weave in as a matter of course. Our only purpose is to give someone who has never searched online before a taste of what the process can be like.

The importance of fields

As you will recall, databases like those on DIALOG, BRS, and ORBIT consist of files, records, and fields. Most other databases use similar divisions, though they may not call them by those names or permit you to search them in the same way. Records are what you are after when you search a database, and fields can be one of the best ways to hit them.

For example, imagine a database created from your address book or Rolodex cards. If there is a field in each record for "Phone Number," you could tell the database software to retrieve every record containing the phone number "800-555-1212." That's not terribly useful. After all, how often do you know someone's phone number but not their name?

Suppose we break up the phone number into more precise fields. Suppose we re-structure the records so that there is a field for "Area Code" and one for "Phone Number." If you were planning a trip to Los Angeles and wanted to be sure to call all of your friends when you're there, you could easily produce a comprehensive list. Simply tell your database software to retrieve every record in the file in which "Area Code=213" or "Area Code=818," since these are the two main codes for Los Angeles. (If you wanted to broaden your coverage to include surrounding suburbs to the north and the south, you might include "Area Code=714" and "Area Code=805.")

Now, look at the abstract in Fig. 11-1. Study it well. This is a record from the ABI/INFORM database summarizing an article that appeared in *Beverage World*. It was retrieved via DIALOG's Knowledge Index. Each line that appears above the abstract paragraph contains one or more searchable fields: title, author, journal name, etc.

Thus, using KI's search syntax (explained in the KI manual), if you wanted to limit the search to just articles that appeared in *Business Week*, you would include the following line in your search statement: JN = BUSINESS WEEK. If you wanted to

Here is an example of a search conducted on DIALOG's Knowledge Index, a system you may use for personal inquiries and practice but not for professional assignments. We began by selecting command mode (indicated by the question mark prompt) and entering the BUSI1 database, ABI/INFORM.

Then we checked the database's inverted index with the EXPAND command and incorporated the target term (E3--DECAFFEINATED) in our search statement (FIND E3 and TEA). The results were promising, so we opted to look at the results with the TYPE S1 command. The first record that came up is shown here.

?BEGIN BUSI1

Now in BUSINESS INFORMATION (BUSI) Section (BUSI1) Database
ABI/Inform_ 71-91/Nov Week 3 (Copr. 1991 UMI/Data Courier)

?EXPAND DECAFFEINATED

Ref	Items	Index-term
E1	3	DECAF
E2	3	DECAFFEINATE
E3	39	DECAFFEINATED
E4	3	DECAFFEINATION
E5	2	DECAFS
E6	1	DECAGW
E7	1	DECAIRIE
E8	8	DECAL
E9	1	DECALED
E10	3	DECALERT
E11	1	DECALOGUES
E12	29	DECALS

?FIND E3 AND TEA

	39	DECAFFEINATED
	411	TEA
S1	8	"DECAFFEINATED" AND TEA

?TYPE S1

00570756   DIALOG FILE 15   ABI/INFORM   91-45107

USE FORMAT F FOR FULL TEXT

Ready to Go - Upscale Iced Coffees and Teas Are Hot

Jabbonsky, L.; Wolf, A. E.

Beverage World v110n1498 PP: 58 Sep 1991 ISSN: 0098-2318
       JRNL CODE:BEV

DOC TYPE: Journal article LANGUAGE: English LENGTH: 1 Pages

AVAILABILITY: Fulltext online. Photocopy available from
       ABI/INFORM 80095.00

WORD COUNT: 688

ABSTRACT:

An increasingly image-conscious populace is moving away from stodgy hot drinks to cold refreshment with an emphasis on convenience and speed. Ready-to-drink iced coffees and teas are poised to take advantage of this trend. The Coca-Cola Nestle Refreshments Co., while unable to discuss specific product-launch timetables,

Fig. 11-1. A complete ABI/INFORM search on Knowledge Index

Fig. 11-1. Continued.

promises a full line of Nestle, Nescafe, and Nestea branded ready-to-serve coffees and teas to be distributed via the Coke bottling network. Helping to create the opportunity for iced teas and coffees in the US is the fact that per capita consumption of soft drinks in the morning has increased 52% since 1985. Several well-known coffee makers are coming out with an array of decidedly New Age offerings. For example, Chock full o' Nuts Corp. has unveiled 3 flavors of Chock o'ccino iced cappuccino in 8-ounce glass bottles as its first introduction to the packaged beverage market.

COMPANY NAMES:
Jolt Co
Snapple Natural Beverage Co (DUNS:06-385-3998)
Coca-Cola Nestle Refreshments Co
Chock full o Nuts Corp (DUNS:00-202-3265)
Lipton Inc (DUNS:00-137-8892)

GEOGRAPHIC NAMES: US

DESCRIPTORS: Beverage industry; Trends; Product introduction; Manycompanies; Niche marketing

CLASSIFICATION CODES: 8610 (CN = Food processing industry); 7500 (CN = Product planning & development); 9190 (CN = United States)

---

limit things further by date, you would include: PY = 1991 or PY = 1989:1991. These two statements specify a "publication year" of 1991 or the range of years between 1989 and 1991.

In addition, the entire abstract is also a searchable field. So if you searched on COKE AND MORNING, you would retrieve this record, since both of those words can be found in the abstract. Now look at the end of the record. COMPANY NAMES, GEOGRAPHIC NAMES, DESCRIPTORS (keywords), and CLASSIFICA-TION CODES are also searchable fields. (We'll have more to say about them in a moment.)

Our point is simply this: The fields in a database record let you fine-tune a search. If databases were not organized into fields, you would not be able to zero in on specific publications, date ranges, or anything else. Just imagine, for example, if you could *not* say to Knowledge Index, "Okay, I want you to look for '1991' in the date field."

Without this power, if you included "1991" in your search statement, you would retrieve everything in the database that contained "1991" somewhere in the record. If an abstract of an article published in 1984 contained the phrase ". . . may take until 1991 before things are straightened out," that record would be retrieved.

Full text as a field

We should note that the full text of an article may also be treated as a field. This is the case in the example shown in Fig. 11-1. Notice that at the very beginning of the record there is a line reading "**USE FORMAT F FOR FULL TEXT**." As you will see in a moment, this record was retrieved by searching on DECAFFEINATED AND TEA. Neither term appears in the abstract, but both can be found when you use "Format F" to view the full text of the article.

In this particular case, then, the entire ABI/INFORM record consists of all the fields we've discussed, including the abstract, and the full text of the article. Together, they form a single discrete unit of information. By displaying only the abstract in Fig. 11-1, we are, in effect, displaying only part of the "complete" record.

Do you have to specify fields?

We know what you're thinking. Suppose you just sign on to a system, enter a database, and type in the word or phrase you are looking for. Suppose you do not tell the database to look at specific fields. What then?

Well, the answer is simple. Like most online database vendors, DIALOG and Knowledge Index are pre-programmed to search certain fields in each database. For example, if you simply key in a search term or phrase on KI, the system automatically searches the title, the abstract, the full text (if available), and the descriptors. On DIALOG, this pre-programmed selection of fields is called the "Basic Index," and it varies with each database. The fields included in the Basic Index for each database are listed in the corresponding DIALOG Bluesheet.

You can tell a system to forget about its Basic Index and zero in on a particular field or series of fields if you like. Or you tell it to search the Basic Index for a database as well as the other fields you specify. Although the specific commands differ, other online systems follow a similar practice.

Special fields

Most of the fields we've discussed so far require no further explanation. We all know what to expect in a date or author or journal name field. Even COMPANY NAMES or GEOGRAPHIC NAMES (see Fig. 11-1) are relatively easy to figure out. But what are we to make of DESCRIPTORS and CLASSIFICATION CODES?

The answer is rooted in the information provider's desire to help you to retrieve records with a high degree of precision. After all, finding and displaying records is what this business is all about. So not only is it the "right thing to do," it is also in the best interests of an IP to make it as easy as possible for you to locate the records you want in its database.

As an example, look at the DESCRIPTORS at the end of the record shown in Fig. 11-1. None of the words found there ("beverage industry," "trends," "niche marketing," etc.) appears in the abstract. Nor, in fact, do they appear in text of the complete article. (We checked.)

Yet someone who was interested in trends and niche marketing in the beverage industry would almost certainly want to see this record. Since none of those words is used in the abstract or the full text article, if these descriptors were not attached to the record, that person might not find it. Descriptors are added to a record by an indexer/abstracter to give you a helping hand. The terms themselves are usually drawn from a special word list or "controlled vocabulary," as explained in Chapter 9.

Sometimes, in addition to indexing terms selected from a controlled vocabulary, a database producer will use subject or topic code *numbers*. These may simply be the U.S. Government's S.I.C. (Standard Industrial Classification) codes you may have heard of. Or they may be some elaborate and very precise system created by the IP. ABI/INFORM and the various Predicasts, Inc., databases, among others, make extensive use of code numbers. There are codes for companies, major topics, sub-topics, "events" like the announcement of a new product, codes for specific types of products, and so on.

The code numbers can be used exactly as you would use controlled vocabulary terms. You look up the topic you want on an IP-supplied list, note the corresponding code, and enter the numbers in your search statement.

Supplementary documentation

Every information provider does things its own way. You can thus expect each database to have its own unique array of fields. The Marquis Who's Who database on DIALOG and KI, for example, has at least five fields dealing with a person's education (degree, name of school, school location, years of attendance, and certification).

The Merck Index Online on DIALOG, a database of chemicals and drugs, has over 40 fields—everything from chemical names to boiling point to refractive index. The database Magill's Survey of Cinema has fields not only for film title, actor/actress, and screenplay author but for running time, video cassette availablility, cinematographer, releasing studio, and more.

The fields a database includes will always be mentioned in the Bluesheets, if it is a DIALOG database, or in equivalent publications on other systems. Keep in mind, however, that Bluesheets and their equivalents are merely capsule summaries intended for quick reference. For a full explanation of how to use, say, ABI/INFORM's classification codes, you will need more documentation.

In almost every case, you will find complete explanations of the type of information you can expect to find in each field in the appropriate DIALOG documentation "chapter" for the database. Database chapters are sold separately at a cost of about $6 each. All such chapters begin with a general explanation of the file and the fields included in its Basic Index. (Remember, the Basic Index is the pre-programmed collection of fields that will be searched unless you specify otherwise.) They then explain each searchable field in turn. The chapters always conclude with several search examples and a list of additional documentation or search aid material that may be available.

We highly recommend buying the DIALOG database chapter for any database you think you may be searching on a regular basis, regardless of whether you will be searching the database on DIALOG or some other system. It is true that the commands used on, say, BRS Search, will be different. But translation usually isn't a problem, and the information a DIALOG chapter provides about a database can be equally useful.

But don't stop with the DIALOG database chapters. Contact the company that created the database to inquire about additional manuals, controlled vocabulary thesauri, code lists, booklets, training materials, and anything else that may be of use.

As we said earlier, the online information industry operates on two tracks when it comes to providing customer service and database documentation. The vendor offers things like Bluesheets or their equivalent and possibly database "chapters." But to get something like a controlled vocabulary thesaurus, you must go to the information provider—the company responsible for creating and maintaining the database.

Of course, you'll have to pay for this supplementary documentation. Indeed, since sales volumes are low, the prices tend to be relatively high. A price of $50 or more for an IP thesaurus or special manual is not uncommon. That may sound steep. But when you consider that the information such supplementary documentation contains can easily save you that much in one or two search sessions, and when you realize that it will help you serve your clients better, the high price is easier to accept. Ultimately, buying supplementary documentation is simply one of the costs of doing business if you are an information broker.

Boolean logic and proximity operators

There are two final points we need to make in this whirlwind tour of online search tools and techniques. The first concerns the matter of "AND. . . OR . . . NOT," or Boolean logic. The manuals for nearly every database vendor system go into much greater detail, but basically, Boolean operators are used to tell the online system what you want. (George Boole, the man for whom this term is named, was an English mathematician who died in 1864.)

Picture yourself standing at a counter talking to a clerk. You want the clerk to get you recent articles mentioning certain American Presidents and energy policy. You might say, "Get me everything you have that mentions Presidents Nixon AND Reagan but NOT Carter OR Ford AND the word 'energy' within one word of 'policy.'"

To qualify for retrieval, an article would have to mention *both* Nixon and Reagan. But if it mentioned Nixon, Reagan, and Carter, the article would not meet your specification and would not be retrieved. Similarly, if the record's only reference to "energy" and "policy" was in a sentence like "The President attacked the policy of imposing import duties with great energy," the record would not be retrieved.

This leads to our second point—proximity operators. As you can see from this little example, specifying ENERGY AND POLICY can produce articles that have nothing to do with the subject of energy policy. As long as both words are in the record somewhere, the record qualifies for retrieval.

That's why most online systems include proximity operators and/or phrase searching capabilities. If you wanted to specify a particular phrase, you might have to put in quotation marks ("energy policy"), for example. Or you might be able to enter a command telling the system to find only records in which TAX OR TAXES occurred within five words of INCREASE.

The tools at your command

There is much, much more to learn about the tools and techniques used in online searching. But already the outline of the process is becoming clear. You can key in a word or a phrase to have the system search its pre-programmed set of fields. You can use additional fields to focus a search on one or more specific aspects (publication date, controlled vocabulary descriptor, special subject or concept code). And you can use operators (AND/OR/NOT, etc.) to control which of these various focal points are considered and in what way.

Online searching really is like standing at a counter and telling a clerk what you want. The difference is that you may or may not know precisely what you want, and you almost certainly don't know every item that the clerk has in the back of the store. So searching becomes an interactive process and a process of successive approximations.

You stroll in and say, "Okay, I'm looking for something in energy policy. Not too old, but with lots of facts, figures and statistics. I'd like it to mention Presidents Reagan and Nixon, but not Carter or Ford. Show me what you've got."

In a twinkling, the clerk tells you that the store has, say 1200 items that meet your specifications. "Well, that's more than I had in mind," you say. "Could you take those 1200 items and tell me which ones mention shale oil and the recycling of automobile tires?"

The clerk might say, "Sorry. There aren't any items in that 1200-unit set that mention both of those topics." You think for a moment and then say, "Gee, that's too bad. I really was looking for an item like that. Well, how about everything I said before, but this time include President Carter."

The process—the "dialog"—between you and the clerk continues as you use the tools at your disposal to turn the dials and fine tune your inquiry. That's what online searching is like. There is no guarantee of success. But it stands to reason that the more you know about the tools and how to use them, the more likely you will walk out of the store with the merchandise you want at a fairly reasonable price.

The five rules in action

Now let's put it all together and look at a real online search. The search was conducted on Knowledge Index since this is the system we suggest you use for your own practice sessions. Once again, you are not permitted to use KI for business purposes. It is strictly for personal use and practice.

We have used KI's command line option since it is closer to what you will face on DIALOG and other major league systems. As noted earlier, KI also offers an easy-to-use, but less powerful menu option. The concepts demonstrated here apply equally well to virtually any command-driven system. The process starts with:

The five rules of search success
Rule 1:   Respect your opponent
Rule 2:   Define your target
Rule 3:   Consider the source: Who would know?
Rule 4:   Don't go online unless you have to
Rule 5:   Know your databases

No problem with Number 1. If you don't have a pretty good idea of what you're up against by now, there's nothing we can do to help you. Now let's invent an imaginary client, say, someone who has developed a new process for removing the caffeine from tea. She's a scientific type with little exposure to marketing, but she wants you to prepare a report of the market for decaffeinated tea. That subject will be your target.

Who would know about such a thing? Well, there might be an industry association of beverage makers. Perhaps they have a study they can send you. Since the main outlet for coffee, tea, and the like is grocery stores, you might check to see if there is a trade group or association of American grocers you could call. What the heck, there's probably even some kind of group responsible for promoting tea consumption, funded by the tea industry, of course. The American Tea Council? It might be worth looking into.

Though we have not checked ourselves, our experience tells us that somewhere in this country there is almost certainly an organization that can send you some information about tea consumption in the United States. It might be a private industry group, or it might be some arm of the U.S. government. (Remember our earlier discussion of the potato expert Matthew Lesko found at the U.S.D.A.? Why not tea?)

Naturally there's no way to tell what the information such groups may provide will consist of. There might be press releases and photocopies of articles published in various trade magazines. It may be nothing but a corporate annual report. But more than likely there will be something you can use: the names of the companies who make or are considering making decaffeinated tea, the names of key people at Lipton or Twinings or whichever companies own those brands. Your next step might be to contact one or more decaffeinated tea manufacturers.

Should you go online? Sure you should. The materials you receive from the firms and/or organizations you've contacted can help you refine your search. But you want to know a lot more about the topic, and a database search is ideal for that kind of application. But which database should you choose?

Before making up your mind, stop for a moment and ask yourself about the kind of information you want. Do you want a *Scientific American* type treatment or the kind of article you'd expect *Business Week* to do? Whatever you decide, by asking yourself these questions you have automatically made the database selection process ten times easier. If you are new to the field, there's no way for you to know which databases cover which publications. But there are people you can ask and, as noted previously, there are directories you can consult.

Here's a professional tip: In general, if you are interested in a business topic, you should almost certainly begin by consulting PTS PROMT or ABI/INFORM or both. These two databases offer superb coverage of business magazines and trade and industry journals. Indeed, they are so good, that no one else even comes close.

Twelve steps to online information retrieval

Yes, it's beginning to sound like a crazy New Age self-help guru has gotten loose on these pages. But lists can be wonderful things, and frankly we know of no better way to cut through the fog that surrounds information retrieval. Let's assume that you have decided to conduct an online search as part of your assignment to investigate the market for decaffeinated tea.

Step 1: Select your database

We've covered this pretty thoroughly. All that remains to be said is that you may eventually want to search *several* databases. Be aware, however, that at some point you're going to encounter diminishing returns. Overlapping coverage is fine since one IP's abstracts can complement another's. But if you search more than a few databases, you can very quickly end up with more information than you can successfully digest, and you will have lost much of the benefit of using electronic information retrieval.

Step 2: Check the vendor and the database documentation

Please, please, please do not omit this step. Discipline yourself to do it every time until you know the database so well you don't have to think about it. Which fields are searchable? Can you search by phrases or must you use words and proximity operators? What kinds of information does each field contain: words, code numbers, dates, controlled vocabulary terms?

Step 3: Meditate

Seriously. You may not be a Ninja warrior preparing for battle, but it's not a bad analogy. If you ride in like a cowboy with six-guns blazing, firing off search terms as they come into your head, you'll stir up a lot of dust, expend a lot of ammunition, and be presented with a hefty bill—but very little relevant information—when you're done.

Think about the topic beforehand. Let your mind run free and flow into the subject. What do you know and what can you extrapolate about decaffeinated tea? What are the names of the companies who are known for selling tea? Have you read anything recently about the popularity of herbal teas? Could there be a connection? Who buys or is likely to buy decaffeinated products? Is there a health angle? And so on.

Try to develop a list of search words that come close to defining what you want. Some searchers try to think in terms of synonyms and word variants. The database thesaurus—if one exists for your target database—can help you there. We prefer an approach that's closer to free-association. Ultimately you'll develop a technique that works best for you.

Think about the source material and types of magazines or whatever you are searching. Then pick the words that you feel could logically be expected to appear in the kind of document you're looking for. The process is similar to writing up a bid specification. The document you want will have this, this, and this. It will be published between these dates. It will deal with such-and-such a topic, and so on.

Step 4: Select your fields

We can't tell you what fields to search since they vary so with the database. The author (AU) field may be virtually useless in a database of general interest magazines, but crucial in a database of book titles. The database documentation is your best guide to selecting the fields most likely to retrieve what you want.

Step 5: Write out your first search statement in full

Don't try to keep all of your search terms and search logic in your head. Free yourself of them by putting them on paper. When you are actually online, you'll have many other things to think about, and unless you're awfully quick, you don't want to be thinking about all the various words and commands you could use while the meter's running.

Keep a pad of paper and a pen within easy reach, as well. You will need them. And remember this professional's trick: Use the macro key function of your comm program or use a macroing utility program to record your first-pass search strategy *before* you go online. That way, you can enter a database and blast your first search statement into it at the touch of only one or two keys.

Step 6: Check the display options and verify how you sign off

The ultimate point of going online is to display the records that your search statements have selected. Make sure you know what formats are available and what pieces of information are included in each format as it applies to the database you're going to search. Again, this is not the kind of thing you want to look up while you are connected and paying for online time. The same thing goes for making sure you know how to sign off. What is the correct command?

Step 7: Set your computer to capture incoming information

This is so important that it's worth the emphasis of making it a separate step. Generally it doesn't pay to keep your printer toggled on during an online session. Printers slow things down and thus eat up connect time. During your search you may want to dump a screen to the printer for easy reference. So leave it on and enabled, but don't toggle the printer echo on from within your communications program.

Instead, open your capture buffer or set your communications program to dump to disk or do whatever else is necessary to put the machine into "record" mode. You can always go back into the file and edit out the portions you don't want with a word processor. In addition, a record of a complete online session can be a wonderful self-teaching tool since you can review it to see where you went wrong, the number of hits on a term that you did not follow up on, etc.

Step 8: Sign on and check the "inverted file"

Systems like DIALOG, Knowledge Index, BRS, and ORBIT maintain files of every searchable word in every database. In the trade, these are called "inverted indexes," and it is really these files that you are searching when you are online. Each keyword in an inverted index is tagged with an invisible pointer identifying the records in which it appears.

It can be extremely worthwhile to look at this list of keywords before you begin displaying records. In fact, most professional searchers would say it is essential. The command to do so on both DIALOG and Knowledge Index is EXPAND followed by the keyword—or first part of a keyword. As an example, take a look at Fig. 11-1. At the top you will see the command BEGIN BUSI1. This tells KI you want to start searching ABI/INFORM. (Database names, codes, and documentation are provided as part of your KI subscription package.)

Note the command: EXPAND DECAFFEINATED. By entering this command, we told the system to look for DECAFFEINATED in the inverted file for the fields in its Basic Index.

Step 9: Enter your first search statement and note the results

Our first and, as it happens, only search statement told the system to look for the "EXPAND" term 3 (E3 or "DECAFFEINATED") and TEA. We could have entered FIND DECAFFEINATED AND TEA with the same effect. It is a small point, but once you EXPAND a term on KI or DIALOG, you can avoid typing it by following the procedure shown here. (This technique is explained in the KI documentation, so if you don't grasp it now, don't worry.)

In checking the results of this command, we see that the word *decaffeinated* appears 39 times in the database; *tea* appears 411 times; and both *decaffeinated* and *tea* appear in eight records.

Step 10: Add qualifiers to narrow the search

Some searchers like to put all of the qualifiers they can think of in their initial search statements. Many of the commands that clutter the vendor system manuals are designed to make this possible. For our money, this makes things needlessly complex.

We prefer to think of searching as a process similar to repairing a household appliance at a well-equipped workbench. There are certain tools (search terms and search logic) you know you're going to need to open the case or remove the housing. But from then on there are no definitive steps to follow. At this point we've got the case off and are peering into the machine's innards to try to get an idea of the situation.

If the initial search command had located, say, 50 or 100 records containing the words *decaffeinated* and *tea*, we would have had to reach for another tool. Through experience, we know that 50 to 100 hits indicates that the search needs to be more sharply focused. It's a good start, but perhaps records should be winnowed further by setting some kind of date limit. Say, just the last two years. If that were the case, one could zero in on this first "set" of records with a command like FIND S1 AND PY = 1991:1992. As the KI manual explains, "PY" stands for "publication year."

Generally speaking, it is not a bad idea to try to narrow a search down until you are left with about 20 records. Though we hasten to add that this is merely a rough rule of thumb. Naturally, everything depends on the subject you are looking into and the database you are using. There are too many other variables in online searching for this to apply across the board. As it happens, in our sample search, we have found eight records, which is fine for our purposes here.

Step 11: Display results

This is the easy part. There's nothing like conducting a search that appears to be on the beam and yields a manageable number of results. Here we merely keyed in TYPE S1 to display all the records in SET 1.

Of course there are variations. KI, DIALOG, BRS, and nearly every other online system offer commands to control how much of each record you display. As discussed earlier, DIALOG and most other information systems charge you a different rate for nearly every display format, under the general principle of "the more you display, the more you pay."

KI is different. All that matters on KI is the amount of time you are connected to the system. So, because a full text record or a "long format" record takes more time to display, viewing it costs a little bit more. "Short" and "Medium" formats are also available on KI.

Step 12: Log off and write your capture buffer to disk

Now log off to stop the connect time clock. On both DIALOG and KI, the official command is LOGOFF, though QUIT, BYE, and OFF also work. Close your capture buffer and write it to disk. Because of the way most personal computers do things, if you neglect this step, you may lose all or part of the material you have downloaded, and the information that has already been written to disk may be rendered inaccessible because the file was not properly closed.

Conclusion

Although we have reproduced only one of the eight records retrieved for our search on DECAFFEINATED AND TEA, all were typical of what one could expect from a search of this type. The abstract shown in Fig. 11-1, and the full text of the article to which it refers, do not provide the ultimate answer regarding the current state of the decaffeinated tea market. But they, and the other seven articles we found, offer good leads to additional information.

Certainly there is a lot more searching to be done. And, budget permitting, a lot more phoning, interviewing, and possibly library research. But as you work through the process, it is important to remember that the definitive article you envision may not exist. With all the information that's out there, it may seem like a paradox that no one has written the one article that can fill all of your needs. But very often that will be the case. As we have said from the beginning of this book, the best way to view online is not as the source of all answers but as the source of many starting points.

Books about online searching

There are many books about online searching. Indeed, if you'd like a current list, you have only to sign on to Knowledge Index and select command mode. Then enter BEGIN BOOK1 to move to the Books In Print database. Key in FIND ON-LINE BIBLIOGRAPHIC SEARCHING. That will produce a set (S1) of about 80 titles or so. Key in FIND S1/ACTIVE to select only those titles still in print. That will produce a second set (S2).

Make sure that your communications program's capture buffer is open so you will record incoming data to a disk file. Then key in TYPE S2/L/1 to see the first record. To display succeeding records one at a time, just hit your T key at the next prompt that appears. To display records 2 through 30, key in TYPE S2/L/2-30.

You probably will not have heard of most of the companies that publish books on this topic. Nor in most cases will you be able to find the books in bookstores. You will almost certainly have to ask the bookstore to order them for you, but with the information the Books In Print database provides, the store will have little problem doing so. Virtually every bookstore in the country has a copy of the print version of *Books In Print*, so they will know how to contact the relevant publishers. You should also check to see if a library has a copy of the book you want to look at.

The book we recommend most highly is Alfred's *How to Look It Up Online* (St. Martin's Press, NYC; 486 pages, $14.95). There is no financial motive in making this recommendation. It is simply that the book was written specifically to show the average person how to take advantage of major league databases. The book was published in 1987, so many phone numbers and prices are out of date. But the core of the book is as relevant as ever.

You might also want to consider *Online Searching: A Primer* by Carol H. Fenichel and Thomas H. Hogan (Learned Information, 1990, $16.95.) You can reach Learned Information's Medford, New Jersey offices at (609) 654-6266.

12

Special Interest Groups (SIGs) and forums

SOME YEARS AGO, A YOUNG MAN CALLED ALFRED TO SEEK ADVICE ON BECOMING an information broker. Sue gets calls like these about five times a day. But Alfred was somewhat surprised. The young man was quite earnest as he said, "Well, I think I'm all set. I've got my subscription to CompuServe, and I'm on my way to PIP to pick up my business cards. I just wanted to touch base to see if you could give me any suggestions on how to market my services."

Authors are under no obligation to serve in loco parentis, but honestly, Alfred didn't know whether to laugh or cry. If you've read the previous chapter, you are well aware that CompuServe, as good as it is, isn't even in the same state, let alone the same ballpark, as the likes of DIALOG and BRS. Nor is GEnie, Delphi, BIX, America Online (Quantum Link), Prodigy, or any of the other consumer-oriented systems. Nor do they try to be, though CompuServe has added several industrial strength databases in recent years.

The consumer-oriented online utilities, however, have one thing the industrial-strength information systems do not have: online Special Interest Groups (SIGs). As mentioned in Chapter 9, these features go by different names on different systems. But they all follow essentially the same format, and they all offer unique information retrieval possibilities.

In this single respect, the aspiring young information broker who called Alfred was way ahead of the rest of the profession. Most search professionals come from a library school background and can operate BRS or DIALOG blindfolded. But most have never heard of CompuServe or GEnie, and those who do know about these systems have no idea how to tap the riches they offer.

It is important to remember once again, that often what you're really after when you go online is a contact—a person you can call on the phone for more information. And, since SIGs are about nothing if not about people, they are often an excellent place to look. Of course, you'll find interesting and useful text files and programs to download as well.

In this chapter, we'll help you get familiar with the basic SIG structure. We'll tell you where to find SIGs, and we'll give you some general instructions on how to use them. The SIGs we'll be speaking of most often are those on CompuServe, where they are called "forums," and on GEnie, where they are called "Round-Tables" or "RTs." In our experience, these two systems offer the greatest potential, though BIX is particularly strong if you're after information on programming or the technical aspects of personal computing.

The basic SIG floor plan

All systems have multiple SIGs, and it is often convenient to think of them as fraternity or sorority houses on the CompuServe or GEnie campus. All SIGs on a given system have an identical floor plan and, in general, this basic floor plan varies little from system to system. Once you know how to use one SIG on one system, you automatically know how to use all the others on that system. And although the actual commands differ, you will have little difficulty translating your skills from one system to another.

You will undoubtedly find that mental images of your "physical location" are very helpful while you are online. Never is this more appropriate than when contemplating a SIG. That's why the image of a frat house or community building is so useful. You can see yourself physically opening the front door and entering the building as you enter a SIG.

After you join a SIG, every time you enter you will be greeted by name and notified of any new forum developments that have taken place since your last visit. The system will display bulletins and announcements prepared by the *sysop* ("sis-op," short for "system operator"). Then you're on your own.

Let's imagine that you've just walked through the "door" of a SIG. On your right is the club message board. It's a very big board, with lots of messages organized into lots of categories and topics within those categories. You might pause for a moment and read any new messages in any or all categories that have been posted since your last visit.

You might want to post a question or an announcement here yourself. Or you may have the answer to someone else's question and scribble them a quick note. You might even disagree with something someone else has said and feel moved to comment at length.

When you're finished there, you might stroll into the lounge ("conference" area) to have a real-time chat with anyone or any group of members there at the time. Most SIGs have regularly scheduled get-togethers during the week, and many invite guest speakers. Individuals as diverse as Steve Wozniak and Barry Manilow have been guests in various SIGs in the past. Indeed, you can never predict when a "name" in a particular field will appear.

If conferencing doesn't appeal, you can go upstairs to the library. There you will find a series of alcoves, each devoted to a particular topic and each containing all manner of useful information, including transcripts of notable online conferences and guest appearances of the past. In most cases, you'll find tons of free, public domain software as well. All of it yours for the downloading. And you can upload any of your own programs or files, usually free of charge.

All this at no extra cost

In almost every case, SIG usage is billed at standard connect time rates or is included with your monthly membership fee. On CompuServe, for example, the minimum connect time rate of $12.80 applies to most forums round the clock. On GEnie, the message board section ("bulletin board" or "BB" in GEnie-speak), is part of your monthly $4.95 fee. You can use these boards as much as you like at no extra charge during non-prime time hours (evenings and weekends). Downloading files on GEnie is billed at $6 per hour, as are your connections to those few RoundTables that are not included in the basic monthly fee. Uploads to SIG libraries on both CompuServe and GEnie are free.

After you've spent some time in a really good SIG you can't help but become aware of all the hard work that's gone into making it what it is. That may naturally lead you to wonder about the sysops and their assistants, and how they are paid for their labors. The answer is that while many of the sysops undoubtedly put in many long, under-compensated hours working on their SIGs, the SIGs themselves are designed to be small enterprises.

CompuServe and GEnie don't charge you extra, but they pay the sysops between 2% and 15% of the connect time revenue generated by the forum. Some individuals operating very popular SIGs routinely earn a six-figure income from their efforts. That's certainly not typical. But more than one sysop has found himself or herself with a tiger by the ears as what started as a hobby turned into a full-time job.

As with anything else, there are sharp, well-run SIGs and there are SIGs that are not so well run. Generally, the policy of compensating sysops works to the benefit of everyone. Sysops who operate their forums in a way that makes subscribers want to come back and spend time there are rewarded financially for their efforts, while subscribers have a wealth of unique places to go and things to do at no extra charge.

Why are SIGs important information sources?

Think back to our description of one entering the clubhouse, looking at the message board, peeping into the conference room, and going upstairs to the library. Now multiply that activity by several thousand people—sometimes, even several tens of thousands of people—for each SIG. Imagine thousands of people each evening doing exactly what you're doing.

At this writing, CompuServe claims some 700,000 subscribers and GEnie claims over 250,000. And while both systems draw most of their subscribers from the United States and Canada, both are also available internationally (Japan, Germany, Switzerland, Australia, etc.). If you add in the subscribers to other online utility-type systems (20,000 here; 40,000 there), you rapidly approach one million people, even allowing for those with subscriptions to several different systems. That's a million people worldwide who are meeting each other online to exchange information—people who would have never met each other any other way.

A wide variety of expertise

Now, admittedly, the mix of interests is heavily skewed toward computer- and software-related topics. But there are lots of SIGs devoted to non-computer subjects as well. For example, on GEnie you will find RoundTables devoted to topics like: genealogy, home offices, legal issues, medical issues, photography, SCUBA, science fiction and fantasy, space issues, travel, television, show business, and freelance writing—in addition to RTs devoted to almost any brand of computer and almost any leading software program.

On CompuServe you will find forums focusing on topics like fish, astronomy, aviation, cancer, wine, coin and stamp collecting, diabetes, education, foreign languages, organic gardening, ham radio, journalism, religion, rock music, and sports. There are even two sections for information professionals in the Work from Home SIG (GO WORK) run by Paul and Sarah Edwards. One section is open to everyone. The other is available only to members of the Association of Independent Information Professionals (AIIP). Again, all of this is in addition to the many computer-related forums. (Please see Fig. 9-3 in Chapter 9 for a list of the forums available on CompuServe at this writing.)

In each of these non-computer SIGs you will find current topics of interest being discussed on the message boards. You will find topic-relevant software to download. And you will find files, like the one on the GEnie SCUBA RoundTable detailing the best places to dive for shells on the East Coast or the one on the CompuServe HAMNET forum offering reviews of the latest ham radio equipment from people who have really bought and used the products.

Magnets for experts

Most important, you will find people you can reach, either by phone or by electronic mail, who can either answer your questions or put you in touch with experts and other field authorities. Online SIGs, in short, act as magnets for people who have a particular interest, curiosity, or expertise. They won't provide everything you need as an information broker. Not by a long shot. But they are clearly too powerful and unique a source to be ignored.

As an example, consider a topic that must be close to every prospective information broker's heart—concerns about becoming self-employed, managing a business, marketing your services, taxes, insurance, and so on. All of these topics are covered in the message section of the Home Office/Small Business RoundTable on GEnie and the Work-at-Home (GO WORK) forum on CompuServe. Figure 12-1 offers a brief glimpse of what you can expect to find in but two of the 25 message categories on the HOSB board on GEnie.

Shown here are just a few of the series of messages you can opt to read on the Home Office/Small Business (HOSB) RoundTable. Messages can range from short notes to medium-length essays. Many contain the names and addresses of suppliers or service providers, along with recommendations of the message author.

The electronic mail address of each participant is automatically made a part of each message he or she creates, so you can reach the person privately using GEnie's electronic mail service. Note that the number of messages ("Msgs") currently on hand for each topic is given in the column at the far right. These are two of the nearly 25 topic categories currently on the system.

Category 2 How to Start a Business

No.	Subject	Msgs
1	About this category	4
2	Professional typing at home	1
3	Publishing a newsletter	124
4	Full time complete wedding service	23
5	Working from the home.........HOW ?	101
6	What about other home based businesses?	50
7	Starting a Home-based Cruise Agency	13
8	Service Oriented Businesses	58
9	Bank Problems	28
10	SRDS Address	2
11	United Home Offices, Inc	20
12	900 and 967 number business	99
13	What do you think of this idea....	120
14	Business Start-up ideas	64
15	Starting and working in a partnership	3
16	College Financial Aid Search Services	49
17	Video Photography--Weddings & Such	11
18	BBS Listing Service	3
19	Ladies' Apparel Manufacturing	7
20	Power Washing	5
24	Getting Gov't/private Grants to startup	22
26	Pricing Services: How much to charge	50
29	Dropshipper or Prime Source?	34
32	Starting a tax preparation business	59
34	Personal Emergency Response Systems	67
36	How to make money with shareware	40
39	How To Start a Business--What To Start	81
43	Buying\Startup of Packaged Businesses	65

Category 3 Managing Your Business Successfully

No.	Subject	Msgs
1	Buying from mail order vendors	33
2	Airfare Tips	10
3	Business Organizations	15
4	Should you turn down small jobs?	40
5	Employees--how to find, hire, fire	14
6	How to stop persistent sales calls	17
7	Unionization attempts: what to do	17
8	How To Cut Mailing Costs	155

Fig. 12-1. Bulletin Board message topics on GEnie's HOSB RT

Fig. 12-1. Continued.

9	Child Care For Profit	2
10	Family Businesses	39
11	Medical practice as small business	40
12	HEALTH INSURANCE FOR SELF EMPLOYED	182
13	Business insurance	41
14	SAFEWARE Computer Insurance Opinions	12
15	Break-Even Pt and Sales Analysis	8
16	Time management...	232
21	Filing Systems...Paper and electronic	28
23	LIABILITY INSURANCE FOR INSTRUCTORS	2
24	Wholesale Suppliers	11
26	Office Supplies	122
27	EMPLOYEE LEASING	19
29	Buying Clubs and Warehouse Shopping	78
30	When the deal goes sour...	20
31	Industrial Small Businesses	19

Looking at libraries

A SIG's "message base," as the comments, messages, and "postings" on its bulletin board are sometimes called, is but one source of valuable information. If you use the system's search function to locate messages likely to be relevant to your search assignment and come up empty, don't automatically leave the SIG. Go check the SIG library as well.

Again, since self-employment is a subject we can all relate to, let's look at the libraries available in the Work-at-Home forum on CompuServe. (GEnie's HOSB has similar files in its library.) As you can see from Fig. 12-2, the "WORK" forum offers some 17 different libraries. A "library," we should point out, is simply a way of making a first cut at classifying files. When you enter, say, Library 9—Accounting, Tax, and Legal in the WORK forum—you are telling the system to concentrate on those files that pertain to that library topic.

You can search a library on the basis of keyword, date, and the e-mail address of the uploader. But the search will be limited to just the files in the library you have selected. On GEnie, in contrast, you can search "ALL Libraries" at once.

You can enter the library section by selecting an item from the main forum menu. This will display a list (shown here) of all available libraries. Pick a library, and a menu will appear. (Here we selected Library 9.) From this menu you can opt to browse and be prompted for a keyword and/or a date.

We chose the keyword TAX and opted not to specify a date. The system searched and then displayed the description of the first file it found. If we had typed ``CHOICES'' as prompted after the description had been displayed, we would have been given the option of downloading the file, continuing to browse, or returning to the library menu.

As explained in Glossbrenner's *Master Guide to FREE Software for IBM's and Compatible Computers*, there are faster, command-driven ways to search a CompuServe forum library. But the results are essentially the same.

Fig. 12-2. Libraries and files on CompuServe's WORK Forum

```
Working From Home Forum Libraries Menu

1   General Information
2   Business Info
3   Specific Businesses
4   Info Professionals
5   Mail Businesses
6   Forum Help Files
7   Getting Business
8   Publishing/DTP/Type
9   Acctg,Tax,Legal
10  Independent Writers
11  Jobs/Telecommuting
12  International
13  United Home Offices
14  Office Hdwr & Sftwr
16  Member Showcase
17  Home Off Computing Magazine

Enter choice !9

Working From Home Forum Library 9

Acctg,Tax,Legal

    1 BROWSE thru files
    2 DIRECTORY of files

    3 UPLOAD a new file (FREE)
    4 DOWNLOAD a file to your PC

    5 LIBRARIES

Enter choice !1
```

```
Enter keywords (e.g. modem)
or <CR> for all: TAX

Oldest files in days
or <CR> for all:

[71420,1465]
1040.RPT            06-Jan-91 14694          Accesses: 6

    Title    :  1040 REPORT
    Keywords:  IRS 1040 TAXES CONGRESS TAX REFORM

    Summary of a report that provides compelling evidence of the need to reform the
    federal tax laws and for Congress to take greater control of the IRS. The report
    brings together the work of several reform movement organizations concerning
    IRS compliance with three pieces of landmark legislation and documents the
    failure of the IRS to comply with its mandate.

Press <CR> for next or type CHOICES !
```

How to use a SIG

For years there has been talk (and little else) in the online industry of introducing a "common command language." The idea is that users would learn one set of commands and be able to apply them on DIALOG, BRS, ORBIT, DataStar, and any other industrial-strength online information system. There has been no such talk in the consumer-oriented online utility field.

Every online utility is different, requiring you to learn a separate set of commands for each systems's SIGs you plan to access. As noted, however, the concepts are the same across SIGs, so this does not present a terrible difficulty. It is true that there are little differences in features and capabilities across systems, but there is enough *de facto* standardization that we can tell you in general how to make the most of any SIG.

Step 1: Get a list of all SIGs on the system

The first step is to get a list of all the SIGs available on the system. Check your system manual for instructions on accessing or searching the index feature. When you do access that feature, search on the appropriate keyword. If you are looking for SCUBA SIGs, search on "SCUBA." But if you want a complete list of SIGs, search on the name the system uses for these features. Search on "FORUM" on CompuServe, for example, and "RoundTable" on GEnie.

Note that the list may or may not be 100 percent complete. Updating files is a persistent problem affecting all areas of the online world. It is always possible that a SIG has been added to the system but its name has not yet been added to the list.

Step 2: Select a SIG of interest

Step 2 is to select the SIG of interest and enter the command needed to get there. The first time you access any SIG you will be considered a visitor. On GEnie this status causes the system to display "Hi, sailor. Welcome aboard!"-type bulletins and announcements. These will not appear the next time you enter.

On CompuServe you will get similar treatment and then be offered a menu, one selection of which is "JOIN." By all means do so. There is no cost in most cases, and if you don't join you may not be able to download any files.

Step 3: Zero in on the library

Step three is to learn how the SIG library works. This is an experience that can make you wistful for the controlled vocabularies of major league information systems. The problem is that any SIG member can upload a file. Since part of the uploading process is a prompt for keywords, and since most uploaders are not information professionals, you can imagine the variety of keywords they use for their files.

One user might use the keyword "IRS," while another might use "I.R.S." But as you know by now, computers are the very definition of literal-minded. So if you search on "IRS," you will not find the file tagged with the word "I.R.S." Alfred once wrote an article for *Database* magazine titled "SIGs: On the Frontier of Civilized Searching," (October 1989). Discrepancies like this—plus the inevitable misspellings of keywords on the part of the uploaders—add new meaning to the term "uncivilized."

The best way around this problem is to download (capture to disk) the complete list of keywords used for all files in a given library. Then sign off and print it out. Circle the keywords of interest and sign back on again to do your search.

The way to do this on CompuServe is to select a library and open your capture buffer. Then, at the library menu prompt, instead of selecting BROWSE or some other menu item, type in the command KEY. This will give you a list of every keyword used in the library and the number of times it appears. Close your capture buffer when the scroll out has finished and key in OFF to leave the system.

There is no comparable command on GEnie. However GEnie lets you call for a "directory" of files. The directory contains two lines for each file in the library, including the filename and accession number, date, number of downloads, and a one- sentence description of what the file is or does.

Step 4: Download a file

Step four is to actually download a file. Again, consult your system manual for the appropriate commands to do this. You will have to know either the name or the accession number of the file, and you will have to know which error-checking protocols your comm program supports. If you are using ProComm Plus on GEnie, for example, the best protocol to choose is ZMODEM. If you are on CompuServe, opt for CompuServe Quick B. In general, steer away from XMODEM when accessing a remote mainframe computer. XMODEM simply was not designed for this kind of connection, even though many mainframe-based systems offer it.

Step 5: Master the message board

Finally, step five is to master the message board. Check your system manual for instructions on searching message topics to find just those that are likely to be relevant to your quest. On GEnie, you can choose to read just those messages that are "new" to you (that is, that you have not read before.) Or you can select individual messages or ranges of messages. On CompuServe, you can read message "threads"—series of messages and replies, and replies to replies.

Conclusion

As a prospective information broker, online utilities like CompuServe and GEnie have the advantage of being very cheap by industry standards. However, they are also very unconventional, again, by information industry standards. If you're going to get into this business, we still emphatically recommend starting with a subscription to Knowledge Index as discussed in the previous chapter. The kinds of searches you do on KI are much closer to those you will eventually do on big systems like DIALOG and BRS than anything you will encounter on GEnie or CompuServe.

However, we strongly urge you to get a subscription to one or both of these systems and learn to search their online special interest groups. You may not want to bet the farm on these features when you are just starting out. But the SIGs on these and the other systems we have mentioned are simply too good to miss.

Alfred has been sailing these waters for nearly a decade, and his books on CompuServe, GEnie, online communications, and getting free software for IBMs and compatible machines can be invaluable aids in making the most of any online SIG. Check at your local library, or order your own personal copies from Glossbrenner's Choice (Appendix D) or from your local bookstore. Please see Appendix B for the addresses to contact to open subscriptions to GEnie, Compu-Serve, and most other online utilities.

In the next chapter, we'll turn to free public bulletin board systems or "BBSs." For a persistent searcher, these too offer a wealth of information and contacts. They have the advantage in most cases of being freely available, except for any long distance charges you may incur. But if you thought searching a SIG was on the wild and woolly side, just wait.

13

Bulletin Board Systems (BBSs)

BULLETIN BOARDS! WHAT ON EARTH ARE YOU TALKING ABOUT? I'M A TRAINED information professional. I know DIALOG, DataTimes, and Dow Jones like the back of my hand. But bulletin boards? What's in it for me?

Possibly nothing. It may very well be that you will never have an assignment where bulletin boards would be helpful. But then again, depending on the question at hand, a bulletin board may hold the only answer to one of your client's requests. It is difficult to tell—bulletin boards cover so many subjects, attract such a wide variety of people, and change so rapidly.

We would be the last to suggest that the 32,000-odd bulletin board systems (BBSs) in the country today are likely to be a prime source of information or leads to information. At the same time, however, it is impossible to deny that BBSs attract articulate, experienced experts in various fields. Unorthodox as they may seem to trained information professionals, BBSs are not only a legitimate information source, in some instances they are the *only* easily accessible information source in some subject areas.

What is a bulletin board?

Now, before we go any further, we must define terms. It is true that the term "bulletin board" is often applied to systems like CompuServe, GEnie, and Prodigy by the lay press. But, as is so often the case, the press does not know what it is talking about. As you know by now, CompuServe, GEnie and their competitors are far more than message exchange systems. Well, real bulletin boards are anything but the products of large corporations. They are very much a private, individual effort.

A real computer bulletin board system consists of the same components everyone uses to go online: a computer, a modem, and a telephone connection. The difference is in the software. Bulletin board software can be thought of as a specialized form of communications program. Instead of allowing the computer owner to dial out, BBS programs are designed to allow other users to dial in. They can thus turn any personal computer into a "host" system. Like the people who run SIGs on commercial systems, the person who owns, sets up, and runs a bulletin board is called its system operator or *sysop* (pronounced "sis-op").

The board's personality

The sysop is also responsible for the board's personality. Indeed, most sysops view their boards as their own unique creations, and they are forever tinkering with them the way some people tinker with souped-up stock cars. Thus, even if you are an experienced user, you never know what you'll find when you sign on. For example, at your option, some boards are capable of putting on quite a show, complete with pseudo-animated graphics, music, and other surprises.

Other boards are more sedate, channeling their originality into the selection of files they offer for download or the lively discussions and message exchanges they host. The sysop can focus a board on any topic he or she finds interesting. Most give their boards a name and publicize its existence throughout the BBS community. Once the word gets out, they have merely to sit back and wait for people with the same interests to call. The makes and models of the host system and the caller's computer are irrelevant since any communicating machine can talk to any other.

It is hard to know how many BBSs are in operation today, though reliable estimates place the number in the neighborhood of 32,000. And that's just in the United States. There are BBSs, or "mailboxes" as they are sometimes called abroad, in many other countries as well. The number and variety of topics covered is breathtaking. For example, here are the names and primary focus of just a few of the boards in operation today:

Big Sky Telegraph	Educational plans and services to rural Montana schools
Catholic Information Network	Early texts and writings of the Roman Catholic Church
Dallas Law SIG BBS	Lawyers forum on legal issues related to telecommunications
Hay Locator	Database of hay and straw suppliers and buyers
Greenpeace Environet	Ecological, disarmament, and related issues
Micro Message Service	USA Today, Newsbytes, and Boxoffice magazines

National Genealogical BBS	Family history and genealogical research
The Second Ring	Online computer magazine index operated by the San Jose Public Library
Colorado West BBS	Ham and packet radio
The Cyber-Zone	Science fiction
The Droid	Online tradewars and baseball games
Gay Community	Message exchange and downloads for the gay community
Midrash	Messianic Judaism, religion, and philosophy
The Silver Streak	Science, engineering, and Turbo Pascal
White Runes of Tinuviel	Tolkein subjects and Dungeons and Dragons

Most sysops operate their boards as a hobby, but even so, running an active board can be a lot of work. There are questions to answer, messages to respond to, programs to test for viruses, and old files to remove. Consequently, some sysops offer download-only systems with virtually no messaging capabilities. These systems can serve as "publishers" of news, information, and selected topic-specific articles, but most act as distribution points for public domain (PD) and shareware software. The number of megabytes of PD software a system has to offer is a mark of distinction in the BBS community, with some boards boasting 75 to 400 megabytes or more. Here the make and model of your machine *will* make a difference, for while Macintosh users can talk to and download programs from an IBM-compatible system, or vice versa, that system will almost certainly offer only IBM-compatible programs.

A narrow pipeline

From an information standpoint, BBSs offer all of the advantages of an online utility SIG. But they have a number of disadvantages as well. The main problem with "boards" is the width of the pipeline. You can dial up CompuServe or GEnie at any hour of the day or night and be virtually certain of making a connection. After all, these systems are set up to handle thousands of users at the same time.

The vast majority of boards, on the other hand, are connected to a single phone line. There is a growing entrepreneurial trend in the field, and some boards do offer 16 or more lines and impose membership fee requirements. ExecPC, for example, is a board operated by a husband and wife team in Illinois. It offers 250 phone lines (1200, 2400, and 9600 bps) and charges $20 for a 3-month subscription. But by and large, most boards are one-line-only, and most levy no fees. This means that if a board is good, the line is very likely to be busy when you call.

Look at it this way. If you assume that a board is "up" (available) 24 hours a day and that each caller spends an average of half an hour per call, the absolute limit on the number of callers per day is 48. When you add to this the fact that the sysop usually has to take the board down (make it unavailable) for a few hours a day for maintenance, the pipeline becomes even more restricted.

Consequently, while bulletin boards have a great deal to offer—every bit as much as a SIG on GEnie or CompuServe, but on a more limited scale—they are not necessarily a reliable source of information and contacts. What do you do, for example, if you need a certain piece of information to meet a client's deadline and cannot get on a board of your choosing? On the plus side, BBSs—especially *local* BBSs—do offer you an opportunity to try out your online and search skills virtually for free.

How to plug in:
Getting lists of good numbers

This is only a brief sketch of the kinds of things you'll find once you enter the BBS world. More than likely, making your initial sojourn will cost you little or nothing. Some bulletin boards do charge token membership fees and issue passwords like a commercial system, but the vast majority are free to all callers. Your only expense will be any long distance charges for the call.

The key thing is to find a list of good numbers, by which we mean numbers that are still connected to operational boards. The attrition rate among new sysops is high. Many novices publish their board numbers only to find that they really don't want to make the required commitment.

As noted, operating a good board can take a lot of time and energy. In addition to routine computer housekeeping, a conscientious sysop will review all uploaded files to make sure no one has put a copyrighted program on the board and make sure that no uploaded program contains a virus. Most also review each day's messages for stolen credit card numbers and other dicey information.

Of course there is also the time spent tuning, tweaking, and tinkering with the hardware and software. Add to this the fact that every sysop is a target of opportunity for all the addlepated computer punks who get their jollies by trying to wreck every board they call, and it's no wonder BBSs come and go with such frequency.

The ephemeral nature of bulletin boards is a fact of online life, however, and it simply means that you must pay particular attention to the freshness of the BBS phone lists you use. Because of this, books and magazines are not usually very good sources. The lead time between the submission of the last bit of copy and the publication date can be three months to a year, and inevitably many of the numbers will be out of service by the time the book or magazine hits the stands. However, there is at least one exception—the FOG/Computer Shopper list.

The FOG/Computer Shopper list

Computer Shopper is a tabloid-sized magazine that regularly runs to 800 pages or more. It makes a valiant attempt at providing editorial content and articles, but people really buy it for the ads. In fact, the demand for advertising space is apparently so great that the publication is in transition at this writing. It's new owner,

Ziff-Davis, is in the process of repositioning the magazine as a publication for people in the computer industry, while it produces a different, but similar, publication called *PC Sources* for consumers.

We bring this up because, while current issues of *Computer Shopper* contain one of the best BBS lists available in print, in the future this list may disappear or move to *PC Sources*. In the meantime, it is worth consulting the most recent issue of each magazine to see if it contains a feature called "Bulletin Boards." This is a 15- to 20-page BBS directory normally compiled and maintained by FOG, a leading user group based in Daly City, California. The group is assisted in its efforts by members of the Public Remote Access Computer Standards Association (PRACSA).

Boards are listed by state and area code and each listing includes a paragraph describing the BBS's special focus, if any. What makes the list so good is that sysops must renew their listings every two months. Those who don't are dropped from the FOG list.

Lists online: The electronic alternative

The main point in favor of a conscientiously prepared printed BBS list is the amount of information it provides. The main disadvantage of all printed lists, aside from the problem of currency, is simply that they are printed: the numbers are on the page instead of in your computer where they belong.

Since you have a modem, however, there's an easy solution. One of the best places to look for bulletin board numbers is on other bulletin boards. Virtually every board will have at least one list of numbers in its file or library area. The richest, most varied phone number collections can be found, however, in the SIG libraries of the online utility systems.

Look for a SIG devoted to telecommunications, bulletin boards, a particular communications software program, or simply to your brand of computer. Use the system to search a SIG data library for lists by specifying one of these two keywords: BBS or LIST. (Please see Fig. 13-1.)

You could also select CompuServe's BROWSE option from the data library menu and simply specify LIST or BBS as your keyword when prompted to do so. You will probably want to search separately on both words to be sure of finding all relevant files.

There are lots of lists in Fig. 13-1 for local and international areas. But notice the special interest lists—desktop publishing, medical science, dating, and nutrition. And pay particular attention to the file USBBS.ZIP. This file contains the best, most current list of boards running IBM-compatible software. It has been continuously issued every month for 90 months to date.

Don't let the "DOS BBS systems" qualifier throw you off. This simply means that if a board on this list offers public domain and shareware software for download, it probably will be for IBM-compatible (DOS) machines. The fact that it is a DOS board has nothing to do with the topics that may be discussed. However, if you are after software, your best bet is to do a similar search in the CompuServe or GEnie SIGs devoted to your machine.

On November 21, 1991, we signed on to CompuServe, keyed in *GO IBMBBS* to get the IBM Bulletin Board SIG, and then keyed in *DL7* to get to Data Library 7--BBS Listings. When we entered *S/DES/KEY:LIST* to scan the database on the keyword LIST and display the matching files and their descriptions, the following were among the files that appeared:

[72470,250]
BBSLST.EXE/Bin Bytes: 149130, Count: 50, 11-Nov-91

> Title   : National BBS List
> Keywords : BBS LIST U.S. CANADA
>
> This file contains a text file listing over 7000 BBSs in the U.S. and Canada. It is a self-extracting file.

[71301,1435]
96LIST.ZIP/Bin Bytes: 101516, Count: 25, 03-Nov-91

> Title   : 96LISTK1 - Nov. 91 list of 9600-capable BBSs
> Keywords : BBS LIST 9600 14400 USR HAYES V.32 FAST USA CANADA
>
> 96LIST is an ASCII text file sorted by area codes and includes   Bulletin Board Systems in the United States and Canada that support 9600 bps and faster callers. The Nov.1991 release lists over 3000 systems reported by SysOps, users and from various other sources, including CIS nodes. Please rename to 96LISTK1.ZIP. Compiled by Ken Sukimoto, Downtown BBS, Los Angeles.

[73137,416]
USBBS.ZIP/Bin   Bytes: 65280, Count: 203, 28-Sep-91(29-Oct-91)

> Title   : USBBS90 - Darwin USBBS list for November 1991
> Keywords : DARWIN USBBS USBBS90 BBS LIST NATIONAL MS-DOS NOV 1991
>
> Nov. '91 edition of the Darwin USBBS list, a nationwide list   of DOS bulletin board systems. Edited by Meade Frierson and updated monthly. The list itself contains instructions on how sysops and others may submit update information for future editions. Please rename to USBBS90.ZIP and discard earlier listings.

[72371,2401]
DUR109.ZIP/Bin Bytes: 2107, Count: 36, 13-Oct-91

> Title   : Durham/Research Triangle Park North Carolina BBS
> Keywords : DURHAM NC RTP BBS LIST
>
> October listings of BBS's in the Durham/Research Triangle Park   area of North Carolina. Lists modem type, hours, BBS software, network addresses.

[24777,416]
ARGENB.TXT/Bin Bytes: 18919, Count: 13, 12-Oct-91

> Title   : Current list of BBS's in Argentina
> Keywords : BBS LIST ARGENTINA OS2
>
> Updated list of BBS's in Argentina, Revised as of October 10th. This time including more BBS'S in the provinces. Any Change known please send a CIS mail or mail into OS2 & Sound.

[71565,1532]
MED069.ZIP/Bin Bytes: 12425, Count: 60, 23-Jun-91

> Title   : Latest Medical BBS List - 06/25/91
> Keywords : MEDICAL DISABLED FIRE EMS AIDS RECOVERY SCIENCE BBS LIST

Fig. 13-1. Lists of BBS phone numbers online

The following list is a list of medical, Fire/EMS, science, alcohol, AIDS and disability related bulletin board systems. All have been checked within the last twenty five days. Contains over 340 international numbers. CHECK IT OUT !!! Edward Del Grosso M.D. Black Bag BBS (150/140) 302-731-1998 CIS 71565,1532 GENIE E DELGROSSO

[71301,2056]
JAPAN.ZIP/Bin   Bytes: 9218, Count: 37, 05-Jun-91

    Title   : Tokyo Japan Area BBS List
    Keywords : BBS LIST JAPAN TOKYO HONEYTREE PROJECT KANJI

Most current list of active BBS's in the Tokyo Japan local. Many Kanji boards, many private boards on US Military bases, and Local Japanese boards in English. Curtesy of the HoneyTree Project.

[71551,436]
DATING.TXT   16-Sep-90 2328   Accesses: 431

    Title   : Dating BBS List
    Keywords : DATING DATA BABE DUDE BABES DUDES SINGLE SINGLES BBS BBOARD LIST

A listing of dating bbs systems. Most are 2400 baud and have guest levels.

[70635,1250]
BLTN15.ZIP/binary   03-Jun-90 5924   Accesses: 76

    Title   : Ventura Professional BBS list of DTP BBS's
    Keywords : BBS LIST VENTURA DTP DESKTOP PUBLISHING

Desktop publishing BBS list from Ventura Professional BBS in CA May 31, 1990

[73557,2532]
OPLINE.TXT   17-Mar-90 167   Accesses: 30

    Title   : OpLine BBS info
    Keywords : HEALTH NUTRITION BBS 812 LIST IN

OpLine BBS: Health and Nutrition Opinion Line Evansville, IN. (812) 477-9607 24 Hours/Daily 1200 and 2400 baud 8-N-1 Features: Personal RDA Profile and Food Analysis

[72135,424]
PARA.LST   20-Dec-89 10359   Accesses: 182

    Title   : list of ParaNet systems
    Keywords : PARANET BBS LIST UFOS

The complete list of ParaNet(sm) Information Service nodes, worldwide. Paranet is an international cooperative of Bulletin Board Systems dedicated to promoting the scientific investigation of UFOs and other scientific anomalies. It comprises the world's largest online database of UFO information, articles, reports, and research studies. Access to all ParaNet boards is free.

How to implement "Attack Dialing"

The best way to "work the boards" is to take advantage of your communications software's dialing directory or phone list. Most comm programs these days let you create lists of numbers to call. Enter the phone numbers once, and you can tell the program to dial them by simply picking an item off a dialing directory menu.

If you're a novice user, start by keying in five or six nearby numbers from a list of BBS systems. Take extra care to get the numbers right or you'll end up with an irate voice on the other end of your line instead of the familiar modem tone. Most programs will record your numbers on disk and let you dial each one in turn by entering a single key selection from the dialing directory menu.

Many programs will also let you specify a list of dialing directory entries for them to dial in turn. If the first number is busy, they automatically dial the second one, and so on until they get a connection. This technique is sometimes called "attack dialing," and it offers the best way to deal with constant busy signals.

If you really get into bulletin boarding you will want to search boards and online utility libraries for any public domain programs capable of *automatically* converting a file of BBS numbers into a dialing directory for your comm program. There is no guarantee that such a program exists for your communications software, but some user may very well have written exactly the program you need. If you're lucky enough to find one, you may never have to key in another BBS number by hand.

ProComm users will find such a program on the Glossbrenner's Choice Comm Pack 2—ProComm Utilities disk. But it will be useful only if you have an IBM or compatible and ProComm. (The full ProComm communications package, version 2.4.3 is on Comm Pack 1.) See Appendix D for ordering information. For more details on the program, as well as hands-on instructions for locating and downloading free programs from BBSs, see Alfred Glossbrenner's *Master Guide to FREE Software for IBMs and Compatible Computers*.

Keeping up-to-date

The only way to really plug into the bulletin board world is to regularly work the boards. But there are a number of ways to keep up-to-date if that is not possible. As you can imagine, BBSers don't spend all of their time on BBS systems. Many of them use the online utilities as a convenient common meeting ground and file exchange. Print publications are another possibility, and one that we especially like is Jack Rickard's *Boardwatch Magazine*. This is a professionally published, full-size magazine that normally runs 60 to 70 pages. Each issue contains hardware and software tips, profiles of interesting boards, announcements of new electronic services, plus an extensive, current list of board numbers. We would not recommend it for a complete computer novice, but if you've had a little experience, you may find that it's just the ticket. The cost is $36 a year (12 issues) or $3.95 per copy. Contact:

Mr. Jack Rickard
Boardwatch Magazine
5970 South Vivian St.
Littleton, CO 80127
(800) 933-6038 (subscriptions orders only)

Conclusion

Bulletin board systems, like the electronic universe as a whole, offer you information, adventure, and a sense of community. Dialing up a board is an ideal and virtually cost-free way to enter that universe. And it's easy, particularly if you follow our advice and put several board numbers in a dialing queue so your comm program can cycle through them seeking a connection.

Once you've plugged in, you'll discover store-and-forward mail systems like FidoNet that can pass your locally uploaded message across the country or even around the world at little or no cost to you. You'll encounter oceans of public domain and shareware software.

And you'll find that the BBS community is so diverse that it can answer virtually any question on any topic or at least help you turn up some expert or contact who can. It's simply a matter of locating a board frequented by the kind of experts you seek.

As you will discover, many different bulletin board host programs are in use, so many of the boards you sign onto will have a unique look and feel. Like the SIGs on commercial systems, however, most boards offer a message area and a file or library area. Most let you operate with menus or with commands. And most have help and instruction files available.

When in doubt about how to use a board, open your capture buffer and key in a question mark (?) at the prompt it presents. The chances are this will lead to the help you need. If it doesn't, try keying in HELP or MENU. You will find the BBS community exceptionally friendly, so don't hesitate to call a board's sysop if you are having difficulty. Many sysops post their voice phone numbers on the BBS greeting screen.

You will also discover that many sysops like to boast about the sizes of the hard disk drives they make available. Believe it or not, disks ranging from 200 to 600 megabytes are not at all uncommon. But if you think that sounds like a lot— 200 megabytes is the equivalent of 100,000 double-spaced pages—wait till you see what's waiting for you in the next chapter. There we will conclude Part Three—Electronic Options and Alternatives—with a discussion of *CD-ROM* (Compact Disk—Read Only Memory).

As a current or prospective information broker, the main question in your mind is the one we put forward at the beginning of this chapter: What's in it for me? It's question that we simply cannot answer. However, there can be little doubt that BBSs are a legitimate information source. And it can be well worth your while to look into this new medium.

14

CD-ROM possibilities

THIS CHAPTER DISCUSSES WHAT MANY FEEL IS THE MOST EXCITING TECHNOLOGY to hit the information industry in over a decade—CD-ROM. It's a technology that lets you put an entire database—or an entire encyclopedia—in your pocket. As an information broker, there is really only one thing you need to know about CD-ROM. It is simply this: With a database on a CD-ROM disk, you can search to your heart's content without being subject to the various charges levied by online database vendor systems.

Thus, if you frequently search a particular database online, purchasing that database on CD-ROM (if available) can be a very cost-effective solution. For the same reason, a CD-ROM also offers new searchers the opportunity for unlimited practice at a fixed price. The commands required to search a given CD-ROM database may differ from those used by an online system. But the search concepts and approaches will be the same.

If you like, you can skip the other details presented here and jump to the end of the chapter where you will find a sampling of CD-ROM titles and the names of two of the leading directories of the products that are available. On the other hand, if you'd like to know a little more about the pluses and minuses and the technology that makes it possible to pack all that information on a little disk, read on.

Too important to ignore

The phrase *CD-ROM* stands for "compact disk, read-only memory." The disks themselves are identical in appearance to the CD audio disks that have all but replaced vinyl records in music stores across the land. They are of interest here because of their incredible information-holding capacities—entire encyclopedias, the text of literally hundreds of books, tens of thousands of images, all packed onto thin plastic disks measuring a mere 4.7″ in diameter.

These days, if you're interested in information, you have to be interested in CD-ROM, since more and more information is being made available in this format. In years past, however, your interest might be merely intellectual. A fascinating technology, yes. But buy one for my own use? No way! I can't afford *that*.

It may be that you still can't afford or cost-justify owning your own CD-ROM reader and CD-ROM disk collection. But recently many things have changed. Equipment prices have dropped to around $400 for a CD-ROM reader. Ever more CD-ROM titles are becoming available, some for less than $100. And performance has improved.

As a professional information broker today, you can't afford *not* to at least consider the possibility of owning and using a CD-ROM system. The topic and the possibilities have simply grown too big to ignore. In the future, if you stick with this profession, we guarantee that you will indeed have a CD-ROM reader and disk library.

As Sue points out, "If you follow our advice and find your own special market niche, you may indeed find that using CD-ROMs can save you a lot of money. Just two years ago I would not have recommended CD-ROMs due to the cost. But CD-ROM prices have come down, while database search costs have gone up. Today, I'd say that if you specialize in any of the technical or medical areas in particular, it can be well worth your while to look into buying appropriate CD-ROM databases. They really are a realistic and cost-effective alternative in many cases."

There's nothing like a real-life example to clarify a point, and Alfred's got the genuine article for you. We'll let him tell it in his own words in the section that follows.

Alfred's most excellent CD-ROM adventure

As many of you know, over the past decade or so I've made a profession of writing books about telecommunications, databases, software, and computers. In support of this effort, I have subscribed to a *lot* of topic-relevant magazines. In fact, I've still got the premier issue of *PC Magazine*, a thin little saddle-stitched affair that bears no resemblance to the perfect-bound monster that now appears in my mailbox twice each month.

Actually, I should say "appeared," since I no longer subscribe to *PC Magazine*. In the computer business that's rank heresy. If you're going to be a computer pundit and author, at the very least you must subscribe to *PC Magazine*, *InfoWorld*, and *PC Week*. You should probably add *PC World* as well, and possibly *PC Computing*. And that's if you're concentrating on the DOS world. If you are concentrating on the Apple Macintosh, at a minimum you need *MacUser* and *MacWEEK*, in addition to *InfoWorld*.

Unfortunately, there are a number of drawbacks to subscribing to all of these magazines. First and foremost is the expense. A one-year subscription to *PC Magazine* costs $45. A subscription to *PC Week* is $160 a year. *InfoWorld* is $110. And so on. Yes, this is simply a cost of doing business, and as with all magazines, special discounts are available. Still, magazine subscription costs do mount up.

So, too, do the magazines themselves. I'm fortunate in having a third floor in my house, and an entire section of it is filled with book boxes of the sort you get when you move. Each box has a label, and each holds issues of a particular magazine, newsletter, or other publication.

It doesn't take too long for a box to fill up, and when it does, I transfer the contents to another box in another part of the third floor. Or I move it out to the barn that serves as our garage. I am loathe to throw out old computer magazines.

An iffy proposition

I know the technology changes awfully fast. I know that any magazine more than a year old is seriously out of date. But I also know that at times I have needed a particularly good in-depth article that appeared perhaps two years ago. And even today, trying to find a copy of a leading computer magazine at a local library can be an iffy proposition. I would much rather subscribe to the magazine itself and hold onto it so it is always there when I need it.

The problem is: How do you locate the articles you need when you are preparing to write, say, a book about hard disk drives? Some articles I remember from paging through the magazine when it first arrived. My memory is far from perfect. Yet if you are attuned to some topic, it is amazing what sticks.

But I don't read or even skim every magazine any more. There simply is not enough time. Consequently, you will often find me seated on a stool on the third floor illuminated by a single bare bulb scouring the tables of contents of relevant magazines. When I find something that applies to the topic I must write about, I mark the page with a paper clip. Later I will photocopy all articles so marked using my big Sharp SF-8260 office copier. The copied pages will be stapled, and the articles will be filed by the book chapter to which they apply. The magazines must then be returned to third floor storage.

This is a laborious process, to be sure, but it is one I have gone through many, many times. As time-consuming as it is, it is still quicker than getting into the car and trying to do the same thing at the library.

I followed this routine in researching my book about hard disk drives for Osborne/McGraw-Hill. But I also added an online component. Ziff-Davis, publisher of *PC Magazine* and many others, produces a number of online databases through its subsidiary, Information Access Company (IAC). I knew about these databases, of course. But I wasn't keen on paying $108 an hour in connect time and nearly a dollar for every record I asked to have displayed on DIALOG or $2 for each full text article I wanted to see.

Computer Database Plus on CompuServe

As it happened, at about this time Ziff-Davis began to offer a product called Computer Database Plus on CompuServe at a cost of $24 an hour, plus $1.50 to $2.50

for each full text article retrieved. Since I was on CompuServe every day anyway to check my mail, I decided to give it a try. (A similar Ziff-Davis database is available via Knowledge Index at $24 an hour, but it does not include full-text articles.)

The Ziff-Davis database was great. I would search for and capture articles published in magazines that I did not have. For those magazines that I knew were in third-floor storage boxes, I would use the system to simply (and cheaply) locate citations. With the article title, page number, and magazine date in hand, it was easy to locate the target magazine and bring it down to the office for photocopying.

To make a long story short, I spent over $300 using Computer Database Plus on CompuServe in this way. That sounds like a lot, but you have to view it in relation to the advance the publisher paid me to write the book, not to mention the *time* this research would have cost me. I certainly looked at it as a legitimate and reasonable cost of production.

What I did not know at the time was that the experience would forever change the way I work. Again, I've been doing this magazine shuffle for nearly a decade. I knew I had to save all those magazines, but the difficulty of finding relevant articles in them had always bothered me. And the magazines were beginning to take over my third floor.

I knew from my reading that Ziff-Davis also had a CD-ROM product called The Computer Library. I had acquired a Hitachi CD-ROM reader in the course of doing a project. So what could it hurt to call Ziff-Davis and ask about The Computer Library? I did, and I was very impressed with all that it offered. I had to take a sharp breath when they told me the price, but I agreed to subscribe.

Nearly a year later I can say it was one of the best decisions I've ever made. The product is now called Computer Select, and it contains the full text of nearly 50 computer-related magazines, plus informative abstracts of articles appearing in over 100 other magazines and newsletters. (Please see Fig. 14-1.)

The full text of each month's issue of the following magazines is available on the Computer Select CD-ROM database. That means *everything*, even letters to the editor. The full-text list here is followed by the publications for which Computer Select offers abstracts. The abstracts may or may not hold enough information to satisfy your needs. But they can definitely tell you whether the full text of a given article is worth pursuing at the library or by some other means. Computer Select, for example, does not offer the full text of *BYTE*, but the full text of this publication is available to you electronically on BIX. Similarly, the full text of *Business Week* or *Forbes* can be found online--or at your library.

Computer Select Full-Text Publications

ACKnowledge, The Window Letter
AI Expert
Communications of the ACM
Computer Conference Analysis Newsletter
Computer Glossary
Computer Language
Computergram International
Computing Canada

Fig. 14-1. Computer select CD-ROM magazines

Data Based Advisor
Datamation
DBMS
Digital Review
Dr. Dobb's Journal
EDGE, on & about AT&T
EDGE: Work
.EXE
Government Computer News
Hewlett
IBM Journal of Research and Development
IBM Systems Journal
LAN Magazine
LOCALNetter
Lotus Magazine
MacUser
MacWEEK
Microprocessor Report
Microsoft Systems Journal
Multimedia Computing & Presentations
Newsbytes
Netware Advisor
Patricia Seybold's Network Monitor
Patricia Seybold's Office Computing Report
Patricia Seybold's Unix In The Office
PC/Computing
P.C. Letter
PC Magazine
PC Sources
PC User
PC Week
Personal Workstation
Release 1.0
Seybold Report On Desktop Publishing
Seybold Report On Publishing Systems
Softletter
Software Magazine
Systems Integration
Tech Street Journal
Technologic Computer Letter
Telecom Dictionary
Teleconnect
Unix Review
WordPerfect Magazine

Computer Select Abstracted Publications

3D
ACM Computing Surveys
ACM Transactions on Computer Systems
ACM Transactions on Database Systems
ACM Transactions on Graphics
ACM Transactions on Information Systems
ACM Transactions on Programming Languages & Systems
Business Week
BYTE
CAD-CAM International
Canadian Datasystems
Classroom Computer Learning
Communications News
CommunicationsWeek
Computer
Computer Communications

Fig. 14-1. Continued.
Computer Design
Computer Graphics World
Computer Reseller News
Computer Security Journal
Computer Systems News
Computer Vision, Graphics & Image Processing
Computer Weekly
Computer-Aided Design
Computer-Aided Engineering
Computers & Operations Research
Computers in Banking
Computers in Healthcare
Computerworld
Data Communications
DEC Professional
DEC User
DG Review
EDN
Educational Technology
Electronic Business
Electronic Design
Electronic Engineering Times
Electronic Learning
Electronic News
Electronics
Electronics Weekly
ESD: The Electronic System Design Magazine
Federal Computer Week
Forbes
Hewlett-Packard Journal
High Technology Business
I&CS (Instrumentation & Control Systems)
IBM System User
IBM Systems Journal
IEE Proceedings Part E Computers and Digital Techniques
IEEE Computer Graphics and Applications
IEEE Design & Test of Computers
IEEE Expert
IEEE Micro
IEEE Network
IEEE Software
IEEE Spectrum
IEEE Transactions on Computers
IEEE Transactions on Robotics and Automation
IEEE Transactions on Software Engineering
Industrial Computing
Industrial Engineering
Information Executive
Information Week
InfoWorld
Journal of Object-Oriented Programming
Journal of Systems and Software
Journal of Systems Management
Journal of the Association for Computing Machinery
LAN Times
Lasers & Optronics
M.D. Computing
Macworld
Microprocessors and Microsystems
MIS Quarterly
MIS Week
Modern Office Technology
NetWare Technical Journal

Network World
Networking Management
New York Times
The Office
PC World
Personal Computing
Proceedings of the IEEE
Publish!
Robotics Today
Science of Computer Programming
Simulation
T H E Journal (Technological Horizons in Education)
Telecommunications
Telecommuting Review: the Gordon Report
Teleconnect
Telephony
Today's Office
TPT-Networking Management Magazine
UNIX World
Wall Street Computer Review
InTech
The Wall Street Journal
Which Computer?

Still more features

The disk also offers a directory containing the addresses, company officers, phone and fax numbers, and financial data for 11,000 computer and software companies. And there is address information on nearly 70,000 hardware and software firms. Plus a database of computer terms and their definitions, and copies of the free programs offered in many issues of *PC Magazine*.

Each disk contains 12 months of data, and a new disk is mailed to you each month. The oldest month drops off the disk as each new month's data is added. Thus the January 1992 disk contains all of 1991. In my experience, the search software that is a part of the disk has continuously improved as well. You can now search Computer Select with all the power available on a system like DIALOG.

The crucial difference

The difference is that with Computer Select's CD-ROM product, you can search at any time of day or night and for as long as you want at no extra charge. You can tag articles you want to copy to your hard disk and print—the product will take care of it, at no additional charge. You are free to make mistakes and explore any avenue of inquiry that happens to occur to you, at no additional charge.

It is a heady feeling, having all of this information at your fingertips. No need to trundle up to the third floor, eyeball one table of contents after another, paper clip pages, and bring them downstairs for photocopying. With Computer Select's CD-ROM, it is all right there.

This is an enormously impressive product. But then, it had better be: A subscription costs $1000 a year. No question, that's a lot of money. It clearly would not pay you to invest in this product unless, like me, you have a continual and constant need for the information it offers. The same applies to other CD-ROM titles, almost all of which are much less expensive.

But if you *do* have that kind of need, consider the fact that a Computer Select subscription costs the equivalent of $84 a month. That's less than a single hour of connect time on some databases. And it is only slightly more than the $75 that DIALOG has for years maintained is the cost of one typical search on its system.

Or consider the fact that if you were to subscribe to all of the 50 magazines and newsletters Computer Select offers in full text, special deals notwithstanding, you would pay much more than that. (Divide $1000 by 50 and you get $20 per publication, far less than even the most aggressive magazine can afford to charge for a yearly subscription.) And you would have all those issues to store in your attic.

If you were to search equivalent databases on DIALOG, you would pay $118 an hour ($1.97 a minute) in connect time and telecommunications charges, plus about $1 for every article you wanted to display. Even at $24 an hour, the price of similar databases on Knowledge Index and CompuServe, there is the inconvenience factor of having to sign on and move to your target database. And the connect time meter is always running.

Even though I wince at the $1000 price tag, having all this information easily searchable at a fixed cost is well worth it. I use it *constantly*, not only in researching an article or a book, but to look up addresses and phone numbers of hardware and software companies, or merely to explore a topic I happen to be interested in. These are things I would never do if I had to go online and pay by the minute each time. I would simply do without.

If nothing else, this CD-ROM has allowed me to reclaim significant portions of my third floor. I have thrown out years' worth of computer publications. Now I save new publications only as long as it takes for them to fill up a single box. Then I pitch them.

There are drawbacks. At this writing, like most online and CD-ROM products, Computer Select does not include graphics and illustrations. Fortunately, for my purposes, photographs and graphics aren't all that important.

Overload! Overload! Mass Critical!

There is also the information overload factor. This is something I've never seen anyone talk about when discussing CD-ROM. The fact is, however, that in the course of researching this chapter for your indefatigable writing team, I found 1581 articles containing the keyword "CD-ROM" on the most recent Computer Select disk. I looked at the titles for all of them, and I selected 84 to be printed.

The result was a stack of hundreds of pages. I had much more information than was necessary, and not all of it was strictly relevant. But since I had it, I went through it, selecting the pieces containing facts most likely to be of greatest interest to a reader like yourself.

Of course, CD-ROM is a very broad topic, and I had in effect said to the database, "Give me everything you have on CD-ROM." I did not have to do that. The search software provided with this and many other CD-ROM products is at least as powerful as the software that drives many online systems. So I could have been much more selective. But, since it didn't cost anything, I decided to go for the whole enchilada.

Still, it did strike me that while my Computer Select CD-ROM made locating and printing the information incalculably easier, it also greatly broadened the scope of the source material. It thus produced far *more* information than I would have come up with had I been limited to the boxes of magazines in my attic. Then again, if you are in the information business, those are the kinds of problems you *like* to have.

The point of it all

The point here is not to urge you to go out and buy every CD-ROM that seems to bear on a query. Certainly the Computer Select disk I like so much is aimed at (and priced for) corporate information centers and public libraries, not for individual professionals. The important thing is to open your mind to the possibility of owning an entire database on disk.

The prices will come down. There will be more and more information made available on CD-ROM in the future. So keep your ear to the ground. At some point in the not too distant future, you will find that it makes good economic sense to buy a database instead of just paying to access it online.

A word about CD-ROM technology

Don't worry. We're not going to make you sit through a chapter-and-verse explanation of how CD-ROMs are created and how they work. Still, it is important to have a very general idea of what CD-ROMs are all about and how it is that they can store such massive quantities of data, if only so you can sound reasonably intelligent when someone asks you how all that information can fit on such a little disk.

The answer is the laser. Laser beams can be focused with incredible fineness, and they can be turned on and off very quickly. These two facts are at the heart of CD-ROM technology. When an inscribing laser beam is focused on a spinning CD and turned on, it makes a very, very tiny pit in the CD's surface. When it is turned off, there is no pit.

Ones and zeros—again!

Thus, as a reading laser beam traverses the CD's surface, at any given second it is over a pit or a solid place on the disk. If it is over a pit, the laser light reflected back from the disk looks one way. If it is over a solid area, the reflected light looks another way. But these are the only two ways the light can appear: either a "pit" or "not a pit;" either an "on" or an "off;" either a "1" or a "0."

Laser disks or CD-ROMs, in other words, are a *binary* medium, just like a hard or floppy disk drive. The reading laser is either over a pit or over a "nonpit." There is no in between. Just like your disk drives, CD-ROMs can record the numbers needed to represent ASCII characters or any other kind of computer data.

What sets a CD-ROM apart is the terrifically fine precision of that laser. The pits and non-pits are much, much smaller than the magnetized or non-magnetized areas used to represent 1's and 0's on a floppy or hard disk. Indeed, it has been estimated that if you were to stretch out the spiral data track of a 4.7 inch CD-ROM, the track would extend to three miles or more.

How many megabytes?

That's about all you need to know about CD-ROM technology. It will certainly satisfy any non-technical person who asks. Accordingly, please feel free to skip ahead to the next section, if you like. The paragraphs that follow are for those who are interested in learning a bit more about CD-ROM technology.

The image of a three-mile long track of data is certainly striking. But let's put it into more conventional terms. Because of the fineness of lasers, a single side of a single CD-ROM can hold 650 to 700 *megabytes* of data. That is the equivalent of more than 1850 five-and-a-quarter-inch 360K floppy disks. A disk of 650 megabytes is also equivalent to 325,000 double-spaced typewritten pages or 650 reams of paper. Or a stack of pages 135 feet high. If you were to transmit all the data on a CD-ROM using a 2400 bps modem, working round the clock, the process would take you 23 days.

Or consider this. The original version of *Grolier's Academic American Encyclopedia* on CD-ROM included the full text, but no illustrations, from the 20-volume printed version. But even these 20 volumes of text occupied only one fifth of the disk's capacity. (The most recent edition of Grolier's Encyclopedia now includes 1500 color plates—VGA required—and a pop-up notepad.) Small wonder that single CD-ROM disks are currently available offering the text of over 100 books on a single subject, like American history.

It is also worth noting, while we are speaking of the technology, that at this writing, one can produce a master CD-ROM for about $2000. Once the master has been created, the cost of pressing a single disk is less than $2. Producing the printed version of the encyclopedia, in contrast, might cost a publisher $10 a book—or $200 for the entire set. And, of course, 20 printed volumes take up far more space and cost much more to warehouse than single CD-ROM disks.

So, given a choice, which would you rather sell if you were the publisher: The printed version at a discounted price of $500 or the CD-ROM version at $400? Your gross profit on the printed version will be $300. But on the CD-ROM version, your profit will be nearly $400. Plus, the CD-ROM version will involve far fewer intermediary costs. Just think what it costs to ship a 20-volume encyclopedia—compared to the 98 cents or so you would spend to ship a single CD-ROM in its jewel case.

The economics of CD-ROM publishing are *very* attractive. Particularly if you are primarily in the business of producing a printed product anyway. For a very low entry fee, you can offer a CD-ROM version of your print product that holds the potential of making you nearly 100 percent profit.

More and more CD-ROMs are being published

It is thus not surprising that the catalogue of CD-ROM titles is growing. In 1989 there were 1418 CD-ROM titles, according to ''The Seybold Report on Publishing Systems.'' By the end of 1990, there were 3000, and an estimated 6000 titles are expected to exist by the end of 1991.

We'll offer a few highlights in a moment. Right now, you should know that some of these thousands of titles are what ''The Seybold Report'' calls ''shovelware.'' This is a reference to the fact that some companies have taken public domain material—like The Bible or the works of Shakespeare—and ''shoveled'' huge quantities of it onto a disk. Such firms have none of the data development costs of an encyclopedia company, which must pay researchers and writers.

Still, having the full text of 450 of the world's greatest books—works by Aeschylus, Aristophanes, Aristotle, St. Augustine, Boccaccio, Cervantes, Chaucer and the rest—on a single *searchable* CD-ROM is an attractive proposition. World Library of Garden Grove, California, (714) 748-7197, offers just such a disk as its Library of the Future Series First Edition for a list price of $695.

The downside today, and solutions for tomorrow

Not everything is hearts and flowers. It never is. Though they have been a factor since at least 1986, CD-ROMs have a number of serious drawbacks. On the purely technical level, using a CD-ROM drive is not like accessing a hard disk drive. CD-ROM drives, you see, were designed for audio compact disks.

Sony and the Dutch electronics giant N.V. Phillips jointly invented CD technology in 1980. Audio was the first application, but binary information was a natural follow-on. CD-ROM drives have a few additional circuits and chips on their controller boards, but the drive mechanism in an audio and a computer CD unit are identical. Not surprisingly, NEC and several other companies now market portable ''Walkman''-style units designed to handle both audio and CD-ROM disks. The Hitachi desk unit Alfred uses offers a stereo headphone jack and volume control dial should you wish to listen to an audio disk when you aren't searching a CD-ROM.

Slow access speeds

The consumer electronics origins of CD-ROMs have had a positive effect in rapidly reducing prices. The same plant production lines used to stamp out Beethoven can be used to stamp out *Books in Print*. But, governed by audio requirements, CD-ROM drives spin at between 200 and 500 revolutions per second (rpm)—compared to the 3,600 rpm of a hard disk.

That makes the CD drives nearly 20 times *slower* than a hard disk. Where a hard disk may have an average seek time of between 10 and 28 milliseconds, for example, a CD-ROM drive may require as much as 500 milliseconds. Where a hard disk may transfer data to your computer at 312 kilobytes per second (kbs), a CD-ROM drive may only be able to achieve 150 kbs.

In other words, if you are accustomed to hard disk speeds, you will find any CD-ROM drive *slow*. Of course, it is largely a matter of what you're used to. If you operate with floppies alone, you won't be quite as aware of the CD-ROM speed difference. But most people have hard disks these days, and most will indeed feel that CD-ROM drives are sluggish.

There is hope for the future, however. Taking their cue from the techniques used to speed up hard drive access, some companies have begun to use disk caches and read-ahead algorithms to greatly improve the effective speed of CD-ROM drives.

Without going into detail, the read-ahead feature causes the drive to automatically read information that you have not yet asked for. It assumes, for example, that if you want to look at one article on a list, you will probably want to see at least one of the next five on the same list. So it automatically reads them and stores them in an area of your computer's memory (RAM) that has been configured as a disk cache.

A disk cache can be thought of as an extension of a disk drive that has been carved out of random access memory. It is the place the system looks at first the next time you call for information. If the information is there, it will appear on your screen with the speed of light. And, while you are reviewing that article, the read-ahead feature will set the CD-ROM drive to reading the next unrequested segment of data. These techniques are not perfect, but they work well enough, often enough to make using a CD-ROM nearly as fast as using a hard disk drive.

The non-writeable problem

You will also hear complaints about the fact that one cannot write to a CD-ROM disk. In our opinion, these objections are groundless. One cannot blame people for dreaming of a removable media costing perhaps $2 a disk and able to hold 650 to 700 megabytes, not when hard drives offering the same capacity currently sell for $1400 or more. But you might as well complain that a horse is not a cow.

A more legitimate problem concerns the matter of updating. As our friend Barbara Quint points out in her magazine, *Database Searcher*, premium online databases are updated daily or weekly. Most other online databases are updated monthly. Most CD-ROM products are updated either yearly or twice a year, or they aren't updated at all.

The way it's going to work in the future (we think)

The seriousness of this limitation depends on the data involved. Monthly subscription services like Computer Select are one answer, though they tend to be pricey. But if you have to have up-to-the-minute information on a subject, you have to go online. CD-ROMs will never match the currency of an online database that is updated on a daily basis. But since many titles are CD-ROM versions of online databases, it can be most cost-effective to use the online version for the latest information and use the CD-ROM version for archival information.

In our opinion, it is not an "either-or" decision. By making their databases available on CD-ROM, information providers have indeed succeeded in cutting out the middlemen (the DIALOGs, BRSs, SprintNets, and Tymnets of the world). And they will continue to succeed, particularly if they resist the temptation to price their products too high.

The process will take many years, but it seems inevitable that a hybrid approach of this sort will become routine. A decade ago, gaining access to the processing power and storage capacity of a mainframe computer was unique. But when you combine today's 80386, 80486, and soon, 80586 computers running at speeds of 33 megahertz or faster with the massive storage capacity of CD-ROM, what you've got is something pretty close to mainframe functionality.

There are even "juke box"-style CD-ROM readers capable of giving you access to six or more disks on demand. In round numbers, that's about three gigabytes of information, easily on a par with a mini-computer and some older mainframe equipment. In fact, it's better than that. An online database computer may have many times that amount of storage, but as a searcher, you will only use or need a tiny fraction of it, probably far less than three gigabytes.

The net-net is that as CD-ROMs become more widespread, online databases will be forced to concentrate more and more on making absolutely current information instantly available. That is the one unique feature online systems can offer. In the future, that will be the most appropriate use of the technology.

An eclectic sampling of titles

With so many CD-ROM titles available, it would be impossible to list even the available subject categories. Instead, we will offer a brief sampling to help demonstrate the depth and breadth of CD-ROM coverage. At this writing, most prices are well beyond the budgets of most information brokers, so we will not bother quoting them. However, you may be able to find many of these titles at your local library, and prices do come down.

If you need a comprehensive list of what's available, see *CD-ROMs in Print* from Meckler Publishing at (203) 226-6967. This book is published each October, and the cost is $50. You might also look for the *Directory of Portable Databases* from Gale Research. Published twice a year (April and October), a subscription to this directory costs $99. To order, call (800) 877-4253. For more information, call Gale Research, Inc. at (313) 961-2242.

Let's start with a quick list of some of the familiar databases that are now on CD-ROM. We can use DIALOG's CD-ROM division (DIALOG OnDisc) as our example. Among other things, it offers the following databases on CD-ROM: the Boston Globe, Aerospace Database, Canadian Business and Current Affairs, Compendex Plus, ERIC, Chemdisc, Kirk-Othmer Encyclopedia of Chemical Technology, Medline (National Library of Medicine), NTIS (National Technical Information Service), Polymer Encyclopedia, San Jose Mercury-News, Standard & Poor's Corporations, Trademarkscan, Thomas Register, and the Los Angeles Times.

This only scratches the surface. In general, you can assume that most major databases now available online either are already available in CD-ROM versions or soon will be. Only you can decide whether a particular CD-ROM database is cost-effective for your business. But if you find that you are searching the same database online again and again, if you find that you are developing a special market niche for yourself, it can certainly pay you to investigate. Check one of the CD-ROM directories we've cited here, or simply call the database vendor and ask for the phone number of the company that produces the database you're interested in. Meantime, here are some less traditional offerings on CD-ROM:

U.S. History from the Bureau of Electronic Publishing. One hundred history books and 1000 images.

Birds of America. Presents both pictures and bird calls.

Mammals: A Multimedia Encyclopedia from the National Geographic Society and IBM. Text, color photos, range maps, animal vocalizations, and 45 full-motion video clips using standard CD-ROM format.

The Physician's Desk Reference (PDR). Contains five PDR volumes. The Merck Manual is an optional add-on.

The Oxford English Dictionary. All 13 volumes.

U.S. Patents from the U.S. Patent and Trademark Office. Abstracts and index data, not the patent files themselves. In contrast, International Thompson publishes Official Gazette/Plus, which has both patent abstracts and images of recent patents.

PhoneDisc USA. A residential phone directory for the whole country, on two disks (East and West) from Compact Publications. More than 90 million residential listings, with name, address and phone number (where available). You can print up to twenty listings at a time for future reference. An autodial feature allows you to dial from the application. Searches can be done on partial names and can be constrained by combinations of area code, ZIP code, state, city, or street.

The American Business Disk. From American Business Information, this disk offers a national yellow pages directory containing more than 9.2 million businesses.

TRW Decision Disk. Business profiles and credit summaries on three million businesses.

The National Portrait Gallery. From the National Gallery of Art in Washington, D.C. Contains 4000 images.

Artfact. Descriptions and prices of artworks sold at the top auction galleries, plus color pictures, all taken from the galleries' catalogs. Updated quarterly.

Books-in-Print. Over 770,000 citations from the printed volumes, plus 100,000 full-text book reviews.

Microsoft Bookshelf. *American Heritage Dictionary*, *World Almanac*, *U.S. Zip Code Directory*, *Bartlett's Familiar Quotations*, *Chicago Manual of Style*, *Roget's Thesaurus*, and more.

Multi-media, the next step

Finally, we must direct your attention to what is undoubtedly the next trend in CD-ROMs and possibly in personal computing in general. It is called "multi-media," a fancy term for using a combination of text, graphic images, full-motion video, and sound to convey information. The audio heritage of CD-ROM technology has been seen as a disadvantage in regard to speed. But it is a major plus for multi-media applications.

By all accounts the most convincing harbinger of this trend is Compton's MultiMedia Encyclopedia from Britannica Software. This product offers 9,000,000 words; 15,000 images, maps and graphs; 60 minutes of sound, music and speech; 45 animated sequences; plus a complete online Merriam-Webster Intermediate dictionary.

You will need a mouse and a VGA display, and a CD-ROM player with audio output jacks or a computer with IBM's speech adapter card. A fast 386-based computer is also recommended.

Compton's MultiMedia Encyclopedia uses a point-and-click interface, though typing is just fine as well. Once selected, the text of your target article appears in a scrolling window. Icons along the left margin indicate the availability of additional material. A camera icon means a photograph is available. Click on it and the screen fills with a high-resolution image.

Other icons include an open book to alert you to a cross-reference. A pair of eyes indicates the availability of a summary. A pair of headphones lets you know that speech or music is available. Full-motion pictures or animation are indicated by a movie camera icon.

When reading an article on human anatomy, for example, you might click on the headphone icon next to text about the heart muscle. That would produce a recording of a heartbeat in your speaker. Click on the camera icon beside the paragraph on joint movement and you'll see an animated sequence of an elbow bending.

Click on any word in the text, and the product will instantly look up that word in its dictionary. If the word is underlined, MultiMedia will *pronounce* it for you through the speaker or voice synthesizer. (The cost of the product, in case you're interested, is $895.)

The next new thing?

It is impossible to know where multi-media will lead. The computer industry is always hungry for "the next new thing," whether that thing or technology is truly significant or not. Without something to hype, the computer press could easily find itself short of topics to write about. For the past few years the drumbeat has been building for "multi-media," so you will certainly be hearing a lot more about it.

It does look as though this may be the genuine article, however. The Compton Encyclopedia has gotten uniformly excellent reviews, and it is really only a preliminary first step. Imagine being able to look up "space shuttle" and click on an icon that would cause the system to show you an actual take-off, complete with sound.

There are already CD-ROMs that will show you a score by Mozart or Beethoven and, at your command, play the measures you have selected, not to mention showing you pictures of the composers and text about their lives. The long-standing respect and affection we hold for online systems notwithstanding, it is difficult to see how any of them can ever compete with something like that.

The price of entry

If you are interested in CD-ROM, in the near term, cost will still be a major consideration. Equipment prices have fallen considerably in recent years. The first CD-ROM drives listed for around $1200. Today, list prices are closer to $600, and "street prices" are lower still. Even so, assuming you can get a CD-ROM drive for $400 or $500, it is not an inconsiderable investment. And then you have to consider the cost of the software—the CD-ROM disks themselves.

In our experience, CD-ROM disks typically sell for at least $100. Some, like the Grolier's Encyclopedia, list for around $400. And, of course, there is Alfred's $1000 yearly subscription to Computer Select.

It seems likely that a CD-ROM drive will eventually become a standard component of even an entry level computer system. But the time is not yet. Today, CD-ROM is not an inexpensive proposition. In our opinion, the best way to acquire computer equipment is to wait until you really need it. The velocity of change in the computer marketplace is breathtaking. By waiting until the last possible moment, you make sure that you get the greatest capability at the lowest price.

There is also the fact that as an information broker you will probably be called upon to range far afield. Unless you specialize in a particular subject, it probably does not make sense to commit always scarce dollars to one or more CD-ROM titles. Still, if you need the information on a regular basis, and if you have enough business to cost-justify it, it could well pay you to take the plunge.

At the very least, this is a technology and a possibility that you have to be aware of as a prospective information broker. And not just with an eye toward acquiring your own CD-ROM capability. More and more libraries are offering CD-ROM titles as an extension of their reference departments.

It is entirely possible that the database you were planning to search on DIALOG is actually available in CD-ROM form at your local library—for free. This opens a whole range of possibilities that simply did not exist only a few years ago. And it's all due to a little 4.7" piece of plastic called a CD-ROM.

Part IV

The business side of information brokering

15

Services to sell

IT IS A CARDINAL RULE OF SUCCESS IN ANY BUSINESS TO KNOW WHAT BUSINESS you're really in. It is thus appropriate to begin this fourth part of this book with a brief discussion of the kinds of services you can expect to offer. We have spent most of our time up to now discussing information gathering. That will always be your bread-and-butter, and we will assume that you have at least a preliminary understanding of what this service is. There are two other services, however, that many information brokers offer as well—"document delivery" and what used to be called "SDI." SDI stands for "Selective Dissemination of Information," but thankfully, the term is being replaced by "electronic clipping" or "alert" services. Here we will use the term Alert Service.

Of course, these services involve information gathering. But it is information gathering of a type that is different from what is likely to be your main line of business. These services may or may not be profitable for you. As Sue says, "You should be able to make money on an Alert Service, but document delivery can be a real sinkhole. It can cost you far more time to locate an article or other document for a client than you can ever charge for the service, if you try to do it yourself. However, as we'll show you in a moment, there are alternatives. So read on."

Whether you make or lose money, however, there are good reasons to consider offering these services. For one thing, they are part of the "full-service" concept many brokers want to project. For another, they offer a natural way to keep your name in front of a client's eyes. And that, of course, can lead to more assignments.

Document Delivery, Yellowsheets, and DIALOG

Document delivery—or "doc del" as it is called in the profession—is basically the service of providing clients with photocopies of documents referred to in an online search. The "document" can be anything from a magazine article to a corporate report to an out-of-print book. The term originated in the days when online systems offered only bibliographical listings of source material pertaining to a particular topic. But, of course, the practice of inter-library loan that preceded "doc del" has been in existence since invention of libraries.

At the time, there were no full-text databases. If you saw a reference to an article in, say, a scientific journal that looked like it might be relevant, you could order a copy using a document delivery service. DIALOG, for example, has arrangements with over 100 doc del services. (Their capabilities and areas of specialty are listed on DIALOG "Yellowsheets.") So if you are on DIALOG and you see a bibliographical citation of interest, it is an easy matter to key in a command telling the doc del service of your choice to send you a copy of the article.

A matter of choice

Choosing the right document delivery service is one of the skills you will develop as a practicing information broker. In virtually every case, you will have to make a decision regarding the doc del house you wish to use. If you have found a citation in a database that provides its *own* document delivery service, then it is often most cost-effective and expedient to take advantage of that fact and order your documents from them.

A top-of-the-head list of database producers who provide doc del services includes ISI (Sci Search and Social Science Search), Engineering Societies Library, Chemical Abstracts, Predicasts, ABI/INFORM, and Compendex. As you would expect, one of the features that makes using an IP's own doc del service attractive is speed. The information provider almost always has the actual documents (magazine articles, reports, etc.) on file. It does not have to go looking for them. For this reason, in-house doc del services can usually offer their doc del services at a relatively low price.

Full service document delivery firms

On the other hand, if you need something that is not referenced online or if the item is from a database that does not operate its own in-house doc del service, then you should order from a "full service" document delivery company. We've dealt with several such firms over the years, including Dynamic Information, Information Express, Infocus, the Information Store, Information on Demand, and Omnifacts. See your DIALOG Yellowsheets for details on contacting many of these firms.

A full service doc del firm will usually be able to obtain anything from anywhere, even if you can't provide them with the complete citation. They typically take longer to deliver the goods than a databases's in-house doc del service because, for the most part, they do not maintain their own document collections. Instead, they rely on their networks of "runners" stationed at or near major libraries.

The service will consult its records to determine which library has the originals of the documents you need. It will then issue an electronic work order to the runner who covers that library. The runner will locate and photocopy the document and either fax or FedEx it to the doc del service's home office. Depending on how you and the company have arranged things, the runner may simply send the item to you directly. Either way, there are all kinds of options, ranging from first class mail to fax to using an overnight delivery service like Federal Express.

Our point here is that mechanisms and organizations already exist within the information industry to locate, copy, and deliver virtually any document you may want. Some documents are easier to get than others. But just about everything cited, whether online or in print, is available as a photocopy of the original. Markups are added and fees are charged, of course.

Competition from the IPs

At IOD, Sue had her own network of library runners to provide document delivery services to clients. It was profitable. Generally there was a gross margin of around 60% on document delivery, compared to a gross margin of about 25% on research. However, you need considerable volume (15,000 requests per month or more) to make that kind of profit margin. There is always the chance that one especially difficult doc del assignment can significantly eat into the profit made on the easy ones. You may find yourself spending far more time on one of these tasks than you can possibly bill for.

It takes a lot of time to build an organization like the one Sue established at IOD, and it certainly isn't something a new information broker should attempt to do today. The market has changed, and, as noted, there is significant competition from the database producers themselves.

For example, ABI/INFORM and Predicasts, two leading databases offering informative abstracts of magazine and trade journals, offer document delivery. (Predicasts will fill requests, but it does not actively promote its doc del services, undoubtedly because it currently offers so much full-text information online.) They will supply a photocopy of any article they reference in their online databases. Their rates are very reasonable. ABI/INFORM charges $11.75 for any article and guarantees shipment within 24 hours if the order is in by 1:30 P.M. Eastern time. Rush service is an additional $5 per order and Federal Express shipment is an extra $5 per article.

There is also competition from small one- and two-person operations, many of which do not pay copyright clearance fees. We strongly advise you to avoid firms like this. After all, one of the benefits that a good doc del house provides, in addition to speed and cost-effectiveness, is freeing you from the liability and overhead associated with copyright issues.

If you are new to the field, you may not be aware of the fact that anyone who provides articles, book chapters, or any other copyrighted material may be required to pay a royalty fee. A doc del firm that does not pay royalties as required can be sued for damages and costs. And if you are a customer of that firm, you may be dragged into the suit as well.

The Copyright Clearance Center

To facilitate the granting of permissions and payment of fees, in 1977, in accordance with the expressed desire of Congress, an organization called the Copyright Clearance Center (CCC) was established. Corporations pay site licensing fees to the CCC to cover photocopies made and distributed internally. Document delivery services are required to pay a fee to the CCC for each document they photocopy. The CCC then passes the fee along to the appropriate publisher.

For example, Dynamic Information of Burlingame, California, (415) 259-5000, has some 26,000 journal titles in its collection, including all the magazines covered by Ziff-Davis's Information Access Company. It charges $10 to photocopy any article in that collection, up to 25 pages. Additional pages are 35 cents each. Copies from other sources start at $12.50 and range up to $25. In every case, the price includes first class postage and up to $4 in copyright clearance fees.

Thousands of publishers participate in the CCC, but every now and then Dynamic receives a request for a document whose publisher is not a CCC member. In those cases, Dynamic contacts the publisher and negotiates a permissions agreement. The phone calls and letters involved make this a labor-intensive process.

They'll give you the hard stuff

When Sue was running IOD in the 1980's, the competition in the document delivery end of the business wasn't nearly as intense. But as more and more database producers began to offer documents from their own collections at cut-rate prices, it became increasingly difficult to make any money offering doc del services.

"We began to get all the tough requests," Sue says. "The ones requiring us to contact the British Museum or some library in Russia. The clients would use the new document delivery services provided by Predicasts and ABI to handle the easy stuff and turn to us for the real toughies.

"The problem was that our rates were established on the assumption that we would get *all* of a client's doc del business. The money we made on the easy ones would offset the money we lost on the really hard ones."

Today, in Sue's opinion, it is very difficult to make money offering document delivery unless you happen to own a "captive collection." Some information specialty firms are in this position, and, of course, many databases are. But for the aspiring information broker, document delivery is not a viable option.

Information Express

Bruce Antelman, founder of Information Express, (415) 494-8787, has come up with an imaginative solution. Bruce combines an in-house collection with a worldwide network of runners. This combination enable Information Express to provide quick service (24−28 hours via the core "captive" collection), and to respond to esoteric and unique requests for information available in only one or two libraries in the world.

The Rugge Group uses Information Express for almost all of its document delivery needs. Information Express charges from $6.85 to $15. The Rugge Group adds an appropriate markup and bills the client.

A convenience, not a money-maker

We should make clear that Sue doesn't view doc del as a profit center. "It's a convenience we offer clients, not something we push. Whether they take advantage of it or not usually depends on the client's access to collections of printed material or the client's familiarity with document delivery services."

If you are working for a corporate information center staffed by a full-time librarian, the chances are that he or she will know about the most economical document delivery services. If the client is not "information wise," if he or she does not have easy access to the doc del mechanisms of the industry, you might consider offering the service at a 50 to 100 percent markup.

The Rugge Group might charge $15 for a document delivered by Information Express at a cost of about $7. If the price of the document is higher, the Rugge Group might mark it up by a smaller percentage. A markup of $8 to $10 is hardly unreasonable considering the time, effort, and handling that goes into obtaining a document, even from a document delivery service. Remember, you are offering the client the convenience of "one-stop shopping." Most clients don't want to deal with the details. They just want "the facts."

If the client balks at the price you charge, fine. Let them get the document elsewhere or do without. Document delivery, in most cases, will not be your primary business.

Electronic clipping or alert services

The information industry is as bad as any other when it comes to jargon. For years, long before President Reagan proposed the Strategic Defense Initiative, the information industry has offered "SDI," or "selective dissemination of information." As noted at the beginning of this chapter, "SDI" is rapidly being replaced with the much more descriptive term of "Electronic Clipping Service" or "Alert Service."

Call it what you will, the concept is not difficult to understand. Suppose you conduct a search on a DIALOG database to find information on, say, the most effective colors to use in packaging a snack food. You do the search today, capture all the information it produces, and prepare a final report. But two weeks from now the database is updated to incorporate citations of articles published in the last 14 days.

For a small fee, you can store your search strategy on DIALOG. Then, when the database is updated in two weeks, DIALOG's computers will *automatically* run that search strategy against the new information. Any hits will be automatically transmitted to your DIALOG electronic mailbox. So when you sign on two weeks from now, you will have a "letter" containing the latest hits generated by your search strategy in your mailbox. DIALOG will also let you store a search strategy and run it yourself at a time of your choosing.

You capture this new information, clean it up as need be with your word processor, and send it to the client along with a bill. That is what an Alert Service or "current awareness" service is all about. It is easy to do, as long as you are certain that your search strategy is the right one to use.

Every online system does things a bit differently, but all major online systems offer some version of an Alert Service. DIALOG calls its version DIALOG Alert. Fees vary with the database but typically range from $4 to about $12 per update and include all charges for the first 25 records. Additional hits are printed at the normal per-record display price.

To calculate your monthly Alert Service expense, multiply the per-update charge by the number of times the database is updated during a month (daily, weekly, monthly, etc.). Updating schedules and Alert fees for each database are given in the DIALOG price list.

Add a comfortable markup

An Alert Service depends on computer technology, and it thus has a "sexy" feeling to it. You can make much of this in selling a "current awareness" service to a client. Figure your costs beforehand, and add a comfortable markup. If you have to pay DIALOG $12 a month, plan on charging your client at least $75 a month for the first 25 records, plus your cost on any records above 25.

Remember, you'll have to pay connect time charges for using DIALOG's electronic mail system to download the hits. You'll have to spend time word processing out all the elements in a record likely to confuse a non-searcher (accession number, keyword descriptors, etc.). Then you'll have to print it out, package it up, and mail it to the client. It's not all gravy, in other words. A lot of processing and handling is involved.

Like document delivery, an Alert Service is not something to build your business on. But it is an easy "add-on" service, and that's how we suggest you sell it. Wait until you have done a search your client is happy with—that way you'll know your search strategy is producing the desired results—then suggest a current awareness service using the same strategy. At the Rugge Group, the cover letter that accompanies most reports to clients notes that the search strategy has been saved (offline), and "if you feel updated information would be useful to you on a regular basis, we can provide it for $X a month or $Y a quarter. Just let us know."

You probably won't get rich on Alert Service income. But offering this kind of service has the extra advantage of helping to keep your name before the client's eyes. Someone who is getting a report from your office every week or every month is much more likely to remember your firm when the next search question comes up.

Conclusion

There are all *kinds* of things an information broker can offer a client. The field is so wide open that we would hesitate to set any limits. But the three conventional services most information brokers offer are information gathering, document delivery, and current awareness or Alert Services. Regardless of where your future takes you, this is an excellent triumvirate to start with.

In the next chapter, we will show you how to create the basic materials you need to project a suitable image so you can sell this triumvirate of services. Then we'll look at how to sell and how to market your services (two different activities entirely!).

16

Projecting an
image of credibility

IN CHAPTER 17 WE'RE GOING TO FOCUS ON THE THINGS YOU CAN AND SHOULD
do to market yourself and sell your services. But before we can get to that point,
you've got to prepare your business materials. You've got to have stationery, business cards, and a brochure designed to sell your services. These components are
not to be taken lightly or treated casually, for they are your basic marketing tools.

Business cards

Like it or not, everyone who hopes to sell his or her personal skills to someone
else is *ipso facto* in the image-making business. The image happens to be one of
yourself and your business, and every piece of paper a client or a prospect
receives from you reinforces it. The image you want to project as an information
broker is, above all, one of *credibility*. When you hand your business card to
someone, you don't want the person looking at it and silently saying, "Hmm,
cheap. I wonder if this is really my sort of person?"

Nor do you want your card to communicate flashiness. Flashy people cannot
be relied upon to be discrete. And discretion and confidentiality are *crucial* in
your relationship with a client.

Your business card should therefore be cleanly designed, quiet, and of the
best quality. If the traditional white card with black lettering is too boring for you,
consider a different colored stock and/or a different ink color. But keep it quiet
and avoid the temptation to get cute.

Stationery

The same thing goes for your stationery. It should be 24 pound, 25 percent cotton bond. This is the kind of paper that carries a water mark (visible when you hold it up to the light).

Paper "poundage," incidentally, refers to the number of pounds registered by a stack of 500 sheets of the 17 × 22" master stock from which letter sheets are cut. The conventional range is 9 to 28 pounds.

Photocopy paper, by comparison, is usually 16 or 20 pound paper, really too flimsy for your professional letterhead.

Good paper costs more, to be sure. But nothing else communicates the same look and feel of quality. It says you care about how clients and prospects perceive you and that you take pride in anything that bears your name.

You will have to decide what information to provide on a business card and letterhead in addition to your name, address, and voice phone number. It is a good idea to use the nine-digit ZIP code for your address since it really will speed up your mail delivery. Call your local post office for details.

A fax number, if you have a facsimile machine, is good to include. In fact, in today's fax-happy world, a fax number is a virtual necessity. You may also want to include your electronic mail addresses. MCI Mail, CompuServe, and DialMail (if you are an active DIALOG or Knowledge Index user) are good choices. Don't include addresses for systems you do not check regularly.

Describing your business

You should also include a line on your business card and letterhead describing your business. There are no hard and fast rules here. When Alfred was more heavily involved in freelance corporate communications and copywriting, he used the simple term "Wordsmithing." This was a deliberate—and effective—attempt to avoid being pigeonholed as someone who specializes in a particular kind of writing.

On her stationery, Sue includes the line "The Rugge Group" followed by the line "Information Specialists and Consultants." Given the breadth of services you may perform, there is no reason to be more specific than that in most cases. In our opinion, the one term you should not use is "information broker." Yes, that's what we all call ourselves. But your prospects won't know what it means, and you risk embarrassment trying to explain it. "I see," your prospect will say, "but what do you 'broker'?"

Hiring a professional designer

One thing you may want to strongly consider when producing your letterhead and business card is hiring a professional designer. This doesn't have to be expensive, particularly if you are not asking for a special logo or other custom device.

Tell the designer that you want your letterhead and business cards to match (same color paper, same color ink, same typestyle, etc.). This again presents a uniform, professional image. You will also want to consider carrying the same design elements through to your brochure. Indeed, we suggest you use the design on *everything*.

As for quantity, if you are just starting out, go with the print shop's minimum. That's likely to be 500 sheets (one ream), and you may want to get 1000 matching Number 10 business envelopes as well. (You will find yourself using your envelopes for everything.) Of course there's a tradeoff here. The larger the quantity, the lower the price. Sue uses about 1000 letterhead sheets and about 2500 envelopes a year. But then, she is well established in the business.

In any case, whether you buy your own paper and take it to the print shop or use the stock it offers, don't forget to get a ream of matching blank paper to use as second sheets. Note that many printers offer package deals that give you letterhead, envelopes, and business cards at a reduced price. So be sure to ask.

Other printed pieces

There is absolutely nothing wrong with using your letterhead as your invoice form. Simply key in the date and the client's address, just as if you were sending a letter. Then draw a solid line several lines below the inside address. Allow a few more blank lines, and type in your billing information (item descriptions, amounts, total due, etc.) just as you would on an invoice form.

Paper for client reports

However, there *are* a number of additional printed pieces to consider, though none of them are crucial. You might consider ordering a ream or two of good grade copier paper printed with a discrete header or footer that displays your address and phone on a single line. Use a colored ink, but don't make the type too large. If you use this special paper for your client reports, you will subtly remind the client on each page that you and your firm are the ones who tracked down and delivered the information.

Of course, there is nothing wrong with using plain copier paper for client reports. If money is tight, you may wish to do so. As an inexpensive compromise, see if your word processing program can supply appropriate headers or footers for each page in a smaller type size than your regular text.

Note and memo paper

Note or memo pages bearing your letterhead design are also a possibility. The printer will create these by cutting an 8.5 × 11" page in half to make 5.5 × 8" sheets. These are ideal for brief notes to clients while you are working on a project for them. Whether typewritten or handwritten, a little three-sentence note looks much better on a note or memo sheet than swimming around on a piece of full-sized letterhead.

Report envelopes and labels

Large, letter-size envelopes are another possibility. The standard size is 9 × 12", though we strongly recommend you consider a size of 10 × 13" to give yourself a bit more room. Whenever possible, you should avoid folding a client report, so you will be sending reports in 10 × 13" envelopes. The slightly larger size will accommodate more pages, in case you have a really big report. And it is essential if you use any kind of report binder or cover.

You may be tempted to have these letter-size envelopes imprinted with your letterhead design as well. That's a nice look, but there's a better alternative. Consider using good looking pressure-sensitive address labels instead. This will give you the flexibility you need. You can use them to address boxes, book mailers, report envelopes, and anything else you send through the mail, except a conventional business letter.

Most print and copy shops offer three or four standard label designs, often in color. The problem is that everyone uses them. To rise above the ordinary, you might consider ordering special labels that use the same design and ink you selected for your stationery.

Do-it-yourself mailing labels

That's probably the ideal solution, and it certainly makes a wonderful presentation. But custom labels are expensive, and they may not be worth the extra cost. A client can be expected to file your cover letters. But the mailing label and the envelope to which it is attached is almost always thrown away.

Often a simple typewritten label will do. But, thanks to the Avery company, an excellent compromise is available. Avery offers a low-cost program called LabelPro that makes it incredibly simple to produce professional-looking labels. (There is a version for IBMs and for Macs.) The program comes with a nice selection of business-related clip art that you may want to incorporate in your label design.

The IBM version will also accept graphics files created by PC Paintbrush or other programs capable of producing a .PCX file. (We have not checked the Mac version, but it is certain to have a comparable capability.) This means that you can scan your letterhead design into the computer and use the resulting file as the basis of your label design. In fact, since copy and print shops have become so computerized in recent years, your printer may even be able to supply the letterhead design as a file. It certainly doesn't hurt to ask.

The only catch to using LabelPro is that the program is designed to use Avery's line of laser printer label sheets. (But then, at this writing, few other companies are producing laser labels.) As noted, versions of LabelPro are available for IBM and Macs and for laser and dot-matrix printers. The list price is $100. For more information, contact

Avery Dennison
Avery Commercial Products Division
818 Oak Park Rd.
Covina, CA 91724-3624
(800) 541-5507
(818) 915-3851

The laser printer alternative

Just as a modem will turn your personal computer into an information machine, a laser printer will turn it into a typesetter. Laser printers typically start at around $850. But their output is so good and the machines are so versatile (and quiet!) that they are almost as essential as fax machines in today's business world.

We will discuss laser printers in more detail when we look at how to equip an office later in this book. What you need to know here is that, if you have to, you can use your laser printer to produce your own letterhead and pressure-sensitive address labels on an as-needed basis. The ideal program to use is a desktop publishing package like Ventura or PageMaker, but you may be able to get by with one of the many "paint" programs (PC Paintbrush, Corel Draw, etc.) since most offer several typestyles or fonts.

Use this approach if you have to keep costs to the bare minimum. But be aware of the hidden costs. No truly powerful desktop publishing (DTP) program is easy to use. So, unless you are an experienced DTP user, you may spend a lot of time preparing your letterhead. And, regardless of how skilled you are, in all likelihood, you will be limited to using black as your ink color. In our opinion, this is not a place to try to save money. Let the pros handle your letterhead design.

Designing your brochure

Finally, you will need a capabilities brochure. A few large information specialty firms produce saddle-stitched booklets on glossy paper with photos. Yours does not have to be anywhere near this elaborately done. Some people use a legal-size sheet of card stock printed on both sides and folded into thirds, so it fits neatly in a Number 10 business envelope. That gives you six narrow "pages" to work with. This is a standard offering at most print and copy shops.

Actually, even that may be more than you need, particularly when you are just starting out. Alfred, for example, uses his letterhead second sheets to list books, articles, and industrial and educational films written, advertising and marketing campaigns designed and executed, and so on. But the pages are laser-printer-typeset, and they are stapled into a heavy-stock report cover.

The easy way to customize your brochure

Sue uses the same technique—letter-sized pages typeset with a laser printer to have a professional look and feel. But she varies the pages depending on the client or the prospect. If you are sending material to someone you have already spoken with, this is really the ideal way to do things. On the other hand, a brochure designed for direct mail—unsolicited by the client—will look quite different. We should note that we definitely do not recommend the direct mail approach. It is far better to establish yourself with a client by phone and then send a more meaty package. That way the prospective client is ready to receive your information and will pay much more attention to it.

If the client knows virtually nothing about information resources and information brokers, one can include sample pages of database output in the brochure to help bring the person up to speed. If the client is more knowledgeable, there is no need to include those pages.

The same thing applies to the pages you include listing your past clients and accomplishments. If you feel that the prospect you are trying to sell is likely to have a special interest in, say, competitive business intelligence, you can include pages that describe your previous work in that area. If you feel the person is more likely to be interested in scientific topics, you can substitute pages detailing your work in science-related areas instead.

Clearly, there are no hard and fast rules about the contents of a brochure, though we offer some strong suggestions below. If you are just starting out, you won't have any previous work to highlight or any past clients to call on for favorable recommendations. But you can produce a list of typical projects. You might say, for example, "Here are examples of the kinds of projects we can execute for you:" and follow with a bulleted list of the kinds of questions you might expect to be asked to explore.

Even if you lack past experience, there may be other achievements you can cite: articles published, awards earned, areas of special expertise, etc. You might include reprints of magazine articles about the crucial role of information and/or information brokering. And, if you happen to have written articles yourself, by all means include reprints of them.

Use your imagination. There really are no rules. However, we strongly suggest that you avoid presenting yourself as a one-person operation. You want your clients to think of you as a *business*, not as a single individual. Therefore, *do not* include a *resume*! If your current resume contains important pieces of information, find a way to work them into the brochure. But do not present the information as a conventional resume.

Above all, remember that your brochure is a *sales* document. That fact should be your guiding principle. This means you must put yourself in your prospect's shoes and try to create a brochure that will convince the person that you are the one to call to discuss his or her information needs. You're smart. You're professional. You have the knowledge and skills to do the job. You are . . . *credible*.

The cover letter

For both Alfred and Sue, as for you, a cover letter on letterhead bond is an essential part of the brochure package. The cover letter should never be more than a single page. And since much of it is likely to be *boilerplate* (material that will appear in every letter) it can be produced rather quickly. Create a master copy and just make a duplicate of it under a different filename each time you need to prepare a letter. Customize the duplicate as necessary for the particular prospect.

You should start by saying "Enclosed is the material you requested," or words to that effect. This serves as a subtle reminder to the recipient that the material is not unsolicited junk mail but information that he or she has asked you to send. Make that point right up front so the recipient does not inadvertently assume that this is yet another mailing destined for the "circular file" of the wastebasket.

Then move on to some sales copy about your firm and what you can do for a client. Close with the friendly statement that you will call the client in a week to answer any questions he or she may have or to further explore how you may be of use to them. For an example of the cover letter prepared by Sue Rugge for The Rugge Group, please see Fig. 16-1.

Later, when you have had time to develop a track record, you may wish to use a folder of the sort that opens to reveal two pockets. Your capabilities brochure could go in one pocket. The other pocket could contain reprints of magazine articles you have written for trade journals (more on this later) or even a sample client report or two. (You must have each client's permission for this.) Be sure to paper clip your business card to one of the interior pockets and add a cover letter.

Shown here is a copy of the kind of cover letter you may wish to create to accompany your sales and capabilities brochure. The text shown here is adapted from a letter used by The Rugge Group. This is the firm's basic letter. When contacting attorneys, private investigators, or other potential clients in special areas, a more focused letter is used. (The types of samples and lists of satisfied clients also vary with the type of letter and potential client.)

Notice how the first paragraph tells the reader what the package contains. The following paragraphs sound a sales theme, highlighting the benefits The Rugge Group can offer.

The letter ends with a paragraph promising to call next week to see if there are any questions. You can adjust this to the situation, but in general, you should plan to call the prospect within about ten days.

Please remember that as with brochures, there are no hard and fast rules regarding cover letters. You can assume, however, that even if the prospect does not read all of the materials in your brochure, he or she will almost certainly read the cover letter. So make the most of this opportunity.

*(The Rugge Group
letterhead logo, address,
and phone number.)*

(date)

Dear -------:

Thank you for your interest in The Rugge Group. We are a coalition of highly experienced, internationally based, information industry specialists. We offer expertise ranging from market research--both primary and secondary--to online and manual information gathering in a wide variety of fields. A list of typical projects and a short description of the capabilities of some of our members is included.

The "average" cost of an online bibliographic search is $450 to $650. We search the online electronic databases appropriate to your subject. (We access over 600 individual databases.) We provide the results in paper or electronic form. The product may be the full text of the pertinent articles, or it may be a reference to where the articles were published and an abstract of their contents. Results can be in your hands within 24 to 48 hours. Same day rush service is also available.

While online searching is a powerful tool, many market research and other types of investigative projects require manual work, including in-depth interviews. Our staff is particularly skilled in the art of extracting

Fig. 16-1. A sample cover letter

Fig. 16-1. Continued.

information from people over the telephone. We formulate the approach for your approval. Then we interview the pertinent competitors, experts, trade association officials, trade journal editors, or people at government agencies. Their opinions and our conclusions are presented to you in narrative form. Budgets for these projects vary widely, but we always work within a prearranged figure. Samples are available on request.

I'll plan to call you next week to explore further how The Rugge Group might be of use to you. In the meantime, if you have any questions concerning our capabilities or would like a quote on an upcoming project, please feel free to give us a call. I look forward to working with you.

Sincerely,

Sue Rugge
Principal

(The bottom line of letterhead includes Rugge Group fax number and electronic mail addresses on MCI, CompuServe, DialMail, and ION.)

Production values

As with your stationery and business cards, production values are important. You want everything you send out to add to your credibility. But as long as your brochure is cleanly designed and produced, it does not have to be elaborate.

Once those conditions are met, the most important thing is what you choose to say in the brochure. Don't tell your audience what you do. Don't say "We search this and that database, and we have document delivery from these 10 libraries."

Your prospects don't care. What they want to know is how you're going to save them time and money.

Benefits, not features

Follow the tried and true principle of selling the *benefits*, not the features. Mention the features, but take the next step for the reader and explain what the features mean to them. Explain the benefits.

Here's a familiar example of a feature: This car gets 35 miles to the gallon on the highway.

And here are some of the benefits: That means you'll save money, particularly on long trips. In fact, on a 100-mile trip, you'll save $X compared to what you'd spend driving your current car. And you'll be able to go longer between fill-ups. Think how much time that will save you.

Examples are the key

One way to make the benefits of what you offer instantly clear is with examples. Examples are crucial. You can explain until doomsday what you do, and then if you say "I did this for so-and-so . . .," something clicks in your prospect's mind.

All of a sudden, *they* begin coming up with the benefits hiring you could provide.

We should add that you will need permission from the client before using his or her name. Never, ever link a client's name with a particular subject without asking permission. That's part of the confidentiality you offer.

On the other hand, it is usually okay to include a list of clients you have served. But under no circumstances can you include a list of satisfied clients without the permission of each and every one of those clients. Information is a sensitive issue, and some clients would just as soon others not know what they are interested in knowing.

Be careful!

The Rugge Group uses client testimonials about the quality and timeliness of its service, without mentioning the actual topic. But large companies usually have policies against endorsing a specific firm. You might find that a large company will let you say "We did thus and so for a major adhesives company in Minneapolis," but not let you say "We did this for 3M."

The bigger the company, the less likely they are to allow you to use their name. In doing her brochure, Sue will call the people she knows well there and say, "We're putting a brochure together. Would you be willing to contribute any of the comments you've made to me over the years. . ." Sometimes they'll say "Sure, tell me what you want me to say." Sometimes they will not be able to give their permission.

We cannot emphasize this enough. Information and information retrieval are *sensitive*. Sometimes, to a client's competitors, even the fact that the company has hired you can be of interest, even if they don't know what you did for the firm. It is imperative to ask before using any client's name in any way in your brochure or sales literature.

Creating a track record

As a brand new information broker, you won't have a track record to cite. So what do you do? Use your imagination. That sounds like a cop-out on our part, but we're serious. Think about the industries and professions you plan to focus your sales effort on. What kinds of questions would they ask? If you don't know the industry very well at first, consult its trade journals and associations.

Use your information retrieval skills to find out about your target industries/professions. What are the hot issues? What's everyone talking about? What kinds of questions might you be able to help them with? Create a few good questions, then research them as if each were an assignment from a client. Keep track of your time and expenses, then figure out what you would have charged each imaginary client.

Now you have a track record. You cannot say you have worked for numerous Fortune 500 companies. But you can say, "In the past we have completed the following research projects," and then list them and the price you "charged." Or you can say, "These are the types of questions we can help you with."

Making it real

One word of warning: Don't try to fake it by not actually doing the research. If a prospective client asks you to name the company you did a certain project for, you must decline in any case since all such names are confidential. But if the client says, "You know, your project on current market trends in the super-premium ice cream market—the one you did for $500—sounds interesting. We have a similar problem here. How did you approach that one?", you had better be prepared to give a credible answer. The only way to do that is to have actually done the search.

You might also consider assembling a few testimonials. Again, you can't fake this, but you can fudge it a bit. You would be amazed, for example, at how many of the blurbs you read on book jackets just happen to come from authors whose books are distributed by the same publisher. You might offer to do a project for a friend, for example, and then ask for a testimonial. Prospective clients won't know that it came from a friend. Testimonials always have more impact if they can be attributed to specific people at specific firms. But if you cannot get permission to do this, you can say "a leading law firm," "a top advertising agency," or whatever other location is accurate and appropriate.

How to get sample brochures

To get ideas for your brochure's layout and contents, you might consider contacting established information brokers and requesting their literature. The source to use for names and addresses is Helen Burwell's *Directory of Information Brokers* (See Appendix A).

As a professional courtesy, you should be up-front with your fellow practitioners. Tell them you are in the trade as well and are looking for additional resources to call on when you are overloaded or when you do not feel qualified to handle a particular subject. Ask them to send you their literature.

Use the information you receive as a guide in preparing your own brochure. Then file it carefully. You can never know when you may need to sub-contract work to one of the people you contact. It is a collegial profession, and not only will your paths cross in the future, the people you meet this way can be an excellent source of friendship and advice.

The question of rates

Should you quote your rates in a brochure? No, you shouldn't. An hourly rate means nothing to a prospect since he or she has no idea of what you can accomplish in an hour.

Instead, present a list of research project examples and the prices you charged. This will give your prospective client a much better idea of what to expect.

A client, once he or she is interested, immediately wants to know what a job is going to cost. But as we all know, every job is different. The only way to come up with an accurate quote is to meet or speak with the client to define the job.

Sue strongly recommends trying to quote by project, not by the hour. Yet, it's important to have some concept of pricing in the brochure because—surprising as it may be—most prospects think your services are more expensive than they really are. That's why a list of sample questions or research projects with a round dollar figure next to each one can be so effective.

Examples from The Rugge Group brochure include:

Determining whether a Hong Kong-based company has any U.S. corporate affiliations	$600
Locating the current address of a specific German physician	$ 75
Identifying an expert witness on pit bull attacks	$700
Researching the technology of electronic color printing	$425

Notice that there is no need to describe who the client was or what he or she received. List the question succinctly and tag it with the price for the information you found. This won't answer all of a prospect's questions about price. But it will certainly give a sense of what your services cost.

At the end of the list, be sure to include a line noting that prices will vary, depending on the scope of your project. Then, as Sue suggests, say something to the effect that "We always work within a not-to-exceed budget." After all, it is possible to do a quick survey of the floor-covering industry for $500 to $600, but it is equally possible to spend $5000 doing an in-depth study of the same field.

Everything depends on how far the client wants you to go. Because of this, it is also a good idea to include a line suggesting that the client give you a call to discuss his or her needs. Then note that you will be happy to give them a free quote after the initial reference interview.

Follow-up phone calls

Finally, always make it as easy as possible for a prospect to communicate with you. Include your address, phone, fax, and electronic mail addresses in the brochure and make sure they are easy to find. Sue's brochures are not intended to be sent as part of a direct mail solicitation. They have always been designed as "tell-me-more" pieces, to be sent after the prospect has been contacted and expressed an interest in the company's services.

The brochure is something the prospect can file away for future reference. And, of course, it can serve as a talking point when you follow up with a phone call. Use your cover letter to tell the prospect that you will call them shortly. Generally, you should call prospects within ten days of the time the brochure arrived on their desks. Don't let the fire of interest you've kindled grow cold. Fan the flames.

Conclusion

One way or another, you've got to have some kind of brochure. It is true that much of your business will come via word of mouth. But whether someone calls you, or you contact someone on your own, you must have some literature you can send. You should not be making sales calls or doing any kind of promotion if you don't have something to respond with.

It doesn't have to be fancy: sample clients and projects, if you've got them; testimonials, if you've got them; and why it's more cost-effective to hire someone like yourself than to do it any other way. Emphasize that you have the expertise to provide thoroughness, and the cost-effectiveness and ability to respond immediately, with *complete confidentiality*.

In the next chapter we'll show you how to use your business materials to both market and sell your services. As you will see, there are all kinds of possibilities. Some of them are plain common sense, and some are limited only by your own creativity and imagination.

17

Marketing and sales
The missing ingredients

NOTHING HAPPENS IN ANY INDUSTRY WITHOUT SALES AND MARKETING. IT IS important to make this point because many prospective information brokers come from an academic or library background where *sales* is a dirty word. These institutions often vigorously engage in marketing and sales activities, but academics call it "development," "client education," or use some other euphemism.

Of course, it doesn't matter what you call it. The fact is that if you don't actively seek out people who are likely to buy your services, you will starve. The world will not automatically beat a path to your door, regardless of how skilled you are at the art of information retrieval.

"Why don't they call?"

There are hundreds of professional librarians out there with all the right degrees and outstanding search skills (both online and conventional), and many of them have told us they simply don't understand why more people don't request their services. These are good, caring, service-oriented men and women, card-carrying members of a helping profession, who happen to have the most important skills in the Information Age.

Yet many of them, at least those who serve in public libraries, spend their days answering the same questions over and over again. "Here, let me show you how to use the *Readers' Guide* . . . Have you checked *Standard & Poor's*? The card catalogue? I'll be happy to show you how it works." It's like forcing Michelangelo to spend his life painting wide-eyed children on cheap black velvet.

The missing ingredients are marketing and sales. "Sell, sell, sell," says Sue, who never leaves home—even to go to the grocery store—without a stack of Rugge Group business cards. "You never know when you will meet someone who may become a potential client."

You never know, so be prepared

Now, no one is suggesting that you buttonhole every fifth shopper and thrust your business card into his or her hands. Nothing of the sort. The point is that as an independent information broker, you and only you are responsible for bringing in the business. And information is such a broad area, that you *never* know when you will encounter someone who needs your services: in the checkout line, seated next to you on an airplane, train, or in a bus terminal, at a cocktail party, while you are on a trip, wherever you happen to be.

If you are an outgoing person who enjoys conversation with others, things will happen naturally. You don't want to press or ever force the issue. But it is always a good idea to ask them what they do for a living so you can get an idea of what they're interested in. That way, when they ask you what you do, you will know how to phrase your answer in a way they will find interesting.

If someone does indeed ask what you do for a living, and if they seem interested, it just makes good sense to be able to hand them a business card and suggest that they call the next time a question comes up. Better yet, ask for *their* business card so you can send them your brochure.

So few information professionals actively pursue marketing that it is no wonder so many of them fail when they try to go out on their own. Remember: You're not holding a gun to anybody's head and forcing them to buy shoddy, over-priced merchandise. You're in the business of helping people solve their information problems using skills and resources you have worked long and hard to acquire. Like any doctor, lawyer, or C.P.A., you deserve a fair price for what you offer.

If, after you have told someone what you do and what you can do for *them*, they don't want to buy, that's fine. But no one's going to know what you can do unless *you* tell them. That is the essence of marketing and sales.

There *is* a distinction between marketing and selling. Marketing generally includes all the things you do to make people aware of your business and the services you offer: market research, the packaging and design of the product, and sales. The coverage is broad. Sales activities, as one element in marketing, are more sharply focused.

Whenever you are contacting a specific person to personally explain what you can do for him or her, you are selling. In this chapter we will look at both activities. In the following chapter, we'll show you how to play some interesting variations on the sales and marketing theme.

Basic marketing activities

Before you do anything, stop and think for a moment about your overall goals. The purpose of all marketing activities is to make potential clients aware of your existence and of the kinds of benefits you can offer. The purpose of all sales activities is to persuade a single individual to agree to pay you money for providing them. As we said, marketing is broad, sales is specific.

We're going to assume that you've got your materials ready—your business cards, stationery, and brochure. These tools are essential. It is foolish to spend time and effort doing any marketing until you have them in place. Do you remember what we said about your materials projecting an image of credibility? Well, marketing covers the techniques you use to stimulate interest and make people ready to receive your image.

That's your goal—to stimulate interest, which you can then convert into a sales opportunity. So let's look at how you can accomplish it. Let's start with standard, conventional techniques.

Personal contacts

The first and most obvious place to start any marketing effort is with personal contacts. A personal contact is usually someone who already knows you, someone who knows the kind of person you are, the kind of work you do, and so on. Often a personal contact is also a personal friend, though that does not have to be the case.

Since every information broker comes to the profession from someplace else, it's a good bet that you have contacts in some other field, profession, or industry. Don't overlook this possibility. Make yourself sit down with a pad and pen and think about the people you've worked with, the people you know, or the people you know how to reach from your "previous life."

As we have been at pains to tell you throughout this book, one of the wonderful things about being an information consultant is that everyone in every line of work will eventually need your services. They may find a way to do without them, probably because they aren't even aware that people like you exist. But the need will definitely arise.

So. Start by contacting your contacts. Tell them what you're doing. Tell them you're going to send them your brochure and several business cards. And ask them if they know of anyone in the office, at the plant, in the industry who might be interested in what you are now in a position to offer.

This is an important technique. The term "networking" (of the non-electronic kind) has come into vogue in recent years. It is based on the certainty that everyone you know also knows people you don't know. But "networks" don't always drive themselves. Often you have to give things a gentle push. So ask: "Gee, Tony, that's great. I know you may not need me right now, but is there anyone else I might call? . . . Judy Johnson? Great idea. I don't think we've ever met. Mind if I use your name?"

What about direct mail?

The next step you might be tempted to consider, after personal contacts, is a massive direct mail campaign. In our experience, this kind of approach *does not work* for information services. But we would love to be proven wrong, and we believe you should leave no stone unturned. If you think you might have a workable approach, here are some of the things you should know.

There are a number of crucial elements to any direct mail campaign. First, you have got to develop a list of people to whom you can send your direct mail piece. The key thing about the list is that the people on it be likely prospects for the product or service you plan to offer.

Any number of companies have made a business out of assembling tightly focused lists. For example, if you manufacture life preservers, you would naturally be interested in everyone who had bought a boat in the last three months. That's the kind of information "list brokers" or "mailing list houses" collect and sell.

A costly numbers game

It sounds intriguing. Wouldn't it be great, for example, to be able to put your sales message on the desk of the managing partners at every law firm in your state? Just think of the business that would generate!

Well, think again. The problem with direct mail in general is the response rate. In most cases, a one to two percent response from a mailing is considered a big success. That's just responses of the "tell me more" variety, and it assumes you are selling a tangible, easily understood product or service (which you're not.) So to even have the hope of generating enough business to make the campaign worthwhile, a company must send out thousands of letters, probably at a cost of at least $1 apiece.

The short answer is that you can spend a lot of money marketing your information brokering firm through direct mail and have nothing—not one single inquiry—to show for it. In our opinion, information services simply cannot be sold in this way.

So forget about buying mailing lists. Concentrate instead on developing a highly focused, *personalized* campaign. Your goal should be to stimulate enough interest on the part of businesses and professionals in your local area to generate a few initial interviews. A small portion of those interviews will lead to assignments. Some will produce results later, as people return to their files and notice your brochure. And many will be like seeds sewn on fallow ground.

Personalized and highly focused

When we say personalized and highly focused, we mean exactly that. Identify specific individuals and prepare a cover letter aimed at each one. That may mean doing some research. What are the biggest law firms in town? The largest ad agencies? What kinds of information needs do each of these professions have? How might your skills be of value? How can you save them time and money or make their efforts more cost-effective? Who is the right person to contact at each firm on your list—the managing partner? The agency president or creative director?

Who should it go to?

Find the right individual—the person you feel is most likely to be in a position to hire you. Contact the person by phone. Then send a letter with your brochure.

Customize your letter to match the requirements of the kind of firm you will be contacting. You would not want to send the same letter to an ad agency that you sent to a law firm, for example. This is yet another example of why Sue advises all brokers to find a particular market niche. It is simply not efficient to try to market to several different industries at the same time.

Notice that we are not suggesting that you create a different letter for every specific firm. We are suggesting that you create a different letter customized to each different *profession* or business. Again, that's part of "personalization." It may be tempting to create a single, general sales letter. But a piece like that will never be as effective as one that speaks to the prospect in the language of his or her own industry or profession.

Get an appointment

Send the letter and brochure. Then follow up with a phone call a week later and try to get an appointment. Getting the appointment is your real goal. The letter and brochure are simply a means of achieving it.

We are emphasizing the goal of getting a personal appointment here because we believe it is important for all new information brokers to experience the face-to-face contact this involves. On a day-to-day basis, however, you will probably do most of your selling over the phone. Often, in-person sales calls simply cost too much time and money relative to the amount of money the prospect is likely to spend with you to make them economical. Notable exceptions include the opportunity to speak to the sales team, the monthly law partnership meeting, the advertising agency creative group, or any other "group" of potential clients.

First class mail

People open First Class mail. That's why so many firms strive so hard to make their Third Class "junk mail" look like First Class letters. They know that simply getting someone to open the envelope is half the battle. If the letter inside piques a prospect's interest after a quick scan, the person will return to the top of the page and read it with care.

So how do you pique someone's interest? You talk about something of interest to *them*. You give them something to chew on—not vague unsupported statements like "We can save you money." Make that statement, then follow up with several examples. Don't just state the feature. Help them *see* the benefit!

If someone wrote to you saying they could save you money, the first question to enter your mind would be: How? If the letter does not answer that question, if it doesn't put some substance behind this assertion, you will be disappointed. The letter writer will have raised your expectations only to let you down.

Let's look at a hypothetical example in Fig. 17-1.

Analyzing the letter

The letter in Fig. 17-1 is merely an example of the kind of thing you might consider. (Turn back to Fig. 16-1 in Chapter 16 for another example.) Your own letter

September 31, 1998

Ms. Anne Howe, Esq.
Dewey, Cheethem, and Howe
1234 Via Dargent, Suite 567
Monmouth Courthouse, NJ 08540

Dear Ms. Howe:

I'm contacting you today because I believe our firm, Questor, Inc., can save you money.

For example, while I'm sure you and your staff are quite skilled at using LEXIS or WestLaw, those skills may not extend to other online systems. As a result, you may be paying far more than necessary for the information you get from DIALOG, BRS, DataStar, and similar systems.

I believe that we may be able to cut those costs substantially, and possibly improve on both the quality and timeliness of the results as well. At Questor, Inc., we specialize in efficient, cost-effective searches of *all* the leading online information systems.

However, while it may be that an online database search will produce the most pertinent results, this is not always the case. It is essential to know when to go online and when to pick up the phone. And when you do pick up the phone, it is crucial to be able to conduct a skillful telephone interview. Otherwise, your call and your time is wasted.

That's why we at Questor Inc. stress our ability to consult *all* appropriate resources, whether they be online, by phone, or in print.

You'll find more details in the enclosed brochure, but the bottom line is this: We can probably save you thousands of dollars a year in online charges and other information gathering activities, while freeing your staff to spend their time doing what they do best.

Of course, there's no way to know for sure whether we can save you money, and if so, how much, until we compare notes. With that in mind, I'll plan to phone your office next week to see about setting up an appointment.

Thank you for your time and consideration. Please don't hesitate to call if you have any questions or if you have immediate needs.

    Sincerely,

    Joan R. Questor

Fig. 17-1. A personalized direct mail cover letter

may be longer or shorter, though you should try not to exceed a single page. Notice that the first sentence gets right to the heart of the matter. It instantly answers the prospect's question: "What is this package all about?" It's about how the firm Questor, Inc., can save you money. Notice too the use of the first person plural possessive. Call it "our firm," even if you are the only employee.

"Okay," the prospect says, "I'm always interested in cutting costs. And I see the person knows about LEXIS and WestLaw, so she must have had some experience with attorney information needs. I think I'll read on. How can this company save me money?''

The letter continues, anticipating the reader's questions every step of the way. It makes the point that Questor, Inc., offers specialized skills that enable it to provide the same information the attorney is currently getting at a potentially lower cost. Notice that—without promising anything definite—the benefits are made real by the phrase "thousands of dollars." The term "costs" is so vapid and indefinite. But everyone can identify with the image of "thousands of dollars."

A bit of guesswork

The phrase "freeing your staff to spend their time doing what they do best" is a guess born of putting yourself into the prospect's shoes. That's part of personalizing your approach. You may have no definite information that law office paralegals at this firm do online searching. The firm might not even have any paralegals. But it is a valid assumption since employing paralegals and having them conduct online searches (among many other things) is the kind of thing law offices do.

If this law firm matches that profile, you will have scored a bull's eye. What you're saying, in effect, is that paralegals and other law office staff don't have the training, experience, and skill to do the most cost-effective online searches. You do, however. So it simply makes sense for the firm to hire you to do what you do best and free the paralegals to do what they do best.

If the firm does not have a staff of paralegals who do online searching, there is no harm in guessing that it does. The reader of the letter in Fig. 17-1 will take it as a sign that you know a thing or two about how a law office works and that's all to the good.

Let the brochure do it

Notice, too, that the letter directs the reader's attention to the enclosed brochure for more information. Opinions vary on how much detail you should include in your cover letter. The answer probably depends on exactly what you are selling. But if you put yourself into your prospect's shoes, you will see that he or she would prefer a brief letter. Unless you've got some absolutely irresistible offer—like how to get free money—don't do your explaining in the cover letter. Concentrate on benefits, make your points cleanly, and get out.

As you are leaving, tell the prospect that you will plan to call the following week. Don't ask for permission. Simply say that you're going to do it. Then make good on your promise.

Remember that the whole purpose of this marketing exercise is to stimulate interest that you can convert into a sales opportunity. Your goal in preparing your letter and sending your brochure is to get into that office and have the opportunity to sell your services face-to-face or, failing that, over the phone. So the follow-up call to arrange an appointment is crucial.

Ideally, there should be a specific purpose to your call. In the sample case, the purpose is to set up an appointment that will let you compare notes on what the attorney is currently paying for non-LEXIS/WestLaw searches with what you can offer. You are offering the prospect a way to determine whether she is indeed paying too much for those searches, and you are doing so at no cost to her or her firm.

"What's in it for me?"

This is much stronger than saying you will call to see if the prospect has any questions. Or that you will call to arrange an appointment to discuss the prospect's information needs. Ugh! Put yourself in the prospect's shoes once again. Would you be enthusiastic about giving up half an hour or more of your day to let some salesperson come in and give you a sales pitch?

"What's in it for *me*?," you'd say. "Why should I give this person my time? Simply so she can make a sales call? Forget it! I've got better things to do."

In our opinion, a weak or vague closing like that is simple laziness. Take the time and make the effort to think of something you can offer. You have got to at least hold out the hope that meeting with you will lead to tangible benefits. The reason you come up with may very well be a smokescreen—for both of you. If you get an appointment, you may find that you spend no more than the first three minutes of a half-hour meeting on your ostensible reason for being there.

The prospect may have other, related concerns. There may be a hidden agenda. But you're there. Face-to-face, person-to-person. You're able to listen—really listen—to the prospect's desires and needs, and you are able to respond in a way that no brochure can ever respond. You are able to *sell* your services and—most importantly—*yourself*!

The follow-up phone call

And what about the dynamics of that follow-up phone call? It's a little scary, isn't it? Well, don't worry. You're not being pushy. If the individual does not want to talk to you, a secretary or receptionist will screen the call. You will be told the person is in a meeting or not in the office today or has read your materials and they are not of interest at the present time, thank you very much.

No harm done. No embarrassing confrontations. No reason, in most cases, not to call back again in a month or so. Sales and marketing are a normal part of business life. Everyone in every business or profession does it in one way or another. Attorneys can't afford to sit and wait for the business to walk in the door any more than you can. So your letters and follow-up phone calls are expected.

You can be personable, pleasant—and persistent—at the same time. Again, you're not selling second-rate merchandise at exorbitant prices. You've got something special to offer. Something that can be a major benefit to the prospect. If she isn't ready to receive it right now, fine. There are lots of other people you can call (and there are!). Sorry we couldn't get together this time, perhaps sometime in the future.

Confidence is the key

This leads to what is undoubtedly the most important aspect of sales and marketing: confidence. There are books and seminars galore about effective sales and selling technique. But the fundamental component in all of them is building up the confidence of the salesperson. That's not always an easy job. To be a confident salesperson, you've got to believe that the product or service you are selling is the best on the market.

As consumers, we all know that much of the time there's not a dime's worth of difference between many products. Understandably, perhaps, many of these "motivational" courses and books are really about the art of self-delusion. The hidden message is that it does not matter whether the product you are selling really is superior. All that matters is that you enthusiastically *believe* it is. Here's how to create that belief. Now go get 'em, tiger!

Happily, absolutely none of this applies to information professionals. Our services and our skills really *are* unique. With all due humility, there is probably no manager or professional on earth whom we couldn't help in some way. They may not be willing to pay for what we can deliver. They may not even be aware that they need our assistance. But that in no way changes the fact that what we offer has a genuine value. It is very much the real thing.

Stop erosion now!

The problem is that you are out there trying to make a living offering this genuine jewel, and no one is buying. Meantime, your rent or mortgage payment is due. The kids need new clothes for school. And your teenager has just wrecked the car. You're desperate. You can't figure out what you're doing wrong. Is it you? Is it your sales materials? Is there something you're missing?

Your confidence begins to erode. You no longer believe in yourself and what you're selling. And it shows. As a result, you sell even less. You become even more uncertain. Your business begins a downward spiral.

There's an old saying that banks are eager to lend you money only when it is clear that you don't really need it. If you need it, the coin purses snap shut. The same general principle applies to selling information services or any other product. If you feel desperate, your prospects will sense that fact, and you will get even less business. No one wants to hire a loser. If you're not confident in yourself, how can you expect a client to be confident in your ability to execute an assignment?

How we wish there were a mantra you could chant or a magic phrase you could utter to shield yourself from desperation like this. But, alas, none exists. Everyone encounters doubts and desperation. The difference is that if you work for a company, you can coast for a while until it passes. But if you are self-employed, it can affect your income.

Competence alone will suffice

On the positive side, after you have been in business for a while, after you have learned your craft, you will eventually reach a point where you are absolutely confident in your ability to make a living, doing something, regardless of what else happens. Remember: Regardless of the business you are in, you don't have to be good to make a living. All you have to be is *competent*. That alone will set you apart from the vast majority of people. It may not make you rich, but you will always eat.

The best practical advice we can offer to ensure that you will remain confident is to suggest that you not put all your eggs in the information broker basket to start. If you have some other source of income, failing to make a sale of your information services may be a disappointment, but it will never be a tragedy. You can say to yourself, "Sorry, Ms. Anne Howe, Esquire, you will never know what you're missing out on," and mean it. End of story. Next case.

Ideally, your other source of income should be something that permits you to be in your office during normal business hours. Your clients are businesspeople, and you must be available when they need you. That means at least between the hours of 9 A.M. and 5 P.M. weekdays. In other words, make information brokering your main "real" job and, if necessary, do something else to earn money after normal business hours.

Basic sales technique

Now let's turn to the sales side of things. Let's assume that your follow-up phone call has resulted in an appointment. To make the most of this opportunity, it may pay to do a little research. See if you can get up to speed on the industry jargon. Find out what are the most widely read journals and magazines, the industry and trade associations, and the leading companies and competitors.

You might check to see if the person you will be meeting has published any articles. If the company has been in the news recently—winning a major suit or landing a new account—that can also be of interest. Don't go overboard. Don't spend a lot of money. (You are perfectly free to use Knowledge Index for this kind of research.) But anything you can find out about the prospect and his or her company can be useful.

If nothing else, these little items are good fodder for smalltalk. And slipping into the conversation a few well chosen phrases based on this information will impress the individual with how interested you are in the firm and/or its problems. It will set you apart from all the other salespeople who pass through the office's doors.

The art of active listening

The key to success in any sales call is to *listen*. Offer your opinions and ideas as appropriate, but above all, listen to what the prospect is saying. What are her concerns? What is he really saying? Forget about your own agenda and about making a sale. What does the person really want?

Alfred has always said that "the hardest part about being a freelance writer is not the writing. It's finding out what the client really wants." Sue readily agrees. "Determining what the client is trying to accomplish," she says, "rather than what he or she thinks you can do is a major aspect of the sales effort."

Some clients will tell you in no uncertain terms. But many prospects have only the vaguest notions. Like all of us when we were infants, they know they want *something*. But they don't know what. They may have a rough idea of what it is. They may be certain what it is not. But they are powerless to express their desires in words.

As an information broker, you will certainly face this problem. But it will be complicated by the prospect's lack of knowledge about what can be done. As Sue says, "People will only ask for what they think is possible. It's up to you to expose them to resources they never knew existed."

That's why you should never take the person's initial request as a precise description of what they want. Always ask "What are you trying to accomplish?" That will open things up and get them thinking about their true goal, not about their assumptions regarding what you can and cannot do for them.

They've no idea what you can do

The best example is the one we told you about briefly in Chapter 2. A client once asked Sue to produce a list of magazines on solar energy. That's a clearly defined request, and it is easy to satisfy. A less experienced broker might have said, "Be happy to," and left it at that.

But Sue said, "Sure, we can do that for you. But I'm curious. Why would you want such a list?"

"So I will know where to look for articles on how to build a solar green-house," the client said. "I like to grow tomatoes, you see."

Sue smiled. "Well, you know, we could get you the actual articles if you want. That could save you a lot of time, and I doubt that it would be too expensive."

The client was simply amazed. "Do you mean all I have to do is say, 'I'm interested in subject XYZ,' and you can get me the latest articles on that topic? That's simply incredible."

It's always fun to be seen as a wizard or a miracle worker. But as simple as it is, this kind of situation comes up all the time. And if you don't handle it right, it can actually hurt your business. People will ask for only what *they* think you can do, when in reality they don't have the slightest idea of the power you can place at their disposal.

Somehow you've got to convey to the client that you are not being nosey and that their needs will be kept in the strictest confidence—but in order to be able to really help them, you need to understand their ultimate goal. That's why we recommend that you always ask, "What are you trying to accomplish?" or use words to that effect.

Sympathize and suggest

You must convince the client that you are there to help and that you have the power to be very helpful indeed. So listen to what they say. Suggest alternatives and possibilities and get their reaction. Then state what you think they want in your own words: "So, if I understand things correctly, what you want is a comprehensive report on everything that has been published in leading trade journals on . . . ." and so on.

We can offer endless scenarios, both hypothetical and drawn from real life. Ultimately, the only way to perfect this part of your skill repertoire is to practice. Get to your interview on time, but no more than about five minutes early (even if you have to drive around or sit in the car). Dress for the occasion. Bring any documents, reports, charts, or other materials that might help you make your case. Concentrate on projecting a professional, credible image.

Then have at it. Go into each interview with a song in your heart. Sure, that sounds hokey. What we mean is that you should approach each interview as if you were about to meet a witty, fascinating, comfortable person whom you just might be able to help with your skills and experience. If you can, great. If not, that's also fine. At the very least, you're going to have an enjoyable afternoon and will undoubtedly learn a great deal.

Human contact

Forget about selling. Forget about the bills at home. You're here to make contact with another human being, which is what life is really all about. Of course you'll talk business. It may be that you will be able to help the person you're meeting. If not, well, there's always the future. Truly, you never know when some contact you made a year ago will suddenly call with a major assignment.

That's the attitude you should take. We are not crazy about the phrase, "Have fun with it." As a denizen of the East Coast, Alfred, for one, feels it's "too California." But one must admit that it summarizes perfectly the way you should approach each and every sales call.

You will find that you get better and better with each interview. You will be able to anticipate the questions people will ask of you, and thus be well prepared to answer them. Strange as it may sound, your mouth will become comfortably familiar with the words and phrases you utter. With each interview you will refine your presentation and the words will flow with greater ease.

After the interview

It is wonderful if your sales call results in an assignment or in a request that you bid on a project. We'll cover what happens next in a later chapter. But if you don't walk away with an assignment, don't give up on the prospect.

Assuming you had a good meeting, write the individual a note thanking the person for the time spent with you. Say you're sorry that you could not get together this time, but that there is always the future.

You don't *have* to do this. And if you do, the elaborateness of your response may depend on how well you hit it off with the individual. The important thing is to keep in mind your goal.

You want to make yourself stand out from the crowd. You want to persuade the prospect that you are different. You are more than a name and address. You are a flesh-and-blood personality in the prospect's mind, with something valuable to offer. You also want to keep your name before the person's eyes.

If the prospect receives an initial letter and brochure from you one week, meets with you the following week, and gets a thank-you note from you the week after that, you will have made yourself a presence in his or her life for the better part of a month. You will have made an impression.

If the interview went well but no business resulted, you may want to keep an eye out for articles or information your prospect might be interested in. It probably will not pay you to seek out such articles. But if you happen to spot something in a magazine or online search, make a photocopy and send it with a brief note to your prospective client. Again, this is a personal touch that just happens to keep your name before the client.

Conclusion

Mining personal contacts, mounting a personalized, highly targeted direct mail campaign, making a sales call, keeping in touch on a regular basis—these are the major elements of a basic sales and marketing effort. You make contact, you explain your services and the benefits they can offer the prospect, and you get the job. If you don't get the job, and you feel the prospect is worth the effort, you keep in touch. When the next job comes up, you will be the first person to come to mind.

In the next chapter we're going to show you how to create variations on those themes. Once you have the basics firmly in hand, you can let your imagination run free into the realm of "power marketing."

18

Power marketing
tips and techniques

THE LAST CHAPTER OUTLINED THE BASIC ELEMENTS OF ANY SALES AND MARKETING program. These are making contact, explaining how the benefits you offer match the prospect's needs, and getting the job. You could describe such a program as: Make contact. Make a good impression (by establishing rapport). Then make the sale and make sure you stay in touch. Virtually every sales and marketing activity you can think of falls under one of those four headings.

These elements are not a secret. Everyone sends out brochures and letters. Everyone tries to get sales appointments. Everyone wants a prospect or client to remember them the next time a job comes up. And we mean *everyone* in nearly every industry.

But not everyone gets good results from a marketing campaign. There are lots of reasons for this. However, assuming you're a pleasant person who bathes regularly, assuming you're competent at what you do, the reason for less than stellar results may be that you are not using the techniques we call "power marketing." The difference between power marketing and ordinary, run-of-the mill marketing is the difference between a thin broth and a hearty stew. Let the others ladle the broth—you dish up a tasty ragout.

And how do you do that? With imagination. With creativity. With energy. It's not the ingredients. And it's not your advertising budget—everyone in this profession is basically in the same boat when it comes to marketing dollars. It's how you put the ingredients together, and the spices you add to make it interesting. It's also how much of yourself you put into the effort. If you're looking for a nice, comfortable, nine-to-five job that makes few demands, you don't belong in this profession!

Start by thinking abstractly. Don't think in terms of placing ads or sending out personalized mail pieces. Think instead of the four elements: Make contact, make a good impression, make the sale, and make sure you keep in touch. Write each one at the top of a page of paper, then find a quiet spot and *think*. Let your imagination run free. Don't stop any thought. There is plenty of time to edit your ideas later.

Thinking free: "Making contact"

For example, consider the element of making contact. Who do you think would be interested in your services? What kind of assignments and projects would you most like to have, and who can give them to you? Forget about what it would cost: How many different ways can you think of to reach these people? What's the wildest and craziest idea you can think of to make contact?

If you did not have a good imagination and if you were not blessed with a certain amount of creativity, you would not be an information broker. So put your innate talents to work for yourself. "Thinking free" or brainstorming is an exhilarating experience. Once you get started, you will find it difficult to stop.

Don't edit yourself. Don't worry about money or time or how outrageous an idea may be. You can never know when something that is clearly out of the question will suggest something else that is not only do-able but devastatingly effective. Have fun with it. (There's that phrase again.)

We will discuss the other three elements in a moment. For the sake of continuity, let's follow this one through. Let's assume that you've got a page or more of scribbled notes. (Use a tape recorder if your hand cannot keep up with your brain.) We'll assume that this list contains every technique you can think of for making contact with the people who are likely to need your services.

A cardinal rule or two

Now we can edit. We can temporarily rule out anything that costs money. That will still leave some very effective options. For example, one of Sue's cardinal rules for making contact is: Whenever possible, try to talk to more than one person at a time. Sending out brochures and cover letters can be expensive. And it can be time-consuming if you follow our advice to "personalize" each letter. But that doesn't mean that it is not necessary. It is.

Joining your local Chamber of Commerce, however, is cheap. Attending Chamber meetings, luncheons, and other functions puts you in touch with businesspeople and professionals.

Another of Sue's rules is to join organizations that put you in contact with your clients—not just your colleagues. Otherwise, you're preaching to the choir. For example, check to see if there are local chapters of the American Marketing Association, the American Chemical Society, or the American Management Association (AMA) in your area. If there are, join them! You may not be a marketer, a chemist, or a manager, but your potential clients are, so make it easy for them to get to know you.

In any organization, you get to know people and they get to know you. Your activities may not lead directly to a project, and it is bad form to make overt sales pitches at meetings. But contacts and friendships evolve naturally, and you never know when someone you met through the Chamber or an AMA meeting will put you in touch with a friend who wants to hire you.

Kiwanis, Rotary, and others

Similarly, it costs you nothing to speak before local organizations like Kiwanis, Rotary, Optimists, and other clubs. Church groups, adult education classes, the local "Y," professional associations, the list of organizations and groups needing luncheon or dinner speakers is nearly endless. And every one of them has a program chairman who is dying to hear from someone like yourself.

It is true that you can burn up a lot of time this way talking to people who are not in a position to hire you. So pick your groups carefully. Alfred once gave three talks in a single day at various branches of the New York Public library. The topic was online information and the idea was to promote a new book on the subject. Only a handful of people showed up at each location, and most of them were retirees with nothing else to do. Any who wanted the book would simply borrow it from the library.

It is difficult to hear a song in your heart when your voice is raw and you're trudging to the subway station in the pouring rain. (It is a well-documented fact that taxicabs in New York change into fire hydrants, street lamps, or otherwise disappear at the first few droplets of an oncoming storm.) But it was a very worthwhile experience.

Alfred didn't speak to a single person who had even the remotest intent of buying the book. But nothing teaches you how to explain a topic to a group of people like actually doing it. You may know exactly what it is you do for a living and the benefits you can offer. But have you ever stood up and tried to explain them?

Before opening on Broadway, many musicals and plays open first "out of town." Holding performances in Boston lets the production company work out the kinks and smooth over the rough spots before hitting the big time. That's what we suggest you do. Before volunteering to speak at the Chamber of Commerce, perfect your act by speaking at other groups. It doesn't matter that there may be no one in the audience who can buy your services. You're there for the practice, they're there to learn something.

THE SPEECH and how to use it

When you have quite literally gotten your act together, it's time to open on Broadway. Though you will never stop perfecting it, once you have given four or five talks about what you do, you will find that THE SPEECH has begun to emerge. You will know the points that should be covered, and you will have discovered the most effective language for doing so. You will have anecdotes, examples, possibly a laugh line or two, whatever.

Now you can use THE SPEECH as a real business development tool. Watch for conferences that come through your city. Renting exhibit space might be warranted if you have the money and the conference topic is particularly germane, especially if you have the opportunity to speak. Most conference organizers are happy to have someone else on their seminar/speech schedule. You might receive a very small honorarium, or they might pay your expenses. But don't count on it. Always remember that you are there for the audience of potential clients, not for the money.

Note that speaking at conferences involves a long lead time, six months at the very least. So check directories of conventions and exhibits and contact the organizers well in advance. There are several such directories, some organized geographically, some by topic. (See Appendix B.)

You might also ask the large hotels in your area for their convention schedules. Don't forget the convention and visitors bureaus, either.

Make the most of the opportunity

Now, here's a real insider's trick. If you do get the opportunity to speak at a convention or meeting of some sort, give serious consideration to signing up for an exhibit booth.

This reinforces your presence, and it gives potential clients an easy way to locate you. Stock the booth with plenty of copies of your brochure, business cards, and other relevant literature—and offer *free searches* to people who stop by.

Yes, that's what we said: free searches. DIALOG, Vu/Text, DataTimes, among others, will provide you with free passwords to demonstrate their services at conventions. Predicasts and Information Access Company will help you, too, even to the point of giving presentations to explain online business resources to your potential clients, free of charge. It goes without saying that you should find a way during your talk to let the audience know about the free searches available at your booth and invite them to stop by.

Declaring your topic

Whether someone asks you to speak or you ask them, you will have a great deal of control over the topic and title. So make it good. Organizations do not want to hear a librarian talking about how to use the library. Tell them instead that you'll be talking about new electronic ways to gather information, even if the techniques you plan to discuss are not all electronic.

The idea is to deliver enough information and examples to show your audience what's possible. If one or two of your examples has a little razzle-dazzle, so much the better. In effect, you want to say, "All *this* is available today in the Information Age." And you want your audience to be thinking, "Wow, there's so much. I'm really glad to know that these things exist. Probably I should hire this person to help me make the most of it."

Many times Sue has given a talk, returned to her office, and had a call from someone who was in the audience. "I really enjoyed your speech today at the meeting," he or she says. "It sounds like you might be the person who could help us with this problem." You can't count on results like that, and sometimes it takes months for an appearance to bear any fruit, if ever. But it happens too often to be accidental.

The basis of your talk will be THE SPEECH, but it is important to customize it with examples and databases that are relevant to your audience at the time. Try for five basic examples from the areas you know your audience is interested in. If possible, you might consider soliciting research questions before the meeting. Then pick one or two of them and incorporate them in your talk.

It is impossible to over-emphasize the importance of good examples. You can spend 15 minutes or more explaining the concept of online searching, and as soon as you say "For example, we were once asked to research the market for water-pumping windmills," they say, "Oh, do you do *that*?" It is as if a 1000-W light bulb went off in their heads. All of a sudden they understand.

Leave time for Q&A

Be sure to leave plenty of time for "Q&A" (questions and answers) at the end of your talk. A Q&A session lets you learn what people are interested in, something you can only guess at when preparing your speech. It can often provide your audience with more relevant information than your prepared remarks. For this reason, Sue typically leaves at least half of the allotted time for questions.

There's just one problem. Every audience is different, and some can be real duds. As Alfred says, "You have to try to sense the audience and adjust your presentation accordingly. Are they responding to what you are saying, or are they bored? If they are bored, and there is nothing you can think of to kindle their interest, then bring the speech in for a landing as soon as you can reasonably do so. Talk only long enough so that people don't feel cheated. Fifteen minutes is about right. Ask for questions, and if none are offered, smile, say your thank-yous, and get off the podium.

"On the other hand, if you look out on a sea of attentive faces, warm to your topic and let 'em have it. More than likely such an audience will produce a lively Q&A session that will probably extend beyond the time allotted for your speech, assuming there's no one else on the dais and no one else is scheduled to use the room.

"One other point. If at all possible, try to avoid getting scheduled either immediately before or immediately after lunch. Right before lunch, people are hungry and distracted. Right after lunch they're often sleepy."

Press releases

Now for some more power marketing. You've scheduled a speech called "Electronic Information: Productivity and Privacy" to be given at some fairly large convention that's coming to town. Don't stop there. What more can you do with what you've got?

You can send out press releases, for one thing. A press release has always got to have a "news peg" or other clear raison d'etre. Your scheduled speech is just the thing. Write the release as if you were a reporter. "The such-and-such organization announced today that Ms. Joan R. Questor will be speaking on the topic of electronic information at their upcoming convention to be held at the Hilton on June 6, 1992. According to Ms. Questor, 'Electronic information holds the greatest opportunity . . .'" and so on.

You may not be aware of it, but a great deal of the material you read in newspapers and magazines originated as a press release. Sometimes a release will be edited to fit, and sometimes it will even be rewritten. But Alfred and Sue have both sent out press releases that have been published *verbatim*.

Talk about free advertising!

You've got to write the release as a genuine news story. See your local paper and favorite magazines for examples. After a while you'll be able to spot a published press release a mile away. There is never any guarantee that a publication will pick up (print) your release. But sending out press releases is not very expensive. And sometimes a reporter will call you to do an interview as a result.

Master's tip: Use Business Wire and PR Newswire

Here's another hot insider's tip. The most productive and cost-effective way to send out a press release is via Business Wire and/or PR Newswire. You may be familiar with these two databases in their online form, but the databases are actually only a by-product of their real purpose. Their real purpose is to deliver press releases electronically to TV, radio, newspaper, and magazine newsrooms.

But you don't have to be a big company to put a release on the wire. For only $250, you can send a press release out to over 1000 newspapers and trade journals. Your release is sent electronically, which means that upon receipt, the editors can "clip" it out and "paste" it right into their publications. (No need for retyping.)

As a bonus, your press release becomes part of the Business Wire or PR Newswire database. That means that it will appear again and again whenever anyone searches those databases for terms like "information broker." Sue uses Business Wire regularly to promote her seminars.

For more information and current prices and conditions, contact:

Business Wire
44 Montgomery St., Suite 2185
San Francisco, CA 94104
(415) 986-4422

PR Newswire National Press Communications Service
150 East 58th St.
New York, NY 10155
(800) 832-5522
(212) 832-9400

Television talk shows

Television talk shows? Surely you jest. Who's going to want me to appear on television to talk about "electronic information?"

You'd be surprised. One of the things that separates a power marketer from everyone else is an appreciation of the need for free editorial material. (The media considers anything that is not paid or public service advertising "editorial," not just the opinion pieces from an editor or station manager.) The purpose of editorial material is to attract an audience so the advertisers who pay the bills can get a crack at them. This is as true for magazines and print publications as it is for television shows and radio programs.

Without good, interesting editorial matter, there is nothing to attract readers/viewers/listeners. So the need is *constant*. As a power marketer, your job is to figure out what you can offer that would be of interest to one of these audiences.

There is a long tradition of interviewing authors with a new book to promote. Alfred has done countless radio interviews, either by phone or in person, and made one or two local television appearances, for example, all of them pegged to the publication of a new book. It is always amazing how enthusiastic and helpful most interviewers are.

Sue has done many interviews as well, with similar results. The media, in short, is eager to help you tell your story because it helps them fill the time or the space between ads and it does not cost them a cent. Never think it is a waste of time to talk to a writer or reporter. Many times Sue has been featured in a story because she spent an hour or more educating the writer. While other people were willing to give the person only five or ten minutes of their time.

You can't be too overt. You can't make a straight sales pitch. But the mere fact that you are there—a member of the Rugge Group or the author of a recently released book—talking about a subject makes the point.

There is only one rule: Whatever you say, you've got to be *interesting*. Your assignment is to hold the audience between ads. If you are boring or self-serving or if your appearance begins to sound like a sales pitch, you will not be asked back. As when preparing a talk before the Association of American Widget Manufacturers, take the time to put yourself in the shoes of your audience. Think of one or two interesting examples you can use before you go on the air. Or before the newspaper reporter calls to interview you. If you can, try to think in "sound bites"—short, catchy ways to express what you do.

Columns, articles, and trade journal pieces

So far we've talked about press releases, talk shows, and the like in connection with the promotion of a specific speech you have lined up at a convention. Obviously, all of these power marketing techniques are available to you at any time, for any purpose.

Sometimes even something as mundane as your getting a subscription to another online system could be sufficient cause for a press release:

FOR IMMEDIATE RELEASE

Questor Search Service Offers Exciting New Feature

Search broker Joan R. Questor has announced that starting immediately her firm, Questor Search Service, will be offering information from NEXIS, a major full-text database operated by Mead Data Central. In making the announcement, Ms. Questor said, "With the addition of NEXIS to our lineup of databases, we are now in a position to provide complete transcripts of the McNeil-Lehrer Newshour, the BBC World Service, and..."

The media won't know that all you did was open a NEXIS account and maybe took a little training. This is one time when the general lack of knowledge of the online world can work in your favor. If you make it sound like a big deal, and if you include several on-target examples, there's a good chance that the media will pick it up.

More free publicity

There are many other opportunities to trade a little time and effort for free publicity. Without wishing to seem cynical, all of them are based on the unending need for free or low-cost editorial material. For example, have you considered asking a newspaper if you might do a column in which you would answer one or two questions each week? Readers would send you their questions. You would make a selection and do the search, then publish the results.

If you get paid for this, it will be only a token amount. Perhaps $50. But since you are providing editorial copy in effect for free, make sure that the paper publishes your name, address, and business phone number at the bottom of the column: "Joan R. Questor is a professional information broker. She can be reached at . . ." You might consider a similar idea for a local radio program.

Trade magazines are another easy mark. Trade magazines have titles like *Ad Week*, *Progressive Grocer*, and *Plunge: The Monthly Magazine of Holistic Plumbers*, and they are unabashedly in the business of promoting products of interest to members of a given profession or "trade." To speak crudely, they are basically advertising rags with a desperate need for editorial copy. Many trade magazines will print *anything* you send them.

Why? Because U.S. Postal regulations state that in order to qualify for Third Class mail status, a publication must maintain a certain ratio of ads to editorial. Alfred once did a regular column for a very fat computer magazine. When he asked the editor how long the columns should be, he was told, "As long as you can make them." The postal regulations were the reason why.

Trade journal articles

A trade journal article can be simply a written variation of THE SPEECH. It is in your own best interests to do a good job. Take the time to customize the opening and the examples so that both speak to the needs of the trade journal reader. But treat the piece as an extended, very subtle ad for you and your services. Also, ask if the magazine would like a photograph and see if you can have the piece copyrighted in your name, not that of the publication. (That way you can reuse it at will.)

You might also consider magazines and newsletters published by associations. As we said in a previous chapter, there is an association for nearly everything. Almost all associations publish some kind of magazine or newsletter, if only to help members feel they are really getting something for the dues they pay. These, too, are hungry for copy. Which, thanks to your computer and word processing program, you can er, uh, "assemble" with relative ease.

How to place an article

If you have never had contact with an editor, you may be reluctant to tap into the goldmine of free publicity that is waiting for you. Don't be. Editors put their pants or pantyhose on one leg at a time, just like you. Most of them genuinely need what you can offer. If they reject your proposal, under no circumstances should you take it personally. Like you, editors have deadlines, commitments, and priorities.

When soliciting an editor he doesn't know, Alfred likes to send a query letter. The letter outlines the proposed piece, cites the reasons why readers would be interested, and generally does a written sales job. Typically, Alfred will follow up with a phone call about a week later.

Sue favors a more direct approach. She'll pick up the phone and call an editor at the drop of a hat. More than likely, she will talk about electronic access to information sources in the publication's subject area. The word *electronic* is still a hot-button. Use it to the fullest, even though we all know that there is much more to information retrieval than going online. There are so many specialized databases that it is relatively easy to find one or more dedicated to the editor's topic.

As Sue says, "I'm not often paid for a trade journal article. The editor usually says, 'If you'd like to get it into the next issue, we need it by such and such a date.' But they usually don't say they won't publish it. It's been my experience that trade journals are pretty hungry for material. But it's not a way to make a living."

Information industry journals like *Online*, *Database*, and *Information Today* are welcome exceptions. They do indeed pay for material. In any case, once you have published something, use it in your brochure. Many magazines will be able to sell you impressive-looking reprints at a reasonable cost. These are almost always preferable to your own laser printout, particularly if they include your photograph. There is nothing like a published article or two to help boost your credibility in the eyes of most clients.

Speaking at company staff meetings

There are many other opportunities to tell your story. One of them is the company staff meeting. You will need to contact someone within the company, of course. When you do, say, "If your company doesn't have any internal information-gathering facility, I can explain the resources that are available." It's always better to present it generically. Talk about the whole industry rather than just your own company and what it offers. Try to position what you propose to do as educational.

And whom should you try to contact to set up such an appearance? It depends, unfortunately. Often information is a stepchild to the rest of the company. Sometimes you have a president who is really information-oriented. Sometimes the president is someone who has come up the financial ladder, and he doesn't care about research. The Director of Research, the Chief Scientist, and the VP of Marketing are probably the three titles you should shoot for.

If you are good on the phone, simply give the individual a call. Or send a letter and follow up with a phone call. As Sue says, "I like to get through to the person, and then say, 'I'll send you some information,' because then they're ready to look at it. If you can't get through on the phone, send a letter, if you think the firm is a good prospect or if you know it does not already have an internal information center."

The local chapter directory of the Special Libraries Association (SLA) will often be able to tell you if a firm has some kind of information gathering facility. The SLA is an organization of about 13,000 corporate librarians. You can join different divisions, like Business or Federal special libraries.

The SLA can be a valuable resource. As Sue says, "The Rugge Group has many special librarians as clients. They're very familiar with the needs of their companies, and they make wonderful clients because we can communicate in a common language. That's a luxury not available with most clients.

"If a company has an information center staffed by a special librarian, that's where you go. You do not try to contact management directly. These folks have a hard enough time selling themselves within their own companies due to the general lack of understanding of information resources. The last thing they need is some outside information broker complicating the process. Fortunately, there are times when, working with a company's special librarian, we can help."

Some local public libraries carry the newsletters of companies in their area, which might be a good way of getting insight into a firm's operations. And a lot of libraries clip newspaper articles. But it may be easiest to call the company and ask, "Do you have a library or information center?"

The best thing is to go after smaller companies that are less likely to have such facilities. Companies with 50 to 100 employees, for example, are usually good candidates. You can get that kind of information about companies in your area from the local Chamber of Commerce, or a Dun's directory, or trade directories.

Advertising

Advertising falls under the heading of "making contact," so let's spend just a moment on that subject as well. In general, advertising does not work for information brokers. Often it is simply a waste of money. If you were selling shock absorbers, kitchen appliances, or lawn care services, things would be different. There is a very large market for such items and services and the entire population fully understands what the product is and does.

Not so with information services. This is a one-on-one, person-to-person sale. It will never be a mass-market item. The best we can all hope for is that our profession eventually achieves the same status and recognition accorded attorneys and accountants. But that day is likely to be a long time coming.

There is at least one exception, however. If you plan to offer a specific database specialty to a client group whose members know what you are talking about, an ad may be effective. The best example we can offer is an ad in a local or state Bar Association publication promoting your ability to search LEXIS or WestLaw. Every litigator and almost every attorney today will know precisely what you mean.

Yellow Pages listings

Still, advertising may be thrust upon you. If you opt to have business phone and business listing (which Sue strongly recommends), you may find that your phone company will give you a listing in the Yellow Pages free of charge. So what classification do you choose?

A few Yellow Page directories have begun to introduce an "information broker" category. In fact the profession recently got its own S.I.C. code. But you have to be careful with Yellow Pages listings. If you specify "Information Bureaus" you may find yourself in with the Polish Tourist Society or the Gray Panthers.

The Rugge Group is listed under "Market Research," a category more people are familiar with. It is always useful to have a line in such a listing to inform potential customers that you do "secondary research." That way they will know you do not offer primary research services like interviewing passersby at shopping malls.

The Rugge Group can also be found under "Information Retrieval and Research Services" and under "Legal Research." In these listings it can be a good idea to indicate that you do database searching or to indicate your particular specialty or emphasis. That way you will not have to spend time dealing with calls from people who don't really know what you do.

Incidentally, there's a book called *Marketing Without Advertising*—$14.95 from Nolo Press—that offers an excellent treatment of this subject. Please see Appendix A for details.

Creating "credentials"

There are many other ways of "making contact," of course. And we hope we have stimulated your thinking in that direction. Not all of them are equally effective in bringing in new business. You will certainly have to decide which are worth your while.

Appearing on a television talk show may not generate a single sale, but it confers a certain status. Just as our parents' generation believed that anything they saw in print must be true, our generation accepts without question the idea that if you appear on television you must be an authority, a pundit, an expert, or otherwise know what you're talking about. As an independent information broker, you can use "credentials" like these to your benefit. So even if the appearance took a day of your time and produced no inquiries or sales, it can still be worthwhile.

Making a good impression

Now let's turn to "making a good impression," the second step in any marketing campaign. What we mean here is paying close, personal attention to your prospective client. Information services are the antithesis of soap, cottage cheese, potato chips, or any other mass-marketed product. If someone is going to buy from you (give you an assignment or project), they are going to do so on the basis of whether they like you, whether they feel that you can do the job, and whether you demonstrate that you are truly interested in *their* problems.

So once an initial contact has led to an inquiry and appointment, consider the ways you can demonstrate your "worthiness" for the job. Go to the library and ask to see clipping files of local newspapers. Then look for references to your target company. Who are its competitors? What trade associations and/or trade publications would they be interested in monitoring? What are the key buzz words and special terms in the industry?

InvesText, //TRACK, and other sources

You might do the research necessary to be able to say, "These three companies seem to be your biggest competitors. We can follow them for you, and give you a list of everything that's been written about them every month for $X."

As you may know, there's a service on Dow Jones called //TRACK that lets you tell a client that "for $75 I can provide the following type of company profile for you on a continuing basis." Your expenses are set, and the client knows that it's going to cost him the same thing every time.

These are simply examples, talking points, items you can bring up during your discussion. They offer tangible information. Your knowledge of their industry is very important in establishing your credibility. That is why it is so important to find a niche and zero in on a couple of industries. It is simply impossible to be an expert in everything or to be all things to all prospective clients.

Of course, you must be careful not to get carried away. There is a wonderful database called InvesText that carries company- and industry-specific reports prepared by many of the leading investment banking firms. But it is expensive to use. There are also patent databases that can be used to discover the patents that have recently been granted to a firm's competitors. But at $300 an hour or more, they are among the most expensive of all databases.

As Sue says, "I might have an example of an InvesText printout and possibly a patent search (depending on the type of company) to show. But I definitely would not run an individual search for a prospective client. There's no point in giving away the information you hope to get paid to deliver."

The most important thing is to tell them what you can do for them. Don't tell them what you do. As we have said before, the mistake many brokers make is to say "We search this and this database, we have document delivery from these 10 libraries." You need to stress the benefits of saving them time and money. The more industry- or company-specific you can be, the better.

In person or on the phone

One key to making a good impression, is trying to put yourself into the prospect's shoes. This is true whether you are going to be appearing in person or plan to call the prospect on the phone. Personal appearances and sales calls can be time-expensive. You owe it to yourself and your business to make several face-to-face calls. These offer invaluable experience.

But at some point you may have to draw the line. A sales call that takes the better part of a day and holds only the possibility of one $500 assignment may not be worth your while. On the other hand, if you sense that there is more business to be had from this firm, you may well decide that making a personal call is worth the investment. Otherwise, try to make a good impression by phone.

Another key component of this step is what we said in the previous chapter: the fine art of listening. Try to "hear between the lines" what the prospect is really saying. Then put your brain, creativity, and imagination into gear to suggest alternatives, options, and possibilities.

Think of yourself as a consultant. By dint of your hard work, you have special knowledge about what can be found in the world of information. You know what's possible. The prospect does not. He or she is turning to you as an expert. So adopt that role. As we have said before, ask them what they are trying to accomplish, not what they want to know. It is your job to educate the prospect on what can be done. And it is crucial that you do so, since people will not ask for things they think are impossible to obtain.

A good and respected friend who spent his entire career as a salesperson, district manager, and sales executive put his finger on it. "Selling," he said as he lit his pipe, "is teaching. A librarian or a teacher is in the business of communicating information and ideas. They help students grasp a certain idea.

"A salesperson's job is no different. It's the same skill. You communicate information to a prospective client and help him see a particular idea. You help him see how your product or your service can solve a problem or fill a need."

Teachers, librarians, lecturers, and anyone else whose job it is to communicate information and ideas *already* have the skills needed to sell effectively. *Selling is teaching*. The chances are you have something else in your favor as well. The fact that you don't come from a "sales background" and are not considered to have a "sales personality" can be a real plus.

Prospective clients will not look at you and immediately say, "Ah, another saleswoman." Or "Will no one rid me of these troublesome salesmen?" Unlike the popular image of a salesman, your goal is not to make a quick hit and move on. You are interested in developing a long-term, service-oriented relationship. Your prospects will sense that.

No guarantees of success

For your part it is important to avoid any implications that you can somehow guarantee success. What you guarantee is to leave no stone unturned in your quest. Remember, you are not selling the answer. You are selling your expertise and your knowledge of the most productive ways to obtain the information we *hope* exists. In order to protect yourself, say that "the project has been done to the best of our ability within your budget limitations." That's perfect, because there's no recourse; if they'd given you more money, you could have done more research.

At The Rugge Group, Sue always tells people that "We don't take on a job unless we feel confident that we have at least a 50-50 chance of finding the information you need." It is up to you as an information professional to refuse jobs that you don't feel you have a reasonable chance of completing successfully. After all, you want repeat business, and you want to get paid, neither of which is likely to take place if you aren't at least partially successful.

If Sue or her associates suggest that a particular question is not a good search candidate and the client insists they go ahead and try, then she'll be sure to get a written agreement or contract. According to Sue, "If we feel at the outset that the client is going to be unhappy, we'll push for a contract. The less knowledgeable the person is, the more trouble we're going to have with them. They assume the answer exists, and they expect miracles."

Make the sale

The hardest part of selling is making the sale. In one sense, everything we have talked about so far in this chapter is "selling." Making contact, doing your homework on a prospect, listening intently, offering alternatives and suggestions. But you'll never make a sale until you "ask for the order." The hardest part of selling, in other words, is asking for the order.

You've had a nice conversation with your prospect. You've explored many avenues together, and you yourself have developed a pretty good idea of what you can do for the person. A "project" has begun to take shape in your mind. Now it's time to ask for the order.

Some information brokers are uncomfortable with this, because making the request forces the prospect to make a decision. They are afraid that they will be seen as coming on too strong or being too aggressive. Or they are afraid that the answer will be "No," the pleasant atmosphere will evaporate, and they will be embarrassed. It would be so much nicer if the prospect would make the first move. If he or she would say, "Joan, we want to hire you to take care of this for us. How does $1500 sound to start?"

Sometimes a prospect will do exactly that. But what if she doesn't? What if he is a man of strong indecision? Then what? You could wait until a year from next Friday and never hear the magic words. You have got to force the issue. Gently, artfully, but firmly. By asking for the order in such a situation, you are actually doing the person a favor. Some people are psychologically unable to decide what they want to do until you give them a choice.

Making the first move

Even if your prospects don't have this problem, they may hold back and wait for you to make the first move. Again, put yourself in their shoes. You are not offering a tangible, nuts-and-bolts product that they can look at and evaluate. You are offering something intangible which, by its very nature, must be customized to their needs. It is *your* responsibility to make the project real before the prospect's eyes. It is *your* responsibility to put a price on it.

Forget everything you may have heard about those sleazy salesperson tricks. Tricks like asking for the order by saying, "Well, Mr. Smith this has been most informative. Did you want this widget in red or blue?" Or "When would be convenient for us to deliver the widget, Tuesday or Wednesday?" The idea behind these approaches is to control the prospect's choices. It is not a question of whether you want to buy a widget or not—your choices are red or blue, Tuesday or Wednesday.

The right way to do it

That is not the way for an information broker to ask for the order, even assuming that any of us could pull it off. The way you ask for the order is the same way you close a meeting. Meetings have a natural rhythm. They start with smalltalk as everyone gets comfortable. Participants then get down to business. At some point it becomes clear that all the major issues have been discussed and several possible plans of action have emerged. The meeting begins to wind down, and it is time for the leader to summarize what has been discussed and make clear everyone's assignments.

As an information broker, you ask for the order by summing up, by outlining the project that has developed in your mind as a result of the discussion, and by addressing the issues of deadlines and price.

For example:

> "Well, Ms. Smith, I think I understand what you need. You'd like us to help you identify your firm's top three competitors and, with your approval, check to see what patents they have applied for in the past year. Let me tell you what I think we can do for you.
>
> "We can start with a literature search and produce a report containing the competitor information, including a D&B search to give you their financials. Because patent searches can be so expensive, I think we should hold off on that part of the project for now. Let's see what develops in the initial phase.
>
> "We can do this part of the job for between $450 and $650, depending on how much information there is. In any case, we will not exceed $650 without your approval. You said you were in something of a hurry. Would next Tuesday be soon enough?
>
> "Good.
>
> "Because this is the first time we have worked with you, we require a deposit equal to 50 percent of the authorized budget. In this case,

that's $325. We can accept credit cards or checks. We will then bill you for the remainder after we are sure you are satisfied with our work.

"I'll fax you a letter of agreement today confirming these arrangements."

Now, was that so bad? Did you get any sense of high pressure sales tactics? Of course not. You're not trying to force anyone to buy something. But you are bringing matters into focus. You are taking positive action to sum up the meeting and guide things to a decision point. To put it another way, as a teacher you have planted an idea in the prospect's mind. Now, like any good teacher, you are motivating the person to do something with it.

A few points on finances

If a new client chooses to send or give you a check for the deposit and they are in a hurry, you can say that you will get started immediately. But make sure that they understand that you will need the deposit (the check) before releasing the results. This is really not a very good approach, and we do not recommend it if you can possibly avoid it.

First-time clients do not know what to expect. They can build up false hopes, be disappointed with the results, and refuse to pay. With a deposit, however, you have a much better chance of getting paid for the whole job. The deposit helps commit the client to the project.

When mentioning a credit card, you can say that you will use it as security (hold it hostage, in effect) and will bill the client for the full amount if they are reluctant to have you actually charge the card. If you take this approach, however, make sure that you check the authorization of the card to confirm that it is indeed "good" before you start work.

"Overcoming objections"

In the vocabulary of professional salespeople, the phrase "overcoming objections" is as common as the phrase "bibcite" or "full-text record" is in ours. It refers to how one deals with questions, roadblocks, and concerns prospects raised at any time during a sales interview. "Does this car have a guarantee?" "Gee, I didn't think this watch would cost so much." "Can I bring this program back if I don't like it?"

Sales courses suggest all kinds of ways to overcome objections, not all of them savory. Distract the prospect, mumble, say you don't know and immediately highlight some other feature. But that's claptrap.

You're a professional, not a street hawker or carnival barker. You don't *overcome* objections. You answer them in a straightforward, scrupulously honest fashion. People aren't fools. They know when you're trying to snow them. And they know that no product or service is absolutely perfect. To pretend otherwise, to have a slick comeback for every objection they may raise, is to insult their intelligence.

It is extremely important that the client understand what the "product" will look like. If they expect a full-blown report, complete with recommendations and detailed analysis, and you send them a bibliography, you are likely to have a hard time collecting the balance due on your bill. Make absolutely sure you both agree on the format of the information "product." If possible, show the client a sample of a similar past project so they will understand what they will be getting.

Don't cut your price

So what happens in the case above if you just get finished saying "do the job for between $400 and $600," and the prospect holds up his hand and says, "Whoa, hold on there. I was thinking more in terms of $100. . .$150, tops,"? Your smoothly flowing closing has been derailed. Now what?

If you are inexperienced or lack confidence in what you're offering, your first instinct will be to cut your price. The perspiration will break out on your brow and you'll go all cold in the pit of your stomach. You've just made a terrible mistake by asking for too much money. And look, the guy's ready to buy at $100. He said so himself. Maybe I *could* do it for that amount.

Forget it! If there was ever a time to get a grip on yourself, this is it. If you've done your homework, you know that the price you have quoted is fair. So stick to it for the work you have said you will do for that amount. If you cut your price now, the prospect will not respect you. You will also find that you have set a dangerous precedent for the future. More important, you will never be able to work for this person—or anyone else at his company—for the fees you need to survive. Word will spread that Joan Questor is good, but be sure to ask her to cut her price. Again we say, forget it! You don't want business like that.

Instead, do what Sue does—improvise by thinking on your seat. The guy's willing to spend up to $150? That is not enough to do anything you will be proud of. Sue, for one, does not accept jobs for less than $250 and even then only in special circumstances.

So counteroffer:

> "I'm afraid we can't afford to do what I've described for that amount. But I'll tell you what we *can* do for $300. We can identify your top three competitors and tell you what they have been up to for the past year. We would not be able to do any patent searching or Dun & Bradstreet reports, however."

If the prospect objects to your counteroffer of a reduced project at a lower price, it is time to start packing your briefcase and getting ready to leave. The person obviously is not going to buy from you.

Of course he may say, "Wait a minute. Hold on there. I think my boss might be very interested in the competitor information you could develop. And I'm sure that if I explained it to her, I could get authorization to spend up to—what was it?— $500?"

At that point, you smile and say, "Great. I really think you'll be pleased with what we can do for you." What you do *not* do is continue with the closing presentation mentioned earlier. There is no question now of offering to forego getting an initial half-payment before starting work. Now you say: "Our terms are half in advance and half on delivery of the material, so we'll need $250 before we can start work. When do you think you can get approval for the budget?''

By posing this last question about budget approval you are again "asking for the order." Or you might say, "How would you like to handle it?" Or, "Do you suppose I could pick up a check tomorrow?" There are many, many other things you could say as well. But notice that all of them ask the person to make a commitment.

Get a commitment

That's the key to making the sale. Make it easy for the prospect to make a commitment to you of some sort. It doesn't have to be a direct order for your services or a direct agreement on your fee. But it should leave no doubt in either of your minds of how things stand between you.

Our retired salesman friend says, "In my business, our rule was never to walk out of an office without a signed piece of paper. An order, a letter of intent, sometimes even a sales contract. I know your business is different. But I also know that if you leave with the prospect shaking your hand and saying he'll definitely call you next week, your chances of doing any business with him are less than 50 percent."

The thing to avoid is a sales interview that flaps to a close without any agreement on a definite course of future action. As we said, some prospects will take the initiative. But ultimately it is *your* responsibility to sum things up, make a proposal, and suggest what should happen after the meeting.

That's what "sales" is really all about. That's how you ask for the order. And don't forget: In most cases the prospect/client is already on your side. The individual would not have agreed to see you without being at least partially convinced that the two of you have something to offer each other.

Two final points

Two final points on sales. First, we have used a face-to-face meeting as our example. But everything we've said applies equally well if you are discussing the project with the prospect on the phone.

Second, we will look at how to price your services in greater detail later in the book. For now, it is important to be aware that pricing works both ways. We've discussed reducing the scope of a proposed project and offering to do it at a lower price.

But if you sense that your quote of "$400 to $600" is accepted without the bat of an eyelash, you might say, "Now, of course, that's for a basic search. If the budget allows, we could also do profiles of the three top executives at each competing firm and assemble all the press releases the company has issued in the last two years. Adding that to the basic search would bring the price to around $800."

Again, this is one of the few times where the fundamental characteristics of the information industry actually work to your advantage. We've said it before: One of the things that makes information services so hard to sell is that information is so nebulous. It is not cut-and-dried.

The good news is that because of this, there really is no limit on what you can offer a prospective client. You might do a $750 project on a given industry or market, for example. But you can always go deeper, go back further in time, check additional databases, search from a different angle. The result might be a study of the same industry or market that you can charge $10,000 for. Truly, information is endless.

As a consultant, you do not want to suggest information likely to be of little value to the client based on what you have learned from your sales interview. Your job is to suggest the *right* information for the problem at hand. But there are always grey areas, things that may not be wholly relevant to the problem but are nonetheless nice to know. If you sense that the prospect would be willing to pay for them, offer them as part of a higher priced "deluxe" package.

Keep in touch

Keeping in touch means keeping your name in front of the prospect's or the client's eyes. It's like a free "current awareness" service for the client or prospect regarding your firm. This is a smart thing to do, for at least two reasons. In the language of finance, you might call it "protecting your investment" and "leveraging your assets." Here's what we mean.

Not every sales encounter (phone or in-person) results in a sale. The parties may be willing, but the budget may be weak. Or there could be a dozen other reasons. The point is that every prospect you talk to represents an investment on your part. You've spent time and money making contact and making a good impression. The prospect knows who you are and what you do. That makes the person infinitely more valuable to you than prospects you have yet to meet.

Protect your investment in this person by making sure that he or she continues to remember you. It takes a large amount of effort to get a wheel to spin, but once it's spinning—once you have overcome its inertia—it only takes a little effort every now and then to keep it in motion. That's why you want to keep in touch with prospects who have yet to buy from you.

The best source of additional business

Once a prospect pays you money, he or she becomes a client. Clients are even more valuable. They are absolutely the A-Number-One best source for additional business. Not only do they know you, they know your work firsthand. You don't have to sell them on anything. The next time there is an information need, they will hire you as a matter of course.

Maybe. If they remember your name. If they think to call you instead of someone else. If they think about information services at all. Clients are like movie stars in this respect. Lot's of people know who *they* are, but they cannot be expected to remember everyone they have done business with. They need to be reminded.

You had to be there

Alfred once worked with a former vice president of Merrill Lynch who found the corporate environment too confining. He left the firm, with a fat, two-year consulting contract and scores of contacts and friends in the financial industry. For several years he and Alfred made a good living producing all manner of corporate communications pieces.

The only problem was that business rarely came in over the transom. Friends, contacts, and satisfied clients did not automatically call with new work. It used to drive the guy crazy. Whenever he would go into New York, he would invariably come back with multiple assignments. Forget about low hanging fruit, the stuff was lying on the ground waiting for someone to pick it up.

But you had to be there. No one, not even well-satisfied clients, was picking up the fruit and tossing it in the direction of Yardley, Pennsylvania. There was simply no way to get around the need to keep in touch. There was no way for this guy to avoid spending about one day a week going after new business in The City.

How to keep in touch

Keeping in touch is very much a part of power marketing. Where it differs from "making contact" activities is in the materials you use. You can only "keep in touch" with people you have already met, worked for, or otherwise dealt with. Thus you cannot send the same direct mail letter and brochure you would send to brand new prospects.

So what can you send? Should you make a personal phone call? Send flowers or salted nuts? This is a great topic for thinking free and brainstorming. So pull out the page headed "Keeping In Touch" and give it a go.

We have a few suggestions to get you started, of course. You might consider sending out a newsletter on a regular basis. The purpose of a newsletter is to keep your name in front of someone's eyes. So make it as self-serving as possible without allowing it to turn into a total advertising rag.

What topics can you cover in such a piece? Say you have a new doc del runner somewhere, new databases that have become available, what's going on, how to use your firm's services more effectively, the "five most important things to tell us when you're ordering documents." You might even include an "Employee of the Month" feature, though when Sue did this in her newsletter for IOD it got to be a jinx—invariably whoever was selected would quit or get fired the next month.

You might do things that focus on the people at your firm. As Sue says, "At IOD we would send a Christmas card with all of us on it, faces and names. Ninety-five percent of the clients never met us. They knew us only over the phone. But sometimes they talked to the same person every day, especially if it was a big doc del client."

Personal notes are also good, particularly if they are attached to some article or other piece of information you have found that is likely to be of interest to the client or prospect. The note doesn't have to be elaborate. And it doesn't have to be on your business stationery.

Alfred's business partner and spouse Emily discovered the ideal solution: imprinted Post-It notes. Ask at your local office supply store. You may find that for a small fee you can have your business name, address, and phone printed on Post-

It notes. You'll have enough room to jot something like, "Hi, Bill. Thought this article would be of interest to you. Hope everything turned out well on the Forbin Project. —Joan." There's no need to say any more, though you might consider clipping your business card to the article.

You are certain to come up with many "keep in touch" ideas of your own. It's definitely worth the time and effort since this is one of those details that make a difference.

How to get more business out of current clients

As we said a moment ago, it is much easier to get more business out of current clients than it is to get new clients. So as part of your keeping in touch activities, ask them if you can come and talk to their staff. They already know you and thus can be certain you're not just wasting their time. Maybe there's some new database or approach to a database that's come out that would be useful. Ask for 15 minutes to describe it to the staff.

If you know they're interested in Japanese technology and a new database just came up that translates all Japanese patents into English within three weeks, you can say, "Now there's a really quick, efficient way to get at this literature." The client may never have thought to ask you to do Japanese patent searching because it's in Japanese, and six months behind. Now that's changed, and you're there to pass on the good news.

You will also find that if you can get one person on your side in a company, they'll do a lot to spread the word about you and your services. You might say, "We've been able to do this for your company in marketing. You may not realize that there are technical resources that would be of interest to your research people. Is there anyone I could call about this?" Hopefully you get somebody fairly close to the top. You want someone who can tell his or her people to call you if they need help.

Discipline yourself to do it

The final ingredient in power marketing is discipline. You may have the best technique and the best materials in the world, but if you do not continue to market—day after day—it will all go for nought. If you stop marketing when you get business, you're going to be on a roller coaster of too-busy-to-market, then no work coming in, so you have to market to get some. Don't allow your newsletter to become aperiodic, for example. Make yourself keep it on a regular schedule.

It isn't easy. Most of us would far rather be online or throwing our minds against some fascinating problem than throwing ourselves into marketing. But it is essential.

For example, plan to spend one day a week or the first two hours of every day engaged in marketing activities. "I always like to do it in the morning," Sue says, "because I'm fresher and sharper. At IOD, I didn't start taking calls or listening to employee problems until 9:30 or 10:00. I'd get on the phone first thing. A couple of times I made calls from home to the East Coast before 8:00 California time, and just stay home until I'd finished them. When you send out a brochure, if you don't follow up within 10 days or so, you've lost the momentum.''

Here's an example of how a typical marketing conversation might go as Sue follows up on a brochure she sent the previous week:

Sue	Did you get our brochure?
Prospect	Yes, it looks very interesting.
Sue	Do you understand what we do?
Prospect	Something to do with information. I guess you can save me money.
Sue	We can save you money, and we can save you time. Time is money as well. What kind of topics have you been dealing with lately?
Prospect	Packaging, in grocery stores. We have a new product, and we want an attractive color scheme. Is there anything you can do to help us?
Sue	Would knowing what psychologists say about color be of interest to you?
Prospect	Sure, if there's some research that indicates how people react to certain colors.
Sue	That's something we can do. We can't tell you what we think is the best color for you, but we can get you what psychologists say about it, and we can also check the business literature to see if anyone's reported on what seems to have worked for them, and why they've changed from one to another, if they have.
Prospect	Well, how much would this cost me?
Sue	Usually we can do a bibliographic search, if we're just checking the published literature, for around $350.
Prospect	A bibliographic search?
Sue	That means giving you a list of articles and an abstract, which is a description of the article, for everything that's been published in the last couple of years. Probably you don't want to go back much further than that in this case, since the research might be changing a lot.
Prospect	Suppose I needed it two days from now. Is there any cost for rush service?
Sue	It depends on where you are. We might have to charge you for Federal Express, but we can normally get a bibliographic search out to you within three days. If you'd like us to go beyond that, to call some of the authors, check libraries and see if any more extensive studies have been done, dissertations and so on, it would probably take another three or four days.
Prospect	And you can also get the articles for me?
Sue	Yes. We think it's better if you look at the abstracts and pick the ones you want. But if you're on a tight deadline, we can look at them and pick, say, the five that seem to be most useful. But if you've got a little bit of time, we think you'll be more satisfied with the documents you get if you pick them out.
Prospect	It sounds reasonable. I think I'd like to take a chance on it. What do we do next?
Sue	Since you haven't used us before, we need a deposit equal to half the budget that you're authorizing. You can do it by credit card or send us a check.
Prospect	Since we're under time pressure, I'd like to do it by credit card. But our company doesn't issue them, and I don't want to put it on my own. Would a purchase order do?

The only time The Rugge Group accepts purchase orders (P.O.'s) is from really major companies. "If a company I've never heard of wants to give me a P.O.," Sue says, "I don't consider it worth the paper it's printed on. So I'd say,

'Because we're a small company, and we have out of pocket expenses like phone and computer time, we do need the money up front.' ''

Day in and day out

These are the kinds of calls you have to make day after day to keep an information business in the pink financially. You sit down at your desk and look through the letters you've sent out in the last week. It's just a stack in chronological order marked ''for follow-up,'' so you start with the oldest one first. You pick up the phone and call.

If the prospect says, ''We don't have any needs right now, but we're interested for sometime in the future,'' you put the letter into another folder with a Post-It note reminding you to follow up on June 1, or September 1 or whenever.

Keep those in chronological order, too. That way when the first day of a new month arrives, you can look through these long-range letters instead of the short-range weekly follow-up file. Keep notes on your calls. ''I make a phone call, and I make a note of when I talked to them,'' says Sue, ''Also what they said. Maybe they said 'We won't know until the beginning of the fiscal year, and that's September 1, but we're really interested.' Or they'll say 'Sometime in the next year,' so you put that one on the bottom. It's just common sense.''

When calling these long-range follow-up prospects, you say, ''You asked me to give you a call in three months. Is anything happening?'' Often the person you talk to really wants to hire you, but can't get the budget or permission from somebody else.

You don't want to keep calling somebody every couple of months if his or her answer the last time you talked to them was ''If I need it I'll call you.'' But you might call them six months later, and say ''I was going through my files the other day. Should I keep you on my list?''

Ask in a nice way, ''Is this ever going to be of interest to you?'' Most people in business are cognizant of other business people's time. They're not going to string you along if there's no interest. And if there is, maybe they'd like to be reminded every three months that you're still available.

When business was slow at IOD, Sue would sometimes suggest to the research staff that they think about who they hadn't talked to or done work for lately, and give them a call. ''It wasn't very organized,'' Sue says. ''But with all the new computer tickler files, it is now relatively easy to keep track of recent clients and instead of simply keeping in touch, call them and directly solicit new business.

''Never forget that your best clients are the people you've already done work for, because they're happy with you. For the most part they don't see your phone calls as a bother. In fact, in my experience, they genuinely appreciate that you're interested in them.''

Conclusion

The essence of power marketing is simply making that extra effort. Use your brain, use your creativity and imagination. *Think* about what you might do in the areas of making contact, making a good impression, making the sale, and making sure you keep in touch.

Power marketers are not passive. They don't simply hang out their shingle and wait for people to walk in the door. They don't necessarily do the conventional, expected thing. They *engage*.

Power marketing takes a lot of energy. You've got to be committed, and you've got to be disciplined. To ensure the health of your enterprise, you must market every day.

There are no guarantees of success. But we can guarantee one thing: There is a market out there for the services an information broker can offer. And it's growing. There is no reason why a share of that market shouldn't go to you—if you're willing to seize it. The power marketing techniques outlined here, augmented by your own creative ideas, will help you do just that.

19

Executing the project
Ten steps to follow

THERE'S A FAMOUS SCENE AT THE END OF THE 1972 MOVIE, *THE CANDIDATE,* in which Robert Redford, after fighting a campaign full of ideals and promise, unexpectedly wins the senate race in California. After the official announcement of his victory, after the smiles and the photo opportunities, Redford retires to a back room with his campaign manager. Then, as the camera moves in for a close-up, he turns to his campaign manager and says, "Now what?" Fade to black. Roll closing credits.

Well, you've got the job. Your power marketing activities have paid off. The client has given you the go-ahead. You've got your first assignment. Maybe you have a milkshake or a white wine to celebrate the occasion before returning to your office.

Now what?

It's a scary moment. You may have done searches before in your former life. But now someone has said, "Yes. I believe in you. Find this information for me. As agreed, I will pay you $X." Now what do you do? Where do you start?

We can't give you exact instructions. Every job and every situation is different, after all. But we can help you come to grips with the process of executing an assignment, regardless of the subject matter or the sources you plan to plumb. And we can offer what we hope will be insightful tips to help you along the way.

The ten major components of any search assignment

The key to so many things in life is "divide and conquer," and search assignments are no different. For example, when you stop to think about it, a search assignment or project falls naturally into ten major phases. These are:

1. Confirmation of the assignment.
2. Think time and strategizing.
3. Assembling the tools and preparing for battle.
4. Making the first cut at the problem.
5. Following up on first-cut results.
6. Organizing and analyzing retrieved information.
7. Packaging and presenting your report.
8. Confirming client satisfaction.
9. Preparing and sending your invoice.
10. Following up if the invoice is not paid on time.

We'll cover the last two steps—preparing your invoice and making sure you get paid—in the next chapter. Here we'll discuss items 1-8. We will also offer some advice on nitty-gritty, but essential, details like search request sheets, search logs, and other prepared forms you will want to use to keep yourself organized.

Step 1: Confirmation of the assignment

We have spoken in previous chapters of the importance of "asking for the order." Confirming the assignment is the very next step. Once the client says "Yes, I'd like to have you do this for me," it is your responsibility to make sure that both you and the client clearly understand what you will do and deliver, and what the client will be charged.

This is in everyone's best interests, and it goes a long way toward preventing problems down the road. The last few sentences on the phone should be a summary of the "order":

Okay, my understanding is that you would like us to do ..., and get the results to you by 10:30 tomorrow morning. You'll pay the Federal Express charges, and we will be sure not to exceed your budget of $500. As we discussed, because of the time constraints, we're limited in what we can do, but we'll do everything possible, starting with the approach we think is going to produce the most results.

The output will be a bibliography with abstracts and some full text.
Does that about cover it?

Notice four things here. First, the summary is followed by a direct question to the client. This gives the individual a chance to once again confirm the agreement and to interject any modifications or amplifications of his or her understanding.

Second, nothing is said here about doing a "complete" search or preparing a "complete" report or anything of the sort. You should take care to guard against using the word "complete" or "all" or any other similarly comprehensive adjective. These are such elastic terms, and you don't want to set yourself up for being liable for anything you may have left out.

Third, notice that the form of the output is clearly stated ("a bibliography and some full text"). You might instead say that "Because of your time constraints, we will only print full text," or whatever else applies to the situation. Make absolutely sure that the client knows what you plan to deliver. Make sure that the client is not expecting a narrative report when you intend to send a bibliography.

Fourth, as is obvious, there is nothing in writing. No contract. No letter of agreement. Sue notes that this was typical at IOD because many clients were in a hurry. They always wanted it yesterday. It is also typical in Alfred's experience as a freelance writer. An editor calls; the assignment is discussed and agreed to; and the paperwork follows later, often after the piece has been written and submitted.

Both Sue and Alfred agree, however, that if you have time to prepare a written proposal, bid, or letter of agreement, you should do so. We have not researched the legal fine points, but it seems safe to assume that in the event of a disagreement, a piece of paper setting forth what you will do and what the client agrees to pay will carry much more weight than the parties' recollections of a phone conversation. Though, if someone is going to cheat you, they're going to cheat you, written agreement or no, which is the best reason to exercise great care in choosing your clients.

Get it in writing, if possible

Nevertheless, if there is time to send a written proposal or letter of agreement, by all means do so. There is nothing to be gained in being specific about the actual databases you will search. Instead, say that you will cover the published literature on the topic, plus the publicly available information via appropriate government agencies, trade associations, trade journal editors, and experts in the field. That kind of statement offers sufficient detail.

Include sentences along the lines of: "The product will be a summary of our phone conversations, with a list of the sources we called, plus a bibliography and any key documents we find. As agreed, the cost will be $500, half payable in advance and the remainder on completion."

In other words, lay everything out clearly: the assignment, what you will do, what the client will receive, what the client will be billed, and so on. You don't have to write a legal contract, but it is in your best interests to cover all the bases and to strive to leave no grounds for misunderstanding.

The more you can cover yourself, the better. The problem is that clients tend to call at noon saying they need information at 8:00 A.M. tomorrow morning. Then you don't really have time to do a conventional letter of agreement. In most cases, you will have to rely on the good faith of the person who has hired you and upon your verbal agreement, though you might suggest that you fax the client a letter of agreement.

In any case, we can't emphasize the point enough: If you haven't done business with a client before, get a deposit! Have them FedEx you a check or take their personal credit card number before spending any of your own money.

This is simply the nature of the business. You must be prepared to work on a verbal understanding. That doesn't mean you have to accept everyone who calls with such a request. If it is an established client, someone for whom you have worked before, there's no problem. But if it is a brand new client, you may have to take a chance. You can turn away a lot of business if you don't have that flexibility.

When to steer clear

There is no cut-and-dried formula we can give you for deciding when to take a chance and when to politely disengage. When you are just starting out, you assume that everyone is as upright and honorable as you are. After you get burned a few times—and you *will* get burned—you develop a sixth sense for people who, no matter how good they sound on the phone, would have no compunctions about leaving you holding the bag (and the bills).

If someone like that calls, someone who somehow just doesn't give off the right vibrations, our advice is to steer clear. If for some reason you feel you have to take the job, at least get half the fee up front. Don't forget that Federal Express works in both directions—a client who is really interested in hiring you can FedEx a check to you immediately.

In situations like these, you are also within your rights to ask for credit references. Never forget that the client is asking you to spend your time and your money doing a search. When the bill from DIALOG arrives, it will not be addressed to the client—it will be addressed to *you*. So if you have any doubts, either "cut 'em loose" or get your money up front.

Step 2: Think time and strategizing

You're off the phone. The assignment has been confirmed, and you are ready to start work. Again, "Now what?" The first thing to do is to focus on the final product you plan to create and submit. If you have done your marketing correctly, you should have a pretty clear idea of what the client wants (and is willing to pay for). It will be several pages of bibliography listing all the material published on a particular topic over the last five years. It will be a handful of pages on which you summarize your phone conversations with several key sources. It may simply be a report of the steps you take to run down the required information and the results (in your own words) of each step.

Or it may be something else. The point here is to ask yourself from the beginning, "What kind of report will best satisfy the client's needs? What elements will it contain?" The outline may change and grow as you get deeper and deeper into the topic, but you will still be working toward assembling the elements needed to meet your overall goal.

Eventually, this will become second nature. As you are selling the job, you will know without thinking the shape the final report should take and the elements it will have to include.

Keeping track: The project folder

At this point, there are two main things you have to worry about. First, you have to worry about keeping your search results, strategy, and notes for a given search in the same place. Second, you have to worry about keeping track of your time and the expenses associated with a given project. Fortunately, there's a single answer to both questions: the lowly manila folder.

You may choose to do things differently, but one way or another, you will have to arrange to keep the materials associated with each project separate. We have always found that manila folders do the trick efficiently and inexpensively.

The search request form

When you are on the phone with the client or meeting face-to-face, you will undoubtedly be making notes on what the client wants and ideas that occur to you on databases to search or sources to call.

You should have a ''Search Request'' form that you automatically reach for whenever you are discussing an assignment with a client. (Please see both Fig. 19-1 and the disk accompanying this book.)

The form becomes your ''work ticket'' or control sheet. In addition to offering space for you to describe the search subject, it should remind you to ask for the client's address, phone number, fax number, the home phone number, a street address as well as a P.O. box so you can send things Federal Express or UPS. Certainly a ZIP code, the date the report is expected, the credit card number and expiration date if you are set up to accept credit cards, and the budget limit.

It should also have spaces for summarizing the costs you have incurred in doing the project and for the sources already checked by the client, if any, to avoid duplicating efforts. The idea is to create a single-page form that makes it easy for you to see all the relevant pieces of information about a project at a glance.

Project reference or search numbers

The search request form/control sheet is the first and most important piece of the many pieces of paper you will probably collect in the course of executing an assignment. To prepare a folder for a job, use a pen or Magic Marker to write a reference number or name on the folder's tab. One technique you might use is to simply write the name of the client or the company on the tab.

Or you might do what Sue Rugge and many other brokers do and simply give the search a project reference number. If you are in the month of May and the year is 1992, make the first four digits of the tab read ''9205.'' Then, if this is your first project in May of 1992, add ''01.'' If it is the second project, add ''02'' and so on. The last two digits refer to projects, not actual dates. The job numbers would then read: 9205-01 and 9205-02.

The type of folder you use is entirely up to you. You might choose ''third cut'' so that each folder has a tab measuring one third of the folder's length. Or you might use single cut, with tabs running the entire length of the folder.

Here is a sample search request form you can use as the basis of your project "work ticket." Please see the text for more information on "Proj. Ref. No." and "Phone Code." You will find a copy of this form on the accompanying disk. Use it as a starting point in creating a search request form/ work ticket for your own operation.

The Rugge Group
Search Request

Name:_____

Company Name:_____

Address:_____

_____

_____

Phone:(___)_____ FAX:_____

E-mail:_____ FedEx:_____

Proj. Ref. No.:_____
Phone Code:_____

Date Rec.:_____

Date Due:_____

Date Sent:_____

Researcher:_____
(date)

Researcher:_____
(date)

Budget:_____

Deposit:_____

Search Subject:

COSTS

Labor:_____

Online:_____

Postage:_____

Phone:_____

Photocopies:_____

Direct:_____

Other (specify):_____
_____

BILLING

Invoice No.:_____

Amount: $_____

Date:_____

Sources already utilized/to utilize:

Referred by:_____

Finder's Fee Y/N:_____ Amount: $_____

CLIENT COMMENTS:

Fig. 19-1. A sample search request form

Since you will probably want to recycle the folders, you may want to use Post-it Tape to cover the tab and then write on the tape. The nice thing about Post-it Tape is that it holds fast yet is easily removable. You will also find Post-it brand removable file folder labels at your office supply store. (The 3M product number is 7770-6.) These are sized for third cut folders.

Of course, you could also use paper clips and hand-written notes instead of folders. The point is not the mechanism but the results. You want to keep all the materials associated with a given project together.

The search log

At IOD, where many projects were being worked on at once, Sue found it imperative to maintain a search log. It is a practice she has carried over to The Rugge Group. A search log is simply a few sheets of paper designed to provide an instant summary of all current projects. (Please see Fig. 19-2 and the accompanying disk.)

It lists the date the assignment was agreed to, the name of the client, the subject, the due date, the person assigned to do the search, the search number, the date the invoice for the search was sent, and the phone code.

Using phone codes is a real master's tip. To keep track of phone expenses for project billing purposes, Sue uses MCI phone codes. For only $10 per month, you can easily assign a two to three digit code to each call that you make. It works like this: You dial the phone number you want to reach. Then you hear a special sound on the line. At that point, you key in the phone code assigned to a particular project. Your call is then connected as per usual.

The search log is a form designed to help you track the progress of your projects. It lets you know at a glance how all of your current projects stand--client name, due date, etc. And it tracks projects from inception ("Date Rec'd") through completion ("Invoiced Date"). Notice how the items on the search log correspond with those in the search request form.

There is no need to let your forms become overly complex. Indeed, we have typed in the information in the first line for clarity, but in actual practice, you will undoubtedly write them in by hand. See the accompanying disk for a copy of this form that you can customize for your own operation.

The Rugge Group Search Log

Date Rec'd	Client	Subject	Due Date	Searcher	Proj. Ref. Number	Invoiced Date	Phone Code
7/15/92	ABC Manuf.	Ultra Process	7/21/92	Jayson	9207-27	7/24/92	65

(etc.)

Fig. 19-2. A sample search log

The payoff comes when you get your bill, since all of your calls will be broken down by their codes. Needless to say, this makes things much easier than making a handwritten note of each call for each project. If you do not currently use MCI phone service, contact your current company to see if they have a similar program. You may find, for example, that Sprint offers a similar program.

You will undoubtedly want to customize The Rugge Group form to your own needs. (Just load the copy on the accompanying disk into your word processor.) Our point is that it is extremely helpful to have not only a control sheet for each job, but also a summary sheet or log. The log will make it easy to keep track of the work status as well as the invoiced status of all jobs, whether you are a one-person or multi-person operation.

Bill for think time

Okay, so you've got your initial notes filed in a folder with a date and project number or client's name on it. Now what? Now you start the clock. Now you take the time to think about the databases you want to search, if any. Now you haul down the online system manuals and catalogues, the databases thesauri, the DIALOG bluesheets, and whatever else you need.

You bring all of your search expertise and experience to bear to hammer out a search strategy. What will your first command be when you sign on to a system? What keywords will you use to conduct your search? Are you sure you know the proper commands to have your search results displayed? What command do you enter to get off the system when you are done?

If it is not to be an online search, whom do you think you should call? How will you get the proper phone numbers? What questions will you ask? How will you introduce yourself?

In essence, you need to create a plan of attack. You need the equivalent of a "business plan" for each search. What's the goal? How do you propose to achieve it? What will you do first, second, third, etc.? It is in the selection of search sources that an information broker's skills really begin to show. Phone work requires considerable artistry, but the actual retrieval from an online database can be equally sophisticated.

The point we want to emphasize here is that all of this time is *billable*. It is true that to an outside observer you may not appear to be really "working." You are not online or at the library. You are not on the phone. You may be taking a break to go to the kitchen and stir the soup or straighten up your office.

But your mind is running all the time. Though there may as yet be no tangible, overt results, you are doing the most difficult work of all—thinking and planning. And, friends, that is *work* in every sense of the word. The time you spend doing it is definitely billable, and you are foolish if you do not treat it as such.

Dealing with simultaneous projects

But what do you do if you find yourself working on several projects at the same time? You're hard at work figuring out how to approach an assignment when the phone rings. It's a new assignment. Or it's someone calling you back with information for a different project. Now you've got to switch gears and talk about that project. When you hang up the phone, your tendency is to forget to note that you'd spent 15 minutes thinking about the first project. Before long, your work day starts oozing through the cracks.

The only answer is to discipline yourself. You make your stopwatch your friend and get in the habit of keeping track of how you spend your time. Of course, you don't have to become fixated on it. Everybody ends up *estimating* time but the more accurate you can be, the better. You will find that you tend to undercut yourself rather than overestimate.

You'll say "I've been sitting here all afternoon, but I've probably just spent two hours on this project." When Pergamon bought IOD, the new management tried to get everyone to keep track in six-minute increments. Tenths of an hour, you know. It drove the research staff crazy. But 15-minute increments is a good target to shoot for. If you take a phone call related to a project, for example, mark down a 15-minute segment, because there are always going to be things you did that you didn't mark down for that project.

Billing time in this manner is nothing new. Attorneys have been doing it from the beginning of time. In fact, numerous time and billing software packages have been published to aid attorneys, accountants, and others in time-billable professions in keeping track of their billable minutes. One product you may want to consider is TimeSlips. Many information brokers swear by it. Versions are available for IBM-compatible and Mac machines. Contact:

Timeslips Cor.
239 Western Av.
Essex MA 01929
(508) 768-6100

Step 3: Assembling the tools and preparing for battle

The word *battle* may seem a bit too strong to describe this phase of the operation—until you actually complete a few projects. Finding information, whether online, on the phone, or at the library, really *is* a battle. You may be confronting what is essentially a force of nature, but it is a contest and struggle nonetheless.

If you expect that a project is a candidate for online searching—which you should know, or sense, off the top of your head—you start by choosing the databases, and checking the database catalogs for any you might not have thought of. We've mentioned printed database catalogues, but online versions are also available.

Never block an idea

But electronic databases are only the starting point. There are also trade associations, newsletters, newspapers, and other sources. All of which should go into your search preparation.

As you are thinking and preparing, you may also come up with ideas that are beyond the scope of the authorized budget. No matter—write them down. Never block or disregard an idea, no matter how off-the-wall it may seem at the time.

When you complete a project and are preparing a cover letter for your report, you may find it appropriate to say, "Additional avenues of inquiry include the following: . . ." It is here that you slug in your other ideas and possibly offer to pursue them for an additional fee. Be specific. Say "for another $300 we could track these down as well."

Sue always makes suggestions for further business. She might suggest more phone calls, mentioning a few additional sources that could be contacted. She might note the possibility of searching other databases that may have been too costly for the first budget. And, she usually offers the possibility of providing the full text of documents referenced in the bibliographic citations.

Everything depends on the client you're working with. But there is usually no reason not to include these kinds of suggestions. Doing so may or may not lead to an additional assignment. But even if nothing comes of it, including additional suggestions demonstrates that you have really committed your mental resources to the client's project.

As you complete this step of the process, you should have all your tools laid out. You have selected the databases you plan to search and confected a search strategy. You have a list of associations to call (or associations' numbers to look up at the library). Everything is in readiness to make a first cut at the problem.

Step 4: Making the first cut at the problem

Rarely will your initial foray against the information dragon prove decisive. It is in the nature of things that information retrieval is a developmental process. You may search a database and find some promising leads. You will spend some time selecting and thinking about these leads and then have at it again, either online or on the phone.

Retrieving information is like extricating a quarter that has fallen behind a counter. First you look at the situation with your flashlight. Then you select a tool—possibly a yardstick—and apply it to the problem. This succeeds in moving the target closer to a position from which you can grasp it. You might then reach for the flashlight again to check the current status. Then maybe you need a stick or a screwdriver or a pair of tongs, or who knows what.

The example is a bit whimsical, but the concept is clear. Information retrieval is an iterative process most of the time. You will use a variety of tools as you repeatedly move the target, examine the current situation, and select a tool to move the target again, with each iteration bringing you closer to your goal.

Often the first cut at an information problem involves an online search. From this search, you learn the names and affiliations of people whom you can phone to get more specific information of the names of still other people to call, or books to read, articles to consult, or whatever. Eventually, you achieve your goal of dredging up the information the client needs and is paying you to retrieve.

What if you get more than you expect? Or less?

When doing a manual search, you should be able to tell within the first hour or so whether your quote was really wrong. If you are online, you can tell much sooner, due to the number of hits you find you're getting.

It is important during the reference interview stage, where you are trying to get a clear idea of what the client wants, to ask how much he or she thinks has been published on the topic in the last five years or so. How much does he expect you to find? A good online search should not produce more than about 20 citations or records in most cases. (The exception would be if the client has asked—and agreed to pay—for "everything.") If you plunge into the project, apply all of your search skills, and come up with several hundred hits, stop immediately.

Sign off the system and consult your notes about the client's sense of how much has been published on the topic in the last five years. If the client said "You'll be lucky to get two or three articles," and you've found 500, something is out of whack. The client could be way off in her perception of the topic. Or you might have misunderstood what she wanted.

Contact the client by phone and read him some representative titles. Ask if they are on the mark. Are they the kinds of things she expected you to find? Also, make sure that you are spelling things correctly and using the correct industry terminology. Be sure to discuss date and language (English? or all languages? or what?) limits, if you have not done so already.

From the client's response you may be able to narrow the search. Or you may decide to print only the last two years of material, instead of the last five.

On the other hand, if you try to find the information and come up empty, get back to the client and say, "The first four resources I tried did not produce what we were looking for. This is going to take longer than I thought." For example, Sue recalls a market study on the parking meter industry. It certainly sounded definitive. How complicated could it be? So Sue offered a low quote.

"It turns out," Sue says, "that there are only two parking meter companies in the United States—and they're not about to talk to anybody else in the world. There were no articles. No trade associations. There was simply no way to get at the information. It hadn't occurred to me when I was quoting my fee on that job that this was going to be the case."

Sue called the client. "It looks like this is much more difficult than I'd anticipated," she said. "These are the things I've tried, and I've gotten absolutely nowhere. It looks like I'm going to have to increase the quote to $600. How important is this to you?"

If the client says yes, then fine. If he or she says, "No it's not that important. No big deal," just stop. You can bill the client for the time spent so far. After all, you had no way of knowing going in that this was a closed industry. Remember, you don't guarantee to get the information. You only promise to leave no stone unturned, within the budget that has been authorized.

That's why it's important to stop early on. You don't want to run up the bill and charge more than necessary when you can see it is going to be a fruitless search. That can cause hard feelings and possibly close off the possibility of future business with the client.

Interaction with a client is very important. The client usually appreciates it, and it shows that you are concerned and that you want to do what the client wants you to do. At the Rugge Group, Sue never hesitates to call the client in the middle of a search. "The only thing we don't do," Sue says, "is let the client come in and sit beside us while we are online. That invariably runs up the online costs, and it can be very frustrating and tense because the client doesn't understand the process. Otherwise, we're very big on client interaction."

If you're a new broker, you might worry about appearing unprofessional. Don't. No one expects you to know the information jungle inside and out. You've been hired to use your special skills to go into the jungle and report what you find. You're like Lewis and Clark sent forth into the Louisiana Purchase to report back what they have found. When he commissioned them for the job, Thomas Jefferson didn't expect Lewis and Clark to already know the territory.

The question of filenames

Now let's look at more of the nitty-gritty details. Every assignment is different. But let's assume that you have decided that an online search is the best first step. You have picked a database and entered a search. You will want to record the process and the information it yields on disk. So what filename do you use?

It's a nuts-and-bolts question. But it's important all the same. In general, you will find it most convenient to use the same date-based number you assigned to the project in the first place.

One broker we know, for example, uses file extensions to classify files on disk. A search for the project she might label 9105-03 would have the filename 9105-03.SRH. The cover letter she eventually prepares for this search might have the filename 9105-03.LTR, while the invoice would be given the name 9105-03.INV.

This has the advantage of keeping everything together. Using DOS, for example, the command DIR 9105-03.* would pull up a list of all files named 9105-03, regardless of the file extension.

You will probably want to develop your own system. But this one, using the year and month followed by the project number, can be very convenient. Among other things, it is much easier to use filenames like 9105-03 than it is to struggle with creating an abbreviation for a client's name. What would you do with "Minnesota Agricultural and Manufacturing Council" for example? How would you distinguish "Exxon Consumer Products Division" from "Exxon Corporate Relations" (if such entities existed)?

Record search costs immediately

It is common sense to try to keep all of the notes and materials associated with a given project together in some form, whether in a folder or on your hard disk. The same logic applies to costs. Most major league databases, like DIALOG or BRS, will tell you what you will be billed for a given search as soon as you sign off.

So write that amount down on a piece of paper you include in your job or project folder: "DIALOG ABI/INFORM—$37.42—5/4/91." The online services will send you an itemized bill at the end of each month, but apportioning costs to various projects can be as challenging as apportioning a phone bill.

Phone interviews or other phone work components are less precise. But here's a tip: Instead of trying to keep precise track of every nickel and dime, adopt a policy of charging a flat amount for each minute you spend on the phone. Your charge should be somewhere between 50 cents and $1 a minute for domestic calls. It all evens out in the end, and this practice is far preferable to spending the time needed to track the cost of each individual phone call. (As noted earlier, for Sue and many other brokers, the phone code service provided by MCI and Sprint can virtually eliminate this problem.)

Use a kitchen timer or a stopwatch instead. Start the timer when your party answers and stop it when the call is finished. Then make a note of the person called, the date, and the time spent on a sheet in your project folder. Some phone sets—we know of models made by Panasonic, for example,—have call duration timers built in.

If you spend money buying books or other materials for a project, make a note of them as well and keep it in your project folder. Again, the idea is to keep everything associated with a project—whether it is search results, phone notes, or expenses—in a single place or filed under the same general heading. Simply record your charges, along with the labor time you spend day by day on the back of the form.

Here's another master's tip: Take particular care to record Federal Express (or other overnight carrier) charges. If at all possible, get your client's FedEx account number and use it when sending material. Most clients are happy to provide this number when asked since they know you will mark up the charge if you have to use your own account number. Using a client's FedEx number can free you from the burden of keeping track of shipping charges on a project and preserve precious budget money.

Step 5: Following up on first-cut results

As we have said, your first run at a problem will probably not produce all the information you need to complete a project. An online search, for example, is often only the starting point.

Your search results may contain important facts and figures relating to your assignment, but the real gold is usually the sources and experts that are mentioned. These are the people you will want to call to get the latest, up-to-the-minute information about what's going on in a particular field.

The same thing applies when your first step is to make a few calls instead of going online. More than likely, each call will produce one or more *other* names or contacts. If your first step is to go to the library, you'll encounter the same phenomenon. One reference book will lead to several others.

At this point you must decide what to do next. That's what we mean by "following up on first-cut results," and often it is the most critical phase of the entire project. You've got to do something more to find the information your client seeks. But what should it be?

You've turned up a list of additional contacts and sources, but not every one of them will be equally productive. Which ones should you pursue? And when should you stop? In an earlier time, one might have said that this is where we separate the men from the boys, though separating the amateurs from the professionals is more to the point.

Who you gonna call?

Let us suppose, for example, that an online search has turned up five people whom you might call for more information. These include: a reporter who has done a particularly insightful article on your topic; a professor who has been quoted in another article; an author who has been quoted in yet another article; and the spokespersons for two companies or institutions that have been referenced or quoted in two other articles.

Who you gonna call? It's an important question because budgets are usually limited. If you had an infinite budget, you could call all five individuals—and the other people and authorities these five suggest in the course of your conversations. Sue has worked on any number of assignments where cost was no object. But they are few and far between and, in any case, are not likely to come your way as a brand new information broker.

Each call you make will take your time. You will have to assume, for example, that you will not be able to reach the person on the first try. So you will have to leave a message. With a bit of luck, the person will call you back. If not, you will have to call again and leave another message. Or you may find yourself engaged in "telephone tag," where each of you calls when the other is not in or not available.

That's why we suggest that, if you have to leave a message, leave as detailed a message as possible regarding what you are looking for. You will have much better luck in getting a return call—either from the person you need to reach, from his or her assistant, or from someone else who has been designated as the person to call you back.

If you are calling from a different time zone, for heaven's sake mention the fact. Sue has lost count of the times the phone has started ringing at 5:30 A.M. because the East Coast caller has forgotten that The Rugge Group is based in California. Also, if you know you are going to be out of the office, suggest a time frame when it is best for someone to return your call. Or ask when would be the best time for you to try again.

In addition, whenever you are successful, you may find that the source gives you part of the information you need but refers you to several other people who are "better qualified" to answer your questions. After finally getting in touch with all five of the sources turned up by your initial search, you could find yourself with ten new people to call. And the game will begin again.

Information, as we have said from the beginning of this book, is nebulous. Its retrieval can be as endless as the root system of a tree stump. Not for nothing is the word *ramifications* derived from the Latin word for *root*. Your challenge is to know which path to pursue and when to stop.

The existentialism of information brokering

Unfortunately, there is no way we can tell you what to do. This challenge is at the very core of the *business* of information retrieval. Given an unlimited budget and an unlimited amount of time, any reasonably bright person can find the information a client needs. The trick is to be able to satisfy the client's request on a limited budget in a short period of time and make a profit in the process.

Only experience can teach you how to decide which leads to follow. And no matter how much experience you accumulate, you will still not always guess right. That professor you think is going to be such a font of information and thus are pursuing through several iterations of telephone tag can turn out to be a real dud once you finally make contact. While that little book with the uninformative title you decided not to look at in the library might contain the very facts and figures your client needs.

All brokers make "right" and "wrong" decisions about which paths to follow. But, through experience, successful brokers have learned how to guess right more often than they guess wrong. The best advice we can give you is to be sensitive to the *texture* of information and to be aware that different sources typically produce different textures.

Reporters, authors, professors, corporate public information officials, and politicians may all have something valuable to say on a given topic. But the texture of the information you get from people in each of these groups will be different. It will also differ within each group as well—a Republican Congressman will have a different view than a Democrat, a professor at a university may have access to more hard data than a counterpart at a small liberal arts college, and so on.

As an information broker, you must *always* think about the source and the texture of the information he or she can be expected to produce. If you do this and if you learn from your mistakes, you will soon find you are guessing "right" more often than not about which paths to pursue.

Know when to quit

Step 5 of the execution process holds another trap for the unsuspecting information broker. Sometimes you can get so wrapped up in a project and your mind can be so thoroughly engaged in the quest that you forget to quit when you should.

It's ironic, but the same inquiring mind, imagination, and thrill of the chase that makes you such a good information broker can also destroy your chances of making a profit.

You simply have to face the fact that information is endless. There will always be other leads you can pursue. There will always be more you can do. The hard part is to discipline yourself *not* to pursue them or do them unless you're getting paid for it. You've got to know when to stop.

Sometimes it's easy. If the client's request was specific—say, the names, addresses, and annual sales of the five leading producers of peanut butter—you will know when you have the information you need.

But suppose the request is less well defined. Suppose it's something like, "What is the projected market for solar energy panels in the United States over the next five years?'' Now, before accepting a job like that you would make very clear what you will do for the budget the client is willing to authorize. But suppose you get into it, do everything "right," and still don't have anything approaching a definitive market projection.

That's fine. You're still not in trouble. You have done what you said you would and can report to the client what you have done and what you have found. You didn't promise that you would *find* a market projection, only that you would use your best efforts and skills to *look* for one.

Now for the twist. Suppose that you have spent the authorized budget and at this point have made an acceptable profit for the time and effort you have expended. The trouble is, you're convinced that if you just do a little more—make one or two more calls, check one more database, or track down one more journal or magazine article—you will have the market projection the client wants.

What do you do? Do you spend more time and money pursuing this target and consequently agree to make little or no profit on the job? Do you phone the client and explain that you don't have what he wants but if he could just see his way clear to authorize a larger budget you're almost certain you can find it? Or do you say, "Temptation, get thee behind me!" and prepare your report with the material you have already collected?

It's a tough call. Depending on the situation, either of these three alternatives could be appropriate. If it is a new client with good prospects for future business, you might decide to go the extra mile, even if it means making no profit.

We do not recommend this. However, there may be times when it is unavoidable. In such situations, your invoice should reflect the costs you have borne. Itemize your total costs, but then charge the fee you and your client agreed upon and add a note to the effect that "We always honor our budget limits. But for future reference, we wanted you to be aware of our actual costs on this project."

Each situation is different, and only you can be the judge. However, if at all possible, we strongly recommend avoiding the above approach. It sets a precedent that is hard to overcome in the future. Your audit trail of what you have done to try to find the information is your best defense. Write it up—in detail—and tell the client what other avenues you would pursue if you had an additional budget of $X. (Be specific.) Do not apologize! You followed the right strategy. The information just wasn't there. The client will appreciate the professionalism demonstrated by this approach.

If you have a longstanding relationship with the client, you might call and ask for a larger budget. The client knows your work and can be confident that you are not stringing him along. If the client indicated that money was tight, you might take the third option and submit what you have.

There are other considerations as well. How confident are you that the market projection actually exists and that you can find it quickly? Given what you knew at the time, did you mistakenly quote too low a figure when you agreed to do the job?

Despite your making it clear that there are no guarantees, if you don't produce the market projection, is there a likelihood that the client will not pay you?

All information brokers encounter dilemmas like these. As a new broker you will probably be inclined to feel that the problem is a lack of skill on your part. And some of the time you will be right. Some of the time you will either earn no profit or actually take a loss on a project. But that's how you learn.

As your experience and skill grow, so will your confidence and self-assurance. You will know whether to go the extra mile or not, and you will know when to call it quits.

Step 6: Organizing and analyzing retrieved information

One mistake new information brokers make is to not leave enough time for sorting, organizing, and generally preparing material for the client. In this industry, this is called *post-processing*, and it can be as time-consuming as retrieving the information in the first place. You might think of it as the first stage in preparing your report.

As an example, consider the DIALOG search we showed you back in Fig. 11-1. There is a lot of garbage that can be removed from this file before the abstract we found is included in a report to the client, though we should note that cleaned up records may be a luxury the client's budget cannot afford. If the budget is extremely tight, you may have to eliminate much of the post processing. Just make sure that the client understands that he or she will be getting a "raw" download.

Actually, you may find that some clients prefer you to leave in the codes. This is often the case with "sci-tech" (scientific and technical information) clients since they tend to be more used to dealing with bibcites than their managers are.

Let's assume, however, that the budget permits you to spend some time preparing the records. Using the record shown in Fig. 11-1 as our example, you would use your word processing program to remove everything from "?BEGIN BUSI1" to the line "**USE FORMAT F FOR FULL TEXT**." You would also remove the lines starting with "JRNL CODE:BEV" through "WORD COUNT: 688."

Leave the code words at the end of the abstract intact (COMPANY NAMES through CLASSIFICATION CODES) since they show why the article was retrieved. You might then neaten up the title and publication information to make it easier to read, possibly even tagging "Beverage World" to print in bold or italics. You may also want to use a bold typeface to highlight key statements in records.

Watch your time!

Cleaning up online search results thus involves a lot of word processing. It isn't difficult work, but can be very time-consuming. Fortunately, there are ways to automate large parts of the process if you have a full-powered word processing program that will allow you to program a single key to execute a number of steps. Please look again at Fig. 11-1 and imagine that you had a dozen records to clean up instead of just one.

You could tell a program like PC-Write to search the file for the first occurrence of "JRNL CODE:", turn on its block marking function, move down five lines, and delete the entire marked block. All of these various keystrokes would be assigned to a single key. From then on, each time you strike that key, the entire sequence will be repeated. In computerese, a series of keystrokes loaded into a single key is called a *macro*.

With the right series of macros, you could make short work of cleaning up the file. Indeed, files of records captured from an online database are often ideal candidates for macros because every record typically has the same standard components. If every record were different, macros would be of little use.

Magazines like *Online*, *Database*, and *Database Searcher* frequently carry articles by librarians and information brokers on how to use specific computer programs for information retrieval and post-processing. In fact, "tradecraft" pieces like this are one of the things many readers look forward to in each issue. So use your budding broker skills and track down back issues to see if there is something you can apply. (Hint: Call up any college libraries in your area to see if they carry these publications.) Please see Appendix A for subscription information.

Preparing non-electronic results

If your project involved phone interviews, you will probably have to write them up as well. You may work from the notes you made while doing the interview or from a tape-recorded conversation. You may or may not want to produce a verbatim transcript. It all depends on the client. Sometimes clients want merely a cogent summary of your phone conversations. Sometimes they are extremely interested in every word that was said and every nuance. In any case, preparing phone notes also takes time. Sue's experience is that it takes as much time to write up the conversation as it did to conduct the interview in the first place.

Exercising selectivity

You are also being paid to be selective. We have said many times that information brokers should leave analysis of results to the client and to experts in a particular subject. It is not our job to tell the client what the information we have found means.

At the same time, most clients do not want to be swamped with information. Years ago, for example, Sue did a consulting assignment for *American Banker* magazine. "I was in New York for a week," she says, "and they were paying me $500 a day. So every night I'd come home and write until 1:00 in the morning.

"I showed the client all the stuff I'd written. And he said 'These are just your notes, aren't they? You're not going to make me wade through all this stuff, are you?' He helped me edit it down for his boss. In the end, I think I only gave him four pages for $2000. It's a lesson I have never forgotten."

It's an important lesson for new information brokers too. Your tendency will be to "justify" your fee by pumping out all the information you can. If someone's paying you $500, by golly, you'll show her what you can do and produce 20 to 30 pages of beautifully printed and prepared text.

Wrong. You may well have to adjust your value system. This is not college or high school, where the number of pages you produced for a term paper somehow equated to the amount of time and effort you poured into the project. This is the business world. Your client usually doesn't want *tons* of information, but rather a succinct summary of the *right* information.

The client isn't interested in how hard you worked or how much time you lavished on the project. Clients are interested in answers and results. If you tell them that producing the information they need or checking to see what's out there on a particular topic will cost $500 and they agree, then that is what they are buying.

But they expect you to be professional. That means tuning yourself to their needs and not burdening them with irrelevant, though copious, information.

So you will have to be selective in many cases. Make sure you have a firm grasp of exactly what it is the client wants. Then act in the client's place as you review the information you have retrieved: Would the client want to see this record? That record is close but not on-target. These five records all say essentially the same thing—perhaps I should include the best record and write up a note that there were four more just like it?

As we have said throughout this book: Put yourself in the client's shoes. So, in a sense, you have to do some analysis. It is not analysis in terms of "I found this, therefore we can conclude that . . ." But it is analysis in terms of "I think the client would be interested in *this* information, but *that* information would be a waste of time."

Step 7: Packaging and presenting your report

The report you hand over to the client is but the tip of the iceberg. We all know the time and effort that went into it that does not show directly. But obviously the tip of this particular iceberg is crucial. The report is the product we have been striving toward from the beginning of the assignment. In every sense of the word, it is the payoff.

What form should it take? How should you bind it? How long should it be? Those are the kinds of questions that will go through your mind. Along with, "I can't believe it. They're paying me $500 for *this*. But it's only four or five pages. I'd better see if I can spruce it up."

As we said a moment ago, of course they're not paying you for the four or five pages. They're paying you for the rest of the iceberg—all the work and expense that went into producing those particular four or five pages. But the tip of the iceberg is important, so what should you do?

The answer is easy: Make it neat, make it clean, make it clear. From a mechanical standpoint, that means that you will need either a laser printer, or a 24-pin dot matrix printer capable of letter quality output, or an ink jet printer. In today's world, nothing less will do. The use of bold, italics, and even different fonts and point sizes now constitute the lowest common denominator in business documents.

If you use a printer like one of these and standard copier paper (no need for expensive letterhead second sheets), no one will fault you for neatness. We've already discussed the need to remove extraneous information from online downloads and other text, so that takes care of making it clean.

Clarity is the real challenge. In preparing your report, whether it is a collection of bibliographic citations and abstracts, phone interview transcripts or summaries, or anything else, you should take great pains to make sure that there is nothing for the client to puzzle over.

There is *no* set form for an information broker's report. So if you need to weave notes into the text to explain or amplify things, do so. Ditto if you need to add diagrams, illustrations, charts, photographs, reprints of magazine articles, or anything else. As long as it is within the budget, if it adds to the clarity of your presentation, it is fair game.

Once again—put yourself into the client's shoes. If you were sitting at his or her desk with the same concerns and questions, what would *you* want to see in a report? That's the key. Every report you do may be physically different, but if you keep this key foremost in your thoughts, every client will be satisfied.

As for packaging, there are a number of alternatives. You might consider using high-quality pocket folders, available from your local stationery store. At the same store, you will also be able to find a variety of acetate report covers and spine clips of the sort you may have used for papers in college.

However, in Sue's opinion, it is important to present the client with a *document*, not a bunch of loose sheets of paper. Your local copy shop can bind a report for you at a cost of between $2 and $3. For her part, Sue spiral binds everything—so it will lie flat—and uses acetate covers. Bound into the report, clients will find a cover sheet on letterhead that states the title of the search, the databases searched and time frames covered, the current date, and the client's name.

Indeed, as your business becomes established, you may decide to invest $350 to $500 in some kind of binding machine. You can get hand-operated machines that will punch a stack of papers and apply a comb to create a comb-bound booklet. Others are designed to mate two plastic rails at the spine of your "booklet." In our opinion, however, there is no need to purchase this kind of equipment when you are just starting out.

There are many less expensive ways to make it neat, clean, and clear. If you will just bear in mind that your report *is* you and your firm in the client's eyes, you will have no problem. In a very real sense, your report is your child, and you want it to look good.

The cover letter

Never send a report to a client without a bona fide cover letter. Unless you are on very familiar terms with the client, a Post-it Note saying, "Here's the report you asked for," simply will not do. The cover letter is the formal introduction of your "performance." It is to your report what Jay Leno or Johnny Carson is to a performer. It sets up the audience and tells them what to expect.

Your cover letter should say in effect, "Here it is—the information you asked for. This is what we did, how we approached the problem. Interestingly, much of the information we found pointed in this direction. But, while we found a lot of information on this, there was very little on that. It may be that exploring additional sources would yield more detail on that. If you are interested, a budget of $X would allow us to follow up these leads.

"If you would like copies of any of the documents referenced here, we can supply them for a small fee. We hope this is satisfactory and that you will consider us again the next time you have an information need."

When you are writing your cover letter, put on your "consultant's hat." You're the search expert reporting back. The enclosed report consists of two sections. You found this, but did not find that. You feel it is curious that there were so many articles on Subject A. You want to draw the client's attention to Point 5. And so on.

Let your report carry the real weight, but prepare the client for what he or she is about to receive. You may also take the opportunity to do a little selling. You could note the promising avenues that you uncovered that might be worth further exploration. You could suggest setting up a current awareness service for the client on this topic. Whatever seems appropriate.

Our point is that the cover letter should not be a perfunctory, "Well, here it is," message. You're about to go on stage, as the client turns to your report, so make the most of the opportunity.

Finally, make sure you get your report to the client *on time*. One of the benefits all information brokers have to offer is timeliness. You will find that many of your assignments come from people who have waited until the last minute to call you. And if they are really in a hurry, you are foolish if you don't charge them extra for "rush" service.

But whether it is a "rush" job or not, it is so much better to come in early than to come in late. If you think they need your report in three days, or you think you can do it in three days, tell them "five days." Then deliver the report on the third day! That kind of performance usually costs you nothing, due to the expectations you have set up, and it pays big dividends in the "miracle-worker" department.

However, note the key phrase, "If you think . . ." You must do your best to sense the client's needs. If you say "five days," they may say, "Forget it. I've got to give my presentation the day after tomorrow." So do your best to navigate this passage carefully.

Step 8: Confirming client satisfaction

Once you have delivered your report, don't make the mistake so many new brokers make and just drop the ball. You're in a service business, and client satisfaction is thus paramount. Send off the report, wait a day or two, then follow-up with a phone call.

Ask the client if the report was received and if it is what he or she wanted. Are there any problems or questions? Is there anything that is not clear?

This is simply good customer relations. The person has hired you to deliver a product. You have done so. Now you are calling to make sure that the client is happy with what you have delivered. It's a good, "old-fashioned" way of doing business. And, of course, it can offer some nice payoffs.

Your follow-up call will impress the client with your concern for his or her problems. But it also creates an opportunity for discussion of additional assignments—whether further explorations of the topic at hand or something else. It gives the client a chance to say, "That current awareness service you mentioned in your cover letter sounds interesting. About how much would that cost and what would we get?"

If there is a problem—if the client is not satisfied—the follow-up call gives you the chance to solve it immediately. No one expects you to be perfect, so problems can and will arise. The key thing is how you handle them. If you do not handle them or do so ungraciously, the "word of mouth" about you and your business will suffer.

If you express concern and do all you can (within reason) to make it right, your client will have nothing but good things to say about you. It's not the problem, in other words, that is the issue. It is how you handle it. If you do it right, the problem will be forgotten, while your courteousness and willingness to help will be remembered.

There's a very practical reason for taking this step as well. The most common reason why people tell you three months down the road that they're not going to pay you is that they were dissatisfied. If you have made a follow-up call shortly after delivering the report, you can say, "Well, I have it right here that our researcher talked to you three days after you got the report, and you said it was great. If you didn't like it, that was the time to tell us."

Sue Rugge values client feedback so much that she has taken the unusual step of including a written critique, a single-page questionnaire, in her reports. Were the people you were working with efficient? Did they make every effort to understand your request? Were you satisfied with the results? Is there anything we can do to improve our service?

On average, Sue gets about 25 percent of these questionnaires back from clients. Sometimes people complain about something that Sue and her searchers had not thought would be a problem or didn't know had occurred. So Sue calls and says thank you for bringing it to our attention.

What if they're not happy?

It is certainly true that by taking these steps, you are laying yourself open for someone to say, "No. I'm not satisfied with your work." That's a chance you simply have to take.

If a client is not satisfied, do your best to understand why. Were they hoping for a lot more information? Did they feel that the report you provided was far off the mark? What are their concerns?

There is no question here of cutting your price or saying, "Then you don't have to pay us." Not at all. At most, you may have to say, "Well if this was not what you wanted, we'll do it again."

Of course, sometimes you just can't win. Sue remembers a client who wanted to open a video store. He wanted a floor plan, and Sue and her staff found exactly that. They called a video store owner's magazine and located an article that included the layouts the client had asked for. They sent it to the client. He was furious. "I wanted a *computer* search," he said.

Sue responded, "Didn't this article tell you what you wanted to know?" He said, "Yes, but I could have done this myself. I could have gone to the library. I didn't need you guys to go to the library."

Sue tried to explain that it is the information broker's job to get him the information in the format best suited to his needs. It didn't do any good. The client never paid.

Conclusion

We've covered steps 1 through 8 of the execution process. In the next chapter we'll look at the last two steps—the "money" steps. From the client's standpoint, the report you produce may be the most important step. But we all know that nothing happens without money. So let's look at preparing and sending your invoice, and dealing with clients who are slow to pay.

20

Pricing, contracts, and billing

THIS CHAPTER IS ABOUT A SUBJECT DEAR TO ALL OF OUR HEARTS: GETTING paid! But not just getting paid. Getting paid *enough* to make sure that you have more money coming in than going out. If you don't do this, you'll be the one going out—of business. We'll look at the fine art of quoting on a job and presenting that quote to the client. We'll look at the kinds of written agreements you may want to have to protect both yourself and the client. And we'll discuss how to prepare and present your bill.

The toughest part of the job

Calculating costs and coming up with a quote on a project is the hardest thing a new broker must do. There are so many things running through your head. With little or no experience under your belt, you really don't know how much time you will have to spend conducting phone interviews or how much money you will have to spend searching online databases. So you don't know what your costs are going to be.

Looking them in the eye

But you have to come up with a price. And here, you're afraid that if you quote too high, you won't get the job. But if you quote too low, you won't make any money. Which means you will actually lose money—since even if the quote covers all of your costs, with enough left over to pay yourself $2 an hour, the overhead expenses of running your business will not be covered.

Then there's that scary moment of actually telling someone what they will have to pay you. It can help to use the corporate "we," as in "We charge . . ." or "Our fee for this project will be . . ." But that doesn't change the fact that you are going to have to look someone in the eye, either literally or figuratively, and ask them to give you money.

Western society in general tries to avoid such situations. We put price tags on store merchandise and post set charges for services on charts. So much for a tune-up, so much for a haircut, so much more if you want a blow-dry, and so on. It's convenient, of course. But it also eliminates the need for someone to peer under the hood and say to you directly, "This car . . . hmm, lemme see . . . I'll charge you $75, plus materials, to tune it up."

No one likes confrontations, and telling clients what they are going to have to pay you has the potential of leading to one. What if they say, "That's outrageous! You can't really mean you're going to charge me $500 for this!"? What if they say, "That sounds a little steep to me. Are you sure you can't do better?" Or, "Oh, I'm sorry. I'm afraid that's out of the question. Thanks for your time. I appreciate your coming in."

Other concerns

You're also worried about results. What if the client doesn't like what you produce? What if she refuses to pay? What if it's your fault, you think, because you weren't skilled enough to do the job? What will your friends, associates, and significant other or spouse say when it turns out that you've failed in your first assignment?

There are worries and concerns aplenty to go around. Each of them is significant—not because they represent truly serious, insurmountable problems, but because you are worried about them. We're certainly not going to tell you to stop worrying and be happy, though you could do worse than to adopt that philosophy. Instead, we're going to tell you how to deal with each of these problems in a professional and competent manner.

How to calculate your costs

Let's start with the matter of coming up with an actual quote on a job. As a new broker, you don't know what your costs are going to be. Established brokers don't always know either. But experience is the best teacher. Every project is a custom product with its own unique requirements. Every assignment holds the potential of involving significantly more work than is initially apparent. The difference is that experienced brokers have done enough projects to have a pretty good idea of what's likely to be involved in most new projects.

They don't know the costs to the penny, but they know enough to quote a pricing range. They also know enough not to take a job unless they are 50 to 65 percent sure that they can find what the client needs. (More on this later.) That means that they can often come up with a quote on the spot, while the client is on the phone or while sitting in his office and asking for the order.

This is not something a new broker should even think about doing. There is no shame in saying, "Yes, Mr. Jones. I believe I understand what you need. Let me check a few sources (or check with my research staff) and get back to you later today with a quote." Most clients *expect* you to handle things this way. If the client were to call up a supplier to place an order, he might be pleasantly surprised if the transaction could be handled in a single call. But he would not expect most suppliers to be able to give him a firm quote right away. Prices change. Items go in and out of stock. Shipping charges have to be calculated and delivery dates determined.

The one thing the client would definitely expect, however, is for the supplier to get back to him with a quote as soon as possible. As an information broker, you can do no less. If it's morning, strive to have the quote by mid-afternoon. If it's late in the day, be ready to present it first thing next morning. If you're running into problems, call the client and explain the delay.

Sharpen your pencil

You would think that, while not necessarily easy, the setting of prices of all sorts in our economy would be simple. Calculate the costs to the best of your ability and add a certain amount or percentage for your profit. But there's more to it than that. If there weren't, professors wouldn't be able to write thick tomes on price theory and teach entire courses on the subject.

What complicates the process, indeed what makes pricing an art, is the perfectly human desire to make as much money as possible for the time and effort expended. You may not feel that way yourself just now, but wait until you've begun expending time and effort on a project before you reach your conclusion. More than likely, you will agree with us when we suggest that it is just plain stupid to charge any less than the market will bear.

That sounds like advice from a 19th century robber baron. And perhaps the shoe would fit if there were any wealthy information brokers or if anyone had ever gotten rich in this profession. As it happens, it's a very socialistic policy, with the "rich" subsidizing the "poor." Yes, charging what the market will bear is the best way to maximize your profits. Make the most you can on every job. But be aware that jobs can differ in their payoff.

Please note that we are not advocating that you provide the same level of service for different prices. But the larger the budget you can persuade the client to authorize—"what the market will bear"—the more work you can do. And the more work you do, the more money you will make.

As the budget goes up, the percentage you spend on outside expenses goes down. For example, with a $500 budget, about 50 percent ($250) might go to pay for online time and telephone work. Yet your out-of-pocket expenses may not be much more than that on a $2500 project. The difference is that on the $2500 project, your $250 in expenses amounts to only ten percent of the total. Not 50 percent. A large portion of the remaining 90 percent is money *in* your pocket for work you perform.

The larger the budget, the more value-added service *you* can provide. Thus, the more profit *you* will make. One good example is the process of preparing raw online search data before sending it off to the client. You may be able to obtain the data for $450 in outside expenses. But if you have a budget of $650 to work with, you can probably afford to spend the time necessary to clean up the results, add bold and italic highlights as discussed in Chapter 19, and possibly do an "executive summary"—some introductory text followed by bulleted quotes that point out the most significant results.

We want to make sure you understand that we are not suggesting that you charge $2500 and spend a mere $250 and change doing the work. For $2500, you provide a package that will knock the client's socks off. It is not a question of whether the work gets done. It's a question of who gets the money, you or DIALOG and other online systems? Many times, for instance, if Sue feels that she knows where to call to get the needed information, she will make those calls instead of using DIALOG or some other online system—even though she knows that the information is available online.

There should be no doubt that the resulting report will be "worth $2500." If you are a good information broker, you will make sure that the client is satisfied. The crucial point is who gets the lion's share of the money the client has authorized to produce this wonderful report—you or DIALOG or someone else?

Base price and quoted price

Pricing is thus a two-stage process. The first step is to come up with as accurate a cost and profit figure as you can. That's your base price. The second step is to ask yourself, "Would the client be willing to pay more than the base price for the kind of value-added work you can do? If so, how much more?" The answer to that question determines the price you actually quote to the client.

Let's look at how to calculate your base price first. (Please see Fig. 20-1.) There is no cut-and-dried formula since there are really no cut-and-dried projects. Each one is different, as we keep saying. Nor is it a matter of precise figures. You'll drive yourself crazy if you try to predict everything down to the penny. And your prediction will always be wrong. Calculate in round numbers, and always round up.

Visualize the steps and estimate costs

Start by analyzing the steps you will have to take to execute the job. How many databases will you have to search and how many records will you have to have displayed? How long will it take you, and what are the connect time and display charges in each case?

For example, an efficient searcher can get in and out of the appropriate databases for about $150 to $200. That range is a good yardstick for a typical subject search. But there are exceptions. With a patent or chemical search, the "yardstick" costs will be much higher. But then, you probably should not be doing those kinds of expensive, specialized searches in the first place. Unless you have been trained in chemical or patent searching, you will often be best off calling upon your information broker colleagues who have had experience in these areas.

How many phone calls will you have to make and how long are they likely to

Here's a form you may want to adapt and use when working up a preliminary base price figure. Notice that the Project Element column consists of each of the steps you feel will be necessary in completing the job. Use the entry labelled "Allowance for direct expenses" to factor in any books, journals, or other special materials you may have to buy and deliver to the client with your report.

Please remember that, as formal as it may look, this form is intended merely to help you organize your thinking. There is no single "correct" way to bid a job. You may not want to add the same percentage mark up to all of your costs, for example. Or there may be costs you feel you should simply pass through and not mark up at all.

This form will get you started. But you will want to use the copy supplied on the accompanying disk to create and print out your own customized version.

Project Element	Est. Hours	Est. Costs
Reference interview (labor)	_____	_____
Strategizing (labor)	_____	_____
Online search preparation (labor)	_____	_____
Online search execution (labor)	_____	_____
Online search execution (costs)	_____	_____
Analysis of results (labor)	_____	_____
Library research (labor)	_____	_____
Library expenses (costs)	_____	_____
Phone research (labor)	_____	_____
Long distance charges (costs)	_____	_____
FAX long distance charges (costs)	_____	_____
Postage (costs)	_____	_____
Document delivery (costs)	_____	_____
Report preparation (labor)	_____	_____
Allowance for direct expenses (books, reports, etc.)	_____	_____
Estimate totals:	_____	
Total charge for labor (Estimated hours times $75):	a. _____	
Markup to be added to costs:		_____
Total charge for costs (Sum of costs and markup):		b. _____
Estimated base price (Add lines a. and b.):	$_____	

Fig. 20-1. A sample base price job estimating form

be? Short ones for quick address and contact information? Or relatively long interviews? Multiply the time you estimate you will spend on the phone by $1 a minute to come up with an estimate of long distance charges.

Will there be document delivery charges involved? If you can estimate the number and type of documents you will have to order, you can check with a document supply house and come up with an estimate for this component.

Will you have to purchase special materials, either for delivery to the client or to enable you to perform a component of the job? You might need to buy a mailing list, a directory, or some piece of database documentation, for example. Will you have to travel anywhere, and if so, what will your expenses be? And don't forget those little expenses like charges for photocopies, postage, and the like.

In short, *think through the job!* On the first few jobs you may find it especially helpful to sit down in a quiet room and visualize each step you plan to take. Write the steps down in order, or use a base price job estimating form like the one shown in Fig. 20-1. (You will find a copy of this form on the accompanying disk as well.) But wait before you try to come up with estimates for each cost.

If you are a real novice at searching, you may want to check DialIndex to get an indication of the volume of material you are going to encounter and which databases are likely to contain it. Don't rule out the possibility of using an established broker in the beginning. The Rugge Group is happy to give free price quotes.

As we have said before, if you do not come from an information resources background, you will learn faster and be better able to satisfy your clients if you use an experienced broker on your first few jobs. New brokers should never forget that establishing a client base must be the Number One priority and goal during the first year.

Counting the time

With the list in front of you, continue your visualization to include estimates of the time you will have to spend on each step. Estimated costs are one component of a quote, estimated labor charges are another. And it is here that we so often cheat ourselves. Not necessarily by failing to charge enough per hour, though that is a problem for some brokers. But through neglecting to charge for all the hours we spend.

As a new broker, you may forget to count the time you spend with the client conducting a reference interview. This is not the time you spend selling or estimating a project; it is the time you may have to spend finding out exactly what the client wants after you have been given the job. Most brokers would not forget to charge for the time they spend searching online, but many fail to count the time spent preparing and planning a search before turning on the modem.

You will also spend time printing out, reviewing, and, budget permitting, cleaning up search results. You'll spend time analyzing and selecting data, whether it is from an online system or books and magazines at your library. And speaking of the library, if you visit its hallowed halls, don't forget to start your meter the moment you start your car to make the trip. (If it's a long drive, count your mileage and include it in your costs at 26 cents or more per mile.)

More time will be involved in writing your final report, and more time printing it, packaging it, and sending it off. You might include a time allowance for making a follow-up phone call once the report has arrived. This is a nice personal touch, but it can be an important opportunity to discuss the results with the client.

Estimate your time in minutes or hours as appropriate. Then convert everything to hours or fractions of an hour. What's the smallest fraction you should use? As we said before, when Maxwell Communications bought IOD, it tried to get searchers to record their time in six-minute segments, one tenth of an hour. It used to drive us all crazy. A more workable approach is to follow the lead of many attorneys, C.P.A.'s and other professionals and bill in 15-minute, quarter-of-an-hour segments.

Adding everything up

When you think you've got a pretty good handle on the elements that are going to cost you money and the number of hours you expect to spend, you will be ready to calculate a preliminary base price number. Again, see Fig. 20-1.

If you are a novice or are otherwise inexperienced in using information resources, this approach can be a big help. However, if you are an experienced reference librarian, you probably will not need to go through each step. Sue tries to find out what the information is *worth* to the client. If they are basing major decisions—such as a decision to acquire a company, enter a new market, or move a plant site—then a four-figure budget is not unreasonable. But if they are just looking for a little background information on a prospective client, then $500 may seem a bit high. The key point is that Sue has had enough experience to be confident of what she and The Rugge Group can do for either budget.

Again, when we speak of "what the market will bear," we mean how much the client is willing to spend on a project. We are not suggesting that you should charge one client more than you would another for the identical amount of work. Whatever you charge, you will earn your money.

But, all things being equal, we would rather have a few clients willing to authorize relatively large budgets than a clutch of clients who are primarily interested in doing things on the cheap. The total dollar figure taken in may be the same, but the amount of non-billable, non-information-related time and effort involved (sales calls, client contact, even hand-holding) will differ considerably.

As you review the form in Fig. 20-1, two points may leap out at you: the markup added to the estimated costs and the price of $75 per hour for labor. Let's discuss both items, starting with the markup.

Mark up your costs

Marking up your expenses ensures that the figures you quote will more closely reflect your *actual* cost for each item. Assume, for example, that DIALOG charges you $50 for a given online search. You may think that's your cost, but it's only part of the story.

You could not have done that search if you didn't own a computer, printer, and a modem—equipment that probably cost you $2000 or more. These components tend to be very reliable, but sometimes they need service. And sometime in the future you will eventually want to replace them. There are also your expenses for database and online system documentation and training. And there is the fact that online systems like DIALOG expect to be paid right away—but you may not get paid yourself for a month or more after paying the DIALOG bill. So at the very least, you are losing the interest you could have earned on that money. That too is a very real cost.

The question then is: Where does the money come from to compensate you for the interest lost or to pay to repair and replace the equipment you need to do online searches?

Protect your profit!

If you bill clients for just the DIALOG charges and your labor charges, there's only one place the money can come from. It has to come out of your labor charges. But your labor charges, as we'll see in a moment, already cover office overhead and other expenses. Thus, if you aren't adding a markup to your costs, and your modem suddenly stops working, the cost of replacing it will ultimately come out of your profit.

Of course, most of this is simply a matter of how you choose to account for things. You could pass online and other costs directly through to the client and just raise your hourly rate to cover equipment repair and replacement costs. Or you could leave your hourly rate the same and add a line item to the costs column labelled "Equipment repair and replacement contingency fund."

Clearly, neither of these two other approaches is likely to look good to the client. So most brokers keep it simple. They estimate their costs and then add a markup of between 25 and 50 percent in each case. The marked-up figures are the ones that appear on the final client bill or statement.

Sue marks up her online costs by a third (33 percent) and other expenses by 15 to 20 percent, depending on the costs. Generally, the lower the cost, the higher the markup. The higher the actual cost, the lower the markup. Buying a book for a client costs you much more, for example, than the actual price you pay for the book.

You have to order it, follow up on the order, have it delivered, and deliver it to the client. Then you have to process the invoice for payment. All of this takes *time*, and time is really the only commodity you have to sell. So don't feel that you are "gouging" the client by adding your markup. You are providing a service—if you didn't spend the time, the client would have to do so—and you are entitled to make a profit on that time.

The key point is to be aware of your true costs in every instance and to make sure that you account for them. There is no information broker's guild rule forcing you to charge a client for all of your true costs. But there is an iron law of business that if you do not know what your true costs are, you cannot know whether you are actually making any money or not. And if you are not making any money, eventually you will go out of business.

If all of this is strange to you, seek professional help. Ask your accountant for guidance. If you don't have an accountant, get one. Your time is best spent finding new clients and executing searches, not preparing tax returns or analyzing costs.

How much per hour?

Now we get to it. As an information broker in the 1990's, you should be charging between $65 and $100 an hour for your labor. (If you are an expert in patent or chemical searching, biotechnology, or the like, $150 is not unreasonable.)

That sounds like a princely sum, doesn't it? Why, at 40 hours a week for 52 weeks a year, it amounts to 2080 hours or between $135,200 and $208,000. Won't the folks back home be proud!

Right. As they say, it's nice work if you can get it. And by the way, why 52 weeks? Aren't you going to take any vacation? Okay, okay, so we take two weeks off and shave the yearly total by a few thousand dollars. While you're at it, since there are no paid holidays when you work for yourself, you'd better deduct another thousand dollars or so. That still leaves some impressive figures.

But what happens if you get sick? Say you're unable to work for a week. And what happens if, God forbid, you develop a serious medical problem? Better shave off some more for your health insurance premiums and your disability insurance (if you can get disability coverage at all as a self-employed individual).

And, by the way, who says that all of the 2080 hours or less you are available for work are going to be billable? Fat chance! The truth is that you will be lucky to be able to bill 50 percent of your time once you are established. When you are just starting out, the figure is more likely to be only 20 percent.

Conferences and professional development

You'll probably want to go to one or more conferences during the year. You may want to take special training in using one or more online systems. Certainly you will want to spend time keeping up-to-date on the field by reading industry journals and trade publications.

Who's going to pay for all this? For the conference registration fees, the travel expenses, the tuition, not to mention the income you'll lose by being away? Who's going to pay you for the time you spend reading your journals? Who's going to pay you for the time you spend marketing your services or trying to drum up new business?

Oh, we see. You'll do these things *after* the regular business day. So, assuming there are no deductions for anything, you're not working just 40 hours a week, are you? You're being paid for 40 hours but are actually putting in more like 50. Gee, we hate to say it, but even before you deduct for all the expenses just cited, your effective hourly rate will be considerably reduced. Forget about your quoted hourly rate. If you are actually working 50 hours a week (2600 a year), and you are making $135,200, your actual hourly rate is $52. Or about the hourly rate you pay the telephone company worker who comes out to install your second or third phone line. And he gets benefits!

Comparable worth?

If comparing yourself to a telephone installer makes you uncomfortable, then let's see how an effective hourly rate of $52 compares to the pay received by people who work for companies or institutions. Start by deducting 33 percent. The rule of thumb is that vacation and benefits increase a corporate employee's compensation by about one third. That means that your $52 an hour compares with a corporate employee being paid about $35 an hour, plus benefits. Assuming a typical 40-hour week for the corporate employee, this multiplies out to an annual salary of $72,800, plus benefits.

In other words, asking a client to pay you at a rate of $65 an hour is the rough equivalent of asking for a salary of $72,800, plus benefits. That's an impressive number, to be sure. But it's a far cry from the six-figure income you may think you were asking for. And don't forget, this accounts for benefits, but not for your non-billable expenses (marketing, conferences, training, travel, etc.). It also assumes that you work *only* 50 hours a week.

The bottom line is this: A rate of $65 or $100 an hour *sounds* like a lot of money. But when you consider the amount of non-billable time you must spend as an information broker; when you consider the lack of benefits (which is to say, the benefits you must buy); when you consider that you must be available for many hours for which you are not paid, $65 to $100 an hour isn't much at all.

You are charging for being available

Finally, of course, the lofty annual income we cited assumes that the jobs and assignments are continuous throughout the year, every year. We all know that's not going to happen. So you're not really making the corporate equivalent of $72,800. With skill, luck, and experience, you might be able to line up enough work to actually earn the equivalent of $30,000 to $50,000, less non-billable expenses and operating overhead.

As we hope you can now see, a rate of $65 to $100 an hour is far from unreasonable. In fact, given all the expenses and self-funded benefits you must deduct from what you receive, you can't afford to charge any less. As our rough calculations have shown, when you charge at that rate, you are making the equivalent of a very average corporate or institutional salary and working many more hours to earn it.

Or consider things another way. Have you ever stopped to figure out the hourly rate you are paying the people you buy services from? Alfred pays Tony, his barber, $12 (including tip) for a haircut that takes at most 20 minutes. That's a rate of $60 an hour. And it's cheap. The cost of a haircut at a fancier place down the road, with tip, is more than double.

Yes, the barber has expenses. He has to pay rent on his shop. He has equipment to maintain. There are advertising expenses. He has to attend conferences to keep up with the latest techniques and styles.

And, while Tony has plenty of work, not every 20-minute segment of his day is always booked. As with an information broker, or anyone else in a service profession, part of what Alfred and the other customers are paying for is Tony's *availability*. If he couldn't make enough when he was busy to carry him through the periods when he is not, Tony would close up shop and seek another line of work. His barbering skills would then not be available to anyone.

Differing rates for differing job components

Of course not every time component of a job should be billed at your professional rate. The time you spend performing clerical tasks (filing, photocopying, etc.) should be billed at clerical rates. The reason is simple. If two brokers are bidding on a job, one charging clerical rates for clerical chores and the other charging the full professional rate, the first broker will come in with a more competitive bid.

It is simply a fact of the marketplace. Since clerical help can be hired at clerical rates, whether you actually hire someone or perform a task yourself, you pretty much have to charge clerical rates for clerical chores. If you don't, someone else will.

But don't cheat yourself! Don't assume, for example, that your post-processing work qualifies as a clerical function. As you read over the results of an online search, getting it ready to send to the client, you are looking for false drops (records that match your search criteria but are actually unrelated to the subject at hand). You may be adding printer codes for boldface type or italics to highlight information you know the client will want to zero in on. You might even be adding comments and call-outs to further add value or otherwise enhance the product.

Post processing often requires skills and a depth of knowledge no clerk can be expected to bring to bear. Therefore it simply does not make good sense—nor is it fair to you—to charge clerical rates for this kind of work.

The second stage of preparing your price

Let's assume that at this point you have calculated a marked-up figure for your costs and a figure for the labor involved (both clerical and professional). Add them together to come up with a preliminary figure, then add something more as a fudge factor. This should be at least 10 to 15 percent, depending on the size of the project. The idea is to build in a little bit of leeway in case things don't go according to plan.

You might discover that you have to do a quick online search that you had not planned on. It might cost you only $20. But if you haven't built in a fudge factor, that's $20 right out of your pocket, since you can hardly ask the client to pay $20 more if you have agreed to a fixed price. There are also small costs that you may forget to pick up or quarter-hour segments that you didn't count on.

Add everything up—costs, labor, and fudge factor—and you will have what we call the base price for the job. This is the price for which you feel you could do the job and both cover your expenses and make a profit. It is, in effect, your minimum. But it does not have to be the price you quote to the client.

In preparing the quoted price, consider what the market will bear. How badly does the client need the information? How badly do you want the job? Is someone else likely to be bidding against you? Is the client likely to become a regular customer once you do this project?

When you've sifted and assessed considerations like these, ask yourself how much more you feel you could charge. It could be $100 more, or $500 more, or some other figure. It is completely up to you. As you gain more experience, you will not only develop a better idea of what a proposed project will cost you, you will also get a feeling for how much the market will bear. Remember, the greater the budget you can persuade the client to authorize, the more you can do for that client and the more profit you will make.

Charge extra for rush service

Also, if the client has asked for rush service, then you must charge extra. How much extra is a function of how much you will be inconvenienced. If you have your week scheduled in a way to let you make all your deadlines without working 19-hour days, and someone calls with a rush request, the inconvenience will be considerable. You will have to put your other projects on hold and possibly risk missing their deadlines. You will have to instantly shift gears and swing into action. At times like that, you may well be within your rights to charge double your normal labor fee.

Even if you do not have anything else scheduled, consider charging extra for a rush job. Clients expect to pay more for this kind of attention. And you certainly don't want to say, "Sure, I can get it to you tomorrow. I wasn't doing anything else anyhow." Rush service is almost universally viewed as an extra for which there is always an extra charge.

For example, Sue added a surcharged of 25 percent of the labor costs for rush service at IOD. So far The Rugge Group has been able to accommodate client deadlines. The group approach makes it possible to avoid putting anyone out when a fast turnaround is required. If one member is busy, he or she says so, and Sue gets another member to do it. However, if yours is a one-person operation, you should definitely charge extra for rush service.

The corporate frame of reference

Experience will also introduce you to an entirely different frame of reference. To us, $500 is a lot of money. There are very few things the average person purchases for $500. But in the corporate world—including advertising agencies and law firms—where you will undoubtedly find many of your clients, $500 is just noise. It is insignificant. If they want the information and that's what you say it costs, that's what it costs. Now, when can you deliver it?

We are by no means suggesting that every job will be $500 or more. We merely want you to be aware that your clients will very likely be operating with a different frame of reference than you are accustomed to, particularly if you came to this profession from a public library, college, or other institution.

If you quote $250 on a job the client is expecting to pay $500 for, you will thus do yourself more harm than good. Instead of jumping at the chance to get your services for half what he expected to pay, your client is likely to wonder what's wrong with you. Maybe you're not confident enough in your abilities to actually do the job. Maybe you're desperate. Or worst of all, maybe you're clearly an amateur. In any case, the client may not respect you or your abilities, however good you may actually be. Sue has found through her consulting that the most prevalent problem for novice "IBs" (information brokers) is their inability to charge what they are worth.

Quote a pricing range

Now, before you contact the client and quote the price you have just calculated, stop and consider the wisdom of quoting a pricing range. Instead of saying, "I can do it for $300," say, "We can do this project for between $400 and $500, with a guarantee not to exceed $500." As you are well aware by now, even experienced brokers cannot be sure what they'll run into once they start a project. Remember how nebulous information is and remember that you have made that point with your client.

Given the nature of information and its retrieval, there is no reason why you should be forced to submit a single, firm price quote for most projects. To do so is to make yourself vulnerable to the unexpected and to risk losing money on a project. By the same token, the client should not be expected to give you an open checkbook.

Quoting a project as a range of prices, with a not-to-exceed guarantee, answers both of these concerns. It protects you both from unexpected expenses. If the project comes in at only $300, you might consider charging the client $400 if it seems appropriate. If it comes in at $450, at least you are protected. Imagine how you would feel if you quoted a firm price of $300 in such a case.

Plus expenses?

You may not be able to get a client to agree to "$400 to $500, plus expenses," though it may be worth a try. Most clients want an outside limit, and "plus expenses" can be too vague. Still, there are certain costs you should definitely strive to get outside the search budget.

The Federal Express charges on a rush job are a good example. If you quote $350 to $400, and the client says, "Okay, but don't go over $400," you might say, "All right. We'll keep it at $400, but then we'll add the FedEx costs on top of that." The client will almost always agree because Federal Express is a specific item. (Better still, ask for your client's Federal Express or other overnight delivery service number.)

It was not uncommon at IOD for Sue and Company to spend $50 shipping materials off to a client. If there was a not-to-exceed limit of $400, and the job cost $350 to execute, that $50 could be all that's left of your profit. If FedEx charges are in the budget, then you'll be sending your profit directly to the company's Memphis headquarters. If the client has agreed that FedEx charges are to be billed in addition to the budget, that $50 will stay put in your pocket.

In general, if there is a cost that is a straight passthrough—where you accept money from the client with one hand and pass it to a supplier or service provider with the other—try to get the client to agree to pay for it, over and above the project cost. And don't forget to mark it up by at least ten percent to compensate your business for the hassle.

What about a minimum charge?

When Sue was running IOD, she established an hourly charge of $75, with a two-hour minimum per job. Even if the job took only one hour, the client had to pay for two. At the Rugge Group, where overhead is much lower, Sue has a more flexi-ble policy. But she still will not consider doing a job of any sort for less than $150, and certainly not less than $300 if any online searching were required. "You can't possibly talk to the client, understand what he wants, execute a job, and prepare a bill for anything less than $150," Sue says, "and that's not very much."

You should definitely set a minimum of at least $150. Whether you decided to make that point with a new client or not depends on the circumstances. If the person calling you is a private individual interested in hiring you for a personal project, you should probably find a point early in the conversation to quote your minimum charge. Individuals may not be aware of how expensive it is to be in business and may be expecting you to charge, say, $25.

If the prospect is seeking to hire you for a corporate project, use your own best judgment. The chances are that the person will be expecting to pay much more than $150, so stating your minimum can seem amateurish.

On the other hand, depending on how the conversation has gone, when the prospect asks you what it's going to cost, you might say, "Well, our minimum fee is $150 per project. Based on what you've told me, it doesn't sound like the total charge will be much more than that. Let me check a few resources and get back to you later today with a more accurate estimate."

We should note here that $150 is at the absolute bottom of an acceptable min-imum. Sue's average project runs between $500 and $650. But you will have to find your own level. Just remember what we said about not charging too little.

Bucking up your confidence

You might as well admit it. The first few times you prepare a bid and present it to the client, you're going to be nervous. It's like learning to ride a bicycle. You can't help being wobbly at first. But before long you master the knack, and from then on going for a spin is simply not an issue.

So what about those first few times? Well, at base you have to accept the fact that you have got to master this part of the job if you want to become an informa-tion broker. Either that, or you'll have to find a partner who can go out and sell your search services. And that partner had better be able to present a price quote with confidence or neither one of you will be in business very long.

Fortunately, there are a number of things you can do to help ease yourself over this initial hump. Call them training wheels, if you like.

Start with your self-image. You are not a librarian forced to smile and be nice to anyone who happens to walk in the door. You are not a back-office research drudge at some company forced to spend your days doing every boring assign-ment company managers throw at you.

You're a professional. You've got the personality, special skills, and talents required to do what so very few others can do. And you're good at it. With a little luck and hard work, those talents and skills will let you be your own boss and run your own company. As much as anyone can ever be, you are in charge of your own life. Unlike your friends and former co-workers, you have elected *not* to trade independence and freedom for the security of a corporate job.

You're more like a lawyer opening his own office or a doctor hanging out her shingle. You're good at what you do. You may feel a bit uncertain about this phase of the job right now, but you've got it where it counts. Besides, you don't *need* this particular job, even if it's the first one you've had a shot at. Another one will come along directly. Don't be afraid that your quote will be too high. If you've done your best to calculate your costs and labor accurately and fairly, and the client says that's too much, then the client simply can't afford the service.

If anyone should be embarrassed, it should be the client, not you. The client is in over his head. He had no business asking you to spend the time and effort coming up with a quote if he wasn't willing to pay a fair price.

You can guard against this outcome by trying to get the client to tell you what type budget they have in mind. If they are coy about the figure and won't answer this query, then be sure that within the first three or four minutes of the conversation you manage to work in the fact that an average search runs around $450 to $650. If you fail to do this, you can easily end up spending 20 minutes or more discussing the project—only to find at the end that the client does not have more than $150 to spend. As Sue says, "This is most likely to happen with individuals and with corporate people who have little authority."

In situations like this, more than likely, the client will not say no. He or she will probably try to appear to be thinking it over and then say, "Yes. That will be fine." If the client says anything else, you've got him covered. Following Sue Rugge's advice, you're prepared to suggest two other alternatives. If the client reacts negatively to your quote, you suggest doing a less extensive search for less money. If the client indicates that your price is inexpensive, you say, "Now, that's for the basic project we discussed. With a larger budget we could also do thus and so."

You might try practicing your presentation on your friends. Do your best to make it real. Seat the friend at a desk and yourself at a chair in front of it and do a little role playing. Encourage your friend to give you a really hard time, raising all kinds of questions, reacting to the price, and so on. Try to get into the spirit of it and improvise your responses. Think of it as your workout before the big event. And have fun with it. (That phrase just will not die.)

Call a broker

There is no substitute for working through the process of preparing an estimate of your costs and labor. However, when you are just starting out, you could consider calling an established information broker and ask that person to give you a quote on the job. That should certainly give you a better idea of what the job should cost and whether your own estimate is way off.

Then go a step further. Add a markup of $100 or so to the quote and take it to the client. When you get the job, hire the broker to do the actual work. Then use a low-cost system like Knowledge Index to do the same search yourself, if possible, and keep track of your time and costs. Comparing your approach and costs with those of the broker you hired will be most instructive. Please remember that you may not use Knowledge Index to actually complete an assignment. So don't forget to adjust for the DIALOG/KI cost difference.

Contracts and agreements

It is the nature of the information brokering profession that the time between the placement of an order and its execution and delivery is usually very short. In most cases, there simply isn't time to spend drawing up and exchanging signed contracts. The client calls and needs it *now*. But you've done work for this particular firm before and you know they're good for it. (For your convenience, should a contract be necessary, you will find a sample contract on the disk accompanying this book.)

Talking to strangers on the phone

If someone you don't know calls up, you may not be quite so willing to take the job. If they have been referred by somebody you know and trust, they will say so in the first 30 seconds of the call. That may be completely satisfactory. If it isn't, you can always call your mutual friend to check the new client out.

If someone calls you out of the blue, perhaps because they heard you speak or saw your ad, you will have to be more cautious. If they need it *now*, quote them your quote and explain that with all new clients your firm's policy is to request half payment in advance and half on delivery of the final report.

If they make remarks to the effect of "What's the matter? Don't you trust me?", you might consider turning the question around. On the contrary, you trust them completely. Just as you expect them to trust you enough to send you half the fee in advance.

"Okay, but how can I get it there in time?" Easy. We accept MasterCard, Visa, or American Express. Or you can send us a check via Federal Express and I'll have it by 10:30 tomorrow morning. No access to Federal Express? No problem. Have your bank wire the funds into my account. Here's my account number and the other information you need. The money will be there within a couple of hours.

If none of this is possible, you should give serious thought to turning down the job. Someone you don't know is asking you to spend your money on their behalf and to take their word that they will pay. Should you believe the person? It's a tough call. We might as well say that everything depends on the "vibes" you get from the phone conversation. Is this person for real or out to take you?

Clients in person

If it is not a rush job, and the person seems a plausible fellow, you might consider preparing a quote and faxing it along with a letter of agreement. The letter of agreement should stipulate half payment in advance and half on completion. When the client sends you his acceptance and a check, you can pretty much assume it's safe to begin work. Please see Fig. 20-2 for a sample letter of agreement. (You will also find a copy of this sample letter on the accompanying disk.)

Letters of agreement can also be useful when you are meeting a client face-to-face. Suppose that a month or two after you made a sales call on the Ajax company, the vice president you spoke with calls. You arrange to go in to meet with her to get a clearer idea of her needs. The meeting goes well. It concludes with

Shown here is a bare bones letter of agreement. It is quite utilitarian and limits itself to just the essential facts. Depending on the situation, you may wish to make your letters more warm and friendly. But do not lose sight of the letter's purpose: to state the project, the deadline, and the fee and payment terms in writing.

If you have business letterhead stationery, there is obviously no need to include your firm's address as we have done here with Questor, Inc.

Questor, Inc.
246 Aedile Acres
Praetor, CA 12354

14 July 1992

Mr. Jasper Jones
ABC Manufacturing Company
54321 Bowvista
Summit, AZ 67893

Dear Mr. Jones:

After our conversation on Monday the 13th, I would like to summarize the project as follows:

Project: A bibliography of articles and books that address the subject of Information Brokering.

Deadline: Tuesday, July 21, 1992, close of business.

Payment: $300 payable half in advance and half on satisfactory completion. Thank you for your business.

Sincerely,

Joan R. Questor
President

Fig. 20-2. A sample letter of agreement

your saying something like, "Good. I'll get back to you today with a quote. Our terms are half in advance and half on completion. Does that pose any problems?"

The point is to politely make it clear that you cannot begin the work until you receive the initial payment. Don't wait until you spend the time preparing your quote to make your terms clear to the client.

If your terms do pose a problem, you will have to decide what to do. The person might say, "That's fine. But we're a big company and it takes at least a week to cut a check. Do you suppose you could get started anyway? I'll do my best to get you a check by next Wednesday." In that case, you may feel that it is safe to start the job. If the person says, "No. I'm sorry, but we never do business that way," you may have to respond, "I'm sorry too, but I can't afford to do business any *other* way."

Don't argue about it. Just bear in mind that attorneys often ask for an initial payment before starting to work. So do advertising agencies. So do management, marketing, and other corporate consultants. Consequently, your request for half in advance should not throw anybody for a loop.

Now let's assume that you have returned to your office. Your terms are acceptable and you can now begin to prepare your quote. Next you call the vice president to present your numbers. If she approves, you say, fine, I'll send you a letter of agreement confirming the details of the project. One of those details, of course, is payment of half the fee in advance and the balance on completion.

Letters of agreement

Once you develop a working relationship with a client, you will no longer need a letter of agreement. Indeed, depending on the circumstance, you may not need one to start either. At some time in your career, however, you will find that a letter of agreement is very helpful.

The purpose of a letter of agreement is to clearly state what you will do, what the client will pay you, and how the payments will be made. Its contents are derived from the details of your conversations with the client. Once you've spelled these details out in writing, there is no excuse for any misunderstanding about what will be done and what will be paid. This is much better than both parties relying on what they think they remember of the conversations.

A letter of agreement may carry less legal weight than an official contract that has been signed, witnessed, and countersigned. But it is still a contract of sorts and it has several advantages over the "official" kind. First of all, it's simple. It is designed to cover broad issues, not every little nuance and possibility. "I agree to do this. You agree to pay me that." End of story. The idea behind a letter of agreement is to obligate you to do the work and the client to pay for it, so it's mutual.

Second, if you haul out an official contract with its party-of-the-first-parts, whereas's, and supplemental terms and conditions, you cause people to draw back. Wait a minute, this looks more serious than I thought. What am I getting into here? They're not getting into anything, but you've inadvertently made them think they are by laying a full-blown contract on their desk.

Third, aside from the presidents of small companies, we can't think of anyone in the business world who is likely to be in a position to sign a contract on the spot. "Oh, a contract. Better put this through 'Legal.'" If you have ever dealt with a company and you think the accounting department is slow to pay your bill, wait till you see how long it takes for the legal department to go over a contract.

And, of course, the legal department will be billing for every hour the newest, greenest attorney in the department spends going over your contract for a $350 project. The legal billing may be charged against your client's division, which will make him real happy.

Finally, take a moment to consider the amounts of money involved here. You may *think* that a full-blown contract gives you more protection than a letter of agreement, but you may be surprised. If a client isn't going to pay you, she isn't going to pay you. It makes not a whit of difference whether you have a contract, a letter of agreement, or a verbal understanding.

But if you have a contract, you could take them to court, couldn't you? Sure you could. In fact, you can take them to Small Claims court without a full-blown contract. Sue Rugge has done exactly that a number of times. And she has always won. But you know what? None of the chiselers ever paid. Getting a judgment against someone and actually collecting are two different stories. It is up to you, the recipient of the favorable judgment, for example, to find a client's bank account and get it attached.

Even if you have a duly executed contract and even if the amount in question is unusually high by information broker standards, say $1000, you probably would not sue a non-paying client. The reason? Legal fees, of course. Filing costs. Plus the hours of lost work time you will have to spend in the lawyer's office and in court.

The majority of the time, it simply is not worth it to sue a client, whether you have a legal contract or not. Given this fact of life and given the difficulties and delays contracts can cause, why bother? In the vast majority of cases a clear letter of agreement is simpler, quicker, and just as effective.

When to insist on a letter of agreement

As we said, you will have to use your own best judgment, but most of the time you will find yourself operating without a letter of agreement. There are times, however, when such a letter is essential, even when dealing with an established client.

If it's a big job, say, several thousand dollars big, or if it is an especially difficult job, prepare a letter of agreement. Sue's rule of thumb has always been that "If I don't think I have a really good crack at it, at least 50%, and maybe more like 65%, I just don't want to take on a job.

"Doing so invites all kinds of negative responses from the client. But sometimes they say, 'I just don't know what else to do, and I really want you to try. If you don't find anything for me, that's okay. I agree to pay.'

"In those cases, I say, 'Because that's not the way we usually function, I'd really appreciate having that in writing.' "

Sue then writes a letter clearly stating their understanding. The letter closes with the line: "If the above reflects your understanding of our agreement, please so indicate by signing below." At the bottom of the letter there will be a line with the person's name and date. Sue then signs the letter and sends it off. The client signs it and sends a copy back to Sue. Nowadays, this can all be done by fax, so timing is not a big problem. Still, it can be a crucial step to take when the client insists you take on a project for which you feel your chances of success are low. Or when the size of the fee is quite large.

What about retainer agreements?

Information On Demand used to offer a retainer package to clients. For a fee of $500 a month, the client was entitled to up to ten hours of research a month (IOD was charging $75 an hour at the time), no per-project labor minimums, and volume discounts on document delivery services. Retainer clients also were assured

VIP service, which meant IOD would do rush work for them without charging a rush surcharge.

It was unquestionably a very good deal. But it was a very tough sell. In all, IOD never had more than two retainer clients at a time during the years the program was offered.

Anytime someone has to sign off on a purchase order that says "I'm going to be paying out $500 a month, and I'm not sure if I can use it, and I'm not sure what I'm going to get back for it," they're very reluctant. That's why, with the exception of the large New York-based firm Find/SVP, nearly every information broker who has tried retainer arrangements has had similarly poor results.

As one broker we know told us, "Hell, it's hard enough to sell most clients on a single $350 project every two months or so. There's no way they're going to pay me $500 every month as a retainer. And a retainer's got to be something like that to even be worth fooling with."

The bottom line seems to be that retainers look like a good deal for both the broker and the client. The broker gets an assured income and flow of business. The client gets guaranteed discounts and preferential treatment. The problem is the same one that affects the entire information brokering industry—a general lack of awareness and insufficient demand.

Hopefully this will change someday. But the time is not yet. Until it does, you will probably be better off developing new business and offering excellent service to your current ones than you will designing retainer agreements and programs.

Offering a deposit account plan is much more feasible, however. If the client puts up, say, $1500 in advance, you will offer him the above advantages. You only charge his account when you actually do the work, so he doesn't lose anything. You get the advantage of cash flow. In short, everybody wins.

Preparing your bill

Once you have completed a project, it's time to prepare your bill. As discussed previously, there is no need to purchase a special form. Indeed, it is déclassé to do so. Use your business letterhead stationery. Type in the date and inside address (the client's name, title, company, etc.), just as if you were preparing a business letter. Skip a few blank lines and do two underlines from margin to margin.

If you have quoted by the project, then you should bill that way. For example: "Floor covering market study. . . $600.00."
(See Fig. 20-3.)

Of course, some clients will ask for a breakdown of labor and expenses. (See Fig. 20-4.) But Sue never starts out that way. As she says, "When you are forced to itemize, you run the risk of questions about costs. Not that this is bad in and of itself. It's just that most clients really don't understand your business."

Still, some clients feel more comfortable with an "itemized" invoice. We put the word *itemized* in quotes because we do not want you to think that this means you must itemize each and every expense, cost, and markup that goes into prepar-

Here is an example of the kind of invoice you may wish to present to your clients. Notice that the invoice does not itemize expenses and that it includes the total project cost, the amount paid in advance, and the balance due.

Questor, Inc.
246 Aedile Acres
Praetor, CA 12354

21 July 1992

Mr. Jasper Jones
ABC Manufacturing Company
54321 Bowvista
Summit, AZ 67893

INVOICE

Invoice No.:90054
Proj. Ref.: 9207-11

Floor covering market study $600.00
Less advance (paid 7/15/92). . . . .(300.00)

Balance due $300.00

Fig. 20-3. A sample "project" invoice

ing your bill. Instead, offer the clients who require it a rough breakdown of the sort shown in Fig. 20-4.

Project and purchase order numbers

Notice that in both types of invoices we refer to the project by subject and number. The subject is important for communication between you and the client, particularly if you are doing several projects for the same client. But you should also refer to the project by some kind of number. Most service organizations (law firms, consultants, ad agencies, etc.) have file numbers for their projects as well. It is important to the smooth flow through of payables to use project numbers of some sort.

If you are dealing with a large company, you will need to include a purchase order (PO) number. (Add a line like this to your invoice: "Purchase Order: X-101-576.") Theoretically a PO is a promise by a company that it will pay you for what you are going to deliver upon receipt of your invoice.

By controlling who can sign off on PO's, companies can control purchases made for the firm by employees. So when you are dealing with a big company, make sure that you get a PO number before you agree to do the job. This ensures that the person who is hiring you has the authority to do so, and that your bill will be processed by the accounting department with minimum difficulty and delay.

Shown here is a sample itemized invoice. Notice the blanks for "Invoice No." and "Proj. Ref" number. These items track with the search request form shown in Fig. 19-1.

Questor, Inc.
246 Aedile Acres
Praetor, CA 12354

21 July 1992

Mr. Jasper Jones
ABC Manufacturing Company
54321 Bowvista
Summit, AZ 67893

Invoice No.:90054
Proj. Ref.: 9207-11

Project: Rent Control Case Law search

Labor:

Attorney: 3.5 hours @ $100	350.00
Researcher: 3.5 hours @ $75	262.50

Online costs: 459.80

Postage:

Federal Express	35.00
	25.00

Phone charges: 11.40

TOTAL: $1,143.70

Fig. 20-4. A sample itemized invoice

The "Bean Counters"

Generally, you can expect to encounter two types of, well, of "bean counters." There are those who feel that computer time is expensive, so they expect to pay a lot for it—but not very much for labor. Then there are those who feel computers are so fast that computer time should not be a large part of the bill. But this group agrees that computers are complicated, so they expect to pay more for labor and less for connect time.

Look at how long it has taken us to explain the information brokering business in this book. There is no way you can hope to ever convey the details of the business to a client. Therefore, as we have said, billing with a single fee is often the best course. After all, attorneys and physicians do it. So why not you?

However, as we said, if you are forced to itemize, there is no need to go into elaborate detail. You should definitely include a line for labor. This would be the number of hours you spent at your professional rate. You should also include a line for your online database charges.

You should have a line for direct expenses as well. It is up to you whether you lump everything into a single figure or break it out to include clerical support, photocopies, copyright clearance fees, postage, long distance telephone, fax, travel, and so on.

Anything you had to buy to be able to pass on to the client should also be given a line. Mailing lists, document delivery charges, books, tapes, maps—whatever. The client does not need to know everything, so use your own best judgment on how much billing detail you'll provide when submitting an itemized bill.

Creating an impression

As you can imagine, it is possible to have an invoice with only three lump-sum line items or one with a dozen smaller line items. Both will add up to the same total, but the impressions they create will be quite different. In most cases it is probably best to be moderately specific. Don't go into too much detail. But use enough to help your client understand all that was involved in executing the project. Unless the project is extremely complex, under no circumstances should your invoice run more than a single page.

It is also a good idea to leave room for a line reading "Please make check payable to . . ." followed by your name and your Social Security number. If you do not include your Social Security number, the accounting department may have to phone you to get it, and your check will be delayed.

Be sure to state your terms as well. Sue uses "Net 30 days," but you can try "Net 15 days" or "Payable upon receipt." However, Sue feels that this is a little pushy. "Some manufacturers will say, '2% 10 days, Net 30,' meaning that if you pay within 10 days, you can take a two percent discount. But we have never found that to work in our business. Customers will take the two percent, but pay within 30 days—not 10—and that wreaks havoc with your accounting system."

How to present your bill

There are at least two schools of thought on the best way to convey your invoice to the client. Whenever Alfred completes a writing assignment, he sends his invoice along with the finished piece. But he includes a cover letter introducing the package and assuring the client that he will do the single revision that was agreed to. Whether a revision was part of the deal or not, the letter concludes with "Please don't hesitate to call if there are any questions," or words to that effect. Many information brokers follow a similar practice.

Sue, on the other hand, likes to make sure the client is completely satisfied before submitting her bill. Within four or five days of the time she sends off a search, she calls the client to make sure the package arrived and to ask if they are satisfied. If everything is fine, then an invoice is prepared and sent. If there are problems, Sue does her best to resolve them, even to the point of having the search done over again.

This is good customer relations, to be sure. But Sue is also careful to make notes on when she made the call and what the client said. "The easiest excuse a client can give 90 days later for not paying you is that they were not satisfied," Sue says. That's why you want to be able to say, "There must be some misunderstanding. We talked to you three days after you received the materials and you said 'Fantastic. This looks like exactly what I wanted.'"

There isn't much a deadbeat client can say to that without looking extremely foolish. Hopefully, the person will be embarrassed enough to expedite payment—especially since the client knows you're going to call again if you are not paid.

How to dun a client

It is one of those curiosities of language that the word "dun" is the first word in the credit reporting agency Dun & Bradstreet, and the verb that describes the process of going after deadbeat customers. No one likes to dun a customer. But it is naive to believe that you will never have to do so. The best policy is to follow Sue's advice and make sure the client is satisfied with your services.

Whether you send your invoice with the project or later, *always* make a follow-up call to the client a few days after the materials have been received. This is a very natural thing to do, since as a professional you will be sincerely interested in whether you delivered what was wanted. You want to provide superb service.

But the follow-up phone call is also the ideal time to uncover any dissatisfactions or problems. Unless you have made a serious error in judgment in taking on a client in the first place, you can assume that the client is not out to deliberately stiff you. If you are not paid on time, it may be because the client is dissatisfied. So find out early and correct the problem quickly.

In other cases, the client may simply be too busy (or somehow think so) to deal with the necessary paperwork to put through your invoice. By calling, and continuing to call, you move your request higher and higher on the client's "must-do" list. Office politics may also play a role. Your client may be having a problem with a superior whose signature is required. Or the superior may simply be out of the office on vacation.

It may be that the client has overstepped his authority. He may be able to sign for expenditures of $500, but not the $750 on your invoice. And he may be too embarrassed to tell you that what he really needs are two invoices of $375 each. Be sure to ask in the beginning if there will be a problem like this.

Obviously, there may be all kinds of other reasons as well. The fact remains though that you have done the work the client contracted with you to do and you must be paid. The most effective technique is to make noise. Start with a gentle, inquiring phone call after the invoice is 45 days old if your stated terms are "30 days." If your terms are "15 days," start calling at Day 30.

Turning up the volume

If you do not get satisfaction, call back two weeks later to turn up the volume. Be aware that some companies as a matter of policy don't pay small vendors like yourself for 90 days. It's outrageous, but there is not much you can do but wait for your money. (Alfred remembers one large company that took about 90 days to pay and then did so with a check drawn on a bank clear across the country. Nice.)

At 90 days overdue, it is time to crank up the campaign. Be polite. But be persistent. Call every week, or even every three days if appropriate. If the deadbeat is always out of the office when you call and never calls you back, consider sending a registered letter. In the letter, inform the deadbeat that if you do not receive your check in seven days, you will escalate to a higher level in the company. At this point you have nothing to lose—you're never going to accept an assignment from this person again and probably not from anyone else at the company.

There are other things you can do, short of taking legal action. You can contact the president of the company with your complaint. You can file a complaint with the Better Business Bureau. It might even be worthwhile to send a complaint to Dun & Bradstreet and other corporate credit reporting agencies. But before you take these actions, make sure that the deadbeat knows you plan to take them if your invoice is not paid.

No one likes to be thought of as a pest. Dunning is not pleasant work and hopefully you will never have to take it to this level. But if you do, remember that someone who claims to be satisfied with your work and still refuses to pay you the amount agreed upon is no better than a common thief. That person's opinion of you for being so persistent is of no significance whatever. You're the one who was robbed.

Watch out for small companies

As we said, big companies won't process an invoice without a purchase order number. But that's not where you are likely to have problems. Where you get into trouble is when you're working with a little company, and you think having a PO means everything's going to be fine. You tend to get stung by small companies—five or ten people—more often than you do by individuals or by large corporations. Individuals tend to be more honorable. Small companies tend to be undercapitalized and often have trouble paying their bills. They tend to think, "I'm a small company too, and if this information broker goes bankrupt, well, I've gone bankrupt too. I've got more important bills to pay."

Of course you can get burned by the big firms too. IOD once had a client who worked for a large company and said he needed the information in a hurry. "Don't worry, I'll get you a purchase order next week. But I need the information right now." Of course he never did, and when IOD went to collect, the person no longer worked there. On further investigation, it turned out that the subject area he needed information on was probably for personal use. The company would not authorize payment, and IOD was left holding the bag.

There is no way to make sure that you are never left holding the bag. In industry in general, the rule of thumb is to assume that two percent of your customers will turn out to be deadbeats. So you may want to allow two percent for bad debt. You may be able to deduct it on Schedule C of your tax return, but always be sure to check with your accountant on tax matters first. Still, it would be better to have the money in hand.

Conclusion

We have covered a lot of ground in this chapter. Everything from how much to charge to how to charge what the market will bear to matters of contracts, letters of agreement, and presenting (and collecting) your bill. Excuse us, ''invoice.'' We have tried to give you the outlines and as many relevant tips and tricks as possible in each case.

But ultimately, you can't really learn these parts of the information broker's job until you've actually performed them. As you gain experience, you will develop your own tips and tricks. You'll discover the things that work for you. Remember that there is no right way or wrong way to do them. But you've got to get paid. And get paid enough to cover your expenses and make a living. If you don't, you won't be an information broker for very long.

Office setup
bonus section

WELL, YOU MADE IT. IF YOU HAVE READ THIS FAR, YOU ARE WELL ON YOUR WAY TO becoming a practicing information broker. But don't stop here. There's lots of excellent information on the accompanying disk that you will not find in these printed pages. Appendices A through E can be found on the disk, for example.

In particular, we want to be sure to draw your attention to a special bonus section about how to set up your own office. Topics covered include when and how to hire an accountant, attorney, or insurance advisor; electrical power and phone considerations; furnishings, of course; plus typewriters, telephones, answering machines, faxes, photocopiers, and personal computers and related equipment. As always, Sue's and Alfred's personal advice can save you time and money in setting up your office.

Appendix F, which can be found in its entirety in printed form later in this book, will tell you how to install the accompanying disk. Once the software has been installed and all the files have been uncompressed, you will be asked to hit a key to call up a menu. From this menu you will be able to view or print all supplied *.TXT files, including OFFICE.TXT. As Appendix F notes, you may key in MENU from then on to bring up the menu.

Conclusion

In closing, we have two words of advice for all aspiring information brokers. First, take it slow. Do not try to set up your office, your business, or your information brokerage all at once with every detail in place. Neither Rome nor anything else was ever built in a day.

Second: Do it! If you are truly interested in the information brokering profession, if we have not succeeded in scaring you out of a passing fancy, then, by all means, take the plunge. We have presented the profession and the field in the fairest, most honest way we know how. Indeed, we have gone out of our way to show you the downside and to disabuse you of any lingering notion that there is easy money to be made as an information broker.

If you are still fascinated by information and information gathering, if you have been bewitched by the power and by the thrill of the hunt, if you simply cannot get it out of your mind, then welcome aboard! You're hooked, as we are, and you might as well admit it.

We cannot promise you that you will be able to make a living at this trade, regardless of your enthusiasm and hard work. But we can definitely promise that you will be in excellent company. Professional information brokers are among the most fascinating people you will ever meet. And they're good friends as well.

We cannot emphasize strongly enough what a collegial profession this is. It is probably not accurate to say that everybody knows everybody else, but that's not far off the mark.

To plug in quickly, read and print out Appendix C on the accompanying disk. There you will find information on the Association of Independent Information Professionals (AIIP). It is only a slight exaggeration to say that everyone who is anyone belongs to the AIIP, and you should too. To delve even deeper into the profession, the tradecraft, and the business side of things, see Appendix E on Sue Rugge's Information Broker's Seminar.

Once again, welcome aboard!

Appendix A

The information broker's bookshelf
Crucial resources and reference works

Important note This appendix is located on the accompanying disk. Please follow the instructions presented in Appendix F for installing the disk. Using the menu that will appear at the end of the installation process, you can easily print or view the file containing this information.

Appendix A pulls together and presents in a single place a listing of the resources that are likely to be especially important to any practicing information broker. It includes information on books that may be important to you in your new profession, online information resources, magazines and newsletters, publisher addresses, and more.

Since you will want to contact many of these companies and vendors, you will find it especially convenient to have the addresses in electronic form. Simply bring the file into your word processing program and clip out the addresses you wish to use.

For those of you who don't have access to a computer, you can order printouts of Appendices A, B, and C from Sue Rugge at the address below. Please include $5 to cover printing and postage. Payment can be made by check or credit card.

The Rugge Group
2670 Mountain Gate Way
Oakland, CA 94611
(510) 530-3635 (voice)
(510) 530-3325 (fax)

Appendix B

Contact points
Online systems, organizations, associations, and trade shows

Important note   This appendix is located on the accompanying disk. Please follow the instructions presented in Appendix F for installing the disk. Using the menu that will appear at the end of the installation process, you can easily print or view the file containing this information.

Appendix B is designed to be used as a quick reference. It makes no attempt to be comprehensive. Instead, it concentrates on the names, addresses, and phone numbers most information brokers need most of the time. There are, for example, over 4000 databases and over 500 online systems. But the two dozen shown in this appendix are the ones you will use for most of your projects and electronic mail communications.

Similarly, most brokers will want to join one or more of the information-related organizations and associations listed. If you can possibly manage it, we also strongly suggest that you try to attend one of the two leading trade shows in our industry. There is no better way to gain an instant appreciation of the depth and scope of the information industry than to attend National Online and/or the Online/CD-ROM conference.

Appendix C

The Association of Independent Information Professionals (AIIP)

Important note   This appendix is located on the accompanying disk. Please follow the instructions presented in Appendix F for installing the disk. Using the menu that will appear at the end of the installation process, you can easily print or view the file containing this information.

Once you become an information broker, you'll want to give serious consideration to joining the AIIP, the Association of Independent Information Professionals. Indeed, we feel that membership is virtually essential. The AIIP is quite simply *the* society of independent information professionals, information providers, and users worldwide.

Appendix C will give you an overview of AIIP, describe the types of memberships that are available and the benefits associated with each, and tell you how to send for your membership application. It will also give you a glimpse of the kinds of benefits you can expect by signing onto CompuServe and entering the Work from Home Forum that serves as AIIP's online, electronic headquarters. You do not have to be an AIIP member to take advantage of this, but once you join, additional areas of the forum will be open to you.

Appendix D

Essential software
Glossbrenner's Choice shareware

THIS APPENDIX CAN SAVE YOU *MONEY*! EVERY SMALL BUSINESSPERSON NEEDS A computer system. That simply goes without saying. And every small businessperson faces three costs in acquiring such a system. There is the cost of the hardware, the cost of the software, and the cost of the time and effort required to learn to use the computer and its software.

There isn't much we can do to cut your hardware costs, other than to recommend yet another Glossbrenner book that will steer you in the right direction. Nor can we have much effect on the time and effort required to learn how to use your system. At least not without recommending still another Glossbrenner book. But here we can definitely cut your software costs to the bone. And the nice thing is that you won't have to give up anything more than a shrink-wrapped package and high computer-store prices.

The reason we can cut your software costs so drastically can be summed up in a single word: *shareware*. As we have noted throughout the book, shareware is software on the honor system. You are supplied with a fully functional program, complete with an on-disk, ready-to-print manual, for a small distribution or downloading fee. If you find you do not care for the product, you are free to erase the disk or pass it on to a friend. But if you do like and use the program, you are on your honor to send the programmer the registration fee he or she requests.

The specifics vary with the program, but generally, you can expect to receive a printed manual and telephone support (often from the programmer him- or herself) in return for sending in the registration amount. You may also get free or reduced-cost updates, and sometimes, even a newsletter filled with tips and information.

Requested fees are small, even tiny, by commercial standards. And, in general, you get a lot more for your money than with commercial products.

If you are a Macintosh user . . .

There is shareware for virtually every brand of personal computer. If you are a Macintosh user, for example, one of the best sources of shareware and public domain software is Educorp. To obtain a free catalogue, contact:

Educorp
7434 Trade St.
San Diego, CA 92121-2410
(800) 843-9497
(619) 536-9999
(619) 536-2345 (fax)

An embarrassment of IBM-compatible riches

If you are an IBM or compatible user, your choices are even more varied. Indeed, you are faced with either an embarrassment of riches, or a painful dilemma. On the one hand, there are literally tens of thousands of IBM-compatible shareware programs available, and they cover nearly every topic or application you can imagine. On the other hand, if you are not a shareware aficionado, how can anyone expect you to choose among 30 or more word processors and text editors or among 60 or more communications packages and utility disks?

To make an intelligent choice—to decide upon the one program you should invest your time and effort in learning—you would have to run and test literally *all* of them. What's more, you could easily spend well over $200 just to obtain the disks from a shareware mail order vendor or to download the programs from CompuServe, GEnie, or a bulletin board.

Shareware, in other words, is a twin-edged sword. The selection of easily available products is unparalleled, and you get to try before you buy. But to make a good choice, you either have to test all of the programs yourself, or you have to rely on someone who has done so for you.

Glossbrenner's Choice

It was to solve this problem that Glossbrenner's Choice was created in 1986. The Glossbrenner's Choice collection makes no attempt at being comprehensive. On the contrary, it is highly selective. To be included, a program must offer something that people really need, and it must be absolutely excellent. Programs are chosen by reviewing all of the offerings in a particular category and personally testing them to find the best one.

As a final step, the programmer is often contacted and interviewed to get a better sense of the person behind the product. Is he or she committed to supporting the program, or are registered users likely to get a disconnected number when they call for help? Are new versions and features planned? How are bug fixes handled, and may we see a copy of the printed manual supplied to registered users?

In short, Glossbrenner's Choice does everything *you* would do if you had the time and knew where and how to look for programs. It thus attempts to bridge the information gap that separates most computer users from the money-saving gems to be found in the vast treasure house that is the world of public domain and shareware software.

If you will trust our judgment, we can save you time, and we can save you money. We can tell you which specific programs we feel are the best in each application category. You can then obtain these programs from online or mail order sources. As a convenience, since we have the software anyway, you can also obtain the programs and disks from Glossbrenner's Choice.

Conventions followed here

Listed next you will find those programs we feel are ideal for most information professionals. The programs are referenced by the Glossbrenner's Choice (GBC) disks that hold them. A GBC order form can be found at the end of this appendix.

Disk names or multi-disk packages are given in capital letters. Please note that the items highlighted here are only part of the complete GBC collection. Consequently, disk numbers are not necessarily sequential. We have organized the disks under eight main headings:

Word processing
Idea processing
Security encryption
Online communications
Spreadsheet and accounting
Database management
Forms creation
Education (DOS and Typing)

Word processing

Selecting a word processing program is everyone's most important software decision. Obviously word processing software is crucial to producing letters, notes, and reports. But, as with all software, your greatest cost is the time you spend learning to use a program. That's why, in our opinion, it is best to forget about the under-powered programs shipped with many computers and spend your time instead starting to master a full-featured product.

The program we like and use—indeed, the program this and many other books have been written with—is Bob Wallace's PC-Write from Quicksoft, Inc. PC-Write has more power than most of us will ever need. But it has lots of pop-up help menus, and the support Quicksoft supplies to registered users is superb. It is a super program from a super company.

PC-WRITE package (PCW 1, 2, and 3—3 disks)

PC-Write (PCW), from Quicksoft, Inc., is the world's best example of the power and benefits of shareware. It is a full-featured word processing program that can go toe-to-toe with any commercially marketed product. But rather than reel off a list of features, we'll let the product's success speak for itself.

PC-Write has been continually updated since its introduction in 1983 and has been licensed by companies like DuPont, EDS, Ford Motor Company, ITT, the Los Angeles Times, MCI, Union Carbide and Whirlpool. Colleges as diverse as Iowa State University, Rutgers, and the University of Hong Kong have licensed it as well.

As a result, Quicksoft's sales have risen dramatically over the years from $17,000 in 1983 to over $2 million in 1991. (Over a million people use PCW worldwide.) And the number of employees has grown from 1 to "27 employees (and 1 cat)," according to a fact sheet supplied by the company. Versions are available for Argentina, Chile, Paraguay, Denmark, Finland, France, Germany, Iceland, Sweden, and the Netherlands, among other countries.

People, companies, and colleges obviously *love* the program. And with good reason—PC-Write is fast, friendly, and flexible. It creates "clean ASCII" files containing none of the strange codes and symbols inserted by many other programs. That means that any other program can use a PCW-created file without difficulty. It also means that you will have no problem sending a PCW-created file via electronic mail.

The program comes with an extensive hands-on tutorial and manual on disk (over 200 pages). It's got a 50,000-word spelling checker, to which you can add your own words. (French, Russian, and German spelling checkers are available separately from Quicksoft for $20 to $30.) PCW provides special support for over 800 printers.

Quicksoft offers a variety of registration options. If you would like to buy just the printed manual, the cost is $49, plus shipping. If you want to buy basic telephone support for a year, the cost is $40. If you want to go for the full package, the cost is $129 and includes a hardcover copy of the manual and full technical support for a year. You will also receive the company's tip-filled newsletter, "Quick Notes," for one year.

Finally, when you do register, you will be given a unique number to be added to the program. As always, you are encouraged to distribute PC-Write to others. Each time one of those people registers, Quicksoft will pay you $25. (This is the original meaning of "shareware," a term and technique that Quicksoft invented. "Shareware" has since come to mean any freely distributed copyrighted software for which the programmer requests a registration fee.)

Disk 1 is the program disk; Disk 2 contains the supplied utilities (mouse support, printer picker, etc.); and Disk 3 includes the spelling checker and on-disk manual and tutorial. Please note that the copies of PCW we distribute do *not* contain a registration number and do not earn a commission of any kind for Glossbrenner's Choice.

Idea processing

If one can have word processing, why not "idea processing?" Why not, indeed, said the creators of PC-Outline. Idea processing is actually a fancy term for using computer software to facilitate getting your thoughts in order. A more accurate, though much more prosaic, term is "outliner."

An idea processor or outliner can be very helpful to an information broker in planning a search assignment and in preparing a client report on that assignment. The shareware program we like best is Brown Bag Software's PC-Outline. (We are not alone in admiring the product—*PC Magazine* made it its Editor's Choice.)

IDEA 1—PC-Outline

PC-Outline is an amazing clone of the commercial idea outlining program, Thinktank. Indeed, many former Thinktank users prefer this shareware product. The program makes it easy for you to sit at your computer and brainstorm without worrying about where everything goes. Just key in your thoughts as they occur to you.

As you proceed, a structure will begin to emerge. You can then use PC-Outline to quickly and easily move your random thoughts into their proper order to produce a really solid plan of action or report outline.

Security encryption

As we have said numerous times throughout this book, confidentiality is crucial to successful information brokering. In many cases, clients will hire you to find information that can help them steal a march on a competitor. Your credibility and your future as an information broker depend on your ability to keep a secret.

In some circumstances, therefore, you may want to encrypt your files. That means turning them into gibberish that can only be unscrambled by the proper program and the proper password. It may or may not be necessary to encrypt the files in your office. But you should never send un-encrypted text of a confidential nature through an electronic mail system.

This is not to imply that someone's reading your mail. To our knowledge, only the IBM/Sears Prodigy system makes a practice of this, and it only applies the policy to publicly posted messages. But the mere fact that someone involved with the e-mail system *could* read your mail if they wanted to makes it prudent to encrypt sensitive information.

ENCRYPTION 1—PC-Code and The Confidant

The two programs on this disk (PC Code and The Confidant) can so thoroughly encrypt a text or binary file that cipher experts from the National Security Agency or CIA would have a tough time decoding the results. If you have the password "key," however, you (or your client) can decrypt files in an instant.

Communications

As you know, information brokers use online communications constantly. If you're not doing an online search of DIALOG, you're sending a letter to someone via MCI Mail, or sending a file to someone else via CompuServe or GEnie. And if you are not doing any of these things, you will at the very least check your e-mail mailboxes at least once a day.

There is no substitute for a fast, powerful, superbly programmed communications or "comm" program. And the one that hundreds of thousands of private individuals, professionals, and companies use is ProComm from DataStorm Technologies, Inc. We have no hesitation in saying that ProComm is absolutely the best comm program in the IBM-compatible world.

The features you are likely to value most will be determined by the kinds and variety of communicating you do. But the one you will probably use most frequently, is the ability to prepare logon scripts that will automatically dial the target number and sign you on to a system. If you like, you can extend a script to execute an entire online session, from sign-on to sign-off. And you can tell the program to execute the script at any time of day, unattended.

Online searchers will also appreciate the "macro" capabilities that allow you to load database commands into nine or more keypress combinations. There is also a built-in scroll-recall feature that lets you capture previously displayed information to disk, in case you forgot to open your capture buffer.

If you are new to personal computer communications, either go to the library or order a copy of Alfred Glossbrenner's *Complete Handbook of Personal Computer Communications: Everything You Need to Go Online with the World*. With this book and with a copy of ProComm, you cannot fail.

COMM 1—ProComm 2.4.3

ProComm, version 2.4.3, is the latest and greatest shareware version of the product. It supports a wide variety of transfer protocols (Kermit, several varieties of XMODEM, YMODEM, CompuServe B and "Quick B," for example), not to mention a variety of mainframe terminal emulations. ProComm 2.4.3 can handle any task you throw at it with ease.

COMM 2—ProComm 2.4.3 utilities

ProComm 2.4.3 comes with several utility programs. But users have written many ProComm utilities of their own. The best ones are on COMM 2, including PRCM-DIR, a program that will parse lists of bulletin board system (BBS) numbers and automatically insert them into the ProComm dialing directory. No need to key them in yourself.

Also included is ZRUN.COM, a program that allows ProComm 2.4.3 to support the new ZMODEM protocol for error-checking modems.

COMM 3—The Communicator's Toolchest

This disk contains a collection of utility programs and add-ons selected to make your life easier online. Among other things, you will find DSZ.COM, Chuck Forsberg's famous program for adding ZMODEM protocol capabilities to nearly *any* communications program. ZMODEM is widely accepted as the best, most efficient protocol for transferring files. It is supported by GEnie and most bulletin board systems.

To use DSZ, you must have a comm program that lets you call an external editor, or one that lets you add external protocols. ProComm, Qmodem, and GT PowerComm are among the shareware communications packages that fulfill these requirements. DSZ also lets you use Forsberg's True YMODEM and XMODEM if the system you're calling does not offer ZMODEM.

In addition to DSZ, COMM 3 contains a program to add CompuServe's B+ ("Quick B") protocol to virtually any communications program, plus a complete ARC/un-ARC package, and a variety of small utilities like COMSTA.COM, a program to tell you how much time will be required to transmit a given file at a variety of baud rates.

COMM 3 also contains Vern Buerg's ARC-E.COM, a program designed to extract the contents of an .ARC file. Utilities to "un-squeeze" and remove files from "libraries" are also included. "Squeezing" and "librarying" are compression and consolidation techniques that pre-date today's archiving approach. But every now and then you will encounter a file that requires one of these utilities.

Also included is DPROTECT, a program to prevent any virus or "Trojan horse" program from writing to your disks without your permission.

COMM 4—ProComm PLUS: Test Drive

ProComm PLUS Test Drive is the fully operational ProComm PLUS package. "PC-Plus," as it is called, goes ProComm 2.4.3 one better. It offers built-in support for ZMODEM, for example, plus support for an even larger number of modems. Its script language is even more powerful and sophisticated than the scripting capabilities of "2.4.3."

The "Test Drive" version offered here lacks only the extensive on-disk manual supplied with 2.4.3. (A large, professionally written printed manual is supplied to registered users of PC-Plus.)

COMM 7—TAPCIS

"CIS" is the abbreviation for "CompuServe Information Service" used most often by CompuServe subscribers. This program, pronounced, "tap-sis," is designed to make it easy for you to deal with electronic mail and make the most of CompuServe forums. (There is even a special TAPCIS forum on the system for online support.)

Using TAPCIS for an online session is a three-step process. First you tell it to sign on. It does so and automatically picks up any waiting electronic mail. Then it goes into the forums you have specified during the configuration process and picks up any messages addressed to you. Finally, TAPCIS signs off and thus stops the connect time meter from running.

You take the second step by reviewing the information TAPCIS has gathered offline. You can then key in replies to e-mail and forum messages at your leisure using the built-in editor.

The third and final step is to turn TAPCIS loose to sign on to the system again and automatically upload your e-mail and forum message replies.

TAPCIS can do lots of other things as well. It can download a list of files and their descriptions in a forum library. You can tag the ones you want when you are offline. TAPCIS will then automatically return to the target forum and download the tagged files for you.

The whole idea behind TAPCIS is to make using CompuServe as easy and cheap as possible.

COMM 8—Aladdin

The best way to describe Aladdin is to say that it is, in effect, TAPCIS for GEnie. It is essential to anyone who frequently uses GEnie's RoundTables.

COMM 10—Compression programs: PKZIP, LHARC, and PAK

Archiving a program's documentation, executable, and other files into a single package offers two advantages to an online user. First, it is much easier to download a single archived file than it is to download all the files associated with a program individually. Second, archiving programs not only pack several files into a single file, they also compress the files so they take less time to transmit.

The one difficulty most users face is that there is no single archiving standard. This means that most online communicators need to have several archive creation/extraction programs available. You will find an .ARC extractor on COMM 3. COMM 10, in contrast, contains everything you need to deal with .ZIP, .LHZ, and .PAK files. There are also a number of utilities that will make un-compressing files much easier, regardless of the technique used.

Spreadsheet and accounting

If there is one overriding, central truth to personal computing, it is this: Not everything that *can* be done by a computer *should* be done by a computer. It is far easier to balance your checkbook by hand, in many cases, than it is to locate, load, and learn to use a program to do the same thing.

On the other hand, selective computerization offers small businesses and professionals the single most promising opportunity to be competitive with larger firms. If you can automate your business projection and accounting functions, you will have more time to spend doing what you do best—gathering information.

If you are a small business with very simple needs, you probably do not need a spreadsheet or accounting program. But if your needs are more complex, you can't do better than the two programs profiled here.

SPREADSHEET 1—As-Easy-As

An electronic spreadsheet, in its simplest form, automates the process of adding, subtracting, or performing other calculations on rows and columns of numbers.

The best quick handle on this type of software is to imagine a tax form that automatically re-calculates itself and produces a new bottom line whenever you change any figure that depends on another figure. Businesspeople use spreadsheet software to answer questions like, "What if the tax rate goes up half a percent? How will that affect our profit on the project at the current bid?" A user can enter a new figure into a spreadsheet model, and all the figures that are derived from it will automatically change.

As-Easy-As, in our opinion, stands head and shoulders above virtually every other spreadsheet program available today. The latest version, version 4.x, makes that statement even truer than before. As-Easy-As will simply knock your eyes out.

One of the features that sets it apart from most other spreadsheets is that As-Easy-As is Lotus-compatible. You can bring virtually any Lotus-created "worksheet" into As-Easy-As and manipulate it as if you had created it yourself. As-Easy-As uses a sparse memory matrix and offers a maximum of 256 columns by 8192 rows. It has over 80 built-in functions for math, statistics, logic, strings, and dates, including user-definable functions. It supports spreadsheet linking to let you relate information in your current worksheet to worksheets on disk.

It's got over 50 pages of help screens built right into the program. Plus, it can generate many different graphs, including: bar, stacked bar, line, XY, and pie chart.

There are dozens of other crucial features as well—none of which will mean anything to you if you are not a spreadsheet user. If you are, however, or if you want to learn Lotus-style spreadsheeting, you simply cannot go wrong with As-Easy-As.

PRINTER 4—On-Side (Sideways printing)

One of the problems encountered by all spreadsheet users is printing. Often the spreadsheet you create is much wider (many more columns) than your printer can produce. That's why Funk Software created the highly successful Sideways program, a commercial package that can print your spreadsheets in what is now called "landscape" mode (on their sides.)

The shareware equivalent of Sideways is On-Side, and it comes from David Berdan and Bill Willis of ExpressWare, one of the country's leading shareware firms. As one would expect, this is a super program that is a must for anyone who uses Lotus and similar electronic spreadsheet programs. It will print text files sideways as well.

ACCOUNTING 1—Medlin's GL, AP, AR, and PR

The abbreviations here stand for General Ledger (GL), Accounts Payable (AP), Accounts Receivable (AR), and Payroll (PR). This is an excellent set of accounting modules for a small business that outgrows its manual systems and needs to computerize.

Mr. Medlin, who divides his time between teaching accounting at the college level and supporting his programs, told us that "most of my registered users need and use only one or two modules. The typical small business writes perhaps 100 to 150 checks per month, and most have many, many fewer General Ledger accounts than the 4,000 that the PC-GL module allows for.''

Mr. Medlin also noted that his software assumes a general knowledge of accounting on the part of the user. This is not to say that you can't use it if you have never kept formal accounts before. But you may want to get a textbook on the subject to use with the program modules.

Database management

Database management software is designed to help you keep track of information. The classic use of a database, for example, is to record items like the names and addresses of your regular clients. But you can also use such a program to track jobs, prepare invoices, and ride herd on your billing. You can use database software to keep track of office supplies, to generate mailing lists, or to generate addresses to be merged into form letters created by PC-Write and other word processing programs. You can use a "DBMS" (database management system) to do anything, in short, that requires the manipulation, calculation, presentation, and retrieval of information.

FILE EXPRESS package (4 disks)

This shareware program carries a voluntary registration fee of $99. But listen to what *PC Sources* [August, 1991] had to say about it:

> File Express has features that make other database programs in its price range seem sickly by comparison . . . When you combine this [mail-merge capability] with a powerful label-writing feature, you have all the functionality required by typical small businesses . . . With superior reporting capabilities and an easy, affordable way to convert to it, File Express is perfect for most small business and home-office applications.

The File Express, v5.x, on-disk manual is 415 pages long, and it includes a tutorial for those who have never used a database program before. Indeed, it is identical to the printed manual registered users receive, except that the on-disk version does not contain illustrations or sample screens.

As for capacity, the program can handle up to 2 billion records per database, 4000 characters per record, and 1000 characters per field. It offers context-sensitive help, mathematical accuracy up to 14 digits, simultaneous sorts on up to 10 fields, and support for over 280 printers.

Expressware has been in business since 1984. At this writing, its annual sales are over $1.4 million dollars. As with PC-Write, it is clear that a lot of people *love* File Express. (Glossbrenner's Choice has used File Express to handle orders since its beginning, nearly five years ago.)

Forms creation

If we liked paperwork, we would not be self-employed. We would be working instead for a large corporation or government agency. Still, as you know from

Chapters 19 and 20, some forms of some sort are necessary to run your information brokering business efficiently. You will find copies of the forms used by The Rugge Group on the disk accompanying this book.

With a little modification by you and your word processing program, these may be all you need. However, there may be times when you require a more sophisticated approach. At those times, you should consider FORMGEN, the program cited below.

GRAPHICS 5—FORMGEN

FORMGEN can best be thought of as a text-creating program that has been especially designed to create forms for your office or organization. It lets you use single keystrokes to enter the double lines, shading, and other characters that can give any form a professional look. You can insert columns, draw lines and arrows, and enter check boxes as easily as if you were typing text—and at least as easily as doing so with a ruler and a pencil.

Included on the disk are a sample work order, expense account, phone message, map, and other prepared forms to get you started. There is virtually no type of form that can't be made to look better using FORMGEN. When you design a form and get it just the way you want it, print it out on your dot-matrix, ink jet, or laser printer. Then use the result as your master and run off a bunch of photocopies.

Education (DOS and typing)

The teaching potential of personal computers has yet to be fully exploited. But the two programs listed next come close. The first is for users who are new to MS-DOS, the operating system software that controls virtually your entire PC. The second is a commercial-quality "typing tutor" program that you must see to believe.

EDUCATION 4—DOS Tutor

The DOS Tutor from Computer Knowledge offers a first-rate introduction to DOS. So many "tutorial" programs load the screen with so much text that you would be better off reading the information in book form. The DOS Tutor, in contrast, is colorful, sprightly, and highly interactive. The program will give you some information and, a screen or two later, ask you to provide an answer based on what it has just told you.

Topics covered include the expanded keyboard, a brief history of computers, an introduction to computers, binary numbers and the CPU, an introduction to storage and input/output devices, DOS operations and commands, subdirectory structure and commands, batch file commands and structure, and a brief introduction to structured programming.

The DOS Tutor is an ideal way to review your knowledge of DOS. Even experienced users will enjoy it, not just to show off their knowledge, but as an example of how a tutorial program should be done.

TYPING 1—PC-FASTYPE

We cannot say enough about PC-FASTYPE. It's fast, flexible, and thoroughly professional. Plus, it's fun to use. If you have never learned touch typing, or if you simply want to boost your speed, PC-FASTYPE is absolutely the best typing tutor program going. You will need either a color graphics card (CGA, EGA, or VGA), a Hercules monographics card, or a Hercules clone. Even if you fancy yourself a truly fast typist, you will get caught up in PC-FASTYPE's drills. And it *does* keep score!

Glossbrenner's Choice order form

Use the order form shown here (or make a photocopy) to order Glossbrenner's Choice disks, replacements for the disk accompanying this book (3.5″ or 5.25″ media), and other books by Alfred Glossbrenner. Be sure to watch for *Glossbrenner's Guide to Shareware for Small Businesses*, coming from Windcrest Books in the summer of 1992.

Glossbrenner's Choice Order Form
for readers of *The Information Broker's Handbook*

Name:_____

Address:_____

City:_____ State:_____ ZIP:_____

Phone:(_____)_____

Make checks payable to *Glossbrenner's Choice*. (U.S. funds drawn on a U.S. bank or international money orders only, please.) Mail to:

> Glossbrenner's Choice
> 699 River Road
> Yardley, PA 19067-1965

Order summary

Glossbrenner's Choice Disks: (Check off names of the disks you want on the back of this form and record the number of disks below.)

Number of disks	*Price*
____ 5.25" disks x $5 per disk	_____
____ 3.5" disks x $6 per disk	_____

Special Offer for Information Brokers: Glossbrenner's Choice Office-Pak. Includes PC-Write, File Express, ProComm 2.4.3, As-Easy-As, and FORMGEN at a 30% savings over the cost of ordering the disks individually.

10-disk set, 5.25" format ($35)	
10-disk set, 3.5" format ($40)	_____

Replacements for disk included with this book:

Information Broker's Disk, 5.25" format ($5)	
Information Broker's Disk, 3.5" format ($6)	_____

Glossbrenner Books (Prices include packing and postage):

The Complete Handbook of Personal Computer Communications, 3rd Ed., 405 pp. ($20.95)   _____

How to Look It Up Online, 486 pp. ($17.95)   _____

Glossbrenner's Master Guide to GEnie, 616 pp. plus Aladdin software and documentation ($41.95)   _____

Alfred Glossbrenner's Master Guide to CompuServe, 432 pp. ($21.95)   _____

DOS 5--Book/Disk Edition, 868 pp. ($52.00)   _____

Glossbrenner's Complete Hard Disk Handbook, 780 pp. plus two software-packed disks ($42.95)   _____

Alfred Glossbrenner's Master Guide to FREE Software for IBMs and Compatible Computers, 530 pp. ($20.95)   _____

Disk/Book Total   _____
Pennsylvania residents, please add 6% Sales Tax.   _____
For shipment outside the U.S., please add $5.00.   _____

Grand Total Enclosed   _____

Glossbrenner's Choice Disks

The following disks are available at $5 each for 5.25" format or $6 each for 3.5" format. Please check the disks you want. Record the total number of disks in the space provided on the reverse side of this form.

Word processing (All three disks are required.)
- ___PCW 1 of 3   *PC-Write 1 (Program)*
- ___PCW 2 of 3   *PC-Write 2 (Utilities)*
- ___PCW 3 of 3   *PC-Write 3 (Reference)*

Idea processing
- ___IDEA 1   *PC-Outline*

Security Encryption
- ___ENCRYPTION 1   *PC-Code 3/4 and The Confidant*

Communications
- ___COMM 1   *ProComm 2.4.3*
- ___COMM 2   *ProComm 2.4.3 Utilities*
- ___COMM 3   *The Communicator's Toolchest*
- ___COMM 4   *ProComm PLUS: Test Drive*
- ___COMM 7   *TAPCIS*
- ___COMM 8   *Aladdin*
- ___COMM 10   *Compression Programs*

Spreadsheet and accounting
- ___SPREADSHEET 1   *As-Easy-As*
- ___ACCOUNTING 1   *Medlin's GL, AP, AR, PR*

Database Management (Disk 4 is not required to run File Express.)
- ___FE 1 of 4   *File Express (Program)*
- ___FE 2 of 4   *File Express (Supplemental Disk 1)*
- ___FE 3 of 4   *File Express (Supplemental Disk 2)*
- ___FE 4 of 4   *File Express (Documentation)*

Forms Creation
- ___GRAPHICS 5   *FORMGEN*

Education (DOS and Typing)
- ___EDUC 4   *DOS Tutor*
- ___TYPING 1   *PC-FASTYPE*

GLOSSBRENNER'S CHOICE GUARANTEE: If the disk supplied with your book, or any disks you order from Glossbrenner's Choice, prove to be defective, we will replace them free of charge. Simply mail the disk(s) to the address on this form.

Windcrest Books assumes no responsibility for this offer. This is solely an offer of the author, Alfred Glossbrenner, and not of Windcrest Books. Please allow 1 to 2 weeks for delivery.

Appendix E

The information broker's seminar
How to make money
as a fee-based information service

THERE ARE TWO PROBLEMS WITH BOOKS: NO SINGLE VOLUME CAN EVER COVER all there is to know about a given subject, and the printed word can never be interactive. You can ask all the questions you want of this book, and we guarantee you it will never answer back. That's why, for those who want to know more, there's the Information Broker's Seminar.

Co-author Rugge has been preparing and presenting her Information Broker's Seminar for the better part of a decade. Each year, it is offered at locations throughout the United States. A one-day course, this program offers a unique opportunity to profit from the experience of one of the pioneers of the information brokering field—and to learn first-hand how to start and operate a successful information brokering service. Seminar topics include:

Small business management

Small business resources
Choosing a business structure
Strategies for starting a business
Managing your cash flow
The ten biggest mistakes in business

The business plan

Purpose of a business plan
Creating the business plan
Questions your plan should answer

Product and service definition

Whether to specialize
Changes caused by changes in the information industry

Marketing and advertising

Sizing up the market
Identifying your target market
Getting clients/keeping clients
Selling in the midst of project overload
Most effective marketing techniques
What your advertising should say

Fees and charges

Setting your fees
Estimating search costs
Credit and collections

Legal considerations

The copyright question
Using contracts
Errors and omissions insurance
Confidentiality

Technology questions

Equipment required

Working information brokers

What they say about the business
Marketing and management techniques that have worked for them

Professional resources

Publications
Professional associations
Conferences
The Information Broker's Resource Kit

Training

Do you need to be a librarian?
Traits of a good database searcher
Traits of a good information broker
Traits of successful entrepreneurs

All seminars run from 9:00 A.M. to 5:00 P.M. and include lunch, as well as morning and afternoon refreshments. The cost of the seminar is $225 with advance registration ($250.00 at the door). The price includes an extensive set of course materials.

For more information on upcoming seminar dates and locations, please complete and mail the included form, or contact The Rugge Group at (510) 530-3635 (voice) or (510) 530-3325 (fax).

The Information Broker's Resource Kit

The Rugge Group also offers The Information Broker's Resource Kit. This is a collection of documents that includes Sue Rugge's latest journal articles on information brokering, plus an annually updated list of books, publications, and newsletters likely to be of interest to any current or prospective information broker.

The Resource Kit itself is free, but postage and handling costs being what they are, The Rugge Group must charge $5 per copy. Please see the order form shown next to send for your kit.

Mail or phone your request to:

The Rugge Group
2670 Mountain Gate Way
Oakland, CA 94611
(510) 530-3635 (voice)
(510) 530-3325 (fax)

- -

____ **Please send me the Information Broker's Resource Kit. I have enclosed $5 to cover shipping and handling. (U.S. funds on a U.S. bank, international money order, or credit card only, please.)**
____ **Yes, please send me more information about The Information Broker's Seminar.**

Name_____
Company_____
Street Address_____
City_____State_____ZIP_____
Province/Country_____
Phone (_____)_____

Visa/MasterCard/American Express:_____
Expiration date: _____
Signature: _____

- -

Appendix F

How to use
the accompanying disk

THE DISK ACCOMPANYING THIS BOOK IS FILLED WITH THE FILES AND FORMS you need to get off to a good start in establishing your own information brokering business. It also contains half a dozen or more utility programs that can make living and working with your PC much easier.

In this appendix, we'll quickly cite the files the disk contains and show you the menu system used to present them. Then we'll tell you how to install the menu system and the software. Finally, we will discuss the various utility programs supplied as part of the menu system.

Forms and files

The disk contains all of the information broker forms presented in Chapters 19 and 20. As we noted in those chapters, our goal here is to make it easy for you to produce forms customized for your own business, without having to start from scratch. All of the text files on this disk (files ending in .TXT) are *pure ASCII text*. They can be brought into any word processing program for editing and customization. You may wish to add codes for boldface and italics or incorporate different fonts, for example.

The disk also contains material not found in the book, including a sample contract, several real-life cover letters, and a complete information broker client report. We have also included relevant material from Appendices A through E. You can use Appendix A to create your own list of reference books and to quickly generate letters to book, magazine, and newsletter publishers. Use Appendix B

("Contact Points") the same way. It is amazing how easy it is to generate a letter if you already have the company name and address on disk.

The menu system

After you have installed the disk, you will see a menu like the one shown in Fig. F-1. The menu is designed to make it easy for you to quickly print out individual files or to view them on the screen. As you can see from Fig. F-1, menu selections A through O offer print options.

To bring a file up on the screen so you can scroll through it, simply hit F3 and then L on the menu that will then appear. The menu system will present you with a list of all its text files. Scroll through the list until you find the one you want to view, and then hit Enter.

To back out of any screen, hit your Esc key. When you hit the Esc key while the main menu is on the screen, the program will ask you if you want to quit. Respond with Y for yes, and you will be returned to DOS.

```
Friday   December 25, 1992  08:00:06 pm        Lite Menu Version 1.8
         The Rugge/Glossbrenner Information Broker's Handbook Disk


                       Information Broker's Disk
    A - Print Letter of Agreement     M - Print Appendix D (Shareware)
    B - Print Sample Contract         N - Print Appendix E (Seminar)
    C - Print Search Request Form     O - Print Lite Menu Instructions
    D - Print Job Cost Estimate Form  P - ==============================
    E - Print Sample Search Log       Q - Print Setting Up Your Office
    F - Print Sample Cover Letters    R - ==============================
    G - Print Sample Broker Report    S - To VIEW files on the screen,
    H - Print Sample Plain Invoice    T - hit F3 and then L on the
    I - Print Itemized Invoice        U - menu that will appear.
    J - Print Appendix A (Resources)  V - ==============================
    K - Print Appendix B (Contacts)   W - Use the ESC key to back up.
    L - Print Appendix C (AIIP)


      F1 - Help  *  F2 - Save  *  F3 - DOS Utilities  *  F10 - Setup
            Press F3 and then L to View Files on Screen
```

Fig. F-1. The Information Broker disk menu

How to install the disk

The accompanying disk is a 5.25″ floppy. You may use it from any drive, though on many systems, Drive A is the 5.25″ drive, while Drive B is the 3.5″ drive. If you do not have a 5.25″ drive on your system, you may order a copy on 3.5″ media using the form in Appendix D. Or you may simply want to take the disk to a friend who has both formats in his or her system and copy it off yourself.

The disk contains two main files: INSTALL.EXE and BROKER.EXE. Place the disk in a drive and key in INSTALL. The program will first prompt you for the disk you want to install the software onto. It will then prompt you for a subdirectory name. The default drive is drive C, and the default subdirectory is C: \ BROKER. You may change either or both of these settings, of course.

When you have responded to the prompts, hit your Enter key. The specified subdirectory will be created on the specified drive, and the file BROKER.EXE will be uncompressed into it. (BROKER.EXE is a self-extracting "archive" file.) The menu system will take a good look around and deliver a prompt at the top of the screen advising you that in the future you may simply key in MENU to bring up the menu. Hit any key at this point, and you will see a screen like the one shown in Fig. F-1. (From then on, though, the menu will come up faster if you do indeed key in MENU.)

If you don't have a hard disk . . .

In preparing this disk, we have assumed that most readers have a hard disk drive. This is a reasonable assumption, since it is simply impossible to use a computer as a business tool without one. If you are still waiting to install your hard drive, however, you're not out of luck. Simply put the accompanying disk in your floppy drive (Drive A) and key in BROKER B:. This will cause the self-extracting program to extract its files onto a disk in Drive B. If you don't have an actual, physical Drive B, don't worry. Your system should prompt you to swap floppies in and out of the one drive you do have until the extraction is complete. (Your Drive B is a "phantom" drive, in computer talk.)

All of the text files and utility programs compressed into BROKER.EXE will fit on a single 5.25″ floppy. However, there is not room for the menu system. (Through a clever bit of programming, INSTALL.EXE copies itself onto the hard drive as LITE.EXE during a hard disk installation and becomes the menu system program.)

Thus, if you have only a single floppy drive, use the command DIR > PRN to send a listing of the files to your printer. (You will have to push buttons on the printer to take it offline, issue a form feed, and put it back online again to make it disgorge the printout.) Files ending in .BAT are designed to print out files ending in .TXT. Thus, keying in LOG.BAT will copy the file LOG.TXT to the printer and give you a hard copy of the Search Log form.

Space does not permit a complete DOS tutorial on dealing with files. If you are a brand new computer user, take the disk and this appendix to a friend with more experience. After reading the information provided here, your friend will be able to show you what to do.

If you have a Macintosh . . .

If you have a Macintosh instead of an IBM-compatible DOS machine, take this disk to a friend who has a DOS machine and ask him or her to extract the files in BROKER.EXE onto a 3.5″ disk. If your Mac is equipped with an Apple FDHD SuperDrive, you will be able to read the .TXT files on your Mac. The SuperDrive can read DOS disks, but you will have to use Apple File Exchange (AFE) to do so. AFE is supplied as part of your Mac operating system, so check your manual for details on how to use it to import a DOS text file.

Alternatively, if you have a SuperDrive, you might look into one of at least two software packages designed to make file importation even easier than the less-than-intuitive AFE. These are DOS Mounter from Dayna Communications and AccessPC from Insignia Solutions, Inc. Both products have a list price under $100. Ask your dealer for more details, or contact the companies at:

DOS Mounter Dayna Communications
50 S. Main St., 5th Fl.
Salt Lake City, UT 84144
(801) 531-0600
(801) 359-9135 (fax)

AccessPC
Insignia Solutions, Inc.
526 Clyde Av.
Mountain View, CA 94043
(800) 848-7677
(415) 694-7600
(415) 964-5434 (fax)

A clutch of useful utilities

The menu program used to present the files on the Information Broker's Disk was written by Marc Perkel of Computer Tyme. It is a customized version of Mr. Perkel's LITE Menu, which in itself is an exceptionally easy-to-use version of his full-powered MarxMenu system. As we will show you in a moment, you can use the files supplied on the accompanying disk to create your *own* menus as well.

First, however, let us tell you about the nine Marc Perkel-written utilities supplied on the disk. Each of these programs can be run directly from the DOS command line, but, for your convenience, we have had them incorporated into the menu system itself. These are the programs that the menu system will access when you hit F3 and choose an item from the resulting "DOS Utilities" menu that will pop up. Here is a quick summary:

D. Marc Perkel's "sweet little directory program." You will never use DIR again. Try it. Just key in D from the DOS command line.

DMLITE. Directory Master Lite is a complete file manager/shell program that lets you view text files, mark files for copying and deletion, rename files, and perform many other DOS functions. It's got a built-in help function you can use for more detailed instructions.

FREE. This program tells you how much memory (all types) and disk space you have, and how much of each is currently occupied. Just key in FREE.

KBD. This "keyboard" program from Marc Perkel's Computer Tyme DOS Toolbox can be used from the command line. But it really comes into its own in a batch file. KBD can be used to toggle your Caps Lock, Num Lock, Scroll Lock, and Print Screen on and off. You can also use it to load up the keyboard buffer with the responses required by programs run from your batch files. Key in KBD at the DOS command line for three screens of information.

LITE. This is the main menu system program. As noted, it is Marc Perkel's "lite" version of his famous MarxMenu program. LITE makes it easy to create professional-quality menus in minutes.

PD. The "Pick Directory" program lets you move to a desired directory by using a graphic tree display or by selecting a name from an alphabetical list of all the directories on your disk. You can also move to a nested directory like C:\ WP \ VENTURA by simply keying in pd ventura, or even pd ven.

As long as the name of the target directory is unique, there is no need to specify the complete path. PD offers many of the benefits of a shell, with none of the drawbacks. PD can also be used to *rename*, remove, hide, unhide, and create subdirectories. Use its built-in help function to get more information.

PIPEDIR. This program is required by PD, but it is also a nifty utility in its own right. PIPEDIR can give you a list of every text file (*.TXT) on your entire disk, for example.

RAMMAP. A program to present a quick summary of what's loaded into your system's memory at the present time.

WHEREIS. This program will locate every filename matching your specifications (complete filenames, wildcards, etc.) on a disk. You might key in WHEREIS CLIENT-A.*, for example, to instantly get the locations (paths) of all matching files on your disk.

How to make your own menus

If you would like to use the LITE.EXE program to create your *own* menus, copy LITE.EXE, D.EXE, and WHEREIS.EXE to a separate directory or disk. Log onto that location and key in LITE. You will be told that you have no menu choices available. So hit F10 to be taken to the set-up screen. Select a slot from A through Z and hit Enter. A menu will pop up prompting you for the screen text and the program you want to be run when someone selects that menu item.

The screen text and the program are the only things that are absolutely required, though additional options are available. LITE will use the D and WHEREIS programs to present you with a list of your directories. Select one, and you will see a list of the files it contains. Select the program file (.EXE, .BAT, or .COM) you wish to have associated with that menu selection. Hit your F2 key to save your set-up information. (It will be saved in a .DAT—for "data"—file.) That's basically all there is to it. You may enter up to 26 (A-Z) selections in this manner.

To back out of any screen, simply hit your Esc key. Also, from the main menu screen, hit F1 for a list of additional commands. As you will see, you can control the colors and the various text items on the menu screen using these additional commands.

LITE.EXE is a truly remarkable program, as are *all* of Marc Perkel's Computer Tyme utilities. They are provided here as shareware, which means that if you like and use them, you are expected to register them with Computer Tyme. LITE is part of Computer Tyme's Tymely Utilities package, a collection of Perkel programs that goes well beyond what you have seen here. The registration fee for a single copy is only $20. See the file LITE.TXT on the accompanying disk for more details. (You can print it out via the menu system.)

You can use your major credit card by calling (800) 548-5353 or (417) 866-1222. Or you can register by mail. Send $20 with your request for the complete Tymely Utilities package to:

Computer Tyme
411 N. Sherman Suite 300
Springfield, MO 65802

Conclusion

Clearly, there is no magic wand we can wave to automatically make every reader a bona fide information broker. With this disk, however, we have tried to make it as easy as possible for you to get *started*. We urge you to print out all of the text files, either using the menu system or the DOS command COPY *.TXT. Then take the time to study them. In particular, study the Sample Cover Letters and the Sample Broker Report.

Every client, and every report, is different. But the collection of cover letters and the sample report provided here will give you a much better idea of the kind of material a successful information broker delivers to a client. Since the letters are derived from actual letters, we have substituted names ("Ms. Jones," "Mr. Roe," etc.) and changed things around to protect the confidentiality of the real-life client.

The specific names, places, and subjects, however, are not the point. Concentrate on the tone of the letters, how they detail the work that has been done, and how they suggest (if appropriate) additional research possibilities. To provide a well-rounded picture, we have included letters sent when a research project was unsuccessful, as well as ones where the client did indeed receive what he or she was hoping for.

Finally, we strongly suggest that you contact the organizations and online services cited in Appendix B. Ask for an information packet, and when it arrives, put it in a file. That's why we've included these appendices on the accompanying disk. With these addresses and a word processing program, you can quickly generate the query letters you need.

Now, if you have not done so already, put the accompanying disk in a drive and key in INSTALL. We think you'll be very pleased with the results.

Additional help

Sometimes disks can be downright troublesome. If you have a problem with the disk included in this book and you can't seem to find the answer anywhere or from anyone, feel free to put your question in writing and send it off to Alfred at

Glossbrenner's Choice
699 River Road
Yardley, PA 19067-1965

Index